T. S. ELIOT AND

T. S. Eliot and Mysticism

The Secret History of *Four Quartets*

PAUL MURRAY
*Lecturer in Mystical Theology
Dominican Studium, Tallaght,
and Angelicum University, Rome*

First published 1991 by
THE MACMILLAN PRESS LTD
Houndmills, Basingstoke, Hampshire RG21 2XS
and London
Companies and representatives
throughout the world

ISBN 0–333–47585–2 hardcover
ISBN 0–333–61406–2 paperback

A catalogue record for this book is available
from the British Library.

Printed in Great Britain by
Antony Rowe Ltd
Chippenham, Wiltshire

Reprinted 1993,
1994 (with corrections)

To Siún

the well known is what we have yet to learn
T. S. Eliot

Contents

Preface

When I first discovered *Four Quartets* I was about eighteen or nineteen, and I had in my possession no commentary nor any critical study of the work on which to rely for assistance. At first, and not surprisingly, much of the meaning of the work eluded me. Yet, somehow, to my astonishment, the poems at once aroused my deepest interest. My attention was drawn and held by their strange 'chamber music'. And the simple hearing of this music probably communicated to me more of the poems' essential meaning than I have since gained from my study of learned, critical commentaries. Eliot himself remarked in 1961:

> Good commentaries can be very helpful: but to study even the best commentary on a work of literary art is likely to be a waste of time unless we have first read and been excited by the text commented upon even without understanding it. For that thrill of excitement from our first reading of a work of creative literature which we do not understand is itself the beginning of understanding. . . . Understanding begins in the sensibility: we must have the experience before we attempt to explore the sources of the work itself.[1]

I first became interested in the question of the sources of *Four Quartets* when, for a period of two to three years at the Angelicum University in Rome, I had the opportunity of studying several major authors in the Western mystical tradition. I found that the more familiar I became with the philosophy and literature of mysticism the more definite was my impression of a unique and profound connection between the mystical tradition and the poetry of *Four Quartets*. And it was, in part, to verify and test my own intuition that I undertook the writing of the present study.

Once I had decided to take part in the critical debate concerning *Four Quartets* I was immediately made aware of an almost overwhelming number of books, articles and reviews on the

All his life Eliot clung with equal force and, one suspects, with almost equal need to his wide-ranging interest in religious mysticism and to his own native hesitancy and scepticism.[8] Eeldrop, one of the fictional protagonists in a fragment of 1917, is described by Eliot as 'a sceptic with a taste for mysticism'.[9] At one point in the debate between Eeldrop and Appleplex, the poet, no doubt with tongue in cheek, has Eeldrop declare: 'I am, I confess to you, in private life, a bank clerk.'[10] At times Eliot apparently made no effort to hide his enthusiasm for the mystics and their writings. One of his fellow students, E. R. Dodds, recalls for instance that when he first met Eliot, 'a young American lately arrived from the Graduate School at Harvard', Eliot talked to him excitedly about mysticism. Both Eliot and Dodds were attending J. A. Stewart's class on Plotinus. 'The membership of the class was initially six', according to Dodds, 'but as Stewart proved to be an unexciting teacher it quickly dropped to two . . . like me, he [Eliot] was seriously interested in mystical experience.'[11]

In the early years in London Eliot not only continued to read books about mysticism, he also came to know a number of authors, among them May Sinclair.[12] He reviewed her book *A Defence of Idealism* for *The New Statesman* in September 1917. 'Miss Sinclair's book', Eliot remarked to his readers, with an air of unusual excitement, 'has all the charm which the fresh and interested mind of an outsider, turned upon the achievements of a technical art or science, can give. . . . Miss Sinclair writes very much to the point in discussing Butler, Pragmatism and Mysticism . . . in fact, it is one of the most interesting books of philosophy that have appeared for several years.'[13] Like Eliot, Miss Sinclair obviously had 'a taste for mysticism'; but, for the most part in her book, she remains quite unimpressed and unconvinced by the ordinary manifestations of mysticism in the West. 'Now it cannot be denied', she argues, 'that Mysticism is suspect. It has a bad history. In fact it has two histories, an ancient and a modern history; and it would be hard to say which is worse.'[14] Sinclair raises in passing serious questions about what she calls the 'violence' and the 'emotionalism' of the language of St John of the Cross and St Teresa of Avila. And of Neo-Platonic mysticism in general, she writes: 'it carried the passion for Godhead to drunken excess . . . [it] is a psychological phenomenon like any other'.[15]

From the time of his Sinclair review until the period during which he composed *Four Quartets*, we can detect in Eliot's prose writings a similar impatience with, and even opposition to, religious mysticism. In 1934, for example, on the occasion of the death of A. R. Orage, Eliot contributed to an obituary number of the *New English Weekly* which was particularly critical of Orage's preoccupation with certain forms of mysticism.[16] Two months later Eliot wrote in his own review, *The Criterion*: 'I deprecate Orage's mysticism as much as anyone does. . . . Had he been a Catholic his mysticism would have repelled; as that of an irresponsible religious adventurer his mysticism was merely smiled at.'[17] Some years earlier there appeared a volume of letters by the Catholic lay theologian and devotional author, Baron Friedrich von Hügel (1896–1924). Eliot's short review of the letters again makes manifest his deep opposition to mysticism.

> When we read enough of his letters we come to think of him as almost a saint, as a minor master of the devotional life. He was manifestly not merely a good man; he had also that more exact and disciplined virtue which comes only from the regular practice of devotion in one of the systematic religions. He was not a great philosopher or theologian. His feelings were exact, but his ideas were often vague. And his mysticism is no longer the order of the day. He belongs to a past epoch, a period of intellectual indistinctness, in which he moved among a host of half Christians and quarter Christians. The present age seems to me much more an age of black and white, without shadows. Mysticism – even the particular Christian mysticism studied by von Hügel – is not the issue of our time. We are able to quote with approval that remark of Bossuet: 'true mysticism is so rare and unessential, and false mysticism so common and dangerous that one cannot oppose it too firmly'. We demand of religion some kind of *intellectual* satisfaction – both private and social – or we do not want it at all.[18]

It might seem that Eliot is opposed here to mysticism in every shape and form. But this initial impression is sharply contradicted by statements he made in numerous other articles and reviews and essays written during the same period. The reason for this apparent confusion is simple; and it is related, paradoxically, to the fact that Eliot's own temperament was rather similar to that of Baron von Hügel. 'I am not a systematic thinker', he confessed in a letter to Paul Elmer More on 20 June 1934, '. . . I depend upon intuitions and perceptions.'[19] In the end one comes gradually to realise that Eliot's intention during this period was not completely to reject mysticism, but instead radically to change and to purify some of his own earlier attitudes to the subject – attitudes he now found unacceptable.

But there are, as it happens, certain constants in Eliot's understanding of mysticism during these years. And they can be summarised under three headings. First of all, Eliot regards mysticism as a path of negation; second, as an 'ecstasy of thought' (and not, therefore, as an effusion of feeling); and third, as an incommunicable vision.[20] To a man of Eliot's somewhat ritualistic and disciplined sensibility, the unrestrained emotionalism associated with certain forms of modern and contemporary mysticism was anathema. He complained in 1930 of 'the warm fog which passes for mysticism nowadays'.[21] And earlier in that same year he wrote:

> There is much chatter about mysticism: for the modern world the word means some spattering indulgence of emotion, instead of the most terrible concentration and *askesis*. But it takes perhaps a life-time to realise that men like the forest sages, and the desert sages, and finally the Victorines and John of the Cross and (in his fashion) Ignatius really *mean what they say*. Only those have the right to talk of discipline who have looked into the Abyss.[22]

Eliot's general criticism was not directed exclusively against his own contemporaries. He also showed himself quite ill at ease with what he called 'that fusion or confusion of feeling of human and divine, that transposition of human sentiment to divine objects which characterises the religious verse of the sixteenth and seventeenth centuries, in contrast to that of the thirteenth century, in which the distinctions of feeling towards human objects and divine objects are preserved.'[23] Mystical ecstasy as it was understood in the twelfth century as, for example, by the Victorines and in the thirteenth by St Thomas Aquinas was, in Eliot's opinion, almost always an 'ecstasy of thought'. In other words, emotion did not dominate, but rather was itself dominated and controlled by the intelligence. In contrast, the mysticism of the poets and mystics of the sixteenth and seventeenth centuries was deeply tainted by emotionalism. St Teresa of Avila,

St John of the Cross and John Donne were all described by Eliot
in 1926 as 'voluptuaries of religion'.[24] And, four years later, in
March 1930, he remarked at the close of his 'Survey of Seventeenth-Century Poetry': 'this Spanish mysticism is definitely sensuous or erotic in its mode of expression; and this sensuousness
pervades the poetry affected by it, as it pervades baroque art'.[25]
The distinction Eliot makes in his *Clark Lectures* and elsewhere
between the mysticism of the thirteenth and that of the sixteenth
and seventeenth centuries may well have been in part suggested
to him originally by the work of the Italian critic Mario Praz. 'No
one is more aware than he', Eliot noted in 1925 (a mere two
months before he delivered his own *Clark Lectures* at Cambridge),
'of the world of difference between the religion of the seventeenth
century and that of the thirteenth. It is the difference between
psychology and metaphysics. . . . Praz has been able to supply
what has been a conspicuous defect of English criticism of Donne:
a comparison between Donne and the metaphysical poets of the
age of Dante.'[26]

As a theorist of mysticism Eliot, as we have seen, placed great
emphasis on the role of the intelligence. As early as 1920 he
wrote: 'the true mystic is not satisfied merely by feeling, he must
at least pretend that he sees'.[27] In spite of this emphasis, however,
Eliot never allowed himself to forget that mysticism is also, in
some sense, a state of spiritual feeling. He refers, characteristically, in 1927, when writing about the poetry of Henry
Vaughan, to that 'perfectly definite experience which we call the
mystical experience'.[28] And, in another context, again speaking
about Henry Vaughan, he writes: 'here and there we seem to
catch flashes of an original and unique vision; of personal
mystical experience'.[29] Henry Vaughan comes nearer than Donne
in Eliot's opinion to being a mystic: '[Donne] was rather the
theologian, or rather the student of theology, and the preacher,
than the mystic. In all of his religious writings there is little sign
of that privacy so characteristic of the mystic, that assurance of
experience incommunicable.'[30]

B.   MYSTICISM AND *FOUR QUARTETS*

Since the publication of *Four Quartets* more than forty years ago, a
remarkable body of critical literature has been produced, compris-

ing books, articles, essays, reviews and unpublished theses. Among Eliot's readers and critics a considerable number have presumed to venture beyond the strict area of 'pure' literary criticism, and with varying degrees of success have given attention to what one might call the spiritual or mystical aspects of the poem. So far, however, there has been no really satisfactory or comprehensive study of mysticism in *Four Quartets*.[31] The originality of the present study derives from its special concentration on this subject.

Perhaps the first and most obvious indication of a mystical dimension in *Four Quartets* is the fact that, although only a very small number of direct quotations are incorporated into the poem, almost all of them are taken by Eliot from mystical sources, from St John of the Cross, for example, and *The Bhagavad-Gita*, from Julian of Norwich and from *The Cloud of Unknowing*. These texts and sources have already been noted and commented upon by Helen Gardner in her invaluable study, *The Composition of Four Quartets*.[32] But the mystical dimension of Eliot's poem extends far beyond these few explicit quotations. It is as much present, for example, in the poem's music as it is in its underlying mystical philosophy. And so numerous and disparate are the springs and sources of the poem's mysticism, and also so well hidden, they can be said to constitute the secret history of *Four Quartets*.

The usual tendency when attempting to speak about the influence of mysticism or mystical philosophy on *Four Quartets* is to confine the discussion to an area somewhere *behind* the work, and to talk only about the mysticism and philosophy of the poet, ignoring completely the mysticism of the work itself. But what I hope to demonstrate in the chapters which follow is that the *style* as well as the intellectual content of Eliot's poem has been directly influenced by the literature of mysticism, and that, to a quite extraordinary degree, the poet's essential method and the poet's mysticism have become one and the same thing.

Four Quartets is a poem and not a prose passage of mystical theology. There are, it is true, a number of central themes or subjects with which one can say the poem is concerned. But Eliot's principal task as a poet has been to draw these various themes and subjects into a new whole, so that what emerges is not another subject, but a poem which is able to communicate the different facets and levels of his own Christian and religious experience. In some of the chapters which follow I will attempt to trace a number of these themes and subjects to their sources in the Christian and non-Christian mystical literature which Eliot had read. This is not to suggest that the themes will be studied in isolation from their poetic context. The peculiar emotional tone or musical quality of a given passage in the poem can sometimes completely alter the original meaning of a borrowed phrase or idea. In other words, the main object of my research is not the precise historical importance nor the full theological significance of these mystical themes in themselves, but instead the theological and the literary meaning they possess *within* Eliot's poem. An analysis of this kind, far from imposing on the text a list of external and irrelevant theological criteria, can in fact throw new light on the originality of Eliot's genius as a religious poet, and on the vital inner structure of his masterpiece, *Four Quartets.*

The proposal to make a 'new' contribution to Eliot studies invites, nowadays, the kind of negative opposition meted out to those critics who persist in offering solutions of problems apparently worked to death. Already in 1949 David Daiches was quietly protesting that everything that needed to be said about *Four Quartets* had been said.[33] And among critics in general there was at that time, it seemed, a growing consensus about the status and meaning of *Four Quartets.* One clear indication of this trend was R. W. Flint's 1948 paper 'The *Four Quartets* Reconsidered', and in particular his remark 'it becomes more and more apparent that the *Quartets* have worn well'.[34] Twenty years later, however, after the appearance of important new work by a variety of Eliot critics, Bernard Bergonzi, in his Introduction to a major collection of their essays, felt constrained to remark: 'The essays by Davie, Kenner, Stead and Donoghue do not provide any kind of consensus, and they throw out more questions about the ultimate meaning and status of the *Quartets* than they resolve.'[35] In Bergonzi's Introduction we find the following statement which represents, ironically, an almost complete reversal of Daiches's statement of 1949: 'The *Four Quartets* have been available for a comparatively short time, scarcely long enough for a true critical perspective to have formed.'[36]

Eliot's use of mystical symbolism and Christian dogma has been interpreted and misinterpreted by critics over the years in many different ways. In particular there has been disagreement about how Eliot's understanding of Incarnation, or the theme of Christian dogma in the poem, relates to the poem's other major themes. Some critics claim that *Four Quartets* is an overtly Christian, even a dogmatic, poem;[37] others are of the opinion that it is only intermittently Christian;[38] one critic finds at the centre of the poem not the Incarnate Christian God but the impersonal God of Greek philosophy;[39] another contends that 'the religious dimension of the *Quartets* is not, as most critics believe, its Christian themes and allusions, but the embodiment of a meditative posture, at times more Hindu and Buddhist than Christian'.[40] This disagreement among Eliot's critics, and the general problem of the status and meaning of *Four Quartets* can only, I think, be resolved now by taking hold firmly of what is, perhaps, the single most difficult nettle to grasp in Eliot studies – namely, the question of the relationship between the poetry of *Four Quartets* and Eliot's mysticism.

C.　THE QUESTION OF SOURCES

In answer to a question put to him in an interview sometime before 1949, Eliot remarked that in the composition of *Four Quartets* he was 'seeking the verbal equivalents for small experiences he had had and for *knowledge derived from reading*'.[41] I have italicised the last phrase for the sake of emphasis. It is normal when reading the work of Eliot to be struck by the depth and extent of his learning. What impresses one in particular is the quality and breadth of his reading in the fields of literature, general philosophy and mysticism. And yet not all of Eliot's readers are impressed by these signs in his work of vast learning and impeccable education. Richard Aldington, for example, complains of 'that abuse of the unacknowledged quotation whereby Eliot became credited with what was not his'. In fact 'we might almost say', Aldington concludes, 'that what is original in his poetry is not good, and what is good is not original'.[42] W. B. Yeats, while voicing a similar complaint in a letter to Dorothy Wellesley, gives full vent to his rage and irritation:

> But Eliot, that man isn't modern. He wrings the past dry and pours the juice down the throats of those who are either too busy, or too creative to read as much as he does. I believe that in time to come he will be regarded as an interesting symptom

of a sick and melancholy age. He has written lovely things. I always ask myself however (being limited in learning) 'Is this or that cribbed from a Greek, an Indian, a Spaniard, anyone you like?' He is not perhaps influenced by the past, he being at pains to tell us so. The question is: *does he crib?*[43]

Unfortunately both Yeats and Aldington have failed to realise that the mere enumeration of influences and sources, no matter how extended it may be, does not exhaust one's overall impression of Eliot's or, indeed, of any other poet's work. The poetry of a man like Eliot makes manifest first and last that process which is always new and always surprising, namely the growth and development of an authentic, unique and living sensibility. To accuse Eliot of literary kleptomania, as Yeats does, is – if I may say so – to betray an astonishing *critical* ignorance of what originality in poetry actually means. 'Talk to me of originality', exclaimed Yeats himself, in a wiser moment, 'and I will turn on you with rage. I am a crowd, I am a lonely man, I am nothing. Ancient salt is best packing.'[44]

Originality today is sometimes thought to demand a complete absence of models and to encourage an outright rejection of all forms of tradition. In fact, of course, what characterises true originality is the capacity or genius to take up and transform an inherited living tradition. 'True originality', Eliot wryly noted on one occasion, 'is merely development'.[45] What matters to the poet more than anything else is the assimilation and transformation which takes place through the unique medium of poetry. Today perhaps we remark too often on the *substance* of a poet's borrowings and ignore – to our own obvious disadvantage as readers – the vital *transformation* which has occurred. I think that what Eliot says of Lancelot Andrewes, applies equally to himself and to his own work: 'His single thoughts are no doubt often suggested by the words he borrows, but the thoughts are made his own, and the constructive force, the fire that fuses them, is his own.'[46] Sources and literary influences do have a certain importance, but not so much for what they are as for the changes they undergo, the stimulus they provide, and the reaction they produce. At this stage in Eliot studies it should, I think, be obvious that the heart of Eliot's poetry, in spite of its massive intellectual façade, is emotion. The thrust of feeling in his work is so alive and powerful it manages almost always to master the borrowed language, the inherited style and the acquired wisdom, making them seem both natural and singular. All the sources are in the end but one source: Eliot himself.

'[P]oetic originality', Eliot once remarked, 'is largely an original way of assembling the most disparate and unlikely material to make a new whole.'[47] And again, in another place: 'We do not imitate, we are changed; and our work is the work of the changed man; we have not borrowed, we have been quickened, and we become bearers of a tradition.'[48] If Eliot fails – and he does of course – to give an elaborate acknowledgment of all his literary debts and borrowings, it is not because he desires to evade the penalty for plagiarism. Rather by this very 'theft' it is obvious that he is employing a deliberate literary device and paying a delicate literary compliment.

An initial sympathy with Eliot's method of composition in *Four Quartets* is, I think, required if one is to understand the mystical character of the poem. For without such basic sympathy, and the ordinary knowledge on which it is founded, one has simply no choice but to conclude that *Four Quartets* is a work of second-hand experience – a sort of pious fraud. '*Four Quartets* is not a mystical poem', argues Dr H. Servotte in a short paper entitled 'T. S. Eliot's *Four Quartets* and the Language of Mystics'.[49] One of the principal reasons put forward to substantiate this claim is that the author of *Four Quartets*, rather than allow himself to suffer a direct, intuitional experience of the Supernatural, will trust himself only to one thing – the Tradition – and to its rather limited intellectual wisdom. 'The mystic has met the Wholly Other, the living God; his experience may have been very brief . . . it may belong to the past, but the memory of it gives him the certainty that it will be given him again. Witness St John of the Cross in his *Spiritual Canticle*.'[50] In contrast, we are informed that if the poet of *Four Quartets* entertains the hope of attaining to a final vision of the Timeless, it is not because he has had some mystical experience of his own in the past, but simply because he accepts blindly what the mystical tradition has told him. In the *Quartets*, therefore, his only task is to integrate 'the writings of many dead writers'. And so 'Tradition, i.e. the experience of others, plays a part here which it never plays in the works of mystics (at least not consciously).'[51] A similar point concerning *Four Quartets* is made by Kathleen Nott in her book *The Emperor's Clothes*: 'the religious experience itself [within the poem] is not intuitional, it is "intellectual", or perhaps I should say "literary". Whatever Mr Eliot's personal experience has been, his poetry refers only to similar or secondhand experiences, as they have been recorded in theological works or by mystics.'[52] It is not our intention here, as I have said before, to try to prove that Eliot's experience was of the same order or magnitude as the experience of St John of the Cross. But what is quite obvious is that Eliot's method of composition is basically the same as that of the Carmelite mystic, and the same also as that of almost every mystical author and poet within the Western mystical tradition. As it happens, we now possess the original love-poem which served St John of the Cross as a model for his religious lyric *El Pastorcico*. The process by which the saint's poem came to be written has been analysed by Alonso Schökel: 'The mystic [St John of the Cross] whose whole life force was polarized by the Lord Jesus, read the poem and felt a living flame. Seeking to confer existence and a communicability to the fire he felt within him, he took the poem, retouched it here and there, and transposed it to a completely new image-context. The result is astounding.'[53] To find that a mystical poem can be related in such a remarkable way to a pre-existent literary source does not, of course, entitle one to call at once into question its mystical character. What matters here, as always, is not so much the substance which has been borrowed but rather the dynamic transformation and conversion which has been quickened by the pressure of a new emotion. The poem itself, as it must, stands independent of its origin.[54]

But why then, the question remains to be asked, should one spend time and effort studying the sources of *Four Quartets* when the mere identification of sources has apparently very definite limitations, and may even prove subversive, in the end, of one's fundamental critical endeavour. The simplest answer to this question is an answer already given, and more than once, by Eliot himself. 'Scholarship' he tells us, 'even in its humblest forms, has its rights.'[55] And so, 'the question of "sources" has its rights, and we must, if we go into the matter at all, inform ourselves of the exact proportion of invention, borrowing, and adaptation. . . . This sort of work must be done to prepare for the search for the real pattern.'[56]

Within *Four Quartets* there are moments when it is possible to recognise the author or the book from which Eliot has 'borrowed'. But trying to decide in an individual case 'the exact proportion of invention, borrowing and adaptation' is by no means an easy task. The alchemy of the poet's mind has transmuted the borrowed phrase or image into a new substance. And thus the quotation which was borrowed is a quotation no longer: it is the poet's own original verse. There are, however, a few exceptions to this rule, namely direct quotations like those from Julian of Norwich and *The Cloud of Unknowing* which remain within *Four Quartets* as recognisable quotations, and are to be understood by the reader as possessing an authority or a stature far greater than Eliot's own. But apart from these quotations it might appear at first that Eliot has abandoned altogether the allusive technique in *Four Quartets*. There are, it is true, certain verbal allusions and reminiscences in the poem but they are by no means as conspicuous as they were, for example, in *The Waste Land*. The allusions now, as Staffan Bergsten explains, are 'not so much to literary works of art as to philosophical and religious conceptions and systems'.[57] Eliot's allusive technique has changed, and the challenge to the reader is not so much the obvious literary quotation but what Bergsten calls 'the hidden sources'.[58] He argues, and I think wisely, that 'the study of isolated, literary allusions often turns out to be a blind alley, whereas the study of philosophical and religious patterns leads straight to the core'.[59]

When seeking to uncover the sources of a poem such as *Four Quartets* there is always a danger that the mere enumeration of sources might, by its very thoroughness, appear to offer itself as a complete explanation of the poetry. But even if, by chance, a well-researched work of source criticism is at first mistakenly regarded as a work of major criticism, its deficiencies and limitations will, I suspect, very soon come to the surface, and be clearly recognised for what they are. To examine the lines of a poem under a microscope – or, as it were, within a scientifically-controlled environment – is hardly to do them justice! Small wonder then that the average critic of English literature is usually reluctant to undertake analysis of this kind. The correct embryology of a poem, fascinating as it may be in itself, simply does not constitute the poem's final pattern or meaning. But it can provide helpful aid at times in the search for this pattern. '[A]ny book, any essay, any note in *Notes and Queries* which produces a fact even of the lowest order about a work of art is', Eliot would argue, 'a better piece of work than nine-tenths of the most pretentious journalism, in journals or in books.'[60] The effort to arrive at knowledge concerning literary sources can do no real harm, therefore, provided always we do not mistake these sources for the inner core of the poem; provided, that is, we do not mistake them for what the poem really means.

More positively, it can, I think, be stated that since the use of literary allusion and quotation is one of the main characteristics of Eliot's poetry, an accurate identification of sources is sometimes, in fact, necessary if the full meaning of his work is to be appreciated. The rich play of literary echoes and the complex music of allusion are essential factors in the art of *Four Quartets* and should not be regarded as accidental or unfortunate. '[T]he echoes', writes Barbara Everett, 'are always there, and to catch them is to give back to these elusive poems that fourth dimension of meaning that is their life, almost their embodiment.'[61]

Part One
'Burnt Norton'
At the Still Point

1

Mysticism and Music

*. . . poetry so transparent that in reading
it we are intent on what the poetry* points
*at, and not on the poetry, this seems to me
the thing to try for. To get* beyond
poetry, *as Beethoven, in his last works,
strove to get* beyond music.

T. S. Eliot, 'English Poets as Letter Writers', (1933)

'[M]ystical illumination', Eliot remarked in March 1933, 'is a
vision which may be accompanied by the realization that you will
never be able to communicate it to anyone else, or even by the
realization that when it is past you will not be able to recall it
yourself.'[1] It is, in other words, an event of the spirit as deeply
mysterious and elusive as it is real. But how then is it possible,
one can ask, for a fully authentic mystic, or for someone graced
by an experience of a mystical kind, to be also a great poet? Will
he not tend to demean in some way and to betray the transcendent gift he has received by straining to express it in words? And
on what basis in any case can he hope to give tongue to that
which is in itself ineffable – particularly when, as it would appear,
only a few broken fragments remain in his memory of the original
experience?

In the complex and difficult struggle to express the Inexpress-
ible, there is, as I think Eliot understood very well, no medium
more satisfying or more suitable than that of music. 'Were he a
musician', writes Evelyn Underhill, a leading authority on mysticism and a contemporary of Eliot's, 'it is probable that the mystic
could give his message to other musicians in the terms of that art,
far more accurately than language will allow him to do.'[2] Eliot was
neither a musician nor a composer of music. But within *Four
Quartets*, as the title of the work itself indicates, he has chosen

17

deliberately to usurp some of the composer's and musician's rights and privileges. '[O]f all the arts', Underhill points out, 'music alone shares with great mystical literature the power of waking in us a response to the life-movement of the universe: brings us – we know not how – news of its exultant passions and its incomparable peace. Beethoven heard the very voice of Reality, and little of it escaped when he translated it for our ears.'[3] Normally when the musicial dimension of *Four Quartets* is discussed there is a tendency among critics to restrict the discussion to the external structure or shape of the poem and to a consideration, therefore, of the way each individual *Quartet* is divided up into five sections just as a musical composition or an actual *Quartet* is arranged in a sequence of movements. Of course the use of this structural device is undoubtedly impressive, but it is only one part of the poem's rich musical identity. Of at least equal importance, surely, is the fact that Eliot's poem, by aspiring to the condition of music, has become a medium for the expression of experiences which might otherwise have remained incommunicable.

A.   THE MUSIC OF IMAGERY

. . . our concern was speech, and speech impelled us
To purify the dialect of the tribe . . .

This statement, addressed to the poet of *Four Quartets* by 'the ghost of some dead master' in 'Little Gidding' deliberately takes up and echoes a line from the French Symbolist poet, Stéphane Mallarmé ('Donner un sens plus pur aux mots de la tribu', *Le Tombeau d'Edgar Poe*). The ideal of Mallarmé, an ideal shared by many other French Symbolist poets, was to purge poetry of all prosaic contamination. 'Some [of their number]', writes Paul Valéry, 'studied how to eliminate descriptions, maxims, moralizing, and arbitrary details; they purged their poetry of nearly all those intellectual elements which music cannot express. Others gave to every object endless meanings that presupposed a hidden metaphysics. They made use of delightfully ambiguous matter.'[4] Such a strangely refined poetry – *poèsie pure* as it later came to be known – was not for Mallarmé a mere *jeu de quilles* but served, in fact, an almost mystical purpose. 'Poetry', he wrote, 'is the expression, by means of human language brought back to its essential rhythm, of the mysterious sense of existence: thus it endows our stay on earth with authenticity and constitutes the only spiritual task.'[5] This task was to be achieved in practice by the assimilation of poetry to music.' How the French poets came originally to be so fascinated by the art of music, and then, as a result, by the unique musical and 'mystical' possibilities of language is explained by Paul Valéry. 'What was baptized *Symbolism* can be very simply described as the common intention of several groups (otherwise mutually inimical) to "reclaim their own from Music" . . . we were nourished on music, and our literary minds dreamed only of extracting from language the same effects, almost, as were produced on our nervous systems by sound alone.'[6] Valéry recalls vividly how the Symbolist poets came away from concerts *overwhelmed*: 'Overwhelmed – dazzled; as though, transported to the seventh heaven by a cruel favour, they had been caught up to that height only that they might experience a luminous contemplation of forbidden possibilities and inimitable marvels.'[7] Even if such an ecstatic transport of delight and of 'cruelty' had, on some occasion, been experienced by Eliot, I doubt if he would have expressed it in quite the same way. But he did risk once, in the late March of 1931, communicating the following confidence to Stephen Spender:

> I have the A minor Quartet [by Beethoven] on the gramophone, and find it quite inexhaustible to study. There is a sort of heavenly or at least more than human gaiety about some of his later things which one imagines might come to oneself as the fruit of reconciliation and relief after immense suffering; I should like to get something of that into verse before I die.[8]

Four years later Eliot had begun the first of his own *Quartets*. And one of the forms he devised during the process of composition to assist the assimilation of his poetry to music he named, years later, 'the music of imagery'.[9] 'One is constantly reminded of music', writes Helen Gardner, 'by the treatment of images, which recur with constant modifications, from their context, or from their combination with other recurring images, as a phrase recurs with modifications in music.'[10] At least some of the enchantment arises from the fact that these images are not fixed. An individual image may have one meaning now and another later. And the full meaning is the effect of one form of the image being mysteriously fused, as it were, with the other. This phenomenon is for the reader of Eliot's poetry a cause of some considerable pleasure and enlightenment. But it is also, one has to admit, a cause of some considerable difficulty for the would-be critic. For how is it possible to name any but a few of the multiple echoes which together compose the meaning of a given passage?

The short lyric which begins 'Time and the bell have buried the day', if read only for itself (in isolation that is from its place within the poem, and from its place within the *music* of the poem) will impress the reader as being merely a work of Romantic protest, a 'Nature poem' concerned with the impermanence of the temporal, and with the poignant ephemeral beauty of the English landscape. It would, however, I think, be a mistake to read through this short lyric, with its terrible imagery of darkness and of death, without recalling the imagery of *spiritual* darkness introduced by Eliot just a few lines earlier in the preceding strophe:

> Internal darkness, deprivation
> And destitution of all property,
> Desiccation of the world of sense, . . .

And when, furthermore, the image of 'the still point of the turning world' is introduced at the close of the lyric, does it not also alert our attention to a hidden depth of spiritual, one might even say *mystical*, radiance?

> Time and the bell have buried the day,
> The black cloud carries the sun away.
> Will the sunflower turn to us, will the clematis
> Stray down, bend to us; tendril and spray
> Clutch and cling?
> Chill
> Fingers of yew be curled
> Down on us? After the kingfisher's wing
> Has answered light to light, and is silent, the light is still
> At the still point of the turning world.

To respond imaginatively to the strength and beauty of this final image, one does not, I believe, have to consult textbooks on mysticism, because a distinctive resonance and meaning (both mystical and philosophical) has already been acquired by the image earlier in Part Two of 'Burnt Norton'. And this meaning, like that which attends upon a musical phrase in a Beethoven Quartet, is not entirely suppressed and is not forgotten. Some readers of 'Burnt Norton' have sought to discover strict allegorical and mystical meanings in the images of the yew, kingfisher, sunflower, clematis, and so on. It has, for example, been pointed out by Grover Smith that 'sunflower' is traditionally associated with Christ, and 'clematis' with the Blessed Virgin Mary;[11] and by Peter Milward S.J., that 'kingfisher is an ancient symbol of rebirth from water, and so of Christian baptism'.[12] But even if, during the composition, Eliot was conscious of making such connections, they do not in the end constitute the true mystical character of his lyric. Other works of mystical literature and poetry may very well depend at times almost completely on the use of such a strict allegorical method – a point Eliot himself, as it happens, was prepared to acknowledge. 'I do not care to deny', he noted in September 1972, 'that good poetry can be at the same time a sort of cryptogram of a mysticism only visible to the initiate; only, in that case, the poetry and the mysticism will be two different things.'[13] In the case of his own short lyric in 'Burnt Norton' the poetry and mysticism have undoubtedly become one thing. There is no interruption between the surface beauty and the inner core of meaning. And this has been achieved by the subtle grace and brilliance of 'the music of imagery'.

Perhaps nowhere else in *Four Quartets* is Eliot's orchestration of meaning more striking, and his use of 'the music of imagery' more apparent, than in the closing lines of 'Little Gidding'. Themes and phrases used earlier in the *Quartets* are here repeated; and the reader is at last able to receive and to hold, as it were, in his mind – if only for an instant – the entire meaning of the poem and the entire music.

> We shall not cease from exploration
> And the end of all our exploring
> Will be to arrive where we started
> And know the place for the first time.
> Through the unknown, remembered gate
> When the last of earth left to discover
> Is that which was the beginning;

> At the source of the longest river
> The voice of the hidden waterfall
> And the children in the apple-tree
> Not known, because not looked for
> But heard, half-heard, in the stillness
> Between two waves of the sea.

The musical effect of these lines depends for its authority and its grace on what Eliot has called 'The contrapuntal arrangement of subject matter'[14] – a technique or method which, in the past, has made available to the composer of genius what seem to be 'inexhaustible resources, owing to the development and super-imposition of certain selected themes, which together lead in the end to the supreme harmony of numbers, enabling us to participate in the ultimate purity of Being'. This last quotation is taken from a work entitled *La Mystique Protestante et Anglicane*, one of the few studies I have read which cast light on the relationship between mysticism and music.[15] 'Bach's music', the author, Dr H. Jaegar, claims, 'is the expression of a kind of mystical experience.'[16] It is, he says, inspired by the mystical theology of the Middle Ages and by the great intensity of the inner life of Martin Luther. 'With the work of Bach, we touch', he says, 'the summit of Lutheran mysticism.'[17]

Johann Sebastian Bach, Stéphane Mallarmé and Thomas Stearns Eliot – three names we are not, perhaps, normally inclined to link together; and yet the work of all three of them bears impressive witness to the fact that 'Music itself may be conceived as striving towards an unattainable timelessness.'[18]

> Words move, music moves
> Only in time; but that which is only living
> Can only die. Words, after speech, reach
> Into the silence. Only by the form, the pattern,
> Can words or music reach
> The stillness, as a Chinese jar still
> Moves perpetually in its stillness.

B.   MUSIC AND MEANING

We are today sometimes inclined to think of great music as being capable of producing in us states of emotion of an unusual depth and intensity. This point of view is, of course, one which is expressed over and over again by the Symbolist poets. But, in the assimilation of *his* poetry to music, Eliot, like Beethoven, was concerned to achieve something much more fundamental than a mere state of emotion. On one occasion, in fact, he even dared to speak about what he called 'the *philosophy* of Beethoven'.[19] '[T]hose of us', he said, 'who love Beethoven find in his music something that we call its meaning, though we cannot confine it in words: but it is this meaning which fits it in, somehow, to our whole life: which makes it an emotional exercise and discipline, and not merely an appreciation of virtuosity.'[20] In marked contrast, Edgar Allan Poe, the father of the Symbolist tradition, delivered the following stern warning to his fellow writers and poets: 'Give to music any undue *decision* – imbue it with any very *determinate* tone – and you deprive it, at once, of its ethereal, its ideal, and, I sincerely believe, of its intrinsic and essential character. You dispel its dream-like luxury: – you dissolve the atmosphere of the mystic.'[21] As early as 1920 we find Eliot openly declaring his dissatisfaction with this effete Symbolist ideal. 'The aim of the poet', he remarked, 'is to state a vision, and no vision of life can be complete which does not include the articulate formulation of life which human minds make. . . . The mystical experience is supposed to be valuable because it is a pleasant state of unique intensity. But the true mystic is not satisfied merely by feeling, he must pretend at least that he sees.'[22] By way of conclusion now let us examine one of the methods Eliot uses in 'Burnt Norton', the first *Quartet*, in order to communicate aspects of his mystical vision and his philosophy.

The *Quartet*'s beautiful second movement opens on a note of paradox. On the one hand, its dream-like quality is suggested by the mysterious joining together and interrelating of opposites; while, on the other hand, its discipline and order are evident in the adherence throughout to a fairly strict system of rhymes and to an inherited octosyllabic metre. The imagery of the first two lines was partly inspired by sonnets composed by Stéphane Mallarmé. This fact, by now well known, has encouraged the belief that Eliot's lyric was deliberately composed in an obscure 'Symbolist' mode; and that, as a consequence, it is not susceptible to too close analysis. What such a conclusion or conviction ignores is that the longer, more discursive and more immediately intelligible part of Section Two, which follows after the lyric, is itself a searching and didactic – I do not say *unpoetic* – commentary and analysis on what has preceded it.

> The effect [Helen Gardner has observed] is like that of hearing the same melody played on a different group of instruments, or differently harmonized, or hearing it syncopated, or elaborated in variations, which cannot disguise the fact that it is the same. The movement opens with a highly poetical passage, in a traditional metrical form. . . . This is followed immediately by an extremely colloquial passage, in which the idea which had been treated in metaphor and symbol in the first half of the movement is expanded and developed in a conversational manner.[23]

I think it worthwhile to point out here that although the method employed by Eliot can, with justice, be described in musical terms, the method as a *literary* method was first discovered and developed by the Spanish poet and mystic, St John of the Cross.

St John's mystical treatises are, without exception, commentaries on his own poems and canticles. This fact impressed deeply the French poet, Paul Valéry, when in 1911 he first read the collected works of the Spanish Carmelite.

> The poetic expression [he noted] serves as a text to be interpreted and a programme to be developed, as well as a symbolic and musical illustration for the treatise of mystical theology. . . . The sacred melody is accompanied by a skilful counterpoint, which weaves around the song a whole system of inner discipline. This set purpose, very new to me, made me think. I wondered what effects could be produced in secular poetry, by this remarkable method which links to the poem its explanation by the author.[24]

Valéry went on to say that the use of this method might well result in developments in the art of literature hitherto impossible.

> There is, in fact, nothing against thinking that the method adopted by St John of the Cross to communicate what one may call the harmonics of his mystical thought, while the thought itself is openly expressed close at hand, could be used in the service of all abstract or deep thought that can nevertheless

provoke emotion. There are such thoughts, and there does exist a sensibility of intellectual things: pure thought has its poetry.[25]

In spite of his great enthusiasm for this 'mystical' method of communication, Valéry was not unaware of the difficulties it might involve for the poet. And certainly had he lived long enough to read some of the searching critical responses to Eliot's later poetry, he would have been confirmed in his view that those poets or writers who employ a method similar to that of St John 'expose themselves to formidable judgments which attack obscurity in the one case and didacticism in the other'.[26]

2

The Philosophy of Stillness

How complete, how intelligent, how well understood, is the philosophy used by the poet, how completely does he realize it poetically; where does he get it from, how much of life does it cover? Such questions we must ask first.

T. S. Eliot, 'Poetry and Propaganda' (1930)

Basic lack of information concerning mysticism is perhaps one of the main reasons why Eliot's mystical attitude, or his philosophy of mysticism, has not always been regarded by critics as fundamental to the inner composition of *Four Quartets*. The tendency in general is to imagine that a work of mystical literature – if it is really authentic – will be characterised by an intense erotic-devotional atmosphere. '[T]he erotic relation between man and woman', writes Dr H. Servotte, '. . . is the common analogy [used by the mystics in their writings] for the relation between man and God.'[1] The fact, therefore, that 'in *Four Quartets* eroticism is conspicuously absent' encourages Servotte to conclude that both the end and the starting-point of *Four Quartets* are different from those of ordinary mystical literature.

One does, it is true, come again and again upon examples of 'the erotic-devotional' in the writings of the mystics. But, although a common genre, it is only one of the many forms of expression to be found in the tradition; and, in Eliot's opinion, not always the most authentic.

> The last canto of the *Paradiso* [he writes] may be genuinely 'mystical poetry'. . . . In that canto Dante is describing, with economy and felicity of words, a mystical experience. But when Wordsworth's great Ode, which is simply great poetry based on a fallacy, or Crashaw's 'St Teresa', which is simply a supreme instance of the erotic-devotional . . . is described as 'mysticism' I cannot agree.[2]

26

The tradition of mysticism or mystical literature towards which Eliot instinctively feels himself drawn is one which presupposes not merely an interior and personal experience, but also a rigorously austere and impersonal understanding or grasp of the Truth. Of the numerous attempts made so far by readers of *Four Quartets* to attain to a simple overall sense of what one might call Eliot's 'mystical attitude' in the poem, to determine in other words within which tradition of philosophy or philosophical literature *Four Quartets* can be said to belong, by far the most impressive in my view is that undertaken by the philosopher and critic, Morris Weitz. In an article entitled 'T. S. Eliot: Time as a mode of Salvation', Weitz argues against those critics who claim that Eliot's philosophical attitude in 'Burnt Norton' is Bergsonian or Heraclitean.[3] He ably demonstrates that Eliot's philosophy of time is, in fact, essentially Christian and Neo-Platonist.

Not all Eliot's readers, however, have been fully convinced by the arguments put forward by Morris Weitz. I will attempt, therefore, in this chapter, and in the chapter which follows, to give greater substance to Weitz's theory by indicating certain important similarities, in thought and in style, between the poetry of 'Burnt Norton' and the work of three Christian Neo-Platonists: first the medieval Scottish mystic and theologian, Richard of St Victor; second, the sixth-century Syrian monk and contemplative of the Negative Way, Pseudo-Dionysius; and third, the fourth-century Christian philosopher and theologian, St Augustine of Hippo. I intend also in this second chapter to indicate how significant it is for 'Burnt Norton' that Eliot should find himself opposed to the philosophy and mystical attitude of the modern French thinker, Henri Bergson.

A. RICHARD OF ST VICTOR AND ARISTOTLE

The prose writings of Eliot which would perhaps have thrown most light on the question of mysticism in *Four Quartets* – 'The Clark Lectures' – were never, in fact, formally published in England, at least not in their original form.[4] One section of the lectures did appear in print, however, in an obscure French periodical in 1927. The essay in question 'Deux Attitudes Mystiques: Dante et Donne' is far from being one of Eliot's most readable works of criticism, but it has a unique importance all the same. In it one can discover what is to be found nowhere else in print, namely an explicit statement by Eliot concerning certain exploratory methods or procedures developed by mystical authors, and their influence on the methods employed by poets such as John Donne and Dante Alighieri. 'I have tried', Eliot states at the conclusion of his article, 'to give some idea of the *rapport* between, on the one hand, the mysticism of Richard of St Victor and the poetry of Dante, and on the other hand, the mysticism of the sixteenth century and the poetry of John Donne.'[5]

Eliot is particularly enthusiastic about the method and style of Richard of St Victor. And here let us pause to note that the qualities Eliot admires in the writings of the Victorine; for example, the resolutely impersonal tone, the absence of any biographical indication, the intellectual seriousness, and the avoidance of all superficial sentiment and feeling, are qualities equally characteristic of that other intellectual mystic whose writings also exercised an influence on the poetry of Dante, Pseudo-Dionysius.

> The most interesting example of a XII-century mystic that I know, and an example which should throw considerable light upon Dante, is Richard of St Victor. Richard was, like the greater philosopher Hugh of St Victor, a Scotsman who became prior of the Victorine monastery. . . . His works occupy the greater part of one volume in Migne's *Patrologia* – no small space; they do not appear to be very well known, and I cannot myself profess acquaintance with any but a small part of them. But the most important, for our purpose, is the *De Gratia Contemplationis*, called the *Benjamin Minor*. This is a treatise on the operations and stages of the mind in proceeding toward the beatific vision.[6]

Eliot then goes on to quote a long passage from Richard of St Victor's treatise. His intention in doing this is not simply to compare from the outside, as it were, the visionary ideal of the Victorine with the poetic vision of Dante in the *Divina Commedia*. Eliot clearly believes that these two 'visions' are somehow intimately related and so he is seeking to present what he calls 'the *rapport* between the mysticism of Richard of St Victor and the poetry of Dante', or in other words, to give an example of 'the sort of thinking and writing which went to the formation of Dante's mind and Dante's style'.[7] 'I should remark also', he writes, 'that the method and the goal seem to me essentially the same as with Aquinas and Dante: the divine contemplation, and the development and subsumption of emotion and feeling through intellect into the vision of God.'[8]

It seems likely that Eliot had a similar 'method and intention' in mind when he was writing the final section of 'Burnt Norton'. This section contains a moment of intense visionary experience:

> Sudden in a shaft of sunlight
> Even while the dust moves
> There rises the hidden laughter
> Of children in the foliage
> Quick now, here, now, always –

Ecstatic or visionary experience of this nature is often thought of as being a kind of liberation from rational modes of thinking, and even as the direct antithesis of logical and philosophical thought. But here the experience of vision is preceded by, and is even seen in some way to be dependent on, a process of disciplined philosophical reflection and meditation:

> The detail of the pattern is movement,
> As in the figure of the ten stairs.
> Desire itself is movement
> Not in itself desirable;
> Love is itself unmoving,
> Only the cause and end of movement,
> Timeless, and undesiring . . .

The 'abstract' and austere philosophy contained in this passage bears a clear and unmistakable resemblance to that of the ancient Greek Philosopher, Aristotle. And this resemblance is not something merely accidental. Eliot is in fact *consciously* working here within the same intellectual tradition of religious mysticism to which he gave so much positive attention in 'Deux Attitudes Mystiques: Dante et Donne'. Note, for example, the following passage from the essay in which Eliot explicitly mentions the Philosopher, Aristotle, by name; and makes explicit also the connection between Aristotle and the religious mysticism of Richard of St Victor and Dante.

> There is a type of religious mysticism which found expression in the XII century, and which is taken up into the system of Aquinas. Its origin is in the Metaphysics of Aristotle 1072b and elsewhere, and in the Nichomachean Ethics. . . . For the XII century, the divine vision or enjoyment of God could only be attained by a process in which the analytic intellect took part; it was through and by and beyond discursive thought that man could arrive at beatitude. This was the form of mysticism consummated in Dante's time.[9]

The particular paragraph in the *Metaphysics* of Aristotle which Eliot has noted here – viz. 1072B – is concerned to establish the nature of the Final Cause and End of all movement in the Universe. 'The Final Cause', Aristotle declares, 'produces motion as being loved, but all others move by being moved.' Furthermore, in paragraph 1072A, the philosopher speaks of desire and of the object of desire, 'that which is in itself desirable'.[10] Compare:

> Desire itself is movement
> Not in itself desirable;
> Love is itself unmoving,
> Only the cause and end of movement,
> Timeless and undesiring . . .

For Aristotle the Supreme Being, the one Unmoving Cause of all movement in the Universe, is Eternal, Unchangeable and Immutable. But this is not to say that His being is inert. Aristotle is careful to attribute to the Supreme Being, or to God, the one activity which he believes to be consistent with continuous actuality, namely intellectual activity or thought. He writes: 'Life also belongs to God for the actuality of thought is life, and God is that actuality; and God's self-dependent actuality is life most good and eternal.'[11] In Aristotle's opinion the actuality of thought or consciousness can be enjoyed in certain privileged moments by the contemplative philosopher; but these moments outside time, moments which involve neither change nor movement, are extremely rare. Eliot himself expresses this Aristotelian notion in an earlier passage of 'Burnt Norton'.

> Time past and time future
> Allow but a little consciousness.
> To be conscious is not to be in time . . .

For the Greek philosopher, it is the nature of the Supreme Being to be *conscious* always.

> [His life] is a life such as the best which we enjoy, and enjoy but for a short time. For it is ever in that state which we cannot be. . . . And thinking in itself deals with that which is best in itself . . . and the act of contemplation is what is most pleasant and best. If then, God is always in that good state in which we sometimes are, this compels our wonder; and if in a better state this compels it yet more. And God is in a better state.[12]

Reading through this celebrated prose passage of Aristotelian philosophy, one is compelled, I think, to agree with an observation once made by the French poet, Paul Valéry: 'there does exist a sensibility of intellectual things: pure thought has its poetry. One may even enquire whether speculation does not always have some kind of lyricism that gives it the necessary charm and energy to induce the mind to engage it.'[13] Certainly, for whatever reason, Aristotelian philosophy has had for many hundreds of years the power to influence Christian sensibility and to engage deeply the Christian mind. But that this influence has always been in the best interests of Christianity is by no means accepted by everyone. The God of Aristotle, although He is depicted as the Ultimate Cause on which the Universe depends, is also understood to be indifferent to, and even perhaps unaware of, the temporal concerns of this world. Is it possible then that Eliot, at the end of 'Burnt Norton', has wholly identified his vision with such an apparently cold and inhuman doctrine? In fact, Eliot's identification with Aristotelian philosophy is not as absolute as it may at first appear. Note to begin with the opening phrase of the final section of the poem:

> The detail of the pattern is movement,
> As in the figure of the ten stairs.

This phrase has already been identified by a number of readers as a reference to the ten steps of the ladder of love described by St

John of the Cross in *The Dark Night of the Soul*.[14] However the phrase, taken by itself, can hardly be said to mitigate in any way the severity of the Aristotelian dogma. More significant, I think, is the short qualifying phrase which is placed at the very end of the poet's meditation:

> Timeless, and undesiring
> Except in the aspect of time
> Caught in the form of limitation
> Between un-being and being.

The subject of this phrase is Eternal Love, the object of human desire and the one Cause and End of all movement in the Universe. This Final Cause is first said to be 'Undesiring', an adjective of which Aristotle himself would no doubt have approved. But the phrase which follows is certainly not Aristotelian. Indeed it would probably have seemed sheer nonsense to the Greek. For what Eliot is referring to here is nothing less, I take it, than that mystery which is called by Christians the Incarnation, the mysterious descent of the Supreme Being, God's eternal Word, into space and time.

B.   THE MYSTICAL ATTITUDE OF HENRI BERGSON

Just before one reaches the 'Aristotelian' meditation at the close of 'Burnt Norton' one is confronted by these four mysterious lines:

> The Word in the desert
> Is most attacked by voices of temptation,
> The crying shadow in the funeral dance,
> The loud lament of the disconsolate chimera.

In a note on this passage, printed in the French edition of *Four Quartets*, Eliot's friend John Hayward draws the reader's attention to the last of the Four Gospels, the Gospel of St John.[15] There, as nowhere else in the New Testament, is to be found the theology of the Word Incarnate. But it would be a mistake, I think, to lift from their context in the poem Eliot's lines concerning the Word and try to read and interpret them exclusively in terms of

Johannine theology. What one must do first of all is to try to come to some understanding of the context in which these lines occur; for it is after all the form and the structure of the poetry – not the underlying theological source – which determines the meaning.

The first part of the fifth section of 'Burnt Norton' is concerned with the nature of art and its relationship to contemplation. Words and music are, as we know, bound up with time. But, unlike other temporal phenomena, the genuine work of art can be said to transcend the limitations of time and to attain even to a kind of timelessness. In Eliot's view, apart from the immediate difficulty facing the artist or the poet, owing to the fact that the medium he employs is always, to begin with, ephemeral, there seems to be yet another burden placed on the medium of language, namely the burden of the Fall.

> Words strain,
> Crack and sometimes break, under the burden,
> Under the tension, slip, slide, perish,
> Decay with imprecision, will not stay in place,
> Will not stay still.

'No wonder', as Jacques Maritain remarks in *Art and Scholasticism*, that 'beautiful things are rare'. And he continues: 'What exceptional conditions must be pre-supposed for a civilization to unite, and in the same men, art and contemplation! Under the burden of a nature always resisting and ceaselessly falling, Christianity has spread its sap everywhere, in art and in the world.'[16] Maritain is repeating here the remarkable theory of Baudelaire which Eliot quoted in his essay on the French poet: 'La vraie civilisation n'est pas dans le gaz, ni dans la vapeur, ni dans les tables tournantes. Elle est dans la diminution des traces du péché originel.'[17]

I think many problems in interpreting 'Burnt Norton' disappear if we take Eliot's 'Word in the desert' as pointing not merely to the historical Jesus, and to the temptations he had to endure in the wilderness, but also to the state of contemporary Christian civilisation and to some of the peculiar temptations and distractions it has to try to cope with in the 'desert' of this age.

> The Word in the desert
> Is most attacked by voices of temptation,
> The crying shadow in the funeral dance,
> The loud lament of the disconsolate chimera.

These are manifestly not the precise historical temptations of Jesus. To what then do they refer? John Hayward, in his notes to the French edition of *Four Quartets*, mentions as well as the Gospel of St John *La Tentation de Saint Antoine* by Flaubert.[18] In Flaubert's final chapter, among the many extraordinary monsters and 'primordial figures', one is in fact described as a 'Chimera'. 'Leaping, flying, spitting fire through her nostrils, lashing her winged sides with her dragon tail, the green-eyed Chimera circles, barks.'[19] It is not the saint of the desert, however, but a giant Sphinx, the symbol of total immobility, that the Chimera is trying in vain to tempt. 'Thee I find perfectly immobile', the Chimera groans in frustration. To which the Sphinx answers: 'the dust flies, cities crumble, and yet my gaze which naught can deviate, remains fixed, gazing through all intervening things, upon a horizon that none can reach.'[20]

Like the Chimera in *La Tentation*, Eliot's 'voices of temptation' are trying in vain to persuade the unmoving and immovable Word that constant change and the endless succession of time, the repetition of that which 'can only die' are what ultimately constitute reality. To those readers who are familiar with modern philosophy these 'voices of temptation' will call to mind at once the philosophical doctrine of constant change whose principal and most original exponent had been the French philosopher Henri Bergson. In Paris, in 1911, Eliot had studied under Bergson at the Sorbonne. But, although he was profoundly affected by this experience, it was not long before he was severely and openly critical of the French thinker, even questioning the sincerity of Bergson's evolutionary optimism. In a short review written in 1916 Eliot even went so far as to say that he preferred Nietzsche's policy in regard to the cosmic flux to that of Bergson. Nietzsche's 'world-will is creative like Bergson's', Eliot pointed out, 'but, more sincerely than Bergson's is without sense or promise'.[21] In another place, Eliot remarked: 'Words like *emergent* and *organism* . . . simply do not rouse the right response in my breast.'[22] By taking this stand Eliot was by no means an isolated figure. Jacques Maritain, who had himself been a student of Bergson in Paris, T. E. Hulme and Wyndham Lewis, were all stridently opposed to certain central tenets in the Bergsonian metaphysic.[23] In 1972, Lewis published a book entitled *Time and Western Man* in which he pointed out that 'Bergson . . . more than any other single figure is responsible for the main intellectual character of the world we live in.'[24] He also asserted that 'Time for the bergsonian or relativist is fundamentally sensation; that is what Bergson's *durée* always conceals beneath its pretentious metaphysic. It is the glorification of the life-of-the-moment, with no reference beyond itself and no absolute or universal value.'[25] Eliot had probably read through Lewis's book long before he wrote *Four Quartets*. He refers to it, in fact, in one of a series of lectures he published in 1934.[26] And it is significant also that when the book first made its appearance in 1927 it received an extensive review in Eliot's journal *The Criterion*.[27] One or two passages from this review article are, I think, worth noting here. It opens with a reference to Lewis's Aristotelianism and to 'his belief in the sovereignty of the intelligence in human affairs'. Developing this theme further in the second paragraph, the reviewer suddenly tosses out a rather unusual image to describe the difficulty of a thinker such as Lewis in the modern world; and I have no doubt that, at that time, it made an impression on the visual imagination of Eliot.

The author, we feel, has been tempted like St Anthony by a very dextrous and protean devil, and his book itself is a *recherche* of Mr Lewis' own *temps passé* which might be given the alternative title of 'Temptations I have overcome'; but unlike most volumes of reminiscences *Time and Western Man* has a unity of theme quite independent of the author's experience. Its signal importance is that it effectively calls attention to the popular doctrine of processional flux which permeates a great deal of inferior philosophy and criticism at the present day. . . . When Mr Lewis went out into the wilderness he encountered the Time-Satan in many strange forms. There was a very impressive set of demons; scientific demons like Darwin and Einstein, and the philosophical demons Bergson and Alexander, striding the Flux.[28]

No less than Wyndham Lewis in *Time and Western Man*, Eliot in 'Burnt Norton' is attempting to come to terms with 'the Time-Satan' of Bergsonian philosophy. The poem opens, in fact, with the poet struggling to think through the implications of the Bergsonian concept of *durée*.

> Time present and time past
> Are both perhaps present in time future,
> And time future contained in time past.
> If all time is eternally present
> All time is unredeemable.

For Bergson, reality is change, that change is indivisible, and in an indivisible change the past is one with the present and with the future. 'Real duration', he writes, 'is what we have always called time but time perceived as indivisible.'[29] If this Bergsonian hypothesis is correct there is no possibility of redemption in time. If time is merely 'the present which endures' or, in other words, 'if all time is eternally present', then indeed 'all time is unredeemable'. And yet for Bergson, what is important is to immerse oneself completely in the senses, in images, in the phenomena, to allow oneself to be lulled by 'the uninterrupted humming of life's depths'.[30] To him the essence of mysticism is little more, it seems, than a total immersion in the present moment.

   This theory of Bergson is rejected out of hand by Eliot. Although for a time Eliot had been a student of Bergson in 1911, he was not, he assures us, infected by the 'epidemic of Bergsonism'.[31] In fairness it has, however, to be said that Eliot's opposition to Bergsonian philosophy probably served to make more coherent and more sturdy the structure of his own 'mystical attitude'. When, for example, in 'Deux Attitudes Mystique: Dante et Donne', he wanted to describe the mystical philosophy he himself admired, he found it both expedient and illuminating to use as his point of contrast the philosophy of Bergson. 'You know', he wrote, 'how the Absolute of Bergson is arrived at: by a turning back on the path of thought, by divesting one's mind of the apparatus of distinction and analysis, by plunging into the flow of immediate experience'. In contrast, the mystical philosophy behind the poetry of Dante involved 'a process in which the analytic intellect took part; it was through and by and beyond discursive thought that man could arrive at beatitude'.[32]

   Here then is the form of mysticism or mystical attitude to which Eliot aspired. And it is, as he had indicated more than once in his published criticism, 'the opposite of Bergsonism'.[33] To the poet of 'Burnt Norton' the essence or the heart of the mystical way is a perception of transcendent Permanence. It is a knowledge of stillness, not a knowledge of motion. And it is only by raising

oneself above the cosmic flux, by calmly refu:
oneself within it, that one can begin to reach
which is ultimately real.

C. THE PHILOSOPHY OF THE POET AND OF THE POEM

The poet or the mystical author, in his attempt at self-expression and self-understanding, will often make use of certain images and concepts inherited from a single philosophical source, or from a number of different sources. The central concept or image in Part Two of 'Burnt Norton' is that of 'the still point of the turning world'. Since this is a 'concept' one can find in the work of innumerable philosophers, ancient and modern, the search for Eliot's precise source or sources is not likely to be an easy task. Perhaps the best thing one can do here is to try to indicate the general philosophical tradition within which Eliot is working.

'There are those', writes Pierre Auriol, a minor Schoolman of the medieval period, 'who use the image of the centre of the circle, in its relation to all points of the circumference; and they affirm that this is similar to the *Nunc* of eternity in its connection with all parts of time. By which they mean that eternity actually co-exists with the whole of time.'[34] Auriol is almost certainly referring here to medieval philosophers such as the Dominican Saint Thomas Aquinas. But what he has to say can be applied also to Dante, to St Augustine, to Pseudo-Dionysius, and to other philosophers and poets in the Christian Neo-Platonic tradition, and before them to the Greek thinker Aristotle, and to Plotinus – and, one can add, in our own time, to the philosopher-poet, T. S. Eliot.[35]

That some of Eliot's ideas and imagery can be traced to the Neo-Platonic literary tradition has, I think, been already reasonably well established. But mere knowledge of the poet's philosophical inheritance and mystical background does not in itself tell us everything that is important about 'the philosophy of the *poem*'. The latter term has been used by Eliot to designate that which can only be found *in* the poem itself, or in other words that which cannot be translated back into abstract concepts or philosophical theories. In contrast, the term 'philosophy of the poet' is understood to mean the philosophy which the poet has either taken over from other thinkers, or has constructed himself prior to the composition of a given creative work.[36] The distinction is, I think, a useful one. Reading through *Four Quartets* one is often struck by the sustained quality of its intellectual vision. But one is also aware that 'the ideas' within the poem are not proposed as abstract theories. They are present rather as facts of experience, elements which go together with all the other elements of the poet's experience to make up the basic materials and substance of his art. Accordingly, the understanding of a philosophical or mystical treatise and the understanding of a poem are two very different things. Knowledge concerning sources can, it is true, be sometimes most valuable, especially in the case of a poem such as *Four Quartets*; but the philosophy or mysticism of the *poem* cannot be reduced merely to the poet's own abstract theorising prior to composition, or to certain abstract, intellectual theories of the poet's chosen masters in philosophy.

Of all Eliot's critics, no one, I think, has understood this distinction better than F. R. Leavis. In a review-article published in 1942 he writes:

> The poet's magnificent intelligence is devoted to keeping as close as possible to the concrete of sensation, emotion and perception. Though this poetry is plainly metaphysical in pre-occupation, it is as much poetry, it belongs as purely to the realm of sensibility, and has in it as little of the abstract and general of discursive prose, as any poetry that was ever written.[37]

The poet of 'Burnt Norton' clearly shares with the metaphysician and the theologian an interest in the concept of 'eternity'. But, as Dr Leavis explains, the terms and concepts familiar to the theologian are never taken up by Eliot as accepted instruments for getting to work with. 'The poetry from *Ash-Wednesday* onwards doesn't say, "I believe", or "I know", or "Here is the truth"; it is positive in direction but not positive in that way.'[38] Those readers who bring to the *Quartets* a certain 'theological equipment' do not necessarily, therefore, have an advantage over the less endowed. Indeed, Leavis warns that their 'advantage' may tend, if anything, 'to disqualify them from appreciating the nature of the poet's genius. They are apt to show too great an alacrity in response; to defeat his [the poet's] essential method by jumping in too easily and too happily with familiar terms and concepts'.[39]

One of Eliot's English critics whose work Dr Leavis openly admired, because it showed a grasp of the poet's 'essential method', was D. W. Harding. Of Harding's review of *Collected Poems: 1909–35* published in *Scrutiny*, Leavis wrote: 'It seems to me pre-eminently the note on Eliot to send people to.'[40] If we read through Harding's review-article we discover that one of the passages he chooses to quote in order to bring to light the nature of Eliot's 'essential method' is the passage in the second section of 'Burnt Norton' which we have already been considering. The passage wonderfully illustrates, in fact, the point being made by Harding, namely that Eliot's method is 'to make pseudo-statements in highly abstract language, for the purpose, essentially, of putting forward and immediately rejecting ready-made concepts that might have seemed appropriate to the concept [of Eternity] he is creating'.[41] The point could hardly be made more succinctly. But there is one minor detail concerning this method, which to anyone familiar with the Western mystical tradition is at once significant, but of which Harding and Leavis both seem to be unaware.

The 'essential method' employed by Eliot is, in fact, no different from the method we find employed in the mystical writings of other authors working within the Neo-Platonic tradition. In particular, I am thinking here of a work entitled *The Mystical Theology* by the sixth-century Syrian monk Pseudo-Dionysius. Here first of all is the passage quoted by Harding from 'Burnt Norton'.

Neither from nor towards; at the still point, there the dance is,
But neither arrest nor movement. And do not call it fixity,
Where past and future are gathered. Neither movement from
    nor towards,
Neither ascent nor decline.

And here is a passage taken almost at random from the fifth chapter of *The Mystical Theology*:

It is not immobile, nor in motion, or at rest,
and has no power, and is not power or light,
and does not live, and is not life;
nor is it personal essence, or eternity, or time.[42]

In both passages, there is the same negation of opposites and the same use of highly abstract language. Also, instead of taking existing abstract ideas and piecing them together in the ordinary way, there is a clear rejection of 'ready-made concepts that might have seemed appropriate to the concept' being created.

Eliot – it hardly need to be said – was familiar with the writings of Pseudo-Dionysius. The Syrian's name is mentioned on several of the 'reading notes' which have survived from Eliot's student period at Harvard.[43] And, in a review published in 1925, Eliot spoke of Dionysius as having had what seemed a direct influence on the poetry of John Donne.[44] The particular text of Pseudo-Dionysius quoted above may have come to Eliot's attention as early as 1923. Paul Elmer More, in his book *Hellenistic Philosophies*, quoted the passage together with a number of other passages from the Syrian, and then commented that it was 'a fair statement of the Plotinian mysticism carried to its ultimate expression'.[45] (*Hellenistic Philosophies* was the second volume in a series by More entitled *The Greek Tradition*. In an obituary note written shortly after More's death in 1937 Eliot remarked: 'It was not until one or two of the volumes of *The Greek Tradition* had appeared that More began to have any importance for me.'[46]) The Dionysian text was also quoted in a book by H. C. White, *The Mysticism of William Blake*, to which Eliot gave a favourable review in 1927.[47] White was of the opinion that Chapter Five of *The Mystical Theology* was 'the most famous expression' within the Christian tradition, of the *via negativa*.[48]

The reason why it has seemed worthwhile here to link the name of Eliot with that of the mystical theologian, Pseudo-Dionysius, is not simply in order to focus attention on another possible source *behind* the poetry. My intention throughout has been to indicate that the source of the poet's 'essential method' in 'Burnt Norton' is the point at which his procedures unite and intersect with those of the mystic.

3

Eliot in Meditation

An extremely complex game of serious–nonseriousness was being played when one day at tea in Tavistock Square, Virginia Woolf needled Eliot about his religion. Did he go to church? Yes. Did he hand round the plate for the collection? Yes. Oh, really! Then what did he experience when he prayed? Eliot leaned forward, bowing his head in that attitude which was itself one of prayer . . . and described the attempt to concentrate, to forget self, to attain union with God.

(Stephen Spender, 'Remembering Eliot', 1965)

The kind of knowledge Eliot derived from his reading of mystical philosophy and literature should not, I think, be understood as something merely abstract or intellectual. It was a knowledge that affected in some degree his entire sensibility. The evidence for this claim is in the meditative poetry Eliot has written. But one can also learn something from a few absorbing pages Eliot composed as a 'Preface' to an anthology of devotional literature entitled *Thoughts for Meditation: A Way to Recovery from Within*.[1] Eliot's immediate subject in these pages is the question of how best to read the work of spiritual authors. First of all, he makes a number of comments on the difficulties involved in the reading of other kinds of literature such as philosophy and poetry:

> Philosophy is difficult, unless we discipline our minds for it; the full appreciation of poetry is difficult for those who have not trained their sensibility by years of attentive reading. But devotional reading is the most difficult of all, because it requires an application, not only of the mind, not only of the sensibility, but of the whole being.[2]

Eliot then goes on to explain, in more concrete and more personal

41

terms, exactly how he himself approaches a work of mystical literature:

> I myself should not choose to read very much at a time. To read two or three passages . . . to attend closely to every word, to ponder on the quotations read for a little while and try to fix them in my mind, so that they may continue to affect me while my attention is engrossed with the affairs of the day: that is enough for me in twenty-four hours, and enough, I imagine, even for those more practised in meditation than I.[3]

Although Eliot wrote this passage some time after he had written the *Quartets* it is clear from other evidence that he had begun the practice of meditation many years before.[4] Awareness of this fact should help us to understand more fully the nature and extent of the influence on Eliot's poetry of the mystical tradition. 'Tradition', he tells us himself, 'cannot be inherited; and if you want it you must obtain it by great labour.'[5]

A.   MEDITATION AND POETRY

Approximately ten years prior to the composition of the *Quartets*, Eliot made a number of observations on the relationship between the tradition of religious meditation and the art of poetry. What interested him in particular, as we have seen, was the relationship between the meditative method and mysticism of Richard of St Victor and the poetry of Dante.[6] But Eliot was also aware, at this time, of the extensive influence of certain methods of meditation on the metaphysical poetry of the seventeenth century. 'Now if you read and study the *Spiritual Exercises* [of St Ignatius of Loyola]' he wrote in March 1930, 'you will find a stock of images which reminds you, and by no mere coincidence, of Donne . . . whose childhood was passed under Jesuit influence.'[7] Since Eliot's article was published, a close reading by scholars of poetry written in the sixteenth and seventeenth centuries in England and elsewhere has already yielded evidence to establish a relationship of similarity and even of dependence between the art of meditation and the *ars poetica*. According to Louis Martz, in his book *The Poetry of Meditation*, 'one period when such meditation flourished coincides exactly with the flourishing of English religious poetry'. And he adds: 'There is, I believe, much more than mere coincidence here, for the qualities developed by the art of meditation . . . are essentially the qualities that the twentieth century has admired in Donne, or Herbert, or Marvell.'[8] In 1921 Eliot published a short paper entitled 'The Metaphysical Poets', and he is now generally acknowledged as the person most responsible for the modern revival of interest in Donne, Herbert and Marvell. What is not so well known, however, is that a few years prior to writing the *Quartets*, he returned again to the subject of the Metaphysicals, only this time his interest was focused particularly on the religious nature of their poetry. (See 'The Devotional Poets of the Seventeenth Century',[9] and 'Mystic and Politician as Poet: Vaughan, Traherne, Marvell, Milton'.[10]) Meditation, as it was understood in the time of John Donne and George Herbert can be said to comprise more or less a distinct phase in the life of prayer. It involves a silent application of one's mind to a supernatural truth in order to realise its meaning, and then gradually, with the assistance of grace, to further realise and incarnate this meaning in one's own life. But how is this different from intellectual study? And is the process of meditation not the same as that of contemplation? First of all, meditation proceeds by discursive steps. Aided by the senses, the memory and the imagination, it constructs a vision of spiritual reality in order thereby to evoke a concrete devotional response. In the act of contemplation, however, such vision comes, as it were, more intuitively, and without a laboured process of reasoning.

The art of meditation is different also from intellectual speculation. Although one of its aims is to arrive at firm convictions concerning some important truth, it is not much concerned with intellectual exactitude. The *discursus* of the intellect and the engagement of the senses and the imagination are merely a kind of preparatory drama necessary for the attainment of concentration and for the arousal of love. As it happens, however, it is precisely this 'preparatory drama', with its disciplined use of imagery and its technique of arousing the passionate affections of the will, which has provoked scholarly interest in the relationship between the techniques of prayer and the art of meditative poetry.

Poetry and meditation are, of course, in no way synonymous. But in the mind and imagination of the creative artist, these two separate and distinct disciplines may sometimes unite in the making of a poem; and, perhaps more by grace of instinct than design, help to create what is now called 'the poetry of meditation' or 'the meditative poem'. For our purposes here, it is important to note that this genre of poetry is not necessarily limited to the seventeenth century. Indeed, Martz puts forward the tentative hypothesis that 'in the poetry of Hopkins, and in the later poetry of Yeats or Eliot, we may find that the individual ways of meditation are guided in part by traditional methods'.[11] Although Martz has *Four Quartets* particularly in mind, his remark has not yet received the close attention it deserves.[12] This is all the more surprising in view of the fact that his proposed definition of 'meditative verse' very nearly defines the opening movement of 'Burnt Norton'.

> A meditative poem is a work that creates an interior drama of the mind; this dramatic action is usually (though not always) created by some form of self-address, in which the mind grasps firmly a problem or situation deliberately evoked by the memory, brings it forward toward the full light of consciousness, and concludes with a moment of illumination, where the speaker's self has, for a time, found an answer to its conflicts.[13]

It hardly needs to be said that there are many different kinds of meditation and meditative poetry. In this chapter our study is necessarily limited to *one* of these methods – viz. the Augustinian method – and to a brief enquiry into the influence it has had on the opening section of 'Burnt Norton'. From the start I should make it clear that the meditative process enacted in this part of the poem is not, in my view, an exercise in religious devotion *simpliciter*. What I do suggest, however, and what I shall try to demonstrate in these pages, is that the poem has been influenced, to some considerable degree, by the traditional art of meditation, and from that source has been provided with a kind of basic discipline and a certain fundamental inner structure.

Towards the end of his book, *The Poetry of Meditation*, Louis Martz suggests that the meditative method which underlies certain parts of *Four Quartets* may owe something to the Ignatian or Jesuit structure of meditation: 'those symbolic landscapes [in *Four Quartets*] can we call them compositions of place?'[14] The idea is certainly an interesting one. But the movement or the structure which we find, for example, in the opening passage of 'Burnt Norton' is much closer, I think, to what has been called by Martz in another place 'the dramatic action of Augustinian meditation'.[15] This structure is, we are told by Martz, significantly different from the 'precise tightly articulated method' of meditation favoured by Ignatius Loyola and his followers. 'I[n] Augustinian meditation there is no such precise method: there is, rather, an intuitive groping back into regions of the soul that lie beyond sensory memories.'[16]

Poetry composed under the impulse of this kind of Augustinian meditation is likely to be somewhat different from poetry composed under the impulse of the Ignatian mode. In the poetry of Augustinian meditation 'the characteristic movement is a mining of associations, a roving search over a certain field of imagery, a sinking inward upon the mind's resources, until all the evocative ramifications of the memory have been explored'.[17] In the eleventh chapter of Augustine's *Confessions* we read: 'Out of the memory are drawn not the things themselves . . . but such words as being conceived by the images of those things, they, in their passing through our senses, have, as their footsteps, left imprinted in our minds'.[18] Compare:

> Footfalls echo in the memory
> Down the passage which we did not take
> Towards the door we never opened
> Into the rose-garden.

At the centre both of Eliot's meditation and that of St Augustine, there is the essential memory of a completely innocent and blissful world, the awareness of a birthright of happiness not yet lost, a paradise within. 'For there is', Augustine says, 'a dim glimmering of light yet unput-out in men.'[19]

For most of us this 'memory' when it happens is an uncertain visitation, a faint gleam that pierces suddenly through our sense of the solid material world, and as suddenly vanishes. We are left with a feeling of intense nostalgia. And yet, very often, our desire seems to have no distinguishable object, no recognisable source. We may even feel constrained to dismiss the entire experience as being merely some kind of an illusion, or an escape. Is this then the experience which is being presented to us in 'Burnt Norton'? The pressure on the poet drawing him back into 'our first world', is it merely the pressure of an unfulfilled emotion, the burden of our common, hopeless nostalgia for 'what might have been'? Or is it, rather, the compelling force of a timeless principle of Love, and the agent therefore of an authentic experience of enlightenment?

There is, of course, no simple answer to this question. And, perhaps not surprisingly, it is a question that has caused considerable division and confusion among Eliot's critics. On the one hand Kristian Smidt tells us that 'in the garden of Burnt Norton . . . the poet has a moment of mystic illumination, a sense of reality and completeness'. And what is more, in Smidt's view, 'The experience now becomes a touchstone of reality and a goal to be sought in all the endeavours of life.'[20] On the other hand, Leonard Unger, whose influential paper on the subject appeared in 1956, is of the opinion that the scene in the rose-garden is 'not genuine but mechanical and devitalized . . . The music is "unheard", and "hidden"; privacy is spoiled by an "unseen eyebeam" and the roses have the "look of flowers that are looked at". The details of the situation have been forcibly willed. . . . The effort is thus one of torment, disappointing in its partial and insufficient revelation.'[21] What we experience in the rose-garden is 'not reality', writes another of Eliot's critics, 'but romantic illusion'.[22] And in a paper by David Hirch entitled 'Eliot's Rose-garden: Illumination or Illusion?', we read: 'The poet suggests a desire for a mystical illumination, but suggests simultaneously that such desire cannot be fulfilled.'[23] One thing common to all these different approaches is, I think, a failure to come to terms imaginatively with the poem's extraordinarily complex and subtle meditative pattern. Once one is made aware of this pattern, at least some of the many difficulties of interpretation begin to disappear, and one's appreciation of the poetry is greatly enhanced. But, it is only, I think, towards the end of the opening meditation of 'Burnt Norton' that one is finally able to make some judgment concerning the nature of Eliot's illumination experience. In the earlier stages the poet himself is distinctly cautious, even, I would say, sceptical. He is determined not to be deceived by the pressure of his desire for 'what might have been'. And in the end it is, of course, precisely this dogged probing and testing of his intuition that gives so much authority and substance to the final vision. But let us not anticipate too much too soon; otherwise we will risk ignoring those aspects or qualities of meditation and exploration that make the poetry so memorable.

B. THE STRUCTURE OF A MEDITATION

'Burnt Norton' opens in an apparently calm atmosphere of intellectual enquiry. The particular view of time being considered seems not to be insisted on by Eliot as his own conclusive insight or personal dogma. On the contrary, the careful placing and use of the words 'if' and 'perhaps' betray in the poet an almost deliberately slow and tentative approach to his subject. Eliot's tone here is one of abstract and cool self-interrogation. But almost at once, with the repetition of the phrase 'what might have been' and in the sudden use of the word 'unredeemable', one can sense the first tremor of some underlying emotional and spiritual pressure:

> Time present and time past
> Are both perhaps present in time future
> And time future contained in time past.
> If all time is eternally present
> All time is unredeemable.
> What might have been is an abstraction
> Remaining a perpetual possibility
> Only in a world of speculation.
> What might have been and what has been
> Point to one end which is always present.

For all their resonance and authority, the last two lines quoted above do not reveal their meaning at once. But rather like an oracle they succeed first in making an impression with their resonance, and only then, as it were, invite us, the listeners, to tease out the hidden meaning step by step. According to one interpretation, this 'end' is the actual present reality at any given moment in our lives. It can be called 'unredeemable' since it is impossible to consider it being other than in fact it is.[24] In support of this view and in order to bring to light what in his judgment is the probable source behind Eliot's oracular phrase, Graham Hough cites Augustine's teaching that our consciousness of both past and future exists only in the present; so there is a sense in which only the present is real. Or, in other words 'that time past and time future have their meaning only in time present'.[25] This interpretation might indeed be obvious and acceptable if, in the relevant passage from the poem, Eliot had spoken of one end which is always the present. But, as it is written, the statement does not refer in any explicit way to the present as such. It suggests rather the immanent presence to what might have been and what has been of some mysterious 'end'.

Just what exactly Eliot means by this 'one end' will be made clear to us later in the poem. For the present, however, it may be illuminating to quote here a passage from St Augustine which, by happy coincidence, very nearly parallels, at one point, the fragment of Heraclitus, which Eliot chose as one of the epigraphs to 'Burnt Norton'. (Heraclitus: 'Although the Word is common to all, most people live as if each of them had a private understanding of his own.') St Augustine first proclaims what, as he says himself, 'we know': 'Thou dost call us therefore to the understanding of God the Word, who is God, with thee God; which Word is spoken from all eternity, and in it all things spoken eternally.'[26] Augustine then goes on to speak of those people who do not understand this mystery:

> They do not yet understand thee, O thou Wisdom of God, and Light of our minds, nor yet do they understand how those things are made by thee and in thee . . . Who shall be able to hold and fix it, that for a while it may be still, and may catch a glimpse of thy ever-fixed eternity, and compare it with the times that never stand, that so he may see how these things are not to be compared together? That he may understand . . . that all which is both past and future is created and doth flow out from that which is always present.[27]

In this passage the phrase 'that which is always present' does not primarily refer to the present moment wherein in some sense we can say the past and the future are contained; it refers rather to the presence of an 'ever-fixed eternity', that 'eternity which ever standeth still' and which as an ultimate end dictates what has been and what will be, and in which, presumably, even the sad sphere of 'what might have been' can expect to enjoy, if not immediate fulfilment for its poignant and frustrated desire, at least a sure hope of being drawn more and more closely towards some final meaning and redemption. It is this theme, namely that of the eternal end which is ever still and always present, to which Eliot returns in Section Two of 'Burnt Norton'. And again in the fifth and final section of the poem:

> Desire itself is movement
> Not in itself desirable;
> Love is itself unmoving,
> Only the cause and end of movement,
> Timeless, and undesiring . . .

Clearly throughout 'Burnt Norton', by a process of conscious and subtle deliberation, Eliot is striving to fix his attention and that of his reader on 'the cause and end of movement', that 'one end which is always present'. But, inevitably, neither the poetry nor the man himself who creates it can sustain for long a fixed and clear vision of that ultimate reality. The problem here is not so much a difficulty in attaining intellectual conviction, but the immensely more difficult task of acquiring spiritual freedom and of putting the sentiments in order.[28] This task is, of course, difficult for everyone. And there are, according to St Augustine, many people who strive 'to have some relish of things eternal while their heart – as yet unstable withal – doth flicker to and fro in the motions of things past and to come'.[29] Eliot in *his* attempt to concentrate his mind on 'things eternal' shows himself distracted, however, not so much by the dimension of things past and to come as by the sad sphere of 'what might have been'. Just at the point when his mind looks to that 'one end which is always present' and having, or so it seemed, already dismissed 'what might have been' as a mere speculative abstraction, that same sad spectre returns to haunt his imagination.

> Footfalls echo in the memory
> Down the passage which we did not take
> Towards the door we never opened
> Into the rose-garden. My words echo
> Thus, in your mind.
>   But to what purpose
> Disturbing the dust on a bowl of rose-leaves
> I do not know.

Due to some failure of nerve or of attention in the poet, the meaning of his experience in the rose-garden, and even that experience itself, seems hardly to have been realised. It is reduced now to mere 'dust on a bowl of rose-leaves' and remains 'a perpetual possibility / Only in a world of speculation'. And yet, emotionally, it would appear, he is tempted to deceive himself and to project back unto the past an ideal vision of fulfilment.

> Other echoes
> Inhabit the garden. Shall we follow?

In spite of his hesitation and scruple, an almost involuntary music in the poetry draws Eliot back into the half-imaginary, half-real world of 'what might have been' and 'what has been'. Moreover, the co-existence of these two spheres of time in the mind of the poet appears to create in his memory a new pattern or series of moving images and presences which together form a kind of hallucinatory and beautiful mirage:

> The pool was filled with water out of sunlight,
> And the lotos rose, quietly, quietly,
> The surface glittered out of heart of light,
> And they were behind us, reflected in the pool.
> Then a cloud passed, and the pool was empty.

This strange hallucinatory atmosphere, with its mysteriously rising 'lotos' and its 'dignified, invisible ghosts', has impressed by far the greater number of Eliot's readers as an evocation of authentic mystical experience. But when we read through the poem in the light of its meditative structure we can see at once that this particular section, far from expressing an intense vision of supernatural reality, represents, in fact, no more than an illusion or an escape. In other words, to use a phrase of Eliot's from another context, its vision is 'immaterial and ghostly, rather than spiritual'.[30] As soon, however, as the few luminous presences in the rose-garden vanish, and the pool is empty, the poet records his first momentary glimpse of the truth, a moment which is 'both an inspiration and a rebuke, a source of consolation and also a source of terror'.[31]

> Go, said the bird, for the leaves were full of children,
> Hidden excitedly, containing laughter.
> Go, go, go, said the bird: human kind
> Cannot bear very much reality.

The recognition of man's innate tendency to be distracted from what is ultimately most real could hardly be made more explicit.

And yet this very capacity for distraction has, it would appear, one distinctly positive aspect. When we look back again to the beginning of our meditation, we discover, perhaps to our surprise, that our first entry into the world of enchantment and illusion was somehow fortuitous. Without it we might never have come to the edge of vision and gained our first real apprehension of the truth. Not once but twice in his meditation Eliot alerts us to this fact when he says that the world of 'what might have been' – illusory and dangerous though it is – can point us to that 'one end which is always present'. This 'world' may in itself be ambiguous and even a sort of counterfeit of the supernatural, but it has the effect all the same of stirring up within us memories and desires at the very root of our being. It is 'our first world' – a phrase which is twice repeated by Eliot. And thus we are being reminded here not merely of the rose-garden beside the house at Burnt Norton but also of the mythical garden of Eden, which according to the legend of Genesis was inhabited before the Fall by 'our first parents' ('There they were as our guests, accepted and accepting'). That a mere image or mirage of 'what might have been' should serve here as a symbol – albeit an ambiguous one – of the Garden of Eden, is no surprise. Within the Earthly Paradise of Dante, as Philip H. Wickstead explains, 'The good that we purposed and never accomplished or that we once knew and have since lost hold of; all that we have been or might have been of good must be a thing that is.'[32]

At least something of the difficulty meditation involves was enacted by Eliot, and more than once, in his earlier poetry. However, unlike the third movement, for example, of 'Ash-Wednesday', which is composed in a prayer form and follows more or less a traditional pattern of Christian meditation, the opening movement of the first *Quartet* is philosophical in tone and is not explicitly religious. In this respect it resembles the art or pattern of meditation favoured by St Augustine.

Western mystics are accustomed to understand contemplation as something which is attained in the silent absorption of prayer; the heart of the contemplative's awareness of God being intuitive and non-discursive. But, for Augustine, at least according to the view of Dom Cuthbert Butler, contemplation is primarily 'an intellectual process – informed, indeed, by intense religious warmth, but still primarily intellectual'.[33] Accordingly, the object of contemplation is sometimes expressed by Augustine in almost abstract metaphysical terms. Describing the climax of one of his own early experiences, for example, Augustine writes: 'In the flash of a trembling glance my mind came to Ultimate Reality, Absolute Being, – that which is.'[34]

Also worth noting is Augustine's famous description of an experience which he shared once with Monica his mother. They were at Ostia and were leaning out of a certain window overlooking the garden. Already, we are told, they had begun a gradual 'inward ascent' by thinking and speaking, marvelling at God's works and discussing with each other concerning that life 'by which all things come to be, both those that have been and those that are to be'. Augustine then continues:

And the life itself never comes to be, but is as it was and shall be ever more, because it is neither past nor future but present only, for it is eternal. And as we talked and yearned after it, we touched it – and hardly touched it – with the full beat of our heart. And we sighed and left there impawned the first fruits of the spirit, and we relapsed into articulate speech, where every word has beginning and ending. And how little, O Lord, it is like unto thy Word.[35]

Here, as in the opening movement of Eliot's poem, the stated object of contemplation, namely that living and eternal Reality, the Word which is always present, is viewed in terms of its relationship to time past and time future. For the protagonist in 'Burnt Norton', however, even a momentary experience of such reality is unbearable. He is prone to be distracted and his inward intellectual ascent to Eternal Life, or to the Paradise within, appears much more hesitant and more subjectively self-conscious than that of Augustine and Monica. But even for Augustine the core of the experience is transitory and is realised only in part and only for an instant. 'We touched it', he writes, 'and hardly touched it (*attigimus eam modice*) with the full beat of our heart.'

In Eliot's poem, as in the method of meditation enacted here by St Augustine and described later, for example by St François de Sales, there is at first 'a simple proposing of the subject for meditation' and then following afterwards an 'imaginary representation' of the same subject.[36] Also, and in spite of certain distractions, this mental and imaginative process attains to a brief moment of illumination. But the experience is, for some reason, unbearable for Eliot, and it is only partly realised. Almost at once, like St Augustine before him, the poet must return to 'articulate speech' and to a prose restatement or recapitulation of the original subject and theme of his meditation:

> Time past and time future
> What might have been and what has been
> Point to one end, which is always present.

The technical qualities of 'Burnt Norton's' opening passage have been examined many times from the standpoint of strict literary criticism, and on at least one issue there is almost complete agreement. Eliot has made use here – and brilliant use – of an intricate, musical technique. To Helen Gardner, for example, the first movement 'contains statement and counter-statement of two contrasted but related themes like the first and second subjects of a movement in strict sonata form'.[37] This analogy with music is unquestionably helpful. But what I hope I have demonstrated in these pages is that the dialectical process of statement and counter-statement in the poem, the discovery together for example of. intense intellectual concentration with more than usual emotional distraction, the placing side by side of the abstract and the concrete, of the dogmatic and the exploratory, and the continual lively attempt to subordinate one faculty to the other – finds a most illuminating and close parallel not only in the art of music but also in the traditional practice and art of meditation and meditative poetry.

Part Two
'East Coker'
The Way of Negation

4

The Ascetic Vision

Yet, take Thy way; for, sure, Thy way is best:
Stretch or contract me Thy poor debtor:
This is but tuning of my breast,
To make the music better.

(George Herbert, 'The Tempter')

A robe of sackcloth next the smooth, white skin.
Such, poets, is your bride, the Muse! young, gay,
Radiant, adorn'd outside; a hidden ground
Of thought and of austerity within.

(Matthew Arnold, 'Austerity of Poetry')

When it was first published in 1940 'East Coker' was considered by many critics to be one of Eliot's most considerable poetic achievements. But this view was not shared by everyone. There was, for example, the following assessment made by an anonymous reviewer in the pages of *The Times Literary Supplement*: 'Mr Eliot is disdainful of many things, of most things. . . . Where Vaughan, whose days were as troubled as our own and little less violent, saw eternity the other night and bright shoots of everlastingness, Mr Eliot sees only the dark.'[1] Unfortunately, many of the disagreements concerning 'East Coker' were, in the beginning, largely ideological. On the one hand, those critics who had sympathy with Eliot's bleak vision of the *via negativa* were inclined to express an almost tribal enthusiasm for the poem. On the other hand, the quite deliberate and unembarrassed expression in the poem of Eliot's Catholic philosophy of disillusion – what the critic George Orwell called Eliot's 'melancholy faith' – did not win much approbation from the more left-wing and agnostic critics. The predictable outcome of this polarisation of

views was that Eliot's poetry was not always read and enjoyed as
poetry, but was used instead as a mere datum in the discussion of
politics, depth psychology and religion. And so, when finally
there appeared in print the sensitive and rigorous critical
response of F. R. Leavis – I refer here to his early review of the
Quartets entitled 'T. S. Eliot's Later Poetry' – the occasion marked
an important turning point in Eliot criticism.[2] Leavis argued – and
argued with impressive authority – that those readers and critics
of Eliot's poetry who did not share the poet's Christian faith or
philosophy were in no way at a disadvantage when it came to
reading the *Quartets*: 'to feel an immense indebtedness to Eliot
and to recognize the immense indebtedness of the age, one
doesn't need to share his intellectually formulated conclusions,
his doctrinal views, or even to be uncritical of the attitudes of his
poetry'.[3] This review was published by Leavis in 1942; and, in so
far as one can judge these matters, it seemed to enjoy an
immediate and powerful influence. But seen now, in retrospect,
there is in this very influence a kind of unexpected and rather
peculiar irony. The fact is that Leavis himself, in at least one of a
number of subsequent studies of the *Quartets*, did not hesitate to
challenge, or at least at times *appear* to challenge, and to call into
question his own wise counsel.[4] This apparent reversal of earlier
attitudes and convictions cannot, it seems, be explained except in
relation to the development, during these years, of Leavis's moral
and religious outlook.[5] With this development, and as gradually
his own intellectual opposition to Eliot's *via negativa* was sharp-
ened, Leavis found it increasingly difficult, as a reader, to
suspend his intolerance of certain of the attitudes of Eliot's
poetry. It became, therefore, more and more difficult for him to
distinguish between the poetry itself and the intellectual or
doctrinal framework which the poetry seemed to invite. But even
to have found himself, in the end, in his last book on the
Quartets,[6] face to face with such a dilemma, is of course a measure
of the human seriousness and honesty of Leavis's engagement
with the poetry. Moreover, the questions which he raises, and in
particular those which refer to the way of negation recommended
by Eliot, cannot be easily or complacently answered, and certainly
should not be ignored by the serious reader.

Leavis's questions and doubts betray, as has already been
pointed out, an intensely moral and even, one can say, a religious
preoccupation. They have the effect of awakening in the reader

serious questions and serious doubts of his own concerning the *Quartets*. First of all there is the question of the relationship between the poetry and the ascetic vision. Because of Eliot's fundamental passion for probity and for self-denial, was there not always a danger, during the composition of *Four Quartets*, that he might render his imagination utterly bereft of its youth and of its spontaneity? In other words, was the language of his verse not likely at some stage to suffer the same fate as that of the Old Testament prophets described by Eric Neumann in his book *Art and the Creative Unconscious*?

> Language, and the language of prophetic religion more than any other, is indeed rooted in the unconscious, with its stream of images; but Judaism and Jewish prophecy were formed by the ethical accent of a consciousness which derived its own central force from its analogy with the central power of the one God. The imperative guidance of this prophetic will so sharpened the intention of the unconscious forces that stood behind, heated it to so white a glow, that the images lost their colours, the variegated flowers of psychic life were turned to ashes.[7]

The second question to be asked concerns the nature of Eliot's own ascetic vision. Does his emphasis on self-denial correspond, for example, to the ordinary teaching of Christian mystics on the *via negativa*, or does it have its source rather in an inherited puritan distaste for life?

Questions of this nature cannot, of course, ever be answered in the abstract. And consequently, as individual readers of Eliot's poetry, we must allow even these questions to be, as it were, interrogated; and our own particular biases and presuppositions to be, themselves, gradually exposed and called into question, by an immediate vital contact with the work in front of us. Otherwise, inevitably, we will run the risk of projecting our own abstract and introverted preoccupations onto the living poem.

A.   A DANCE OF DEATH

The slow, elegaic meditation with which 'East Coker' opens is based largely on the second chapter of *Ecclesiastes*; and, like its

source, it powerfully evokes the permanent cycle of change in the
order of time.

> Houses live and die: there is a time for building
> And a time for living and for generation
> And a time for the wind to break the loosened pane
> And to shake the wainscot where the field-mouse trots
> And to shake the tattered arras woven with a silent motto.
> In my beginning is my end.

East Coker is, in fact, a small village situated near Yeovil in
Somerset. It holds for Eliot certain personal associations, being
the place from which his own ancestor, Andrew Elyot, emigrated
to America in the seventeenth century. In the second paragraph
of the poem we catch a glimpse of the poet-protagonist somewhere on the outskirts of the village, in a 'deep lane/Shuttered
with branches'. The time of day is late afternoon; and the weather
is warm and sultry. After the close of the second paragraph,
however, there is a sudden change of mood and a change of
tempo. Our attention is now drawn away from the warm
atmosphere of the daytime; and we are invited instead – as if
already inhabiting a kind of dream-state – to hear and to perceive
a new midnight world of sound and vision.

> In that open field
> If you do not come too close, if you do not come too close,
> On a summer midnight, you can hear the music
> Of the weak pipe and the little drum
> And see them dancing around the bonfire . . .

Eliot suggested once, in a letter to Professor Haüsermann, that
the imagery of these lines 'though taken from the village itself,
may have been influenced by recollections of *Germelshausen*'
which he said he had not read for years.[8] *Germelshausen*, by
Friedrich Gerstärker, is a story of a village which, being placed
under papal interdict, was condemned almost to extinction. But
once every hundred years, we are told, 'it resumes for the space
of one day its ghostly revelry, and then sinks again under earth'.[9]
In Gerstärker's account, the 'lost village' is visited, on the
occasion of one of these centennial appearances by a stranger
from a completely different world. Observe here how a mere

fragment of remembered reading is made to serve so well the creative imagination of the poet.

From other sources it is clear that, as a young man, Eliot was keenly interested in the question of the preternatural. At Harvard University, for example, he expressed the view that 'illusion', 'hallucination' and 'superstition' were subjects which, in themselves, deserved philosophical attention.[10] And in 1920 we find him responding with enthusiasm not merely to the 'remarkable and original sense of language and the music of language' possessed by William Blake, but also to the English poet's 'gift of hallucinated vision'.[11]

The opening section of 'East Coker' deserves, I believe, to be compared with one of the cantos of Dante's *Inferno*. The fact that such a parallel has not been indicated before now by other literary commentators can be easily explained. Eliot is not concerned here, as he was in 'Little Gidding', to find an approximation to the *terza rima*. And what is more, at least as far as I am aware, there is not a single Dantean echo worth noting in the entire passage. It may seem somewhat strange, therefore, that I should want to introduce here the name of Dante. But let us remember a point Eliot has already made clear, namely that 'the important debt to Dante does not lie in the poet's borrowings', and that 'the greatest debts are not always the most evident'.[12]

The famous episode in Canto v of the *Inferno* when Dante meets with the two lovers, Paolo and Francesca, is referred to several times by Eliot in his critical work. And we find at least one deliberate allusion made to it in the early drafts of 'Little Gidding'.[13] Probably because of the profound tenderness of Dante's treatment of the two lovers, and because the scene itself is so wonderfully imagined, it is, very often, as Eliot remarks, 'the first Episode that strikes most readers'.[14] But, for Eliot, 'it is not the "greatness", the intensity of the emotions, the components, but the intensity of the artistic process, the pressure, so to speak, under which the fusion takes place, that counts. The episode of Paolo and Francesca employs a definite emotion, but the intensity of the poetry is something quite different from whatever intensity in the supposed experience it may give the impression of.'[15] The intensity of the poetry resides, above all, in Francesca's attractiveness in damnation.[16] It is because of this that Dante's feelings are divided. On the one hand, he is aware that Francesca is guilty of the sin for which she is condemned, and that she has herself

freely chosen her terrible fate. But, on the other hand, he is, it
would seem, half-beguiled by the romantic, plaintive figure of a
girl hopelessly in love. The complex nature of the encounter has, I
think, been very perceptively described by A. C. Charity.

> Francesca acts as romantic (or romanticising) literature upon
> Dante, and makes of him, like herself, an 'aesthete' . . . she
> tells how she and Paolo came to this 'doloroso passo' precisely
> by the means which now lead Dante to the point of tears. 'Noi
> leggiavamo' – it was literature – 'di Lancialotto come amor lo
> strinse' – and romantic literature at that ('We were reading how
> love constrained Lancelot'). But they took it for life. They
> translated it, or tried to translate it, into the sphere of existence.
> And they found that the amorality of the love in the book
> became immorality in existence.[17]

Listening to Francesca's plaintive story, the reader's own subjec-
tivity, as much as that of Dante, should be affected by both pity
and by fear. 'For we see ourselves in Francesca, as Dante saw
himself, and must therefore pity her. And we should see through
ourselves, as we look at her, to what will be our end, if our self-
identification with her persists, and are therefore invited to fear.'[18]
'The poem', Charity goes on to conclude, 'does aim, and per-
sistently, to provoke the reader into implicit self-criticism.'[19]
    Section One of 'East Coker' has, I believe, a similar aim and it
employs a similar method. To begin with, we can note how Eliot
deliberately presents himself in the common likeness of man. His
intention is precisely the same as that of Dante, namely to lead us
towards a kind of 'implicit self-criticism'; to 'a new and shocking
valuation of all we have been'. And we can note also the use by
Eliot of certain Dantean 'images of vision'. Like his master, Eliot is
describing here an experience or an encounter that is not wholly
of this world. The medieval poet, before he speaks directly with
the ghosts of Paolo and Francesca, sees in their company other
'lovers' being carried along, two by two, through the storms of
Hell – 'more than a thousand shades . . . knights and ladies of old
times'. Here again A. C. Charity invites us to note how *literary* is
the quality of the romanticism to which Dante responds: 'the
phrase "le donne antiche e i cavalieri" with its peculiar redolence
of the chivalric romance accentuating the "literary" element in
these people's appeal'.[20] In Eliot's poem, the immediate and

central object of visionary attention is also the communion and 'necessarye coniunction' of pairs of lovers:

> Two and two, necessarye coniunction,
> Holding eche other by the hand or the arm
> Which betokeneth concorde.

Reading this passage for the first time one cannot but be affected by the quality of its romanticism. The source of the passage, incidentally, is a celebrated Tudor essay by Sir Thomas Elyot.[21] The archaic spelling of the original text has been deliberately retained by Eliot; and he has preserved also much of its delightful imagery and music. At first, one is spellbound by this country vision and by the sound of 'the weak pipe and the little drum'. But gradually, as the music advances forward, a note of discord is heard. The emphasis is less and less on the civilised harmony and beauty of a courtly dance. And, instead, one begins to perceive and hear the earthly, animal rhythms of the dance of nature and the dance of death.

At the close of the paragraph, the ghostly dancers, with their mirth and their music, 'Earth feet, loam feet', are unceremoniously dismissed by Eliot as 'dung and death'. A deep silence follows. And then, arising as it were out of the depths of his own spirit, Eliot records a feeling of quiet, ecstatic freedom.

> Dawn points, and another day
> Prepares for heat and silence. Out at sea the dawn wind
> Wrinkles and slides. I am here
> Or there, or elsewhere. In my beginning.

This silent ecstasy is something quite different from the sudden 'swooning' of Dante at the close of the fifth Canto. For there, although Dante's viewpoint is in no way dictated by mere sentiment or by romantic enthusiasm, he is all the same so overcome with pity for Francesca and for her ghostly lover that he falls down in a dead faint before them. Eliot's interest, on the other hand, is, it would seem, to extricate himself as much as possible from the plight of those caught on the wheel of successive time,

> The time of the seasons and the constellations
> The time of milking and the time of harvest

The time of the coupling of man and woman
And that of beasts.

He wrote in 1929, 'A great deal of sentiment has been spilt . . .
upon idealizing the reciprocal feelings of man and woman
towards each other . . . ignoring the fact that the love of man and
woman (or for that matter man and man) is only explained and
made reasonable by the higher love, or else is simply *the coupling
of animals*.'[22] This kind of blunt statement has understandably
provoked a negative reaction among some of Eliot's readers. But
the severity of it is, I think, partly mitigated by other statements
which reveal an awareness of the permanent truths of Nature,
and an acceptance by Eliot of the 'wisdom of the countryman
rooted in village tradition and the life of the countryside and the
procession of seasons'.[23]

If we look again at the opening section of 'East Coker', and read
it through carefully, we will find, I think, that the emphasis
placed on the inevitability of death and decay in the human
order, is to some considerable degree balanced by a fascination
with, and an acceptance of, the earthly rhythms of living and of
generation. It is, in fact, precisely the underlying tension between
these two conflicting attitudes in 'East Coker' that first arouses
our interest, and thereafter holds it right through to the end of
the narrative. For no matter what Eliot's ascetic or dogmatic
intentions may have been prior to composition, the poetry as we
have it, is much too complete, and also much too 'human' in its
rich complexity, to be reduced to the mere bare bones of an
ascetic ideal.

B.   THE GOOD FRIDAY LYRIC

The poet Samuel Taylor Coleridge remarked on one occasion that
'a combination of poetry with doctrines is one of the characteristics of the Christian muse'.[24] And reading through Eliot's
unashamedly dogmatic lyric ('East Coker', Section Four) one is, I
think, compelled to agree with him. Eliot's lyric has not by and
large been much appreciated. And the reason, perhaps, is that
the work is concerned largely with the expression of abstract
theological thought. It betrays little or nothing about the subjec-

tive emotional state of the poet. As modern readers we are, of course, as Coleridge also understood very well, impressed particularly by the revelation of the poet's mind, 'producing itself and evolving its own greatness'.[25] We tend in general to think that 'the mind or subject [is] greater than the object'.[26] And so when, in the course of a long poem, an idea or a image is introduced merely for its own objective truth or beauty, 'It at first seems [to us] a discord'.[27]

The objective subject matter of Eliot's lyric is the unbroken link which exists between human suffering and the suffering of Christ on Good Friday. Apparently one of the immediate sources of Eliot's inspiration was his practice of meditating on the Sorrowful Mysteries of the Rosary, the final meditation of which recalls the agony and death of the Incarnate Word on the cross. (According to Raymond Preston, Eliot remarked to him once that the Good Friday lyric was 'probably influenced by the practice of the rosary and in particular by the Sorrowful Mysteries'.[28]) Normally one would expect that a poem so directly influenced by devotional practice would be characterised by an atmosphere of intense personal emotion. Instead, the insight born of Eliot's meditation is expressed through a series of unusual intellectual conceits as outrageous in their way as those employed at times by the seventeenth-century devotional poet Richard Crashaw, or by John Donne.

'Donne's great innovation in his choice of language', Eliot remarked in a paper he composed in March 1930, entitled 'The Devotional Poets of the Seventeenth Century', 'is his replacement of the stock vocabulary of Elizabethan poetry, what we may call its mythology, by a new mythology drawn from philosophical, theological, legal and scientific terminology.'[29] Eliot then went on to remark, and with an eye no doubt directed towards some of his own work as a poet: 'A similar attempt at renovation appears in some of the poetry being written today.'[30] If one compares Eliot's lyric with, for example, the modern section in *The Oxford Book of English Mystical Verse*, one can at once appreciate the effort he has made to replace 'the stock vocabulary' of modern religious verse with 'a new mythology' drawn in this case from the world of medical practice and modern hospital care.

> The wounded surgeon plies the steel
> That questions the distempered part;

> Beneath the bleeding hands we feel
> The sharp compassion of the healer's art
> Resolving the enigma of the fever chart.[31]

The far-fetched association of the dissimilar (the linking of Christ's task with that of a medical surgeon and, later in the lyric, the over-elaboration of the hospital metaphor) has, on occasion, been judged one of the worst lapses of taste ever committed by Eliot. But 'the conceits of poetry', we are informed in an anonymous review of *The Poems, English, Latin and Greek of Richard Crashaw*, 'have always a somewhat impertinent flavour when religion is the theme . . . they can be used with a kind of apologetic playfulness to exhibit by implication the poet's conscious inadequacy'.[32] Eliot himself in 'A Note on Crashaw' observed, 'Crashaw's images, even when entirely preposterous . . . give a kind of intellectual pleasure – it is a deliberate conscious perversity of language, a perversity like that of the amazing and amazingly impressive interior of St Peter's.'[33]

There is one poem by Crashaw which, when it is set alongside Eliot's lyric, serves almost at once to sharpen our understanding of Eliot's austere Christian vision. The poem, *Temperance, or the Cheap Physician*, is concerned largely with the pursuit of good health (it is not a religious work!) and it was apparently prompted by a translation into English of a book by the Jesuit Leonard Lessius called *Hygiasticon: Or the Right course of preserving Life and Health unto extream old Age*. Crashaw is anxious because his Reader has been made the dupe of a number of quack physicians, handing over vast sums of money ('the dear treasures of thy life') to pay for what Crashaw calls with biting sarcasm 'Th' Oraculous Doctor's mystick bills'. If the Reader would instead take Nature as his sole physician, and follow a proper regimen of diet, he would be able, Crashaw promises him, to live unto a ripe and harmonious old age.

> Wouldst see blithe looks, fresh cheeks beguile
> Age? wouldst see December smile?
> Wouldst see a nest of roses grow
> In a bed of reverend snow?
> Warm thoughts, free spirits, flattering
> Winters self into a spring?

In summe, wouldst see a man that can
Live to be old, and still a man;
Whose latest and most leaden houres
Fall with soft wings, stuck with soft flowres?
And when lifes sweet fable ends,
His soul and bodie part like friends:
No quarrels, mumures, no delay;
A kisse, a sigh, and so away?
This rare one, Reader, wouldst thou see?
Hark hither, and thy self be he.[34]

This worldly wisdom, the notion that, given the proper conditions, one can look forward with reasonable certainty to a calm and serene old age, is to the poet of 'East Coker' nothing more than 'a receipt for deceit'. His outright rejection of the idea is expressed, at first somewhat obscurely, in the short lyric which begins, 'What is the late November doing / With the disturbance of the spring', and then more straightforwardly in the longer more prosaic passage which follows:

What was to be the value of the long looked forward to,
Long hoped for calm, the autumnal serenity
And the wisdom of age? Had they deceived us,
Or deceived themselves, the quiet-voiced elders,
Bequeathing us merely a receipt for deceit?

Like Richard Crashaw, Eliot can see, as in a vision, one season mingling with the other ('Late roses filled with early snow'). But, to him, such a disturbance of the seasons is a sign *not* of peace and order – as it was in Crashaw's *Temperance* – but of disorder and anarchy. The seventeenth-century poet is trying to wean his Reader away from a dependence on certain unnatural and expensive drugs (which had been recommended by the Oraculous Doctor) to a reliance on Nature herself, and on the cheapest and most efficient physician of all, the simple virtue of Temperance. Crashaw points out the paradox that the expensive drugs his Reader takes to cure his illness will in the end bring about only 'a costlyer disease'. By way of contrast, Eliot is seeking, in his Good Friday lyric, to awaken his readers to their need, not for a *natural* but for a *supernatural* life. Only the wounded surgeon, the divine physician, he declares, can heal us. And once again, in strange contrast and parallel with Crashaw, Eliot points out the paradox that if we, who are sick, really desire to be cured, 'our sickness must grow worse'.

The *form* of Eliot's Good Friday lyric was adapted from a baroque mystical lyric, *En una noche oscura*, by St John of the Cross. 'Eliot's intention in taking up the baroque mode was not', A. D. Moody writes, 'to celebrate the disorder manifest in its violence and excess, but to correct it.'[35] But the *content* of Eliot's lyric also represents, I believe, a correction of the baroque religious attitude. Take, for instance, the fourth stanza, in which the mysterious disease from which the poet suffers is described in terms of a feverish cold.

> The chill ascends from feet to knees,
> The fever sings in mental wires.
> If to be warmed, then I must freeze
> And quake in frigid purgatorial fires
> Of which the flame is roses, and the smoke is briars.

That these images of burning and freezing refer, at least on one level, to the experience of passionate love, is rather coyly hinted at in the final evocation of the roses and briars. But reading through the original notes Eliot made for stanza four – the only stanza, as it happens, in which the personal pronoun 'I' is used – we are left in no doubt at all about the fundamental nature of the disease Eliot is suffering from. The phrase 'ill of love', he jotted down first. And then, he wrote:

> I am cold
> – must be consumed in fire
> I faint with heat
> – must be frozen in the lonely north.[36]

In terms of *content* as distinct from form, stanza number four, I now suspect, was adapted not from St John of the Cross' lyric *En una noche oscura*, but from the work of another Spanish mystic altogether called Sor María de la Antiqua. The poem or the lyric in question is entitled *The Sweet Laments and Contradictory Sentiments of the Soul as it faints away for love in search of its Beloved*:

For my good I suffer an ill,
Of which I do not expect to be cured:
For my happiness consists
In that ill's increase.

I suffer a sweet fever
With which I burn and am delighted
With a continual thirst
Not of water but of fire.

For the penetrating wound
With which my breast burns,
Only the hand who wounded me
Can give the remedy.

Various things happen to me
With which I burn and freeze:
I fear and hope at one point
I laugh and weep at the same time.

I feel a delightful restlessness
Which I understand and do not understand:
Perchance I sleep, keeping vigil,
And perchance sleeping, I am awake.

Tell him, then seraphim
My spouse and sweet Master,
That for his love I live,
And to die of it is my desire.[37]

The conscious and insistent play of paradox in Sor María's devotional lyric is obviously not a mere arbitrary device. It is something demanded by the quality and strength of her own passionate religious emotion. Eliot's almost complete suppression of such feeling in 'East Coker', Section Four, his deliberate elimination, that is, of the erotic–devotional element, while it certainly leaves the mystical paradoxes intact, manages at the same time to cut them off from their most immediate and most spontaneous artery of life. For unlike other forms of devotional and mystical verse, the baroque mode seems to demand the naked expression of feeling if it is to succeed. Without such feeling, the intellectual play of paradox will at times appear merely clever, or even, as is the case here in Eliot's Good Friday lyric, somewhat wilful.

C. POETRY AND ASCETICISM

To those readers who feel they cannot but admire the power and precision of Eliot's language in 'East Coker', the statement Eliot makes in Section Two of the poem – 'The poetry does not matter' – must come as something of a shock. But it is not, of course, the only statement of this nature which is made in *Four Quartets*. When at the height of his career as a man of letters Eliot meets with 'the ghost of some dead master' in 'Little Gidding' the acknowledgement he receives from the dead man, the crown of honour which is, as it were, placed on his head is, to say the least, a most unusual tribute. For it consists, among other things, in the strange discovery that 'honour stains', and that he, the living poet, must soon expect to experience great pain and great sense of loss, 'As body and soul begin to fall asunder'. What is more, the clear implication of the ghost's message to Eliot is that Eliot's own earlier preoccupation with the purification of language is now to be set aside as of relatively minor importance. From this time onward Eliot is to concern himself first and last with 'the purification of the motive'.[38]

A similar moral seriousness of purpose and marked dissatisfaction with exclusively literary pursuits also characterises the religious attitude of the poet Henry Vaughan. In his introduction to *Silex Scintillans: Sacred Poems and Private Ejaculations* he complained about authors who aim 'more at verse than perfection'.[39] And in his poem 'The Garland' he openly confessed how, in his youth, he also allowed himself to be caught up by worldly distractions, 'Appointing error for my page / And darkness for my days'.[40] The young poet's flirtation with the ways of the world is, however, soon to be interrupted by a stern and unexpected rebuke.

> But at the height of this career
>   I met with a dead man,
> Who noting well my vain abear,
>   Thus unto me began:
> Desist fond fool, be not undone,
>   What thou hast cut today
> Will fade at night, and with this sun
>   Quite vanish and decay.

The wreath of flowers with which Henry Vaughan had hoped to crown himself in this life is, the ghost informs him, doomed to wither. In another of Vaughan's poems entitled *Idle Verse* the mature and sober-minded Christian addresses thus the poetry he wrote as a young man before his conversion.

> Let it suffice my warmer days
>   Simpered, and shined on you,
> Twist not my cypress with your bays,
>   Or roses with my yew;
>
> Go, go, seek out some greener thing,
>   It snows, and freezeth here;
> Let nightingales attend the spring,
>   Winter is all my year.[41]

The rose and the yew. These two images represent for Vaughan and for Eliot the two extremes of life and death, the freedom and the colour of youth on the one hand, and the solitude and asceticism of old age on the other. For Vaughan there can be no communion, this side of Paradise, between them. But, for the poet of 'Little Gidding', who seems, in his own winter poem, deliberately to take these two images from Vaughan in order to correct them.

> The moment of the *rose* and the moment of the *yew*-tree
> Are of equal duration.

That Eliot's cryptic lines contain an ironic reminiscence of Vaughan's poem *Idle Verse* is further indicated by the fact that in Section Five of 'Little Gidding', the section in which the lines occur, Eliot's main preoccupation is with the perfection of a poetic language.

> And every phrase
> And sentence that is right
> .   .   .   .   .   .
> is an end and a beginning
> Every poem an epitaph.

Although it is, I think, obviously true that the pressure of Eliot's dogmatic concerns, his preoccupation in particular with the demands of the Christian *via negativa*, has added a considerable strain to his already almost Herculean struggle with what he called once (in an astonishing phrase) 'the natural sin of language',[42] it is also equally true that neither of the poet's two most basic impulses (his desire to speak out about the need for ascetic purification, and his desire to make 'pure' music) has succeeded in cancelling out the other. For, in the end, both his art and his asceticism have somehow benefited, I believe, from their long 'intolerable wrestle'. Thomas Merton, the Trappist priest and poet, once wisely remarked:

> Religious ascetics have something to learn from the natural asceticism of the artist: it is unselfconscious, organic, integrated in his art. It does not run the risk of becoming an end in itself. But the artist has also something to gain from religious asceticism. It not only raises him above his subject and his material but above his art itself.[43]

D. THE POET 'BETWEEN TWO WORLDS'

'I am assumed', Eliot remarked in 1937, 'to have an intimate and affectionate acquaintance with the limbo and lower regions in which the secular moves: a knowledge of objects towards which the theological mind is not often directed. My qualification is the eye of the owl, not that of the eagle.'[44] One year earlier, in 1936, Eliot published his first *Quartet*, 'Burnt Norton'. And in its central section his acquaintance with at least one of 'the limbo and lower regions in which the secular moves' was made manifest. For in Section Three Eliot's deliberate poetic strategy was to evoke first of all an image of the dimly-lit London Underground and of its hurrying passengers:

> . . . the strained time-ridden faces
> Distracted from distraction by distraction
> Filled with fancies and empty of meaning
> Tumid apathy with no concentration
> Men and bits of paper, . . .

There is in this 'place of disaffection' neither ordinary daylight nor that interior or spiritual darkness necessary 'to purify the soul'. And yet for Eliot the surest way out of the modern Limbo, the way to attain true wisdom, is not, it seems, to return back to the everyday world. Instead, we are advised to go to a level far beneath the Underground itself.

It is at this point, we are told, that the Negative Way properly begins, and here the soul has its first purifying experience of the *new* darkness. In the corresponding third section of 'East Coker', the central theme is also that of interior purgation. Once again, the description by Eliot of the Negative Way is preceded by a peculiarly disturbing, almost apocalyptic vision of the modern secular city. But it is a vision in which Eliot discovers his most original and most sustaining metaphor for the dark night.

> O dark dark dark. They all go into the dark,
> The vacant interstellar spaces, the vacant into the vacant,
> The captains, merchant bankers, eminent men of letters, . . .
> And cold the sense and lost the motive of action.

Here, in this last line, we have the hinge on which the passage turns. Until this point Eliot has not hesitated to assume the mantle of a prophet and to upbraid, from a safe ascetic distance, the folly and the manners of the secular world. The tone of his discourse has been elitist, preacherly and uncompromising. But with this telling psychological detail ('cold the sense and lost the motive of action') the poet is, for a moment, reminded of his own personal nullity, the fact that he also has his place with the 'eminent men of letters', and that with them he is now facing helplessly into the darkness.

> And we all go with them, into the silent funeral,
> Nobody's funeral, for there is no one to bury.
> I said to my soul, be still, and let the dark come upon you
> Which shall be the darkness of God.

Not for the first time in the *Quartets*, one is here, I think, made aware of Eliot's extraordinary ability to make use of a single phrase, or of a sentence, to shift – all of a sudden – the direction of his poem from one world of experience to another, or from one level of intellectual meaning to another. And he achieves this by a superb control of pace, of imagery, and of what he himself has named elsewhere 'the music of ideas'.

The two worlds of experience are, in this case, the modern secular world and the world of interior self-negation and contemplative stillness. Naturally enough, the transition from one world to the other is somewhat abrupt. And yet, at the same time, there are indicated in Eliot's poem a number of surprising continuities between the two worlds. Note in particular that the unspecified darkness which threatens to engulf 'the captains, merchant bankers, eminent men of letters' etc., seems almost to merge into and to become one thing with 'the darkness of God'. For Eliot, as also for the ghost of 'Little Gidding', these two worlds appear for a moment to have 'become much like each other'. And it is therefore hardly accidental – though still of course rather surprising – that the phrase Eliot employs to evoke the spiritual state of his own secular peers, 'cold the sense and lost the motive of action', very nearly parallels his earlier, harrowing description in 'Burnt Norton' of the *via negativa*:

> Desiccation of the world of sense,
> Evacuation of the world of fancy,
> Inoperancy of the world of spirit.

Clearly these small similarities and continuities represent a serious effort on the part of Eliot to bring much closer together what are often judged to be two quite separate and quite distinct dimensions of life, namely the secular and the religious.

When, later in the third section of 'East Coker', Eliot comes to describe in some detail his own experience of 'the darkness of God', he does not employ explicit religious imagery. Instead, with impressive strategic subtlety, he makes use of three unexpected similes, each one of them taken from the everyday world of secular experience. First, the strange sense of 'darkness on darkness' that is felt in the theatre when 'lights are extinguished' and you can hear 'the hollow rumble of wings' as the brilliantly painted façade is being moved away; second, the sudden feeling of emptiness and even panic that is experienced by travellers in the Underground when their tube train 'stops too long between stations'; and finally, the sense of vacancy or 'mental emptiness' that is endured in hospital 'when, under either, the mind is conscious but conscious of nothing'. The ease, in this passage, with which Eliot is able to mediate between the two superficially diverse and conflicting worlds is remarkable.[45] It affords us tangible proof of the strength and quality of his poetic imagination, and no less tangible proof – if proof in fact were needed – of his religious genius.

The ordinary strength of the majority of religious poets in the Catholic tradition is founded on a conviction that God is the source of all that is good and lovely and perfect in this world. Their poetry is, in other words, a poetry of affirmation, and it proceeds by what has been traditionally named the *via affirmativa*. But is such a poetry of affirmation possible in the modern city where, according to Hopkins, 'all is seared with trade; bleared, smeared with toil; / And wears man's smudge and shares man's smell'?[46] Is it possible today to 'see the Living God projected from the Machine'? This striking phrase occurs in a short poem or psalm written by the Welsh Catholic poet David Jones. And, in the same poem, as it happens, we find also clearly stated an authoritative and poignant answer to our own first question: is the poetry of affirmation, or a Franciscan poetry, possible in the modern secular city?

> I have said
> to the perfected steel, be my sister and for the
> glassy towers I thought I felt some beginnings
> of His creature, but A, a, a, Domine Deus, my
> hands found the glazed work unrefined and
> the terrible crystal a stage-paste . . . Eia
> Domine Deus.[47]

The contrast between this passage by David Jones and the passage we have been considering in 'East Coker' does serve, I think, to underline the very considerable originality of Eliot's approach. Eliot's intention in 'East Coker' is not, of course, to confuse or to equate the mystical experience of self-negation and self-emptying with the vacuity and emptiness of life in the modern city. But what he does seem to suggest is that this very darkness and emptiness, although abhorrent in itself, does not have to remain always an obstacle between society and God. Even the experience of the absence of God in the world can somehow be transformed through the discipline of prayer and meditation. And, what is more, for the man who is in search of God, it can come to be understood and accepted as an opportunity for spiritual purification, a first step, as it were, along the difficult path of the *via negativa*.

5

Mysticism and Incarnation

It is by the Christian dogma of the Incarnation that it [mystical philosophy] has best been able to describe and to explain the nature of the inward and personal mystic experience.

(Evelyn Underhill, *Mysticism*, 1911)

Shortly before the third and most controversial *Quartet* was published, Eliot sent a draft-copy of the work to a few of his friends and invited them to read and to study it. One of these friends, Geoffrey Faber, after he had read carefully through the poem, asked Eliot what precise meaning was intended in the poem's final section by the use of the theological term 'Incarnation'. The word occurs at the climax of a paragraph also noteworthy for the fine evocation by the poet of certain small experiences of illumination.

> For most of us, there is only the unattended
> Moment, the moment in and out of time,
> The distraction fit, lost in a shaft of sunlight,
> The wild thyme unseen, or the winter lightning
> Or the waterfall, or music heard so deeply
> That it is not heard at all, but you are the music
> While the music lasts. These are only hints and guesses,
> Hints followed by guesses; and the rest
> Is prayer, observance, discipline, thought and action.
> The hint half guessed, the gift half understood, is Incarnation.
> Here the impossible union
> Of spheres of existence is actual,
> Here the past and future
> Are conquered and reconciled, . . .

Although Eliot replied immediately and positively to other suggestions and queries from his friend Faber, he decided, on this particular occasion to make no comment whatsoever.[1] The reason for his silence is not, I am persuaded, that Eliot considered the enquiry somehow irrelevant or meaningless, but rather that the only possible reply he felt he could make to such a fundamental question had, in fact, already been made *within* and *by* the poem itself.

Four Quartets can be thought of as a mode of comprehending through words the meaning and the mystery of the Word Incarnate. One method Eliot employs in order to communicate this meaning, is to relate the dogma of Incarnation to certain striking and significant experiences of illumination. The task is not an easy one. This is due principally to the fact that Eliot himself is a Christian author writing in an age of unbelief and scepticism. Those readers of the poem, who already share something of his dogmatic convictions, will perhaps find little or nothing to complain about in the equation made, within the poem, between faith and imagination. But, the more 'secular-minded' readers will tend to adopt a rather different approach and will be much less easily persuaded that Eliot has found a satisfactory mode of comprehension for his dogmatic vision. One such critic, Graham Hough, in an interesting paper entitled 'Vision and Doctrine in *Four Quartets*', goes so far as to state that 'the poetry of the *Quartets* falls short of its purpose'. Eliot has failed, Hough believes, to make valid the link 'between the temporal, sensory illumination and the timeless Christian revelation'.[2] My primary objective in this chapter will be to determine the extent to which this negative judgment of Graham Hough is valid. I will be concerned, therefore, with trying to understand first of all the true nature of Eliot's illumination experiences in *Four Quartets*, and then with trying to establish just what it is Eliot wishes to suggest, in the fifth section of 'The Dry Salvages', when he uses the term 'Incarnation'. At the end of the day it is, of course, for the individual reader to decide for himself just how successful Eliot has been in the communication of his dogmatic vision. But, before a final judgment is given, a judgment that may otherwise, perhaps, be too hasty or too negative, one should not fail to pay serious attention to the celebrated cryptic advice from Alexander Pope:

> A perfect judge will read each work of wit
> With the same spirit that its author writ.

TWO TYPES OF MYSTICISM

ɔf 'doctrinal Christianity' which Graham Hough ɾegard as the most authentically Christian, is one which ᴜdes among its central tenets 'a doctrine of immanence' and which allows also for 'a kind of Christian natural sacramentalism'. If the work of any author is to be considered genuinely Christian, therefore, it must, according to Hough, like the work of George Herbert (and, one might add, Gerard Manley Hopkins) be able to recognise and to celebrate the immanent presence of the Eternal in time; in other words, a 'poetry that can accept and love the manifest surface of the natural world, and use it and enjoy it, transfigured in the light of the religious apprehension'.[3] Whatever else this is, it is clearly not an overall definition of the poetry of *Four Quartets* – a point Hough himself is at pains to emphasise. But Hough also suggests – and I think mistakenly – that this was, in fact, the kind of affirmative Christian poetry Eliot was *attempting* to write in the *Quartets,* and that when Eliot failed in this endeavour, failed that is 'to see God in all things' and to assert or to express a positive vision of 'the Timeless immanent in time', his failure was due to nothing other than the negative character of his own sensibility: 'The configuration of his [Eliot's] imaginative life in the *Quartets* [his obsessive preoccupation that is with "the emptiness, futility and ugliness of the time-bound life"] seems to work *against that which he wishes to assert'*.[4] At the conclusion of Hough's paper we read: 'Eliot was a poet and a Christian, but he was never a Christian poet – as George Herbert was a Christian poet. . . . In Eliot the poetic imagination and the Christian confession do not interpenetrate.'[5]

Why this conclusion must, I think, be rejected is because 'the Christian confession' of Eliot, or 'that which he wishes to assert' concerning the timeless Christian revelation, is a doctrine altogether different from the one Graham Hough would seem here to have ascribed to him. For there are two very distinct forms, within the Christian mystical and theological tradition, under which Christian poets have been accustomed to conceive Divine Reality. The first of these – what one may call the doctrine or the poetry of immanence – is quite obviously what Hough has in mind when he speaks of a 'poetry that can accept and love the manifest surface of the natural world, and use it and enjoy it, transfigured in the light of the religious apprehension'. But there is, as I have said, a second form of Christian doctrine and expression – namely, the doctrine or the poetry of transcendence – and it is this second form that can be said to characterise both the completed poetic structure of vision in *Four Quartets* and also the poet's own doctrinal spirit and intention *prior* to the composition of his major work.[6]

The doctrine of transcendence insists on an almost total separation of the human and the divine, of the temporal and the eternal worlds. God, or the Supreme Being, is thought of as being separated from our world of multiplicity and variety by an immeasurable distance. And thus, the path of the man who is in search of religious perfection, or in search of God, must literally be a *transcendence*, it must be a path of painful self-negation, a journey 'inward and upward' through a long series of trials and temptations.

> In the middle, not only in the middle of the way
> But all the way, in a dark wood, in a bramble,
> On the edge of a grimpen, where is no secure foothold,
> And menaced by monsters, fancy lights,
> Risking enchantment.
> 'East Coker', Section Two

The doctrine of transcendence, when it is most radically expressed, as in the mysticism and poetry of Richard of St Victor and St Augustine, Pseudo-Dionysius and St John of the Cross, teaches the Christian contemplative to shut fast the door of his senses, and to turn all his attention away from the created, external world. It teaches him, moreover, 'to sit still' and to wait in darkness, within the innermost part of his being, until that very darkness can become 'the darkness of God'.

> Internal darkness, deprivation
> And destitution of all property,
> Desiccation of the world of sense,
> Evacuation of the world of fancy, . . .
> 'Burnt Norton', Section 3

In contrast, the doctrine of immanence invites the Christian contemplative to look confidently outward towards the material universe that surrounds him, and through all his senses to perceive in the great power and beauty of Nature the immanent presence of God.

> Look at the stars! Look, look up at the skies!
>   O look at all the fire-folk sitting in the air!
>   The bright boroughs, the circle-citadels there!

These lines are taken from the opening stanza of Gerard Manley Hopkins's poem, *The Starlight Night*.[7] And in another, no less astonishing poem by the English Jesuit, we read:

> . . . now, barbarous in beauty, the stooks arise
> Around; up above, what wind-walks! What lovely
>   behaviour
> Of silk-clad clouds! has wilder, wilful-wavier
> Meal-drift moulded ever and melted across skies?
>
> I walk, I lift up, I lift up heart, eyes,
>   Down all that glory in the heavens to glean our Saviour;
>   And, éyes, heárt, what looks, what lips yet gave you a
> Rapturous love's greeting of realer, of rounded replies?
>
> And the azurous hung hills are his world-wielding shoulder
>   Majestic . . .[8]

Hopkins's vision is indeed remarkable. And one can find almost nothing in *Four Quartets* to compare with it. But this does not mean that Eliot is not in any sense a visionary poet. It means simply that whereas the Jesuit's vision of Nature is that of a poet of immanence, Eliot's visionary grasp and understanding of the relationship between God and Nature is that of a poet of transcendence.

Take, for example, the following passage from the third movement of 'East Coker' in which Eliot describes an experience of illumination with reference to certain scenes taken from Nature. The passage occurs shortly after an austere exhortation – spoken by the poet to himself – to remain still and to wait patiently within 'the darkness of God'.

> So the darkness shall be the light, and the stillness
>   the dancing.
> Whisper of running streams, and winter lightning.

The wild thyme unseen and the wild strawberry,
The laughter in the garden, echoed ecstasy
Not lost, but requiring, pointing to the agony
Of death and birth.

Although one may, at first, be inclined to read this passage as if
Eliot intended his images to carry the same significance as 'the
azurous hung hills' or the 'silk-sack clouds' in Hopkins's poem, a
brief analysis of the actual structure of vision in the *Quartets* will
demonstrate beyond any question that Eliot's intentions are
altogether different from those of Hopkins. Eliot almost never
allows his imagination to rest – much less to exult – in the
'barbarous' beauty of Nature. He is determined to walk 'by a way
wherein there is no ecstasy', determined, that is to say, to go
beyond the limited, time-bound states of Nature, so that in the
end he might enter into the free, transcendent realm of the
Timeless.

So complex in its organisation is the expression of Eliot's vision
within *Four Quartets*, one is inclined normally not to speak about
it in diagrammatic terms. But we can, I think, discern within the
poem – although not with scholastic exactitude – three separate
stages in the development of Eliot's mystical awareness. First, an
initial response, or an awakening, to certain physical and spiritual
conditions or states familiar to the poet. Depending on what the
particular object in view is – it may, for example, be no more than
the drab futility of city life, or else perhaps one of those small
sensory illuminations Eliot describes in 'Burnt Norton' such as
'The moment in the arbour where the rain beat' – this first stage is
usually characterised by either a feeling of 'partial horror' or by a
feeling of 'partial ecstasy'. The second stage is marked by the
advent of interior or spiritual darkness. Here the poet is struggling to avoid the extremes of false elation and morbid depres-
sion. He is learning to take his first steps along the difficult, inner
path of the *via negativa*. And finally, just when the darkness
seems to be almost total, and when the Self has at last become
detached from 'the things of sense', there occurs at the innermost
point of the spirit what one may call an advent of the true,
mystical illumination. 'Illumination', writes Evelyn Underhill, in a
study of mysticism with which we know Eliot was familiar, 'is the
contemplative state *par excellence*. It forms, with the two preceding
states, the "first mystic life". Many mystics never go beyond it;

and, on the other hand, many seers and artists not usually classed amongst them, have shared, to some extent, the experience of the illuminated state.'[9]

The language employed by Eliot, and by other poets of transcendence, to communicate this third stage in the development of mystical awareness is always a language of paradox. For although the central object of the mystical poet's attention, at this third level, may well have little or nothing to do *immediately* with the life of the senses, or with Nature as such, the words and the images he uses in order to evoke the reality of the Transcendent, and to make the Spiritual visible, are inevitably taken or 'borrowed' direct from his experience of the sensual world. They are, in fact, paradoxically, the very same words and images he used originally to describe 'the temporal sensory illumination' experienced at what I have called the first level of his awareness of Nature.

We find in the tenth book of St Augustine's *Confessions* one of the most beautiful and most celebrated examples of this kind of mysical writing. I will quote from the text at some length for it serves, I think, to underline the point that Eliot's use of paradoxical language – the metaphorical transference in Section Three of 'East Coker', for example, of a certain group of images from one world of reality to another – is not some kind of newly devised poetic technique or method. It is, instead, as it has always been, in every age, the most practical and most obvious means of expression available to the mystical poet.

But what do I love when I love my God? Not material beauty or beauty of a temporal order; not the brilliance of earthly light, so welcome to our eyes; not the sweet melody of harmony and song; not the fragrance of flowers, perfumes, and spices; not manna or honey; not limbs such as the body delights to embrace. It is not these that I love when I love my God. And yet, when I love him, it is true that I love a light of a certain kind, a voice, a perfume, a food, an embrace; but they are of the kind that I love in my inner self, when my soul is bathed in light that is not bound by space; when it listens to sound that never dies away; when it breathes fragrance that is not borne away on the wind; when it tastes food that is never consumed by the eating; when it clings to an embrace from which it is not severed by fulfilment of desire. This is what I love when I love my God.[10]

In the central section of 'East Coker' under consideration, Eliot, like St Augustine, in order to communicate a spiritual vision, employs the language and imagery of each of the five physical senses: the sense of hearing ('whisper of running streams'); the sense of touch ('the dancing'); the sense of smell ('the wild thyme unseen'); taste ('the wild strawberry'); and finally sight (the 'winter lightning'). A casual reader of the *Quartets*, unaware of the literary and spiritual tradition within which the poet is working here, might very easily miss the point at issue and imagine that Eliot is talking about no more than a few profound experiences of Nature, 'mere secular epiphanies'. In fact, of course, what Eliot really wants to assert and to demonstrate by the use of such concrete language, is that the interior or spiritual realm he wishes to attain – after his long and difficult journey through the dark night of purgation – has the same immediacy and is no less real than the everyday world revealed to us through our senses.

Eliot is, therefore, I repeat, an artist of vision. And so, to appreciate the true contours of his visionary landscape, one must learn not only to suspend, if necessary, one's disbelief, but also to approach certain parts of the *Quartets* with the humility and the quiet attentiveness of a stranger entering into a new world.

B.   THE MEANING OF INCARNATION

The images Eliot uses to describe the experience of illumination in the third section of 'East Coker' reappear, together with a number of others, in the final section of 'The Dry Salvages'. In their new context they are, I think, intended to refer both to Eliot's third level of spiritual awareness – i.e. the mystical state properly so called – and also, and perhaps especially, to those profane states of nature which characterise Eliot's first level of awareness, and which are, of course, states familiar to every human being.

> . . . the moment in and out of time,
> The distraction fit, lost in a shaft of sunlight,
> The wild thyme unseen, or the winter lightning
> Or the waterfall, or music heard so deeply
> That it is not heard at all, but you are the music
> While the music lasts.

In Henri Bremond's cogent analysis of mysticism, *Prayer and Poetry*, a work Eliot read with interest and enthusiasm before the composition of *Four Quartets*, the French author has much to say that is instructive concerning these 'profane states of nature'. In them, he says, 'we can decipher the great lines and discern the image and rough sketch of the mystical states of the soul, properly so called'.[11] Significantly, the first example Bremond chooses to isolate is that same rapt absorption in music, referred to above in 'The Dry Salvages'. Bremond describes how, 'while listening to a melody, the effort to understand relaxes, and the soul simply delights itself in the beauty which it divines'.[12] *The effort to understand relaxes*. Bremond is at pains to point out that the moment of inspiration only takes place after a long distress of intellectual and practical labour. It is in a sense, therefore, really no more than the visible fruit, or the realisation, of what has already been acquired 'in the order of *thought* or of *action*'.[13] Eliot in 'The Dry Salvages' has a similar idea, and he expresses it in almost the same words:

> These are only hints and guesses,
> Hints followed by guesses; and the rest
> Is prayer, observance, discipline, *thought* and *action*.
> (Emphasis added.)

One does not find in Bremond's study, however, the extraordinary claim which one discovers at the very heart of Eliot's vision:

> The hint half guessed, the gift half understood, is
> Incarnation.

Eliot, being a devout Christian, has not hesitated to acknowledge openly his belief that 'the fullness of Christian revelation resides in the essential fact of the Incarnation',[14] or, to use Graham Hough's words, 'that the central event in universal history occurred in Palestine in the reign of the emperor Augustus'.[15] One should not conclude from this, however, that 'since Christianity as a matter of historic fact is no longer the Faith common to all', Eliot's poetry *necessarily* occupies a position of 'sectarian dogmatism'.[16] First of all, the vision or doctrine of Incarnation, enunciated in the *Quartets*, is not one that can be reduced to a mere abstract formula, or to an intellectual statement of belief concerning an historical event. And second, the poet of the *Quartets*, however strong his own personal convictions may be, does not require us to accede to even one part of his own belief. For Eliot knows very well that if a poem is to have its full impact – even a philosophical poem such as the *Quartets* – it is not necessary that the reader be persuaded of *what* the poet believes but only *that* the poet really believes in what he is saying.

One can be aided, I think, to an initial understanding of Eliot's doctrine of Incarnation by consulting, in detail, a number of passages from a work entitled *Mysticism* by Evelyn Underhill. This book was first published in 1911; and we know that Eliot took copious notes from it when he was a young student at Harvard University.[17] Many years later, in England, Eliot came to know Evelyn Underhill personally. When she died in June 1941 he was engaged, as it happened, in the composition of his last *Quartet*. He broke off the manuscript draft to write, as part of an obituary notice, the following warm tribute:

[Evelyn Underhill] concerned herself as much with the practice as with the theory of the devotional life – her studies of the great mystics had the inspiration not primarily of the scholar or the champion of forgotten genius, but a consciousness of the great need of the contemplative element in the modern world . . . she helped to support the spiritual life of many more than she could in her humility have been aware of aiding.[18]

Discussion so far concerning the meaning of Incarnation in *Four Quartets* has centred largely on the question of whether or not Eliot was thinking of 'a specific moment in history' or merely of 'the constant ingression of spiritual reality into time'.[19] But surely Eliot's idea was to include both of these two possible meanings, for they are in no way incompatible. 'The Incarnation, which is for traditional Christianity synonymous with the historical birth and earthly life of Christ, is, for mystics of a certain type, not only this but also a perpetual Cosmic and personal process. It is an everlasting bringing forth, in the universe and also in the individual ascending soul, of the divine and perfect life.'[20] In these lines from Underhill's *Mysticism* one should be careful not to overlook the phrase: 'mystics of a certain type'. Already, in the earlier part of this chapter, I have emphasised the distinction between those Christian mystics who profess a doctrine of Immanence and those who profess a doctrine of Transcendence. Generally, the former tend to look upon the Incarnation as an event that has not only made possible but indeed necessitated an affirmative, sacramental vision of reality. For them the task of the mystical poet, and his privilege, is to celebrate the presence of God in the temporal realm, and 'to accept and love the manifest surface of the natural world'. The timeless realm of Truth is sought not so much *outside* this world as *within* it. And every finite manifestation of beauty that the mystic perceives, through his senses, is regarded as a manifestation of the divine.[21] Thus a true link is forged between 'the temporal sensory illumination and the timeless Christian revelation'.

This mysticism is obviously the chosen path of poets such as Gerard Manley Hopkins and George Herbert. But it is not – I must repeat again – the path or the way of mysticism pursued by T. S. Eliot. And nor is it Eliot's particular way of understanding the Incarnation. (Significantly, one can find among the notes Eliot took from Evelyn Underhill's *Mysticism* (pp. 279–81) the warning 'that vision through the senses is imperfect, capricious, often a delusion'.[22]) The aspect of the Incarnation Eliot gives most attention to is not the descent of the divine plenitude into the depths of human nature (the way of immanence), but rather the slow difficult ascent of human nature upwards into the divine realm (the way of transcendence). 'What poetry must do', Eliot wrote in an article published shortly after the completion of *Four Quartets*, '. . . is a kind of humble shadow of the Incarnation *whereby the human is taken up into the divine.*'[23] It is, I think, rather significant that one or two of the images Eliot uses to evoke the different stages of his illumination experience, point precisely to this kind of total, inward transfiguration and absorption:

> The distraction fit, lost in a shaft of sunlight,
> The wild thyme unseen, or the winter lightning
> Or the waterfall, or music heard so deeply
> That it is not heard at all, but you are the music
> While the music lasts.

For Eliot the entry of the Timeless Word into time has indeed achieved a final redemption for mankind. But the meaning of this redemption and its good news therefore is not, perhaps, what one might have expected. Eliot does not believe for an instant that man can begin now, at last, to live out his life on earth as if he were already inhabiting a kind of earthly, sensual paradise. On the contrary, if time past and time future are in some sense thought to be 'reconciled' with the realm of Eternity, it is *only* because – through the Incarnation – they have been finally 'conquered', and are, as it were, almost wholly absorbed into a world of transcendent Spirit. (In the Incarnation, writes Evelyn Underhill, 'the imperfect and broken life of sense is mended and transformed into the perfect life of spirit'.[24]) For Eliot it is this same process of spiritual transformation that takes place – at least to some degree – in every instant of achieved illumination. Thus, at 'the still point' of the mystic's vision, in that calm and imperturbable realm high above the limited time-bound states of nature, Time itself – what Eliot calls in 'Burnt Norton' 'the waste sad time' – and, with it, all the illusions of the temporal world are also thought finally to have been 'conquered'. Here, then, is the really fundamental level of meaning, and the fundamental level of comparison, at which Eliot has sought to make valid the link between his various experiences of mystical illumination and the Christian dogma of Incarnation.

6

The Influence of St John of the Cross

But perhaps the best subject for discussion . . . is St John of the Cross. I really feel you are overbold in your criticism of one who is crowned with so much authority. But that is a long subject to discuss in a letter.

(Eliot to Paul Elmer More, 17 February 1932)

The name of St John of the Cross first occurs in notes which Eliot made when he was still a student at Harvard from 1908 to 1914.[1] But it was not until about ten years later, in the period immediately preceding his conversion, that Eliot began seriously to read the work of the Spanish Carmelite.[2] At first, although he was greatly impressed by the mystical teachings of St John, Eliot was by no means convinced that St John was a great poet. This judgment was based on a comparison which he made between St John's work and the mystical poetry of Dante.

A genuine mystical statement [Eliot noted in 1927] is to be found in the last canto of the *Paradiso*; this is primarily great poetry. An equally genuine mysticism is expressed in the verses of St John of the Cross; this is not a statement, but a riddling expression; it belongs to great mysticism, but not to great poetry.[3]

In contrast to the austere intellectual structure of Dante's *Divina Commedia*, Eliot thought he detected in the verses of St John 'a strong vein of what would now be called eroticism', and in Eliot's view this aspect rendered St John's verses somewhat opaque and, worse, 'liable to the indignities of Freudian analysis'.[4]

It was not so much the poetry, therefore, but rather the mystical doctrine, the somewhat dry and abstract prosework of St

John which first attracted Eliot and which in time came to exercise a certain influence on the composition of *Four Quartets*.

Because in the view of many people today, the asceticism of St John of the Cross and that of T. S. Eliot are both somehow life-denying and therefore dangerous, I will try in the pages which follow to give an outline of St John of the Cross's understanding of the *via negativa*, indicating at the same time the extent to which this classical theology of negation is reflected, or fails to be reflected, in the poetry of Eliot.

A. THE LANGUAGE OF PARADOX

The latter part of the third section of 'East Coker', with its tantalising paradoxes and its austere teaching, is very much indebted to the thirteenth chapter of St John's prose treatise, *The Ascent of Mount Carmel*.[5] Eliot himself, in fact, refers to this 'borrowing' in a letter written in May 1940 to Professor H. W. Haüsermann.[6] Strange to say, however, on the subject of the transformation of St John's prose into the poetry of *Four Quartets*, no one seems to have examined very closely the nature and extent of the changes introduced by Eliot into St John's text. Are these changes to be understood merely as an indication of Eliot's concern for the music of his poetry? Or is there not perhaps some other explanation more immediately related to the meaning of St John's text and to Eliot's desire as a poet and as a thinker to alter and to transform that meaning? Let us begin first by looking at the original prose passage of St John. It consists of four paradoxi-cal sayings or maxims which have as their primary focus of interest and concern the realities of pleasure, possession, being and knowledge:

> In order to arrive at having pleasure in everything
> Desire to have pleasure in nothing.
> In order to arrive at possessing everything,
> Desire to possess nothing.
> In order to arrive at being everything,
> Desire to be nothing.
> In order to arrive at knowing everything,
> Desire to know nothing.[7]

These four statements are then followed by four other paradoxical sayings which seem to repeat the same idea in a slightly different form.

It may well be worth noting here in parenthesis that this particular series of maxims was also quoted by Eliot's close friend and fellow American, Paul Elmer More, in one of the chapters of his book *The Catholic Faith*. Every echo one can detect in *Four Quartets* from the work of St John of the Cross, is also to be found in this chapter by More. There is included, for example, a brilliant summary of St John's doctrine of the dark night of the senses and the dark night of the spirit, and also a reference by More to the *ten* 'steps of the ladder of love, by which the soul, ascending from one to another, rises upwards to God' – a passage which recalls 'the figure of the ten stairs' in Section Five of 'Burnt Norton'. Eliot referred more than once in his prose writing to More's book, *The Catholic Faith*. And although he certainly did not agree with everything More said relating to the Spanish mystic, the few remarks which his friend made concerning St John's paradoxical sayings may well have encouraged Eliot to introduce a paraphrase of some of these sayings into his own poem.[8] 'And so we arrive', More wrote in his chapter on Christian mysticism, 'at that strange glorification of what in the tongue of the older English mystics used to be called "naughting", and in the Spanish of our author is chanted in prose that trembles into poetry.'[9]

> In order to arrive at that wherein thou hast no pleasure,
> Thou must go by a way wherein thou hast no pleasure.
> In order to arrive at that which thou knowest not,
> Thou must go by a way that thou knowest not.
> In order to arrive at that which thou possessest not,
> Thou must go by a way that thou possessest not.
> In order to arrive at that which thou art not,
> Thou must go through that which thou art not.

The debt of Eliot's 'East Coker' to this passage in St John must be apparent to even the casual reader. But place Eliot's initial statement of paradox beside these dark sayings of John of the Cross and immediately there are two important differences to be noted. Eliot's passage reads:

> In order to arrive there,
> To arrive where you are, to get from where you are not,
> You must go by a way wherein there is no ecstasy.

Eliot's statement is paradoxical first of all because the experience of ecstasy which, it would seem, one is here admonished either to avoid or to repress, had been most vividly and most memorably expressed and affirmed by Eliot in a short passage only a few lines earlier. St John, in *his* passage, makes no comment whatever on the subject of ecstasy. Moreover, the second paradoxical element in Eliot's statement, the idea that one must always keep strictly to the path of detachment, only in the end to arrive at the point where one already is, is an idea which one does not find expressed – at least not in this form – by St John.

The remainder of this concluding part of Section Three of 'East Coker' divides neatly into two sections, with three paradoxical sayings or maxims in each section. The first of the four dark sayings of St John of the Cross is, for some reason, excluded by Eliot. But he does repeat twice over, and in precisely the same order, St John's three other statements of paradox:

> In order to arrive at what you do not know
>   You must go by a way which is the way of ignorance.
> In order to possess what you do not possess
>   You must go by the way of dispossession.
> In order to arrive at what your are not
>   You must go through the way in which you are not.
> And what you do not know is the only thing you know
> And what you own is what you do not own
> And where you are is where you are not.

The reason, I suspect, why Eliot does not present a completely literal rendering of St John's maxims is that his central and almost exclusive concern, *at this stage of the poem*, is with the purification and negation of the interior life of the spirit. St John's maxims are, by contrast, intended to be much more comprehensive. They describe both the dark night of the spirit – i.e. 'the method whereby the spiritual faculties are voided and purified of all that is not God, and are set in darkness concerning the three virtues [faith, hope and love]';[10] and also the dark night of the senses – i.e. the method whereby 'the soul has gradually to deprive itself of desire for all the worldly things which it possessed, by denying them to itself; the which denial and deprivation are, as it were, night to all the senses of man'.[11] The exclusion from Eliot's poem of St John's first maxim with its reference to the negation of pleasure is an indication, perhaps, that Eliot wants to set aside, for the moment, the question of the purification of 'sensual and exterior things', and to concentrate instead on the purification of the three spiritual faculties, *understanding, memory,* and *will.* In this way, St John's three remaining statements of paradox can be immediately and neatly related to what Eliot had said earlier about the necessity of waiting without *thought,* waiting without *hope,* and waiting without *love.*

> You say I am repeating
> Something I have said before. I shall say it again.

The earlier formulation in Section Three of 'East Coker' of the doctrine of St John of the Cross – the passage, that is, concerning faith, hope and love – was also, I now suspect, based on a specific chapter in *The Ascent of Mount Carmel* (vol. 2, ch. 6). Instead, however, of attempting here to give a full presentation of this chapter, it may be sufficient for our purposes to quote from Paul Elmer More's brief summary of St John's teaching – a summary which we can be quite certain Eliot had read.

> Faith, says St John, denudes and blinds the understanding, teaching us to recognise what cannot be acquired by the light of nature and reason. . . . In like manner hope empties the memory of its content and thus deprives the imagination of the material out of which it might construct a visible edifice for the future. For hope is ever conversant with that which is not and by possession ceases to be. We must hope, yet forbear every attempt to realise that for which we hope. And, lastly, charity empties the will of all positive striving, since the soul must learn that of itself it has no capacity for true love, even for true love of God. We must be in a state of charity, but with no object of desire.
>
> Thus the spiritual virtues induct the soul into a second and deeper night, through which stretches the *via contemplativa.* The darkness here is not accidental, like that which frustrates the efforts of the meditative man to realise the Infinite by his finite capacities, but fundamental – the obscurantism of one who extinguishes his own light that he may be illumined by rays from a fount far beyond his knowing, the voluntary passivity of one who waits for Grace to accomplish that for which he has no potentiality.[12]

It is just such a programme as this which Eliot outlines in the
third section of 'East Coker':

> I said to my soul, be still, and let the dark come upon you
> Which shall be the darkness of God.

Here the ideal of purgation which he is striving to attain is
something far beyond and above the limits of ordinary experience. And yet, Eliot's language – like that of St John – remains
lucid, almost prosaic:

> I said to my soul, be still, and wait without hope
> For hope would be hope for the wrong thing; wait without love
> For love would be love of the wrong thing; there is yet faith
> But the faith and the love and the hope are all in the waiting.
> Wait without thought, for you are not ready for thought: . . .

Although discursive reflection, illusory hope and false love must
all be negated, 'there is yet faith', Eliot assures us. And by
implication we are given to understand that the true virtues of
hope and of love are also, in some way, present in the act of
contemplation. Just how this is possible and how it is to be
understood St John of the Cross explains in *The Ascent of Mount
Carmel*: 'The soul waits', he tells us, 'without making any particular meditation, in inward peace and quietness and rest, and
without acts and exercises of the faculties – memory, understanding and will – at least, without discursive acts, that is, without
passing from one thing to another.'[13] Eliot's primary intention in
Four Quartets is, of course, different from that of St John of the
Cross. The inherited ascetical schema of the dark night of the
spirit, for example, (the plan, that is, which involves the purification of faith, hope and love) is not employed by him as an
instrument for interior or spiritual growth except perhaps on one
or two notable occasions; and of these 'East Coker' Section Three
is, to my mind, the most impressive.[14]

An almost completely different interpretation of this passage
has been proposed recently by Eloise Knapp Hay. In her book,
Eliot's Negative Way, she writes, 'the dark night of the soul . . . is
hardly dealt with at all in *Four Quartets*'.[15] And again: 'Burnt
Norton, and the three Quartets that follow it, deal almost
exclusively with the first night, the dark night of sense.'[16] This

judgment is based, if I am not mistaken, on at least one or two minor misconceptions. Hay distinguishes first of all, and quite correctly, the two nights of purification according to the teaching of St John of the Cross: first the night of the senses (for beginners or novices); and second the night of the soul or spirit (for proficients or contemplatives). But to this distinction, the Carmelite mystic added a second. The night of the senses and the night of the spirit have both, he tells us, a two-fold aspect: active and passive. Accordingly, even the first night, the night of the senses for beginners, includes an experience of *passive* purification.[17] So, whereas Hay is perfectly justified in stating that 'the beginner's way is active', she is mistaken in her view that what distinguishes it from the dark night of the soul is 'the passivity of the second'.[18] Probably as a direct result of the hard line of division which Hay has drawn between the two nights (a line far more absolute than that drawn by St John of the Cross himself) she is compelled to conclude that 'the dark night of the soul [i.e. the night of the contemplatives] . . . is hardly dealt with at all in *Four Quartets*'. And in support of her point of view, when Hay comes to discuss the third section of 'East Coker', and to Eliot's paraphrase of St John's maxims, she writes: 'it seems important to note that this paraphrase is from *the way for beginners* – the middle way – of the *Ascent of Mount Carmel* (I, xiii, II), not from the way for contemplatives in the *Dark Night of the Soul'*.[19] But, as it happens, immediately before St John commits his maxims to paper in *The Ascent of Mount Carmel*, he makes it quite clear that his dark sayings are applicable both to the dark night of the senses and to the dark night of the soul or the spirit.[20]

Eliot's dependence on St John of the Cross is clearly much greater than has generally been realised up to the present. But also clear, after one has carefully compared St John's text in *The Ascent* with Eliot's poetry, is the fact that Eliot is not content simply to repeat in paraphrase St John's doctrine. Instead he has deliberately made certain minor adjustments in St John's text in order to emphasise one aspect of the Saint's teaching, namely that aspect which has to do with the necessity of voiding the three spiritual faculties of understanding, memory and will. And so, in order to attain to the state of true faith, one has to learn, Eliot is telling us, to wait 'without thought, for you are not ready for thought'. And in order ultimately to possess what one is now denied, one must learn to 'wait without hope / For hope would be hope for the wrong thing'. And finally, in order to allow human desire and human love to be informed and purified by God, one has to learn to wait even 'without love / For love would be love of the wrong thing'. Eliot's unembarrassed dependence here on the language of scholastic psychology is somewhat surprising. This language has, it is true, a number of obvious virtues to recommend it, and not least the useful and rare virtue of intellectual clarity. But for most people today the language of Scholasticism or the Scholastic idiom has already become a moribund or a dead language; it presents therefore an almost insuperable barrier to understanding. That Eliot should have been able to introduce such material into a modern poem, without it seems too much difficulty, is remarkable; and it serves to remind us yet again of the strength and flexibility of his poetic talent.

B.   THE THEOLOGY OF THE DARK NIGHT

It is one of the most notable of St John's achievements as a mystical author and theologian that he was able to explain what other mystics and theologians before him had only been able to describe. His most celebrated theme, and the one to which in his writings he returns again and again, is the state or the process which is called simply 'the dark night'. In this process there are, as we have already noted, two principal stages or, as it were, two principal kinds of night: the dark night of the senses and the dark night of the spirit. St John explains:

> For the understanding of this it must be known that, for a soul to attain to the state of perfection, it has ordinarily first to pass through two principal kinds of night, which spiritual persons call purgations or purifications of the soul; and here we call them nights, for in both of them the soul journeys, as it were, by night, in darkness.[21]

Ordinarily, darkness means a certain absence of light. But when St John of the Cross states that God is 'dark night to the soul in this life', he is not thinking of the absence of light, but rather of that plenitude of light which is God's presence, and is a light so dazzling it appears, temporarily, to blind the eye so that the soul is able to see nothing but darkness. 'One of the frequent characteristics of Christian mysticism has been', Eliot wrote in August 1930, 'a use of various imageries of light and darkness, sometimes indeed of a light which is at the same time darkness; such imagery is used by St John of the Cross, perhaps the greatest psychologist of all European mystics.'[22]

In the early stages of the soul's journey towards God, the darkness which the soul begins to experience is, we are told, merely the result of simple mortification and self-denial, 'the which denial and deprivation are, as it were, night to all the senses of man'.[23] Eliot refers to this experience in 'Burnt Norton' as

> . . . darkness to purify the soul
> Emptying the sensual with deprivation
> Cleansing affection from the temporal.

According to St John, the experience of the dark night can be either active or passive: *active* in so far as the soul journeys along the way of purification by means of personal effort; *passive* in so far as the soul does nothing in an active way but suffers all passively. These two ways, the one of action or movement, and the other of rest or of stillness, are both sternly proposed to us by Eliot in the first of his *Four Quartets*:

> Desiccation of the world of sense,
> Evacuation of the world of fancy,
> Inoperancy of the world of spirit;
> This is the one way, and the other
> Is the same, not in movement
> But abstention from movement; while the world moves . . .

In almost every respect, the statement of the negative way in this passage recalls the ascetical teaching of St John of the Cross, and in particular his insistence on the necessity of being both in spirit and in body completely detached from one's affection and desire for 'the things of this world'. 'The soul that is affectioned to the beauty of any creature is', according to St John, 'the height of deformity.'[24] His asceticism demands, therefore, the complete annihilation of every kind of natural desire. The soul must be 'deprived of the pleasure of its desire in all things', of every pleasure, that is to say, that comes to it through the five senses of sight, taste, smell, hearing and touch. But that is not all. 'The soul must not only be disencumbered from that which belongs to the creatures, but likewise, as it travels, must be annihilated and detached from all that belongs to its *spirit.*'[25]

These are hard sayings, and the more one thinks of them the harder and more brutal they seem. How is it possible, one begins to wonder, that a man who is universally acknowledged to be a saint, can make assertions that *seem* unequivocally to deny the traditional Christian belief in the goodness and integrity of natural creation? This question is one that, for many years, has puzzled many of St John's readers. Unfortunately, a full and satisfactory treatment of the problem is not possible within the limits of the present study. But it should be possible to give at least some indication of St John's own understanding of the problem, and then afterwards, perhaps, to compare his insight into the theology of negation with that of Eliot.

The first and most important thing to note is that St John's negative way has, as *he* sees it, one purpose only, and that is the attainment of union with God. His asceticism is, therefore, from beginning to end, supported and sustained by a profound and an intense *theological* vision. It would hardly be appropriate, therefore, to think of it as a merely arbitrary or a merely punitive discipline. Thomas Merton explains:

> His whole asceticism is basically a question of choice, of preference. And we cannot understand what he is talking about if we do not see what the choice really is. On the one hand, the love and the will of God: on the other, the love and the gratification of self. But what do these alternatives mean *in practice*? If we merely take them in the abstract, then the asceticism of St John of the Cross becomes something mechanical, cold, soulless and inhuman: a kind of mathematical exclusion of all spontaneity in favour of dreary and rigid self-punishment. But if we see what he is talking about in the concrete, it is quite a different matter. For on the one hand, we have the confused, dissipated, and unruly urges of our undisciplined desire, which draw us into a state of blindness, weariness, distraction and exile from God. On the other hand there are the very real and very urgent inspirations of the Holy Spirit of Divine Wisdom, that 'loving, tranquil, lonely and

peaceful sweet inebriator of the spirit. Hereby the soul feels itself to be gently and tenderly wounded and ravished, knowing not by whom, nor whence nor how' (*Living Flame of Love*, iii, 38, Vol. III, p. 181). One who does not genuinely experience in himself the reality of these two alternatives cannot fully appreciate the ascetic teaching of St John of the Cross. However, even those who are not themselves mystics can profit by reading his works, if only they remember to see them in perspective.[26]

According to St John's logic, 'two contraries . . . cannot co-exist in one person'.[27] And so, as long as the soul remains enslaved by its desire and its affection for the things of this world, it cannot attain even to the beginnings of an awareness of the infinite beauty of God. 'When the soul is clothed in these affections, it has no capacity for being enlightened and possessed by the pure and simple light of God.'[28] This does not mean, of course, that the natural world is considered by St John to be something evil in itself. The problem is not the world as such but rather the soul's inordinate and unspiritual attachment to the world. Fortunately, on this point, St John's teaching is both lucid and unequivocal. He writes:

> we are not treating here of the lack of things, since this implies no detachment on the part of the soul if it has a desire for them; but we are treating of the detachment from them . . . it is not the things of this world that either occupy the soul or cause it harm, since they enter it not, but rather the will and desire for them.[29]

This Johannine principle is borne out in a particular way by St John's mystical poetry. For it is quite unthinkable, surely, that any man who completely despised natural creation would be able, at the same time, to compose a work such as St John's *Spiritual Canticle*, a poem in which so many of the beauties of the created order are sung and celebrated.

In St John's pages, there is no suggestion that he had been driven to follow the negative path because life, as he knew it, was hateful and disgusting to him. On the contrary, as his life and as his work bear witness, the Saint's lively and wholehearted dedication to the way of asceticism – 'this dark night, accomplice of the hopes of the light of day' – was inspired and sustained by his dogged conviction of being 'led by God for love of Him alone, enkindled in love of Him upon a dark night'.³⁰ He describes the stanzas on which his two mystical treatises, *The Ascent of Mount Carmel* and *The Dark Night of the Soul* are based as 'stanzas wherein the soul sings of the happy chance it had in passing through the dark night of faith, in detachment and purgation of itself, to union with the Beloved'.³¹ When we read in St John that all the being of the creatures is *nothing* compared to the infinite beauty of God, we must understand that St John is deliberately employing the mystical language of paradox and that his use of the hyperbolic expression '*nada, nada, nada*', is not, therefore, to be taken literally. St John does not mean that the created world is, in itself, empty and meaningless, but rather that in spite of its great natural beauty there still remains between this world and its Creator a profound metaphysical gulf and an immeasurable abyss.

On the level of abstract theory, Eliot seems to have understood very well this aspect of St John's theology. In an essay printed in 1930, for example, he noted: 'Only those have the right to talk of discipline who have looked into the Abyss.'³² In practice, however, Eliot's motives for wanting to enter upon the negative path were not as clear or as unambiguous as those of St John. At one stage, in fact, in a private letter to his friend Paul Elmer More, Eliot confessed: 'I am one whom this sense of void ["the void that I find in the middle of all human happiness and all human relations, and which there is only one thing to fill"] tends to drive towards asceticism or sensuality, and only Christianity helps to reconcile me to life which is otherwise disgusting.'³³ Here, Eliot's painful honesty and painful self-knowledge command both our sympathy and our respect. But the paragraph remains, for all that, a disturbing document. And one begins to wonder if, at this time, St John of the Cross was not a dangerous guide for someone with Eliot's unhappy and introverted temperament. Eliot himself admitted as much many years after he had completed writing the *Quartets*. In reply to a query from an American correspondent on the subject of St John of the Cross, he wrote:

My opinion is that for the ordinary person like myself some acquaintance with the work of such a great mystic of the spiritual life as St John is desirable, if only to acquire the highest criteria, but that for actual devotional practice for those no further advanced than myself, such a master is so far advanced as to be even dangerous. Lesser writers can be more helpful and safer for the ordinary man.[34]

So, by way of conclusion, it has I think to be admitted that in spite of considerable 'borrowing' from the ascetical and mystical traditions, not too far beneath the surface of Eliot's lines, and present even between the premises of an otherwise rich and profound theology, one can sense the pressure on Eliot the man of his own Jansenistic temperament and his Puritan inheritance. For however straightforward it might seem at first to be converted in one's mind to a theological point of view – in this case to the ascetical theology of St John of the Cross – the conversion of one's emotions and the attainment therefore of an *authentic* spiritual freedom is clearly a much more subtle and a more difficult task.

Part Three
'The Dry Salvages'
Visions and Revisions

7

Mysticism under Scrutiny: The Influence of Søren Kierkegaard

Every work of art adheres to some system of morality. But if it be really a work of art, it must contain the essential criticism on the morality to which it adheres. . . . The degree to which the system of morality, or the metaphysic, is submitted to criticism within the work of art makes the lasting value and satisfaction of that work.

(D. H. Lawrence, *Phoenix I*)

Four Quartets is generally understood to be the work of a Christian artist with a consistent religious and moral vision. Accordingly, although it is accepted that Eliot's terms of reference widen from one *Quartet* to another, the possibility that he may in mid-course have actually begun to change his mind on a fundamental issue is almost never considered. And yet this is, I believe, the only true and possible explanation for the rather confused tone of hesitancy and ponderousness one has come to associate with Eliot's third *Quartet*.

The poem concludes with a short reflection on the relationship between the Incarnation and certain small experiences of illumination. These experiences, together with the language Eliot uses to describe them, are without exception familiar to us already from the first two *Quartets*. Indeed it is initially somewhat puzzling that in spite of the meditation on mysticism referred to above, there are, in this third *Quartet*, no new illumination experiences recorded by the poet. This fact alone should be enough to alert us to the possibility that Eliot may perhaps be in the process of changing his mind on the very subject which, until now, has been to him of such vital interest and importance, namely the question of the illumination experience.

:t on this apparent change of attitude on the part
s one fundamental issue which must first be
 iding demanded by a poem such as *Four Quartets*,
 theological content, is of a different kind from that
 an ordinary passage of theology. The words Eliot
uses, u.. ges, the ideas, and even the theological dogma to
which he refers, invite us not merely to think and judge, but
somehow to intuit or, as it were, to 'feel' the truth of the poem. If,
at times, in this chapter, we seem not so much concerned with
'feeling' this truth as with judging and thinking about it, this is
due to the limitations imposed on us by our topic. At best, what
we can hope to achieve is only an adequate, not a full, literary
response to the poem.

A.   MYSTICISM AND MEANING

We receive the first clear indication of a change in Eliot's way of
thinking about mysticism when, in Section Two of 'The Dry
Salvages', he begins to question his own earlier attitude to the
past.`

It seems, as one becomes older,
That the past has another pattern, and ceases to be a mere
    sequence—
Or even development: the latter a partial fallacy
Encouraged by superficial notions of evolution,
Which becomes, in the popular mind, a means of disowning
    the past.

These lines have been interpreted by several critics, including F.
R. Leavis, as 'an unchallenging dismissal' by Eliot of development
and evolution.[1] But surely it is made clear in the poem that Eliot's
'dismissal' is directed merely towards certain '*superficial* notions of
evolution'. He does not declare himself intolerant of every single
theory of human progress and development. What is more, the
poet's main preoccupation, at this stage, is not with the theory of
evolution at all, but rather – as he himself indicates – with one of
his own earlier attitudes to the past, that attitude of peculiar
disdain which found its most unequivocal expression in the
celebrated, closing lines of 'Burnt Norton':

Ridiculous the waste sad time
Stretching before and after.

This view of time past and time future as no more than 'a mere sequence' was in fact queried by Eliot for the first time in the concluding section of 'East Coker'. The point he made then, he chooses to repeat almost word for word in the third *Quartet*. So obviously what he desires to say is of some considerable importance. And this remains true in spite of the somewhat casual tone he seems to adopt in 'The Dry Salvages'. Contrary, therefore, to what Dr Leavis has suggested, the following short phrase from the second section cannot, I believe, be read as a mere 'inadvertent carry-over'.[2]

It seems, as one becomes older,
That the past has another pattern, and ceases to be a mere
   sequence—

Compare it, for example, to this passage from Section Five of 'East Coker':

As we grow older
The world becomes stranger, the pattern more complicated
Of dead and living. Not the intense moment
Isolated, with no before and after,
But a lifetime burning in every moment . . .

Eliot has come at last, it would seem, to realise that any theory of mysticism which regards the sphere of time past as 'a mere sequence', and which would, therefore, direct all a man's energies towards the simple attainment of a state of ecstasy, or a state of 'holy' indifference, is in large part mistaken. For, as much as those 'superficial notions of evolution' mentioned in 'The Dry Salvages', this no less superficial notion or concept of mysticism is, in the end, but another 'means of disowning the past', and a means also of escaping from the demands and responsibilities of the present.

Inevitably, this questioning by Eliot of his own original theory of mysticism must, at first, have posed a real threat to the inner harmony and momentum of *Four Quartets*. The fact, however, that it did not in the end radically undermine the overall unity of

Four Quartets is due, I think, to a rather brilliant and subtle shift of position on the part of Eliot. For, although in 'The Dry Salvages' he is prepared to admit that he had, at first, misunderstood the true nature of the illumination experience, he is extremely careful not to reject outright as an illusion, or as a fraud, the mystical experience itself. All that is required now, he tells us, is that the original meaning we gave to the experience be revised.

> . . . the sudden illumination –
> We had the experience but missed the meaning,
> And approach to the meaning restores the experience
> In a different form, beyond any meaning
> We can assign to happiness.

At the end of 'The Dry Salvages' the original state or states of illumination are incorporated into a new and complex under-standing of the relationship between time and the Timeless. They are no longer regarded, as they once were in 'Burnt Norton', as being capable in themselves of 'redeeming the time'. For they are 'only hints and guesses, / Hints followed by guesses'. The real contemplative or mystical gift is now, for the first time, acknow-ledged to be not so much the ability to transcend the limitations and the horror of time – in order thereby to escape into the realm of the Timeless – but rather the grace and the strength 'To apprehend the point of intersection of the Timeless *with time*'.

> . . . something given
> And taken, in a lifetime's death in love,
> Ardour and selflessness and self-surrender.

The response of 'the saint', who is of course for Eliot *the* authentic contemplative, is indeed a kind of ecstasy. But it is the ecstasy of self-forgetfulness and of true service, not that of a mere psycho-logical enthusiasm.[3]

Seen now in the light of this new mysticism of the saint, the experiences of mystical or quasi-mystical illumination recorded in 'Burnt Norton' are no longer regarded as having quite the same importance. For, obviously, when compared to the life of the saint, there is little to distinguish them from the ordinary profane states of nature familiar to 'most of us'. It is, I am persuaded, primarily for this reason that Eliot does not bother in 'The Dry

Salvages' to record any new experiences of illumination. Within the short fourth section, for example, instead of attempting to recreate for us a moment of ecstatic personal vision, as he did so beautifully in the first *Quartet*, he is content simply to articulate a very brief and modest prayer of supplication to the Virgin.

At the heart of the first *Quartet*, 'Burnt Norton', there is a desire on the part of Eliot to raise himself as far as he possibly can above the flux of time. And indeed so central is this preoccupation that, as I have already indicated – and without, I think, undue exaggeration – 'the still point' of the work is the point at which the poetry and the mysticism become one thing. There are commentaries on *Four Quartets* which seem to take it for granted that the mystical attitude indicated here at the end of 'Burnt Norton' remained Eliot's fundamental attitude throughout each of the three remaining *Quartets*. But, in fact, already towards the end of the second *Quartet*, the original concept of mysticism, with its peculiarly negative view of time past and time future, is judged by Eliot to be unacceptable and in need of serious revision. He does not thereby reject mysticism completely, any more than he *completely* rejects the theory of evolution. What he does begin to question, however, and to revise, is his earlier 'superficial notions' concerning the meaning of the mystical experience.

B.   A KIERKEGAARDIAN PERSPECTIVE

But why this change? And why should the effects of this change be so much in evidence in 'East Coker', and in the *Quartet* which follows? Can it be, perhaps, that in the years intervening between the composition of 'Burnt Norton' and the later *Quartets* Eliot, as he grew older, simply ceased to feel and to know as he had once known the experience of intense illumination? This idea or theory has been suggested by the critic, C. A. Bodelsen. Commenting on the passage in the fifth section of 'East Coker' which begins, 'Not the intense moment / Isolated, with no before and after', Bodelsen writes:

> As Eliot elsewhere [Burnt Norton v.33–9] speaks of the intense moment as the only thing in life that matters, the rest being only 'a ridiculous waste sad time stretching before and after',

these lines can hardly mean that he deprecates such experiences, but rather that he knows that one ceases to have them as
one grows older, as Wordsworth complained in *Intimations of
Immortality*.[4]

A more satisfactory explanation in my view has been put forward
by A. D. Moody. He underlines the impact on Eliot's poetry of
the outbreak of war in 1939.[5] ('Burnt Norton' was, one must
remember, completed in 1935, and 'East Coker' not begun until
1940.) Faced with the many new demands and responsibilities of
living in a war situation, Eliot's principal preoccupation was not
so much to transcend the physical world, but rather, in a sense,
to enter fully into the world of history. '[I]f I share the guilt of my
society in time of "peace" ', writes Eliot, 'I do not see how I can
absolve myself from it in time of war, by abstaining from the
common action.'[6] Speaking of the general influence of the War on
the *Quartets*, A. D. Moody remarks that 'the poetry [written after
1939] is not so metaphysical as that of 1925–35: its concern is
rather to penetrate than to pass beyond the physical world. The
difference can be indicated by observing that the mind of the
wartime *Quartets* is not haunted by what might have been, but
concentrated upon what has been.'[7]

Moody's observation is, of course, entirely valid. But there is a
further point or factor, not mentioned by Moody nor, to my
knowledge, by anyone else, in relation to Eliot's change of
attitude to mysticism, which casts at least an equal light on the
question. It has to do with the influence on Eliot of the modern
theological debate, and with the remarkable, exploratory writings
of the nineteenth-century Danish theologian Søren Kierkegaard.
Although Kierkegaard's influence on *Four Quartets* may not, in
the strict sense, be provable, it is certainly, I would say, *guessable*.
And if his work merits close attention here, it is not so much as a
literary source more important than others, but rather as a source
which represents a particular theological attitude of mind, and
one which is also characteristic of Eliot's poem.

'Theology', Eliot wrote to his friend Paul Elmer More on 10
August 1930, 'is the one most exciting and adventurous subject
left for a jaded mind.'[8] Other references to the discipline of
theology can be found scattered throughout Eliot's prose-work
and correspondence. But what one does not find is an attempt by
the poet to compose his own systematic theology. 'I am not a

systematic thinker. . . . I depend upon intuitions and perceptions', he confessed to his friend on 20 June 1934.⁹ And,
elsewhere in the same letter: 'I am painfully aware that I need a
much more profound knowledge of theology for the sort of prose
work that I should like to do.'¹⁰ When at one point More, the
religious philosopher, presumed for some reason to query the
system of punctuation his friend had used in 'Ash Wednesday',
Eliot, the poet, replied with sardonic playfulness: 'Why, my dear
More, are you so foolish as to discuss seriously with a mere
ignoramus like myself questions of philosophy and theology and
then go for me on the one subject on which I know more than
almost anyone living. I am quite aware that I am a minor romantic
poet . . . but if there is one thing I do know, it is how to
punctuate poetry.'¹¹ Here there is, of course, little more than an
exaggerated mock-humility on the part of Eliot. But Eliot did
obviously believe at the same time that More's gifts for theology
were very much greater than his own. On the death of his friend
in 1937 Eliot wrote:

> In the later volumes of *The Greek Tradition* [by More], and in the
> acquaintance and friendship subsequently formed, I came to
> find an auxiliary to my own progress and thought, which no
> English theologian at the time could have given me. The
> English theologians, born and brought up in surroundings of
> private belief and public form, and often themselves descended
> from ecclesiastics, at any rate living mostly in an environment
> of religious practice, did not seem to me to know enough of the
> new world of barbarism and infidelity that was forming all
> about them. . . . I might almost say that I never met any
> Christians until after I had made up my mind to become one. It
> was of the greatest importance, then, to have at hand the work
> of a man who had come by somewhat the same route, to almost
> the same conclusions, at almost the same time, with a maturity,
> a weight of scholarship, a discipline of thinking, which I did
> not, and never shall possess.¹²

The influence of the work of Paul Elmer More and that of certain
other religious thinkers and theologians was important not only
for Eliot's religious development, but also, I believe, for the
development of his later religious poetry. If one wanted to give a
full presentation of Eliot's theological position at this time, one

would certainly have to take into account his long-standing interest in Neo-Thomism, and his enthusiasm for the work of the French Catholic layman, Jacques Maritain.[13] But given the limitations of the present study, it seems wiser to concentrate attention exclusively for a few pages on the work of the nineteenth-century philosopher and theologian Sören Kierkegaard.

In the January 1936 edition of Eliot's journal *The Criterion* we find a review by T. S. Gregory of E. L. Allen's excellent study, *Kierkegaard: His Life and Thought*.[14] (Incidentally, the major works of Kierkegaard were all available at this time in French translation. And a considerable number of them were also beginning to appear in English.[15]) On 24 June 1938 Eliot wrote to Rayner Heppenstall regarding a delay in the appearance of Kierkegaard's *Journals* which Eliot had hoped Heppenstall would review for *The Criterion*.[16] In the end, Heppenstall reviewed Kierkegaard's work, *Purify Your Hearts*, and also a critical study of the Danish philosopher by Walter Lowrie. The review appeared in *The Criterion* in October 1938.[17]

Some months earlier, when, as editor, Eliot received the review, he wrote to Heppenstall to express his gratitude.[18] But perhaps the most telling indication of Kierkegaard's influence on *Four Quartets* is the reference Eliot makes to Kierkegaard in a draft lecture entitled 'Types of English Religious Verse', which he composed in or around the year 1939 by way of preparation for a British Council tour of Italy. Unfortunately, because of the war situation in Europe at that time, and the inevitable difficulty of travelling to the Continent, this absorbing talk was never in fact delivered. But it has survived, I am glad to say, among the rich collection of unpublished manuscripts at King's College Library, Cambridge. The talk is, by any standards, a work of quite unique significance: first of all, because it was composed at the same time as *Four Quartets*; and second, because in it Eliot speaks about the probable development of modern religious poetry. '[T]he religious poetry of our time', he tells us, 'will be concerned primarily with giving poetic form to theological thought.'[19] Among the two or three names of theologians and religious thinkers whose work, it is suggested in the lecture, should prove to be of some importance for the development of modern religious verse, we find listed the name of the Danish Protestant theologian Søren Kierkegaard.

The scope of Eliot's lecture, including as it does a survey of the tradition of English religious poetry from the time of Queen

Elizabeth I until the modern period, is of course far too vast to allow for any closely argued critical commentary. Nevertheless, Eliot does find time to raise one interesting question about the religious poets of the seventeenth century and their predecessors – a question which has puzzled and fascinated several generations of literary historians. '[W]hy should half a dozen poets with a genius for the theatre appear in one generation, and another half dozen whose genius expressed itself in the religious lyric, a generation later?'[20] One factor of notable importance in this situation was the availability to poets such as George Herbert, John Donne and Richard Crashaw, of certain works of devotional and mystical interest. The writings, for example, of the fourteenth-century mystical authors, Richard Rolle and Julian of Norwich, might well have been included, Eliot suggests, in the libraries of Donne and Herbert. And Crashaw, as is now well known, read and studied with enthusiasm the mystical writings of the Spanish Carmelite St Teresa of Avila. But the point to which Eliot gives greatest emphasis is the influence on the literature of the period of violent religious controversy.

> Most of the theological writing of the time – and the quantity, in England as elsewhere, was enormous – was apologetic and controversial. It is my belief that the religious poetry of the seventeenth century, both Roman and Anglican, is deeply affected by a new religious warfare both physical and intellectual. It is perhaps significant that the first of the sequence of religious poets was Robert Southwell, the Jesuit priest martyred in 1595.[21]

If 'religious warfare' can, in the seventeenth century, have such a vital influence on the development of religious verse, there is no reason to deny the possibility of a similar influence in the modern period. And, significantly, Eliot himself believed that 'perhaps since the early seventeenth century there has been no age of such acute theological controversy as our own'.[22] The controversy or debate in which Eliot took the greatest interest at this time was not the old debate between the Anglican and Roman Catholic factions but rather the struggle between two 'new' schools of theological thought, the Liberal Protestant school, which has its roots in the early nineteenth century, and the Neo-Orthodox school, which regards Søren Kierkegaard as its forerunner and prophet, and Karl Barth as its founder and principal apostle.[23] The main thrust of Eliot's sympathy was undoubtedly with the Neo-Orthodox group. But of course Eliot never sought to attach himself completely to any one theological camp or coterie.

To some of Eliot's readers, perhaps, the idea that *Four Quartets* may have had its origin, or even a part of its origin, in Eliot's intense opposition to and intense dislike of Liberalism, will seem somewhat far-fetched. But one should note, in this context, the unexpected observation Eliot made just two years before he wrote the first of the *Quartets*, an observation that concerns another religious author, the Jesuit poet Gerard Manley Hopkins. The enthusiasm which, apparently, many critics feel for this poet, Eliot confesses he cannot altogether share. And why? Because to him it seems that 'from the struggle of our time to concentrate, not to dissipate; to renew our association with traditional wisdom; to re-establish a vital connection between the individual and the race; the struggle, in a word, against Liberalism: from all this Hopkins is a little apart, and in this Hopkins has very little aid to offer us'.[24] If we turn our attention back now to Eliot's unpublished lecture, 'Types of English Verse', we find that in the final paragraph Eliot begins for the first time to speak about what he calls 'the probable direction of religious poetry in the immediate future'. Because he is presumably reflecting, in this paragraph, on the direction his own poetry was taking at the time (he had, after all, just completed 'Burnt Norton' and was on the point of beginning 'East Coker') the passage is of very great interest indeed, and it certainly deserves to be quoted here in full.

> The tendency [in 'the religious poetry that is being written today'] is towards something more impersonal than that of 'the last romantics', and I think away from decorative or sensuous aestheticism. It will be much more interested in the dogma and the doctrine; in religious thought, rather than purely personal religious feeling. The precursor of this attitude was T. E. Hulme killed in 1917; he was not a religious poet, but his critical ideas took this direction. In more recent times has come an increasing attention paid also by laymen and even by men outside the Church, to scholastic philosophy; and among the younger English theologians, a revival deeply influenced by Thomism, and to some extent by Karl Barth and Kierkegaard. Hence it is to be expected that the religious poetry of our time will be

concerned primarily with giving poetic form to theological thought, and will tend to have more kinship with that of the seventeenth century, than with that of the nineteenth.[25]

Placed in the company of Barth and Kierkegaard, T. E. Hulme might seem at first to be the odd man out. But he was, of course, an intrepid opponent of Liberal Humanism. 'What is important', he declared once in a passage quoted by Eliot in 1929, 'is what nobody seems to realize – the dogmas like that of Original Sin, which are the closest expression of the categories of the religious attitude.'[26] And he continued: 'It is not, then, that I put up with the dogma for the sake of the sentiment, but that I may possibly swallow the sentiment for the sake of the dogma.' And again: 'I hold the religious conception of ultimate values to be right, the humanist wrong.'[27]

In the context of our present enquiry, the first question to ask is this: did Eliot's apparent interest in the work of the Danish philosopher and theologian Søren Kierkegaard have any direct bearing on his own change of attitude to mysticism? Or, in other words, was his own earlier scepticism about religious and mystical experience in some way re-awakened by his contact with the work of the Danish thinker?

Søren Kierkegaard is himself sometimes thought to have been a kind of mystic. But the idea, or the suggestion, is not one that he would have much appreciated. 'I am', he declared openly in his first major published work, 'an enemy of mysticism.'[28]

> I do not doubt that in religious mysticism there is to be found much that is beautiful, that the many deep and earnest natures who devoted themselves to it have experienced much in their lives and were thereby qualified to give counsels and directions and hints which are of service to others who venture upon that perilous path; but in spite of all that, this path is not only a perilous path but a wrong path.[29]

What particularly distresses Søren Kierkegaard in the life of the mystic is that there is absolutely nothing which seems to be given greater importance than the moment of ecstatic bliss – which Kierkegaard calls 'the luminous moment':

> he has tasted the whole bliss of it and now has nothing to do but wait to see if it will come again in just as much glory. . . .

Reality is for the mystic a delay, indeed a delay of so perilous a sort that he almost incurs the danger that life may deprive him of that which he once possessed . . . for here the significance of life is conceived as a moment not as succession.[30]

Again, in the same section of *Either/Or*, Kierkegaard writes: 'It is appalling to read a mystic's lament over the dull moments. Then when the dull moment is past comes the luminous moment, and thus his life is constantly changing, it has movement indeed, but no development. His life lacks continuity.'[31] It may well be the case that Eliot's poetry in *Four Quartets* is not in any way *directly* influenced by the texts I have been quoting from the Danish theologian. But Kierkegaard's criticism – so clearly and so distinctly outlined in *Either/Or* – is, with very few exceptions, the same criticism and the same doubt Eliot himself expresses in the fifth section of 'East Coker'.

> As we grow older
> The world becomes stranger, the pattern more complicated
> Of dead and living. Not the intense moment
> Isolated, with no before and after,
> But a lifetime burning in every moment
> And not the lifetime of one man only . . .

Kierkegaard's fundamental objection to the life of the mystic can be summed up in one phrase: 'The whole world is a dead world to the mystic.'[32] He finds it difficult to accept 'the *isolation* in which the individual [mystic], heedless of every relation with the given reality, would put himself in immediate rapport with the Eternal'.[33] Such an attitude is, in Kierkegaard's opinion, nothing less than 'a deceit against the world in which he lives, against the men to whom he is bound by obligations and with whom he might have come into relationship if he had not been pleased to become a mystic'.[34] (The ideas expressed here by Kierkegaard may first have been brought to Eliot's attention by Walter Lowrie's study which was reviewed by Heppenstall in *The Criterion*. 'S. K. frequently and emphatically affirmed', wrote Lowrie, 'that he enjoyed no mystical experiences, no direct relationship with God. In the Second Part of *Either/Or* he allows the judge to argue at length against a mystical conception of religion, and over his own name he frequently repudiated it. Such utterances are congenial to Barth and his school . . . it is easy to perceive that his motive for opposing mysticism was sympathy with the common man.'[35])

What demonstrates the true value and the lasting satisfaction of *Four Quartets* is that Eliot allows his own mystical attitude to be radically criticised and even in part rejected *within the work itself*. Thus, in the concluding section of 'East Coker' Eliot makes an attempt to cancel out, as it were, the original sad comment made at the end of 'Burnt Norton' ('Ridiculous the waste sad time / Stretching before and after'). And also, in one of the very first draft notes for 'The Dry Salvages' we know that he jotted down the following brief sentence, which does, I think, make plain the nature of his new vision and his new Kierkegaardian determination, namely, 'To get beyond time and at the same time, deeper into time.'[36]

Finally, it has to be said that the moment of illumination or 'the luminous moment' does retain a certain importance both for Kierkegaard and for Eliot – provided, of course, its significance is never exaggerated.

> In the case of a healthy man [writes Kierkegaard] this instant of isolation will not be long, and such a momentary withdrawal is so far from being an illusion that it rather increases the inwardness of the earthly relationship. But what may be wholesome as a transient factor becomes a very serious sickness when it is one-sidedly developed.[37]

An Italian friend of Eliot, Alessandro Pellegrini, noted in an article he wrote shortly after an interview with the poet in 1949: 'Religious faith is for Eliot a mode of transcending historicism while remaining in its ambit, and his faith issues out of historicism almost as if to try and remedy its limitations'.[38] One of the subjects discussed by the two men during their long conversation was the idea of the 'solitary' or the solitary individual as it occurs in Søren Kierkegaard's work. Pellegrini noted down afterwards:

> Eliot reminded me that, for us moderns, we must speak of a desire to attain faith rather than its possession. His words recalled to me similar ones of Kierkegaard. I told him so. Certainly it was not by chance that so different a formation, and at a century's distance apart, led to related conclusions.[39]

C. THE RECOVERY OF DREAD

In the second section of 'The Dry Salvages' one can sense a definite shift of attention away from 'the moments of happiness', away, that is, from the sphere of religious mysticism and illumination, to the sphere of intolerable human misery and human dread.

> Now, we come to discover that *the moments of agony* . . .
> are likewise permanent
> With such permanence as time has.
>   (Emphasis added.)

F. R. Leavis has argued, and I think mistakenly, that this passage is 'lacking in inevitability and functional point'.[40] But surely Eliot's lines follow on directly and immediately from his own earlier statement that time past is not to be thought of as 'a mere sequence'. Time past survives; it leans over into the present, and thus 'the agony abides'. For Eliot, however, it is not simply the sphere of time past that weighs down on the individual. There is also, as we will see later, the weight and even the awesome dread of 'The point of intersection of the timeless with time'. The *moment*, explains E. L. Allen, in an excellent paraphrase of Kierkegaard's teaching on the subject,

> The *moment* at which the individual stands might be symbolised by the point at which a descending line impinges on one running horizontally. As an existing person, he stores up the past within himself and moves forward constantly into the future. And the *moment* is not a section of time, but an atom of eternity. It is *krisis* – a judgment on time. It brings the present and us who are in it under the constraint and claim of the Absolute, and it opens the future before us as a Promised Land or a waste howling wilderness – as we choose! It thus gives to the future a new significance; the future is as it were the incognito of eternity. This is a clean break with Greek thought, for which eternity lay in the past and was to be recovered by recollection.[41]

The sense of forward, spirited momentum at the close of 'East Coker', the new determination there to launch out on to 'the vast waters' of the Unknown, also clearly represents, I believe, 'a clean break' with the Greek thought and mysticism of 'Burnt Norton'. But if this is indeed the case, how then are we to explain what appears to be the almost complete loss of such momentum in the third *Quartet*? Again, I believe that Allen's paraphrase of Kierkegaard can throw a certain light on the problem. For it seems to me that Eliot's partly forced adventure into the new life of the spirit follows closely the map or the model first established by Kierkegaard; it repeats, that is, the same stern process of education from inner dread to the asceticism of religious belief.

> It is by decision and action, bold decision and fearless action, that we translate into the language of time the ideals which eternity has revealed to us. Here I stand, therefore, an individual human being with a unique life-history. My feet are on the threshold of the future, and God's voice speaks to me here and now. Here, where I stand, I come under his absolute requirement. Am I willing to venture, to risk myself on a new event, something which does not as yet exist but which my own free act will bring about? . . . the individual longs to go forward, yet at the same time he hesitates, shrinks back, is afraid. In a word, he dreads. Dread is a man's reaction to his destiny, fear before the dignity of his own nature. In the last resort, it is not things one dreads, but oneself. . . . A man seeks to escape from himself, but can find no way to do it.[42]

Kierkegaard's understanding of 'dread' as 'a desire for what one fears . . . an alien power that takes hold of the individual'[43] is notably echoed by Eliot in an essay published in 1937: 'We desire and fear both sleep and waking: the day brings relief from the night and the night brings relief from the day: we go to sleep as to death and we wake as to damnation.'[44] For Kierkegaard, man's most characteristic and most profound dread is a fear of the darkness, of the Unknown, of the Unconditional, of God.

> Man has a natural dread of walking in the gloom, what wonder then that he has a dread of the Unconditional. . . . No night and no deepest gloom is half so dark as this gloom and this night, wherein all relative ends (the common milestones and signposts), wherein all relative considerations (the lanterns which else are a help to us), wherein even the tenderest and

sincerest feelings of devotion – are quenched. . . . for otherwise it is not unconditionally the Unconditional.[45]

Certain expressions that Kierkegaard uses here, and elsewhere, might seem to suggest an experience akin to that of the Carmelite mystic St John of the Cross. And indeed a relationship between the two has already been noted by a number of commentators.[46] One has, however, to remember that the very starting point of Kierkegaard's long and dark journey towards God, his peculiarly strong susceptibility to dread and to bleak despair, find no real parallel in St John of the Cross's temperament or situation. The Carmelite chose, it is true, to follow the difficult path of the *via negativa*. But his motives for doing so, unlike those of the Danish thinker, were not prompted by feelings of desperation, or by any sudden experience of existentialist despair. St John would never, I think, have composed the following brief reflection, which Kierkegaard wrote once on the subject of his conversion:

> I was so deeply shaken that I understood perfectly well that I could not possibly succeed in striking the comforting and secure *via media* in which most people pass their lives: I had either to cast myself into perdition and sensuality or to choose religion absolutely as the only thing – either the world on a scale that would be dreadful, or the cloister.[47]

Eliot made a similar comment in 1928 concerning some of the factors that led to his own conversion. He remarked with amazement at the existence of certain people for whom religion is wholly unnecessary. They seem, he said, to miss nothing,

> to be unconscious of any void – the void that I find in the middle of all human happiness and all human relations, and which there is only one thing to fill. I am one whom this sense of void tends to drive towards asceticism or sensuality, and only Christianity helps to reconcile me to life, which is otherwise disgusting.[48]

Inevitably, perhaps, many readers will incline to the view that dread or despair, when it is experienced to this degree of intensity, is nothing more nor less than a form of mental illness. But neither E. L. Allen nor Søren Kierkegaard would agree.

Despair [*they* say] is the secret malady from which all suffer. Who has not been guilty of this failure before the challenge of eternity? The sole difference between men is that some know from what it is they suffer, while others do not. Woe to that man for whom the consciousness that he is sick makes his sickness doubly terrible! Woe above all to him who has seen that his despair also is before God![49]

One year after E. L. Allen's book on Kierkegaard was reviewed in *The Criterion*, Eliot himself found an opportunity to make an equally sharp observation on the common, universal bondage of human misery. Thus, introducing Djuna Barnes's *Nightwood* in 1937 he wrote:

the book is not a psychopathic study. The miseries that people suffer through their particular abnormalities of temperament are visible on the surface: the deeper design is that of the human misery and bondage which is universal. In normal lives this misery is mostly concealed; often, what is most wretched of all, concealed from the sufferer more effectively than from the observer. The sick man does not know what is wrong with him; he partly wants to know, and mostly wants to conceal the knowledge from himself.[50]

This observation is, of course, the very same observation which is made in the second section of 'The Dry Salvages' when Eliot is discussing the permanence of human agony and the reality of dread.

> We appreciate this better
> In the agony of others, nearly experienced,
> Involving ourselves, than in our own.
> For our own past is covered by the currents of action,
> But the torment of others remains an experience
> Unqualified, unworn by subsequent attrition.
> People change, and smile: but the agony abides.

That the object of this meditation is something more than the mere *empirical* fact of human suffering is, I think, made clear in the lines which follow:

> Time the destroyer is time the preserver,
> Like the river with its cargo of dead negroes; cows and
>   chicken coops,
> The bitter apple and *the bite in the apple*.
>   (Emphasis added.)

A 'clue' to the meaning is contained in that final image – an image which has for centuries been associated with the doctrine of Original Sin, or with the fall from grace of 'our two first parents'. Indeed, one cannot help beginning to wonder at this point if the entire second section is nothing other than an attempt by the poet to provide a kind of emotional equivalent for the Christian doctrine of the Fall. The fact that the emotion or the feeling most often evoked is one of dread is not, I think, very surprising. And it may, in fact, point yet again to the influence on Eliot of Søren Kierkegaard. For it is not uncommon, in the works of the Danish thinker, to come upon statements such as the following: 'The nature of Original Sin has often been examined, and yet the principal category has been missing – it is dread.'[51]

> Where is there an end of it, the soundless wailing,
> The silent withering of autumn flowers
> Dropping their petals and remaining motionless;
> Where is there an end to the drifting wreckage,
> The prayer of the bone on the beach, the unprayable
> Prayer at the calamitous annunciation?

'Of all men', writes E. L. Allen paraphrasing Kierkegaard, 'it is the genius who is most exposed to dread. For no other do the Sirens of the future sing so enchanting a song, yet no other sees as he does where *the bleached bones lie scattered on the rocks.*'[52] The image of 'the bone on the beach', the symbol, one may presume, of the stark emptiness of our human condition, appears in both the first and the last stanzas of Eliot's haunting lyric. 'There is no end', we are told, to:

> The bone's prayer to Death its God. Only the hardly, barely
>   prayable
> Prayer of the one Annunciation.

Again in Allen/Kierkegaard we read: 'Man's condition is hopeless, and only a miraculous divine intervention can free him from his bondage.'[53] Eliot's emphasis in 'The Dry Salvages' on the futility and the emptiness of every human endeavour is so insistent that the reader may feel forced to come to the conclusion that, whatever else Eliot has achieved, he has not been able to communicate a positive Christian vision. However, Denis

Donoghue, who is by universal acclaim one of Eliot's finest readers, has demonstrated in his essay 'Eliot's *Four Quartets*: A New Reading' that the negative emphasis in 'The Dry Salvages' forms part of a very deliberate Christian strategy.

> Eliot's problem in *Four Quartets* is a strategic one; how to evacuate practically all the areas in which his readers live. . . . The critique is religious, dogmatic, and Christian. Eliot's hope is to clear a space, or if necessary to take over a bombed-out area, and there to build a new life of the spirit; to realize 'the idea of a Christian society'.[54]

Such an undertaking is difficult enough for those who are committed public apologists for Christianity, such as Blaise Pascal and Søren Kierkegaard. But think how difficult a task it must be when, like Eliot, one is also a poet, and when it seems one can *only* declare one's dogma by a process of 'rejection and elimination', by striving consciously in other words to make all the many secular substitutes appear fraudulent and incomplete. It is, I suppose, small wonder that we read towards the end of Professor Donoghue's critical study the following wry sentence: 'How the non-believer reads this poem, I cannot say'.[55] Certainly if, in *Four Quartets*, the apologetic method of rejection and elimination is the *only* method of strategy Eliot can use as a poet in order to make tangible and to make real the Christian dogmas of Incarnation and Annunciation, then his finished work – when it is viewed as it must be, of course, as a *poem* and as nothing else – is bound to be judged by the 'secular' readers, and by others as well, as less than satisfactory.

But, in practice, Eliot does not, I believe, limit himself to a mere intellectual or dogmatic strategy. Take, for example, the way Eliot introduces into the second section of 'The Dry Salvages' the theme of 'the one Annunciation'. There is, first of all, it is true, an attempt by the poet to undermine confidence in secular man's usual optimism concerning the future. Such optimism Eliot regards as a kind of wilful distraction from what is now our most fundamental fear and our dread, the fear that our future, like our past, may be 'littered with wastage' and have no destination. Man's condition is so hopeless, according to this view, that time cannot be redeemed without 'the miraculous divine intervention' of the Word, without 'the one Annunciation'. At the end of Eliot's lyric, however, the reader is not simply confronted, out of the blue, as it were, by an abstract statement of Christian belief. There is, also, another extremely subtle and, I think, effective *poetic* strategy employed, but one that has not, so far, been accorded due recognition by Eliot's critics. And it is in virtue of this strategy, I believe, that Eliot has been able to communicate in 'The Dry Salvages' not only an abstract *intellectual* 'solution' for man's distress, in the form of a Christian dogma, bút also and most important of all *what it feels like, in practice, to believe in the Christian dogma of Annunciation.*

For Eliot the fundamental emotion that is awakened by *his* belief in the Annunciation, is one that is strangely akin to that emotion of dread or terror we all feel at the thought of our approaching death. And because this primitive, human emotion is one that is familiar to all of us, Eliot deliberately takes it up, and uses it to describe the much less familiar, though no less vivid, *feeling* of Christian belief. Thus 'the hardly, barely prayable / Prayer of the one Annunciation' – Annunciation, that is, with a capital 'A' – is presented by Eliot as being *emotionally* akin, although of course spiritually opposite to 'The bone's prayer to Death its God'.

> The prayer of the bone on the beach, the unprayable
> Prayer at the calamitous annunciation.

(By verbal and musical association, a similar link is also suggested in 'The Dry Salvages' between the ringing of the 'Perpetual angelus' – a sound which is, of course, traditionally associated with the Annunciation – and 'the tolling bell' of destruction and death, heard for the first time at the close of the poem's magnificent opening section.) In emphasising this somewhat perverse and yet, from the artistic point of view, courageous link between Christian dogma and the human emotion of dread, Eliot may well have been encouraged again by the example of Søren Kierkegaard. 'His [Kierkegaard's] misery', we read in a review printed in *The Criterion* in 1936, 'was the shadow side of the supreme paradox, the Incarnation.'[56]

At the close of the second part of 'The Dry Salvages', an intense feeling of dread is once again evoked by the poet. And this time, significantly, Eliot takes up an image he had already used once before in his verse-drama *The Rock* as a means of describing the

Incarnation. '[T]he ragged rock in the restless waters' may appear harmless 'On a halycon day', but it is regarded here by Eliot as something ultimately perilous and even terrifying.

That the feeling of dread should be thus made to serve as an analogue for the experience of Incarnation may seem like a kind of wilfulness on the part of Eliot, a wilfulness to the point of absurdity. For surely the fact of Incarnation must mean to those who believe it that God, the Father, because he loved the world so much gave or sent His only son to redeem it. This view, although it is certainly the most popular theological notion of Incarnation is not, I repeat again, the view of T. S. Eliot nor that of Kierkegaard.

> Salvation is not at all by the good news that God so loved the world, but by the self-contradictory proposition that the eternal has become. [*sic*] The Incarnation is the actualisation of the impossible, the absurd confronting us as fact! Christ, therefore, is a challenge rather than a revelation. But he is an intellectual challenge. He is a stone of stumbling and a rock of offence, a riddle to which our understanding need never hope to find an answer.[57]

By way of conclusion I should like now to draw attention to a point already made in the introduction. Even given the evidence, internal and external, available to us at present (including the new evidence from the unpublished manuscripts at King's College Library, Cambridge) one cannot state *conclusively*, that Kierkegaard has had any great or significant influence on *Four Quartets*. Kierkegaard is not even, necessarily, one has to admit, a 'source' more important than others. But his work does merit particular attention all the same. For by keeping it constantly at the back of one's mind when reading through *Four Quartets*, and by using it as a kind of yardstick, or point of comparison (as I have attempted to do in this chapter) certain aspects of Eliot's original Christian and poetic vision – aspects hitherto neglected or ignored by other readers – are suddenly highlighted, and are brought, perhaps for the first time, clearly into focus. Thus, for instance, Eliot's intense obsession with dread and with Original Sin in the third *Quartet*, an obsession regarded by many critics and readers as being somehow subversive of his determination as a Christian artist to seek out a new mode of comprehension for the Incarnation, this very obsession, which to others, appears a distinct disadvantage, is to Eliot himself the very ground or bedrock on which he has been able to begin to construct and to recreate a new 'concept' of the Christian dogma. For, like Søren Kierkegaard before him, Eliot has not hesitated to contemplate a system 'according to which the Fall would be the dark shadow cast by the Incarnation'.[58] And, what is more, by use of an unexpected and, I think, courageous poetic strategy, he has even dared, after the manner (or should one now say the *example*?) of Søren Kierkegaard, to suggest that 'dread, as it has been the precursor of sin, may also become a schoolmaster to lead men to redemption', and that 'In the very moment when he [the individual] sinks into the abyss of dread, his feet touch the solid rock of God's providence.'[59]

8
The Brahmin and Buddhist Influence

*To call ourselves disciples of the Buddha or believers in Brahma –
as some unstable minds are prone to do – would be superstition
and not spirituality; yet to each of these peoples we may turn for
strength and consolation.*

(P. E. More, *Bhartrihari; A Century of Indian Epigrams*,
1899)

On one occasion when Eliot was discussing the influence from
outside Europe upon European literature he remarked:

In the literature of Asia is great poetry. There is also profound
wisdom and some very difficult metaphysics. . . . Long ago I
studied the Indian languages, and while I was chiefly interested
at that time in Philosophy, I read a little poetry too; and I know
that my own poetry shows the influence of Indian thought and
sensibility.[1]

Again, on another occasion, when asked by Ranjee Shahani in an
interview, 'Which Indian books and writers have impressed you
most?', Eliot replied, '*The Upanishads* and the *Bhagavad-Gita*'.[2]
Exactly at which stage in his life this interest in *The Upanishads*
was first awakened we do not know. But we do know that when
he was still a student at Harvard University Eliot received from
his tutor in Indian Philosophy, Professor C. R. Lanman, a book
entitled *The Twenty-Eight Upanishads*. (This book is now in the
Hayward bequest at King's College, Cambridge.) Later that year,
in August and October, Eliot also acquired two books by Paul
Deussen, *Upanishads des Veda* and *Die Sutras des Vedanta*.[3]
  In spite of the fact that, by his own admission, Eliot was left
feeling somewhat confused after his first initiation into the mazes

125

of Indian philosophy, the records at Harvard University indicate that during his two graduate years Eliot covered a most impressive range of texts, 'and that, apart from one A minus his grades in Indian studies were all A'.[4] Eliot's early interest in the *Upanishads* was shared by his great mentor and friend, the Anglican philosopher Paul Elmer More. On the subject of More's *Marginalia*, Eliot wrote in a last letter to his friend on 11 January 1937: 'What touches me most closely is a suggestion, here and there, of a spiritual biography which if I may say so without presumption, is oddly, even grotesquely, more like my own, so far as I can see, than that of any human being I have known.'[5] In *Marginalia* More had spoken of 'the religious impulse' that drew him (as later, of course, it was to draw Eliot) towards the work of the Western poet Dante Alighieri and also towards the *Upanishads*.[6]

Traces of the *Upanishads* are already detectable in some of Eliot's early poetry. In Part Five of *The Waste Land*, for example, – the section entitled 'What the Thunder said' – Eliot has chosen to adapt for his own purposes a fairly well-known text from the *Brihad–Aranyaka Upanishad*. He acknowledges this adaptation in a short explanatory footnote. He gives first a rough translation of the three Sanskrit words, 'Datta, dayadhvam, damyata (Give, sympathise, control)', and then writes: 'The fable of the meaning of the Thunder is found in the *Brihadaranyaka–Upanishad*, 5,1.'[7] Another section of *The Waste Land* actually takes its title from an eastern text: 'The Fire Sermon' of the Buddha.

While Eliot was engaged in writing *The Waste Land* he apparently felt himself drawn towards the Buddhist religion. Stephen Spender recalls: 'I once heard him say to the Chilean poet Gabriela Mistral that at the time when he was writing *The Waste Land*, he seriously considered becoming a Buddhist.'[8] One reason why in the end Eliot chose not to take this step was the extreme difficulty he had in comprehending from a Western philosophical standpoint the complex religious and philosophical texts of Hinduism and Buddhism.

A good half of the effort of understanding what the Indian philosophers were after – and their subtleties make most of the great European philosophers look like schoolboys – lay in trying to erase from my mind all the categories and kinds of distinction common to European philosophy from the time of the Greeks. My previous and concomitant study of European philosophy was hardly better than an obstacle. And I came to the conclusion . . . that my only hope of really penetrating to the heart of the mystery would lie in forgetting how to think and feel as an American or a European: which, for practical as well as sentimental reasons, I did not wish to do.[9]

The Eastern studies Eliot undertook left him 'in a state of enlightened mystification'; and he declared that 'the influence of Brahmin and Buddhist thought upon Europe, as in Schopenhauer, Hartmann, and Deussen, had largely been through romantic misunderstanding'.[10] This statement was made in 1933. And in that same year Eliot described the enthusiasm for Eastern philosophy in the work of the humanists, Irving Babbit, Ezra Pound and I. A. Richards, as 'a deracination from the Christian tradition'.[11] These negative comments did not represent in any way a lack of respect on the part of Eliot for the wisdom of the East. All that he was sceptical about was, simply, the possibility in the West of our understanding and assimilating this wisdom. But Eliot's attitude changed radically within the space of seven or eight years – the period in fact during which *Four Quartets* was composed. Thus, in 1940, the year in which 'East Coker' was published, he observed that 'Christianity in its decayed forms could learn much from the East'.[12] And in 1941, when he again took up the question of the humanists' interest in Eastern philosophy, and expressed again certain of his reservations, he was careful enough on this occasion to add: 'I would not, however, minimize the importance of their [the humanists'] contribution in reminding us of the need for a Christian examination and understanding of Eastern thought, which the Christian philosophy of the future cannot afford to neglect.'[13] Likewise, in a paper on Goethe delivered in 1955, Eliot placed very considerable emphasis on the necessity of committing oneself to a particular religion or to a particular philosophy. 'But,' he immediately added – and the qualification is, I am certain, equally characteristic of his attitude – 'wisdom is λόγος| ξυνός the same for all men everywhere. If it were not so, what profit could a European gain from the Upanishads, or from the Buddhist Nikayas?'[14]

Given, therefore, the fact that during the making of the *Quartets* Eliot became more optimistic about the possibility, in the West, of philosophers and thinkers assimilating the wisdom of the East, how in practice did this change of attitude affect the composition of *Four Quartets*? Is it possible that in spite of what Eliot stated in his criticism, and may have sincerely believed at a conscious level, he has, in fact, through the medium of his poetry, taken up the cause of the *Universalists*, those 'who maintain that the ultimate and esoteric truth is one, that all religions show some traces of it, and that it is a matter of indifference to which one of the great religions we adhere'.[15] Or, to put the question in another way, to what extent and in what precise manner can we say that the experience proper to Hinduism and Buddhism is relevant to Eliot's poetic and mystical vision in *Four Quartets*?

A. 'BURNT NORTON'

In a short essay Eliot composed in 1930, he drew attention to two medieval mystics of the West, and went on to remark on the similarity in general thought and style between their work and that of the Eastern mystical tradition.

> The mysticism of the thirteenth and twelfth centuries was intellectual and international: two of the greatest medieval mystics, as is not generally observed, were Scots: Richard and Hugh of St Victor. The mystical treatises of Richard of St Victor are as dry and abstract as those of the great Indian expositors of mysticism. They use imagery, certainly, but always clearly as analogy. They separate positively the human from the divine.[16]

Eliot's almost obsessional horror of the transient world, his persistent desire in 'Burnt Norton' to attain to a point of stillness or changelessness, brings him close to the 'negative' spirituality of Buddhism, and to certain of the early chapters in the *Bhagavad-Gita*. Take, for example, his meditation on 'the still point of the turning world' in Section Two. I have already indicated in my second chapter how this passage, with its paradoxical negation of opposites, can be seen to parallel, in a most striking manner, Chapter Five in *The Mystical Theology* of Pseudo-Dionysius.[17] However, Dionysius' path to the Ultimate Truth follows exactly the same route that has always been recommended to the Buddhist and to the Hindu within their own separate traditions.

And so it is with a certain justification that J. Estlin Carpenter could write in his book, *Buddhism and Christianity: A Contrast and a Parallel*:

> Dionysius passing behind the eternal relation of the Father and Son, the Infinite Thinker and his Everlasting Thought, fixed his gaze on the Abyss of Being containing both. No intellectual notion could be formed of it. As the Superessential Essence it admitted of no definition, could be expressed in no predicate. Dionysius dared to call it a Reason that did not reason, a Word that could not be uttered, the absolute Non-Existent which is above all Existence. Here is the Christian equivalent of the Buddhist 'Void'.[18]

The idea of the Eternal Truth of the Imperishable as a 'thing' which completely transcends the pairs of opposites can also be found in the Hindu Scriptures.[19] A direct reference to this teaching occurs in a story by May Sinclair which Eliot printed in *The Criterion* of October 1923. Towards the end of the story, which was entitled 'Jones's Karma', we come upon the following passage:

> When you talk of free-will and bondage you talk of the pairs of opposites. You are free and you are bound also. . . . But so long as you affirm the reality of the pairs of opposites you are subject to illusions. . . . Notwithstanding, there is a path of perfect freedom. When it is indifferent to a man whether he is himself or not himself, whether he lives or dies, whether he catches the cholera or does not catch the cholera . . . he escapes from desiring and undesiring, from the pairs of opposites, and from the chain of happenings and the round of births.[20]

About ten years later Eliot made a passing reference in *The Criterion* to 'Jones's Karma', so the story by Sinclair had obviously not been forgotten.[21] What it means in practice to follow to the end 'the perfect path of freedom' and to attain to a state above and beyond the pairs of opposites, is thus described by Eliot in his meditation concerning 'the still point':

> I can only say, *there* we have been: but I cannot say where.
> And I cannot say, how long, for that is to place it in time.

The inner freedom from the practical desire,
The release from action and suffering, release from the inner
And the outer compulsion, yet surrounded
By a grace of sense, a white light still and moving, . . .

Far from being made aware by the poetry of a vast distance
dividing the Christian from the non-Christian worlds, we are, as
readers, initiated in 'Burnt Norton' into the truth that the Word is
common to all. And, what is more, we discover, perhaps to our
surprise, 'how frequently contemplatives of religions and civiliza-
tions remote from each other are saying the same thing'.[22]

Later, in the fifth section of 'Burnt Norton', there is a brief
reference made to 'The Word in the desert', and this phrase
alludes, presumably, at least on one level of its meaning, to the
Incarnate Word. 'I take for granted', the poet remarked in 1937,
one year after he had completed 'Burnt Norton', 'that Christian
revelation is the only full revelation; and that the fullness of
Christian revelation resides in the essential fact of the Incarnation,
in relation to which all Christian revelation is to be understood.'[23]
In the same essay Eliot also expressed the view that the dogma of
heaven and hell is as essential to Christianity as the dogma of
Reincarnation is to Buddhism. It is therefore of some interest to
note that in 'Burnt Norton' Eliot also makes an explicit allusion to
the states of 'heaven and damnation / Which flesh cannot
endure'. Other possible 'Christian' echoes can, after careful
scrutiny, be detected in the poem. But one does, I think, have to
search for them. And even then I have the impression that they
are few and far between.[24]

But although there are only a small number of *explicit* Christian
allusions in 'Burnt Norton', the underlying influence is, undoubtedly, I would say, that of Christian Neo-Platonism, the tradition
mediated to Eliot through the works of St Augustine of Hippo,
Pseudo-Dionysius, Richard of St Victor and St John of the Cross.
In the West it is this intellectual and spiritual tradition, with its
emphasis on the reality of the Eternal, its awareness of the horror
and the burden of time, its dedication to the search for enlightenment, and its enthusiasm, at least in the early stages of the
mystical ascent, for logical and philosophical reflection, which is
nearest in character and in spirit to the great mystical traditions of
the East. Eliot, by working mainly, therefore, within the tradition
of Christian Neo-Platonism, cannot have found it such a difficult

task to incorporate into the inner structures of his poetry and philosophical thought certain echoes and traces of Hindu and Buddhist mysticism.

It is, obviously, of considerable importance, when commenting upon *Four Quartets* from a philosophical standpoint, to keep in mind that what we are reading here is a poem and not some obscure essay in comparative mysticism or comparative religion. A philosophical theory is one thing in the context of a poet's or a writer's intellectual formation. But it is something quite different when it is found woven into the inner structure of a living poem. Accordingly, certain basic differences which may emerge within the context of an abstract philosophical discussion, and may seem at times to be almost irreconcilable, can in fact be reconciled, Eliot believes, within the context of a poem. 'Different philosophies, or opposed philosophical opinions which cannot in the philosophical area of discourse be maintained at once, may . . . be united and *poetically* reconciled.'[25] The *Quartets* do not present us – any more than the *Upanishads* or the Buddhist *Nikayas* present us – with a systematic or wholly consistent philosophy. They were written down over a period of some eight to nine years, and as a result contain trends of thought differing among themselves in some respects. And yet one can say that there is a sense throughout of an underlying unity. And, in the end, when one has read slowly and carefully through the entire work, it is the shared common ground between the different approaches that remains impressive.

B.   'EAST COKER'

In 1937, one year after the completion of 'Burnt Norton', and three years before the appearance of 'East Coker', W. B. Yeats had occasion to write an introduction to *The Ten Principal Upanishads* in which he remarked how, 'Between 1922 and 1925 English literature, wherever most intense, cast off its preoccupation with social problems and began to create myths like those of antiquity, and to ask the most profound questions'.[26] When Yeats made this statement he was thinking in particular of the work of philosophical authors such as T. S. Eliot and Aldous Huxley. But he mentioned also in his 'Preface' the work of 'a still younger generation', whose primary interest, he believed, was the 'pursuit of meaning'. These authors, said Yeats, 'have thrown off . . . the old metaphors, the sensuous tradition of the poets . . . but have found, perhaps the more easily for that sacrifice, a neighbour-hood where some new Upanishad, some half-asiatic masterpiece, may start up amid our averted eyes'.[27]

The first draft of 'East Coker' contains the following somewhat mysterious passage:

> The mind must venture
> Where it has not been, be separated
> For a further union, a deeper communion,
> Aranyaka, the forest or the sea . . .[28]

The phrase 'Aranyaka, the forest or the sea' was rubbed out by Eliot before publication, but what, we might ask, was it doing there in the first place? In John Dowson's *Classical Dictionary* 'Aranyaka' is defined as 'belonging to the forest'.[29] Indian mysticism, in the form in which it has come down to us today, had of course its origin in the experience of the primitive forest sages, whose wisdom is recorded in the books known to us as the *Upanishads*. These ancient people lived through a period of history which has often been compared with our own situation today. 'It was a period', writes one commentator, '. . . of questioning like ours – questioning of the value of outward rites, of myth, even of theological reasoning if it is not related to intuition and experience.'[30] According to Dowson's *Classical Dictionary*, the word Aranyaka(s) also refers to actual writings by the forest sages.

> Certain religious and philosophical writings which express the mystical sense of the ceremonies, discuss the nature of God, etc. They are attached to the Brahamanas, and intended for study in the forest by Brahmans who have retired from the distractions of the world. . . . The Aranyakas are closely associated with the Upanishads, and the names are occasionally used interchangeably: thus the Brihad is called indifferently Brihad Aranyaka or Brihad Aranyaka Upanishad. . . . In one sense the Aranyakas are old, for they reflect the very dawn of thought; in another sense they are modern, for they speak of that dawn with all the experience of a past day. There are passages in these works unequalled in any language for grandeur, boldness and simplicity.[31]

It was perhaps for reasons such as these that Eliot chose to quote from the *Brihad-Aranyaka Upanishad* in the concluding section of *The Waste Land*. And perhaps for these reasons also that he chose to refer to 'Aranyaka, the forest' in the first draft of the concluding section of 'East Coker'. It is, moreover, my own conviction that this same book deserves to be considered as one of the sources of 'East Coker'. In particular, I have in mind the following brief stanza from the *Brihad-Aranyaka Upanishad*, Chapter Four:

> Blind darkness enter they
> Who delight in unwisdom.
> Into darkness blinder yet
> Go they who delight in wisdom.[32]

In Sections Two and Three of 'East Coker' Eliot deliberately places close together for the sake of comparison two different experiences of darkness and two different kinds of wisdom. First of all there is the wisdom which is the accumulation of 'knowledge derived from experience', the wisdom of 'the quiet-voiced elders'. But this wisdom – or, at least, so it seems to Eliot – is, by its nature, ephemeral and illusory, and is in a sense therefore no wisdom at all, but 'only the knowledge of dead secrets / Useless in the darkness into which they peered / Or from which they turned their eyes'. The true wisdom which, in Eliot's view, is 'the only wisdom we can hope to acquire' is *the wisdom of humility*. Corresponding to these two ways of knowledge or two wisdoms, there are also two different experiences of darkness. On the one hand, there is the almost terrifying sense of void, the darkness of 'the vacant interstellar spaces' into which Eliot – stern moralist and visionary that he is – can see so many of his own contemporaries beginning to enter:

> O dark dark dark. They all go into the dark,
> The vacant interstellar spaces, the vacant into the vacant.[33]

And, on the other hand, there is the even blinder darkness of true wisdom into which the contemplative may be drawn, in stillness and self-denial. And this darkness Eliot calls 'the darkness of God'. (In the *Brihad-Aranyaka Upanishad* one of the stages in the process of a man's enlightenment, or of his awakening, is described paradoxically as that condition 'when he has fallen into

a deep sleep and is conscious of nothing at all'.[34] Compare in 'East
Coker', Section Three, the phrase used by Eliot to evoke the
divine darkness: 'when, under ether, the mind is conscious but
conscious of nothing'.)

I have already examined in Chapter Six the influence of the
Carmelite mystic, St John of the Cross, on Eliot's understanding
of the divine darkness. But it now seems possible that Eliot was
also influenced here, at least to some small degree, by the *Brihad-
Aranyaka Upanishad*. One can even detect in the series of paradoxical statements at the close of Section Three of 'East Coker' – the
section most heavily indebted to the doctrine of St John of the
Cross – one or two traces of Upanishadic or Brahminic mysticism.
Take for instance Eliot's first statement of paradox:

> In order to arrive there,
> To arrive where you are, to get from where you are not,
> You must go by a way wherein there is no ecstasy.

To my knowledge one does not find anywhere in the writings of
St John of the Cross the idea or the notion that one's real aim in
keeping strictly to the path of detachment and in not allowing
oneself to be distracted even by the experience of 'ecstasy', is to
be able to arrive in the end, with a full and calm realisation, at the
point where one already is. Yet this remarkable statement of
paradox is, as it happens, one that is commonplace in Brahminic
mysticism.[35] The eighth-century Hindu philosopher, Sankara, for
example, whose writings deal for the most part with the religious
and the philosophical speculations of the *Vedanta Sutra* and the
Upanishads, views the final attainment of mystical liberation 'not
as a return to what has been left, but as a sudden awakening
whereby the soul learns that she has never been what she seemed
to be, or has cared for what seemed to attract her, but has always
been what she now knows herself to be'.[36] There is an interesting
text, also from one of the *Upanishads*, quoted in a brief essay by B.
N. Chaturvedi as 'proof' that in the third section of 'East Coker'
Eliot was attempting to unite the teachings of the *Upanishads* with
the teachings of the Christian poet and mystic, St John of the
Cross.

> The negative way to the attainment of the Absolute [writes
> Chaturvedi] is emphasized in the third verse of part II of

Kenopanishad: 'It is known to him to whom it is unknown. It is unknown to those who know well; and known to those who do not know'. This is the humility of non-knowledge and of the complete renunciation of the self which enables one to merge oneself with the Brahman. This is what Eliot also emphasizes at the end of the third section of *East Coker*:

> And what you do not know is the only thing you know
> And what you own is what you do not own
> And where you are is where you are not.[37]

Of all the *Quartets*, 'East Coker' is generally thought to be the most concrete and the most distinctly personal. In part this is because the title itself is the name of the Somerset village which was the home of the Elyot family for some two centuries before Andrew Elyot, the poet's ancestor, set out in 1667 to travel to the New World. T. S. Eliot's decision, three centuries later, to return to the place of his origins is, no doubt, the expression of a deep-rooted personal and psychological need. However, the return to East Coker is not permitted by Eliot – at least not within the confines of the poem – to become an occasion for historical or personal self-affirmation. On the contrary, the poet's empirical ego, and the professional mask he has chosen to wear for years in the public eye, are now judged, it would seem, to be hypocritical and even illusory. The poet is shown in the third section of 'East Coker', for example, to have taken his place among the 'vacant' nobodies of the world, among 'The captains, merchant bankers, eminent men of letters' etc. And he seems there to be almost wilfully insistent on the fact of his own personal nullity:

> And we all go with them, into the silent funeral,
> Nobody's funeral, for there is no one to bury.

Elsewhere in the poem Eliot will again turn on himself and turn also on each one of us with words of sharp, purposeful meaning. We may, he writes, 'like to think / That we are sound substantial flesh and blood'. But we are, in fact, whether or not we realise it, hopelessly caught in the succession of the time past and time future. And we are allowing ourselves, each day, to be reduced by distraction and by enchantment to a mere shadow-image or ghostly caricature of our true selves.

Throughout the first part of 'East Coker' Eliot succeeds, and with perhaps more assurance than ever before, in making us conscious of the fixed cycles of change and decay in the human and non-human worlds. What we see being enacted before us is that process whereby the empirical self, or the finite personality, is hypnotised and is taken captive by the blind, inexorable rhythms of human generation and human death. But there is also for Eliot another dimension of the Self – let us call it the impersonal or the archetypal Self – which remains somehow above and beyond the space-bound and time-bound cycles of generation. The reality of this 'other' Self, its immeasurable calm, is felt particularly I would say at the close of the first movement.

> Dawn points, and another day
> Prepares for heat and silence. Out at sea the dawn wind
> Wrinkles and slides. I am here
> Or there, or elsewhere. In my beginning.

From a number of points of view, including that of the Christian mystical tradition, the implications contained within this final statement are quite startling. In order, I think, to find anything *immediately* comparable one has to go outside the Western mystical tradition altogether, and read certain fundamental texts in the early *Upanishads*. (At the same time, however, it has to be said that in the view of a considerable number of modern thinkers, including Aldous Huxley, this doctrine of the Self is *not* confined to Hinduism, but is in fact part of a perennial and universal philosophy which has among its few notable Christian exponents mystics such as Meister Eckhart, Ruysbroeck and St John of the Cross.[38])

In the *Brihad-Aranyaka Upanishad*, the higher Self of a man, his innermost essence or *atman*, is shown to be mysteriously identified with the unchanging and ever-present ground of the universe, *Brahman*.

> In the beginning this universe was the Self alone – in the likeness of a man. Looking around, he saw nothing other than himself. First of all he said: 'This is I'. Hence the name 'I' came to be. . . . In the beginning this universe was Brahman alone, and he truly knew himself (atman), saying: 'I am Brahman'. And so he became the All. Whichever of the gods became aware of this, also became that All: so too with seers and men.[39]

One of the chosen symbols in the *Aranyaka Upanishad* for the eternal state of 'beginning' or oneness is the sea, or the ocean. 'An ocean, One, the seer becomes, without duality: this, sire, is the man whose world is Brahman.'[40] Helen Gardner in her book *The Composition of Four Quartets* was somewhat ill at ease with Eliot's decision to place the image of 'the sea' beside that of 'the forest' in his first draft. '[T]he "forest or the sea" are not', she writes, 'imaginatively equal alternatives in this context [i.e. the context of the "collocation of eastern and western mysticism"]. The forest is to eastern asceticism what the desert is to western; but Eliot's sea-image is personal, with no historic or cultural associations.'[41] If, however, one thinks back for a moment to the use of the sea-image in Section One of 'East Coker', and to its affinity there with the use of the same image in the *Brihad-Aranyaka Upanishad*, Chapter Four, the meaning and thrust of Eliot's cryptic phrase, 'Aranyaka, the forest or the sea' is, I think, at once made clear.

The phrase, 'In my beginning', is used by Eliot a number of times in 'East Coker', Section One. And likewise, in the *Brihad-Aranyaka Upanishad*, almost the same phrase is found repeated over and over again. In both cases, I believe, the intention is the same: namely, to emphasise the reality of the eternal and unchanging state of Being in which the true or higher Self abides.[42] It is, therefore, one might say, the actual voice of that true or higher Self which, throughout 'East Coker' Section One, addresses itself to 'the temporal aspect of the soul' or to the empirical self.[43] Most commentators I have read so far on *Four Quartets* interpret the phrase 'In my beginning is my end' as being descriptive simply of mankind's imprisonment in the fixed cycles of generation and decay. But the true meaning of the phrase has to do rather, I believe, with that state of being which is permanent and unchanging, and with the higher Self's ultimate independence, therefore, of the temporal realm.

> *In my beginning is my end.* In succession
> Houses rise and fall, crumble, are extended,
> Are removed, destroyed, restored, or in their place
> Is an open field, or a factory, or a by-pass.
> .   .   .   .
> *In my beginning is my end.* Now the light falls
> Across the open field, leaving the deep lane

Shuttered with branches, dark in the afternoon,
Where you lean against a bank while a van passes,
And the deep lane insists on the direction
Into the village, in the electric heat
Hypnotised.

(Emphasis added.)

The phrase 'In my beginning' is, as it happens, the note chosen
by Eliot on which to end the first movement. But it is also, as
James Johnson Sweeney has observed, the theme which domi-
nates the entire work. 'Like a musical phrase it is woven back and
forth through the entire texture of the composition, now stated in
one key of meaning, now in another.'[44] Set alongside it there are
numerous other thoughts and impressions of life and death and
generation. These seem to come and go like lesser motifs or like
lesser themes. But the single phrase 'In my beginning' remains
throughout the fundamental note that underlies, and blends
together, all the other lesser notes and meanings. Thus one can
say that in this opening movement of 'East Coker', as perhaps
nowhere else in Four Quartets, the surface music of the poetry and
the profound depth of the philosophy, or the mysticism, have
indeed become one thing.

So striking and impressive is the poet's use of musical counter-
point and 'blending' that the overall composition might, I believe,
even bear comparison with certain forms of traditional Indian
music. This idea may at first seem somewhat fanciful. But it is
not, I think, unusual in Indian literature to come upon statements
such as the following from the Collected Works of the modern
Hindu mystic and saint Ramana Maharshi: 'The monotone persisting through a Hindu piece of music, like the thread on which
beads are strung, represents the Self persisting through all the
forms of being.'[45]

C.   'THE DRY SALVAGES'

Because in the first two Quartets there are no explicit quotations
from Brahmin or Buddhist sources, the task we have undertaken
so far of trying to speak about possible Eastern antecedents for
Eliot's poem has necessarily been limited to the realms of con-

structive hypothesis and imaginative guesswork. But, in Section Three of Eliot's third *Quartet*, with the sentence beginning 'I sometimes wonder if that is what Krishna meant', we come upon a passage which alludes directly and explicitly to one section of the Indian epic, *The Mahabharata*, namely the *Bhagavad-Gita*. Helen Gardner in her first book on Eliot, which was published in 1949, expressed some surprise at Eliot's decision to include the *Gita* passage:

> Though it is perfectly in consonance with the poem's theme of annunciation to use these great scriptures which bear witness to man's recognition of the divine, it might be objected that to introduce Krishna at this point is an error and destroys the imaginative harmony of the poem, since it is precisely in their view of history and the time process that Christianity and Hinduism are most opposed.[46]

More recently, however, in her book *The Composition of Four Quartets*, Gardner would seem to have overcome her initial doubts and hesitations. She now realises that whereas Eliot quotes Krishna's teaching on the subject of disinterested action and the doctrine of re-incarnation, he completes this teaching in his own way and thereby radically alters the original meaning.

> Krishna declares 'Whatever state (or being) one dwells upon in the end, at the time of leaving that body, that alone he attains because of his constant thought on that state of being'. Krishna means that the mind of a man as it is at the time of death is fructified in the next life of that man, i.e. when he is reborn. But Eliot translates the idea into his own [Christian] terms. The 'fructification' here is in the lives of others, and the one 'action' that can fructify in their lives is the disinterestedness with which man acts not the actions themselves.[47]

Of all the Eastern texts Eliot read, the *Bhagavad-Gita* in particular seems to have made a deep impression on him. He referred to it once as 'the next greatest philosophical poem to the *Divine Comedy* within my experience'.[48] But Eliot's recourse to the wisdom of the *Gita* represents far more, I am persuaded, than a mere polite or scholarly acknowledgement of one of his own life-long intellectual interests. It is, instead, related to an urgent need within Eliot himself, and to a need which he now felt, perhaps, more acutely than he had ever done before. For at this particular stage in his life Eliot was coming gradually to realise, and with a new sense of horror and of dread, that the past is alive in every moment, and that there is simply no way of escaping its burden. No matter how hard one's effort at asceticism, or how high and exalted one's *isolated* experience of mystical illumination, in the end, inevitably and horribly, 'the agony abides'. One's only hope, therefore, it would appear, of attaining to a true liberation from the past, is, the poet now realises, the acceptance of a new path of enlightenment based on the direct and saving intervention of the Incarnate Word. But this new awareness of man's need for divine grace, although it obviously prompted Eliot to make more explicit than before his allusions to Christian dogma and to Christian belief, in no way encouraged him to turn his back on the wisdom of the East. On the contrary, his dependence for instruction and enlightenment on both Hindu and Buddhist sources, is, if anything, more striking in the later *Quartets* than it is in 'Burnt Norton'.

The main reason for this remarkable dependence by the Christian poet on the non-Christian East, is, I think, related to Eliot's new and ever-deepening awareness of the permanence of agony. A truly profound awareness of human agony, and of suffering in general, also characterises the wisdom of both the Hindu and the Buddhist sages. For them the only true startling point of meditation, and the first step, therefore, towards authentic enlightenment – enlightenment for the Hindu sage being almost synonymous with 'the yoga of action', and for the Buddhist sage with 'right action'[49] – consists *not* in the rejection of the past, or in any kind of 'mystical' escape from the past, but rather in the compassionate wisdom of an 'even mind', and in the calm and complete acceptance of all the burden of time past as it leans now into the present.

Within the closing meditation of 'The Dry Salvages' we can see realised finally, as perhaps nowhere else in the religious poetry of the West, the living integration of Eastern philosophy and wisdom with one man's authentic Christian experience and Christian belief. Eliot begins, first of all, by speaking of the mystery of Incarnation; and without any hesitation he declares it to be the saving 'point of intersection' for time past and time future.

> Here the impossible union
> Of spheres of existence is actual,
> Here the past and future
> Are conquered, and reconciled,
> Where action were otherwise movement
> Of that which is only moved
> And has in it no source of movement –
> Driven by dæmonic, chthonic
> Powers.

The statement is remarkable. But in spite of its astonishing claim, and its unique authority, it still remains to be completed by the poet:

> And right action is freedom
> From past and future also.

First of all, then, we hear the public expression of Eliot's Christian belief in Incarnation: a statement both lucid and unambiguous. But then, and almost in the same breath, as it were, we hear pronounced a second statement by Eliot concerning 'freedom'; and this time it expresses in code, or in shorthand, Eliot's own private debt of gratitude to the Eastern tradition.[50]

D. 'LITTLE GIDDING'

The influence of Eastern poetry on poets living and working in the West, is for the most part through translations. We have impressive evidence of this fact in the composition of *The Waste Land*. Having placed beside a text from the Buddha's *Fire Sermon* a text from *The Confessions* of St Augustine, Eliot remarked in a footnote: 'The collocation of these two representatives of eastern and western asceticism, as the culmination of this part of the poem, is not an accident.'[51] And *a propos* of his borrowing from the *Fire Sermon* he remarkd further:

> The complete text of the Buddha's Fire Sermon (which corres-ponds in importance to the Sermon on the Mount) from which these words are taken, will be found translated in the late

Henry Clarke Warren's *Buddhism in Translation* [*sic*] (Harvard Oriental Series). Mr. Warren was one of the great pioneers of Buddhist studies in the Occident.[52]

Years later, in the composition of *The Cocktail Party*, Eliot dipped into Warren's *Buddhism in Translations* for the famous admonition of the Buddha: 'Work out your salvation with diligence.' The phrase is quoted no less than three times in Act Two of *The Cocktail Party*. First, by Sir Henry Harcourt-Reilly to Edward and Lavinia: 'Go in peace. And work out your salvation with diligence.'[53] Then, by Reilly to Celia on the occasion of her departure for the sanatorium which in the end will lead her on to the plague-stricken mission of Kinkanja: 'Go in peace, my daughter. / Work out your salvation with diligence.'[54] And finally, by Reilly again to Julia on the subject of Celia's fate:

> And when I say to one like her
> 'Work out your salvation with diligence', I do not understand
> What I myself am saying.[55]

In 'T. S. Eliot and Buddhism', Harold E. McCarthy traces the statement 'Work out your salvation with diligence' to a line from the *Mahāparinibbāna-sutta* of the *Dīgha-nikāya*. The short axiom was spoken apparently by the Buddha (the Tathāgata) when on the point of death.

> Then The Blessed One addressed the priests –
> 'And now, O priests, I take my leave of you; all the
> constituents of being are transitory; work out your
> salvation with diligence.' And this was the last
> word of the Tathagāta.[56]

In the central section of 'Little Gidding' there is a further echo of Warren's *Buddhism in Translations*. In the *Anguttura-Nikaya*, a text also translated by Warren, and one with which Eliot was familiar from his student days,[57] we read,

> There are three conditions, O priests, under which deeds
> are produced.[58]

The three conditions mentioned are covetousness, hatred and infatuation. Later in another text which begins with the same opening phrase, this particular trio is replaced. The conditions mentioned are freedom from covetousness, freedom from hatred, and freedom from infatuation. The opening passage of 'Little Gidding', Section Three, is likewise largely concerned with the subject of detachment. It begins:

> There are three conditions which often look alike
> Yet differ completely, flourish in the same hedgerow:
> Attachment to self and to things and to persons, detachment
> From self and from things and from persons; and,
> growing between them, indifference . . .

This central section of 'Little Gidding', with its thoughtful and clear-headed reflections about detachment from one's country and from one's immediate kin is, to a considerable degree, prepared for by the passage which precedes it. For in the All-Clear passage the ghost of 'some dead master' invites Eliot to enter by his own choice and, as it were, 'like a dancer' into the flame of purification. The link between the two passages is thus seen to be fairly straightforward. In an earlier draft of the ghost's speech, however, this link was obviously intended by Eliot to be far more significant and more profound. Instead of the three 'gifts reserved for age' the ghost had in fact originally delivered an instruction to the poet on how to become detached, through meditation and memory, from those who are most near, even in this life.

> So, as you circumscribe this dreary round,
> Shall your life pass from you, with all you hated
> And all you loved, the future and the past.
> United to another past, another future,
> (After many seas and after many lands)
> The dead and the unborn, who shall be nearer
> Than the voices and the faces that were most near.[59]

The idea is a peculiarly disturbing one. And it is, I would say, quite foreign to the average Western mentality. But it is an idea that is commonplace in the early Buddhist Scriptures. Take, for example, the following well-known text from Ashvaghosha's poem on 'Nanda the Fair'. In it the Buddha explains to Nanda 'how to deal with thoughts concerning family and homeland'. He proceeds first of all by asking 'Who is a stranger, who is a relation?':

> Delusion alone ties one person to another. For in the past the person who is now one of your own people happened to be a stranger to you; in the future the stranger of to-day will be one of your own people. Over a number of lives a person is no more firmly associated with his own people than birds who flock together at the close of day, some here, some there. Relatives are no more closely united than travellers who for a while meet at an inn, and then part again, losing sight of each other. . . . Men, indeed, make and break affections according to their interests. As an artist becomes enamoured of a woman he has himself painted, so the affection, which a person has for another with whom he feels at one, is entirely of his own making. As for him who in another life was bound to you by ties of kinship, and who was so dear to you then, what is he to you now or you to him?[60]

Given the evidence that is available at present, one cannot be certain that Eliot had this particular Buddhist text in mind when composing Sections Two and Three of 'Little Gidding'. All we do know for certain is that he was familiar with the early literature of Buddhism. 'I am not a Buddhist', he wrote in 1933, 'but some parts of the Early Buddhist Scriptures affect me as parts of the Old Testament do.'[61] There are, as it happens, a number of small indications in *The Cocktail Party* which seem to suggest that Eliot was familiar with 'Nanda the Fair'. In particular, certain passages spoken by the Unidentified Guest (Sir Henry Harcourt-Reilly) recall to mind the text by Ashvaghosha which I have quoted above. Reilly explains first that 'we die to each other daily'.[62] And thus, although in friendship and in marriage, we may like to imagine that we are living and meeting with someone 'most near' and most familiar to us, we are in fact, at every moment, face to face with an almost complete stranger.

> What we know of other people
> Is only our memory of the moments
> During which we knew them. And they have changed
>   since then.
> To pretend that they and we are the same

Is a useful and convenient social convention
Which must sometimes be broken. We must also remember
That at every meeting we are meeting a stranger.[63]

The poem of Ashvaghosha, 'Nanda the Fair', like so many other
late and early Buddhist texts, is concerned with the practice and
the art of meditation. One of the aims of this practice is, as we
have seen, the attainment of a state of detachment from one's
immediate kith and kin. And this state of 'indifference' is
achieved within the Buddhist tradition by what is called 'the
knowledge of death and rebirth' and 'the recollection of former
lives'. In the *Visuddhimagga* or *The Path of Purity*, an early Buddhist
text concerned with meditation, we read:

> He [the sage in meditation] recalls his manifold former lives –
> one birth, or two births, or up to 100,000 births or more, and
> many world cycles and aeons: 'There I was, that was my name,
> that was my family, that was my caste, such was my food, this
> was the happiness, this the suffering I experienced, this was
> the duration of my life-span. Deceased there I was reborn
> elsewhere, and there had this name, etc.' It is thus that he
> recalls his manifold previous lives, with all their modes, in all
> their details.[64]

Compare now this text from *The Path of Purity* with the instruction
concerning recollection delivered by the ghost to Eliot in the first
draft of 'Little Gidding'.

> Remember . . . the essential moments
>   That were the times of birth and death and change,
>   The agony and the solitary vigil,
> Remember also fear, loathing and hate,
>   The wild strawberries eaten in the garden,
>   The walls of Poitiers, and the Anjou wine,
> The fresh new season's rope, the smell of varnish
>   On the clean oar, the drying of the sails,
>   Such things as seem of least and most importance.[65]

In both Eliot's poem and in *The Path of Purity*, there is an
emphasis on 'the essential moments' of birth and death and also
an emphasis on those moments that seem much less important

'with all their modes' and 'in all their details'. To my knowledge Eliot never referred directly to the *Visuddhimagga* or *The Path of Purity* by Ashvaghosha. But we can, I think, be fairly certain that he was familiar with the poem. It was, in fact, one of the early Buddhist texts critically edited by Henry Clarke Warren and brought out after his death by Eliot's tutor at Harvard, C. R. Lanman.

Eliot did speak openly, however, and more than once, of a version of the life and teaching of Buddha entitled *The Light of Asia* by Sir Edwin Arnold. This work was composed in verse, and it may well have been one of the minor sources on which Eliot drew during the composition of 'Little Gidding'. In 1944 he wrote:

> I came across, as a boy, a poem for which I have preserved a warm affection: *The Light of Asia*, by Sir Edwin Arnold. It is a long epic poem on the life of Gautama Buddha: I must have had a latent sympathy for the subject matter, for I read it through with gusto, and more than once. I have never had the curiosity to find out anything about the author but to this day it seems to me a good poem, and when I meet anyone else who has read and liked it, I feel drawn to that person.[66]

Certain minor echoes from *The Light of Asia* have already been detected in Eliot's verse-drama, *Murder in the Cathedral*, and in *A Song for Simeon*. James S. Whitlark writes in a short contribution to *Notes and Queries*: 'It is interesting that although Eliot had access to Buddhist works both in translation and in the original (through his graduate studies at Harvard), he made use of Arnold's eccentric version of Buddhist ideas to enrich the thought of his markedly Christian verse, perhaps because *The Light of Asia* is itself a striking amalgam of Buddhism and Christianity.'[67]

On page 62 of *The Light of Asia*, Arnold describes how we, as men and women, are 'bound upon this wheel of change / Knowing the former and the after lives'. (The phrase 'bound upon the wheel' occurs in another place in Arnold's poem – page 139: 'If ye lay bound upon the wheel'. And it is interesting to note here that this same phrase can be found also in two places in the first draft of *The Waste Land*: 'London, your people is *bound upon the wheel*' (emphasis added).[68] At one point in Sir Edwin Arnold's epic poem the Buddha is asked how it is that he has been able to recognise the Sâkya girl at a first glance. He explains at once that he had in fact known her in a former life:

Thus was I he and she Yasôdhara,
And while the wheel of birth and death turns round
That which hath been must be between us two.[69]

And again, later:

Unto me
This was unknown, albeit it seemed half-known
For while the wheel of birth and death turns round
Past things and thoughts, and buried lives come back.[70]

When the ghost in 'Little Gidding', Section Two (the first draft)
invites Eliot to 'Remember . . . the essential moments / That were
the times of birth and death and change', he describes the process
in terms of moving around on a kind of circle or wheel:

So, as you circumscribe this dreary round,
Shall your life pass from you, with all you hated
And all you loved, the future and the past.[71]

In his final version of the All-Clear passage, Eliot dropped
altogether the ghost's instruction concerning the usefulness of
meditation for those who are still bound on the wheel or the cycle
of 'birth and death and change'. He replaced it instead with what
is arguably one of the most achieved passages of lyric poetry in
Four Quartets, namely the description of the 'gifts reserved for
age'. As a direct result of dropping out the first speech of the
ghost, however, the link Eliot had originally forged between
Sections Two and Three of 'Little Gidding' is much less impressive. For, in the first version, Section Three reads as nothing less
than a purposeful attempt on the part of Eliot to practise the
method of meditative remembrance in which he had been
instructed by the ghost.

This is the use of memory:
For liberation – not less of love but expanding
Of love beyond desire, and so liberation
From the future as well as the past.

The ghost's prophetic assurance to Eliot that, through the practice
of meditation and 'memory' his present life would begin, in some

sense, to pass away from him, with all he hated and all he loved, 'the future and the past', achieves its fulfilment in the vision of 'Little Gidding', Section Three:

> See, now they vanish,
> The faces and places, with the self which, as it could,
>   loved them,
> To become renewed, transfigured, in another pattern.

By the attainment of this state of detachment from immediate kith and kin, and from those 'who were most near', Eliot reaches out in imaginative and compassionate awareness – as the ghost had also foreseen – to the dead and to the unborn, to 'people not wholly commendable / Of no immediate kin or kindness'. Furthermore, the meditative process enacted here is, in every detail, the very same process recommended and described in the early and the late Buddhist Scriptures.

Eliot's use of a largely Buddhist method of meditation in 'Little Gidding' is surprising, especially in view of the comments he made on meditation in a paper published in 1937. In this paper he took the opportunity to criticise a posthumous essay on Buddhism, and a translation of *The Dhammapada*, by the American humanist Irving Babbitt. The main objection levelled against Babbitt's essay is the same objection levelled by Eliot against a *Peace Pamphlet* by Aldous Huxley in which, Eliot claims, we find Huxley 'advocating the practice of "meditation" (to which Babbitt also was devoted)'.[72] The neat line of division Babbitt draws between the meditative method of Buddhism – which, of course, he would happily recommend – and the underlying metaphysical and theological luggage which he thinks we can today easily discard, is a line of division Eliot finds very curious indeed. The doctrine of Reincarnation, for example, one of the underlying assumptions of every Buddhist experience, is a doctrine that cannot, Eliot argues, be so easily forgotten about: 'it is as essential to Buddhism as the future state of heaven and hell are to Christianity'.[73] Babbit's attempt to disengage the practice of meditation from its natural religious and theological context is, in Eliot's view, a rather dangerous and futile exercise. And, apparently, no less suspect is the argument put forward by Aldous Huxley and quoted here by Eliot that, 'Meditation is a psychological technique whose efficacy does not depend on previous theological belief.'[74] On the subject of Irving Babbitt's 'purified' Buddhism, Eliot has this to say:

> it is an artificial Buddhism – not only purified but *canned*: separated from all the traditional ways of behaving and feeling which went to make it a living religion in its own environments, which make it a religion possible for every level of intelligence and sensibility from the highest to the lowest. It therefore has something in common with the *psychological mysticism* that is a phenomenon of decadence rather than of growth. This is the mysticism which seeks contact with the sources of supernatural power, divorced from religion and theology; the mysticism which must always be suspect, and which sometimes springs up in cults whose aims are not far removed from those of magic.[75]

And on the subject of Aldous Huxley's theory of meditation, he writes:

> I am certainly not one to deny that 'meditation is a psychological technique whose efficacy does not depend on previous theological belief'. I only maintain that if it neither depends on previous theological belief nor leads towards it, then it is a technique that must be very suspect indeed. It may turn out to be merely an occult means of getting one's own way.[76]

The meditative process enacted in 'Little Gidding', although influenced in a number of different ways by Buddhism is not directed towards, nor ultimately dependent on, belief in orthodox Buddhist doctrine. Eliot has not fallen, I think, into the error which he himself so much abhorred of trying to wrench the psychological technique of meditation out of its natural religious and theological context. Instead, he has taken the underlying Buddhist doctrines – i.e. the doctrines of Karma and Reincarnation – and by a series of small and subtle transformations, changed them into something different, something nearer in fact to his own orthodox Christian vision.

The promise made by the ghost to Eliot in the first draft of 'Little Gidding' that 'the dead and the unborn . . . shall be nearer than those who were most near', might at first hearing seem to imply some kind of belief in the Buddhist theory of Reincarnation. However, in the lines which follow, the ghost refers immediately to the dimension of 'grace' (a dimension not normally included in the Buddhist system) and also to the fact that, in time, each man has only *one* life and *one* history.

> This is the final gift of earth accorded –
> One soil, one past, one future, in one place.
>   Nor shall the eternal thereby be remoter
>   But nearer; seek or seek not, it is here.
>   Now, the last love on earth. The rest is grace.[77]

The use of the word 'love' in this context should serve to remind us here again of Eliot's fundamental Christian attitude (It is surely significant that the short phrase quoted in 'Little Gidding' from the English medieval text *The Cloud of Unknowing*: 'With the drawing of this Love and the voice of this Calling', emphasises the dimension of grace and the aspect of love.) The radical, one might almost say ruthless, detachment from one's own kith and kin, recommended in some of the early Buddhist Scriptures, is not simply taken up and repeated by Eliot without qualification. For the Buddhist, such radical detachment is thought to be necessary in view of the fact that the individual has not *one* life but many lives to lead. And so, the ties of affection and friendship that bind him or her to one family and to one homeland, in this life, and to another in the next, are but mere illusions, and should possess therefore no binding force whatsoever. For Eliot, in contrast, the human individual has only 'one soil, one past, one future, in one place'. Although Eliot does believe that detachment 'from self and from things and from persons' is necessary, he does not recommend to us for a moment an attitude of indifference. On the contrary, the mystical liberation and the salvation to which he aspires demand, he tells us, 'not less of love but expanding / Of love beyond desire'. We have, therefore, unlike the Buddhist, no need to enter once again into the cycle of Samsara. The Timeless is near to us. Our last chance of love, on earth, is *now*.

Within the Buddhist tradition there are a number of texts which would seem to indicate that the Buddha will himself intervene 'at the end of time' to save people from the wheel of Samsara. But, in general, the emphasis in Buddhism is not on divine grace, but on the need for active personal effort if one is to achieve salvation.

On 13 March 1940 Eliot wrote: 'The Christian West . . . has held a doctrine of divine grace unknown to the Orient. . . . I believe, of course, that Christianity is right; but Christianity in its decayed forms could learn much from the East'.[78] In the first draft of 'Little Gidding' Eliot sought to incorporate this idea of 'grace' into the poem by adding to the end of the third section a short traditional prayer to Christ the Saviour:

> Soul of Christ, sanctify them,
> Body of Christ, let their bodies be good earth,
> Water from the side of Christ, wash them,
> Fire from the heart of Christ, incinerate them.[79]

These lines were subsequently deleted and in their place Eliot used two beautiful short quotations from *The Revelations of Divine Love* by the medieval English mystic Julian of Norwich:

> And all shall be well and
> All manner of thing shall be well
> By the purification of the motive
> In the ground of our beseeching.[80]

I have already quoted Eliot as saying that 'Christianity in its decayed forms could learn much from the East'. The statement is well worth pondering. For in spite of what I have said so far concerning his attitude to the Buddhist doctrine of Reincarnation, there is a sense in which Eliot is prepared, like the Buddha, to speak of 'a number of lives' for the individual person, since as he says in the third *Quartet* 'the time of death is every moment'; and thus every day and even every moment of every day is itself a kind of death and a kind of rebirth, 'an end and a beginning'.

So far in this chapter we have succeeded in tracking down a small number of possible Eastern antecedents behind Eliot's poetry. But we have also, I think, been made gradually aware, in the process, that the distinctly Christian dimension of Eliot's spirituality is far more apparent in the last three *Quartets* than it was in 'Burnt Norton'. A new emphasis is given to the reality and necessity of the Incarnation. And we find references being made to Christ 'The wounded surgeon', to the Holy Spirit and to the Blessed Virgin. Also, as one might expect, this new awareness of supernatural grace, the sense, that is, of the importance of the divine intervention in human history, has an immediate bearing on Eliot's understanding of mysticism. For the attainment of union with God, or with the Divine, is now no longer thought to be the mere result of one's own personal effort at asceticism and contemplation. It is, instead, acknowledged at last to be dependent, even from the beginning, on Divine grace. But this does not mean, of course, that as the work progresses Eliot no longer looks to the East for inspiration and instruction. On the contrary, the evidence I have pieced together in this chapter indicates, beyond any doubt, that Eliot's use of Hindu and Buddhist sources was at least as extensive towards the end of the work as it was at the beginning. And, what is more, in the last two *Quartets*, Eliot takes greater care than ever before to discriminate in his use of Eastern sources, and wherever necessary to translate, with a painstaking exactitude, the Hindu and the Buddhist philosophy and experience into his own original Christian vision.

As a Christian, Eliot never allowed himself to believe for an instant that Truth was something confined to his own religious tradition. 'No one', he wrote in 1941, 'should assert that wisdom is to be acquired only from the study of Christian authors'. But then, at once, he went on to make the following cautious qualification: 'wisdom is one thing without Christian wisdom, and another thing with it; and there is a sense in which wisdom that is not Christian turns to folly. Furthermore, wisdom is no substitute for faith.'[81]

9
Mysticism and Magic

When the familiar scene is suddenly strange
Or the well known is what we have yet to learn,
And two worlds meet, and intersect, and change . . .

By whom, and by what means, was this designed?
(T. S. Eliot, 'To Walter de la Mare', 1948)

On 19 January 1935, shortly before Eliot began work on 'Burnt Norton', he made public something of his own attitude to magic by quoting with approval Fr Herbert Thurston's statement that 'for the mass of mankind spiritualistic practices are dangerous and undesirable'.[1] Six years later in his third *Quartet*, 'The Dry Salvages', Eliot again repeated this judgment and gave it the stamp of his own moral and poetic authority.

To communicate with Mars, converse with spirits,
To report the behaviour of the sea monster,
Describe the horoscope, haruspicate or scry,
Observe disease in signatures, evoke
Biography from the wrinkles of the palm
And tragedy from fingers; release omens
By sortilege, or tea leaves, riddle the inevitable
With playing cards, fiddle with pentagrams
Or barbituric acids, or dissect
The recurrent image, into pre-conscious terrors —
To explore the womb, or tomb, or dreams; all these are usual
Pastimes and drugs, and features of the press:
And always will be, . . .

The list seems exhaustive and Eliot's opposition to all forms of magic seems clear. But is it clear? Is there not another sort of magic not listed here of which Eliot is in fact a notable exponent? I am thinking in particular of that element in poetry which Eliot calls 'the magic of verse',[2] an element which is described in one of his shorter poems as 'The whispered incantation which allows / Free passage to the phantoms of the mind'.[3] The fact of meeting in 'Burnt Norton' and in 'East Coker' with such 'phantoms' and again in 'Little Gidding' with 'the ghost of some dead master' has persuaded a number of commentators that in spite of what Eliot may wish to assert to the contrary he is in fact 'writing from direct spiritualistic acceptance'.[4] This perception of Eliot as a devout spiritualist is scarcely credible. But what sort of judgment, if any, can we make about the poem itself and its composition? Does its magic have its source merely in Eliot's feeling for the incantatory element in poetry, or is it not perhaps related in some way to the language and literature of the occult tradition?

Before we turn our attention to this question let us look first at some of the reasons behind Eliot's concentrated attack on Spiritualism in 'The Dry Salvages'. It is obvious, first of all, that the poet's most immediate and primary concern, as he comes to the end of his third *Quartet*, is to make a statement about mysticism which will be both accurate and illuminating. But in order to do this properly he finds it necessary to clear the ground, as it were, by attacking head-on those idols and fetishes of magic which more, perhaps, than any other phenomena in the contemporary world, usurp the place of true mysticism. 'Magic wants to get', wrote Evelyn Underhill, 'mysticism wants to give.'[5] This is the fundamental difference between them. 'In magic the will unites with the intellect in an impassioned desire for supersensible knowledge. This is the intellectual, aggressive, and scientific temperament trying to extend its field of consciousness, until it includes the supersensual world.'[6] In contrast, the mystical temperament desires 'to surrender itself to Ultimate Reality; for no personal gain, to satisfy no transcendental curiosity, to obtain no other-worldly joys, but purely from an instinct of love'.[7] What Eliot is seeking in *Four Quartets* (and the phrase is his own) is 'a mysticism not of curiosity, or of the lust for power, but of Love'.[8]

> . . . something given
> And taken, in a lifetime's death in love,
> Ardour and selflessness and self-surrender.

So mysticism is one way, and magic is another, of making contact with the unseen. They are, in a sense, almost opposites. But the frontiers between these two ways or two methods are not always distinct. Here, in 'The Dry Salvages', Eliot has obviously drawn as sharp a line as possible between them. But elsewhere in *Four Quartets* there are a number of interesting points of contact and similarity, and it is to these we should now turn our attention.

A.   'AS ABOVE, SO BELOW': MEDITATION AND THE OCCULT

Probably no single section of *Four Quartets* invites more immediate comparison with occult theory and practice than the haunting 'axle-tree meditation' which comes almost at the beginning of 'Burnt Norton':

> Garlic and sapphires in the mud
> Clot the bedded axle-tree.
> The trilling wire in the blood
> Sings below inveterate scars
> Appeasing long forgotten wars.
> The dance along the artery
> The circulation of the lymph
> Are figured in the drift of stars
> Ascend to summer in the tree
> We move above the moving tree
> In light upon the figured leaf
> And hear upon the sodden floor
> Below, the boarhound and the boar
> Pursue their pattern as before
> But reconciled among the stars.

If this short lyric can be said to have a purpose – over and above its task of simply being resonant and beautiful – that purpose has in part been obscured by those critics who insist on reading the work as a mere *Symboliste* fantasy. The images of mud and garlic, of wars and sapphires, of axle-tree and stars, etc., might seem to have no other bond between them than that which the poet has himself miraculously devised. But in fact Eliot's particular combination of images, the linking together, for example, of herbs and precious stones and the suggestion of a mysterious correspondence between what is happening here on earth 'in the mud' and what is happening 'among the stars', repeats a pattern of meditation and a form of vision which has for generations been familiar to practitioners of the occult. '"As above, so below" has ever been the maxim of the occultist.' This pronouncement was made by Dion Fortune in her book *Sane Occultism*.[9] And she noted further that by 'applying the maxim, "As above, so below", we shall find that a thing which is true on any place of the cosmos is true through the whole of its correspondences'.[10] What this means in practice is that even natural substances such as herbs, plants and precious stones have stars or planets corresponding to them in the heavens. Indeed every animate and inanimate object in the natural world possesses what is called a sympathetic magic and draws down to itself from its parent star or planet a continual effluvia of magical influences.

> It is further maintained [we read in *The Encyclopedia of the Occult*] that occult vision permits someone specially trained in such matters to 'see' from the form of a natural object or entity, what this influence (or series of influences) is. The influence, stamped on the natural plane in a form which can be read by someone proficient in the occult script, is called the signature. A knowledge of what the signature of a natural thing is may be regarded as the first step in almost any alchemical, astrological or magico-therapeutic practice.[11]

Of all the phrases which occur in Eliot's long list of spiritualistic practices in Section Five of 'The Dry Salvages' there is only one phrase, namely 'observe disease in signatures', which in order to be fully understood seems to require an explanation from the author. Various interpretations of the phrase have, of course, been put forward by readers and critics over the years. But all, I think, have been quite wide of the mark. C. A. Bodelsen, for example, made the following rather interesting but erroneous suggestion in his book *T. S. Eliot's Four Quartets*: 'Eliot may have in mind the attempts to draw conclusions about Shakespeare's last illness from the signatures on his will.'[12] When Bodelsen's book was published Eliot contacted the author, and in his letter he offered the following comment:

> I was not thinking of Shakespeare's signature or that of anyone else, but was using the word in a much more obscure and

possibly not permissible sense. The definition is found in the large Oxford Dictionary as no. 4 of the meanings of signature, and I would quote this example which is given there. 1697 'Whether men, as they say of plants, have signatures to discover their nature by, is hard to determine'. Another example from 1748, 'There are some who think herbs the fittest for curing those parts of a man's body, to which they bear some sort of resemblance, commonly called a signature.'[13]

At the centre of Eliot's 'axle-tree meditation' is the image or symbol of the tree itself. It has on occasion been suggested that this image may be 'a concealed symbol of Incarnation and that "bedded" and "tree" unite manger and cross.'[14] This interpretation may not be incorrect. But Eliot's use of the meditation-symbol invites, I think, more immediate comparison with the diagram of the Tree of Life which is to be found in the Jewish *Cabala*, and which in the West (in a revised and expanded form) is well known to every practitioner of the occult. 'The aspirant', we read in *The Mystical Qabalah*, 'who uses the Tree as his meditation-symbol, establishes point by point the union between his soul and the world-soul.'[15] What is more, the centre of equilibrium of the whole tree represents a particular phase of meditation. 'It is this Sphere on the Tree', writes Dion Fortune, 'that is called the Christ-centre, and it is here that the Christian religion has its focussing-point.'[16] Two images are considered central to this occult meditation. They are 'the new-born Child in the manger at Bethlehem' and 'the Sacrificed God'.[17] 'By such meditation', Fortune tells us, 'it is possible to equilibrate the warring elements in one's own nature and bring them into harmonious balance.'[18]

The 'warring elements' in Eliot's meditation are represented by 'Garlic and sapphires.' According to occult theory the star which corresponds to the sapphire stone is one of the fifteen fixed stars and it is called 'Alhaiot'.[19] I had at first attached no particular significance to this fact until I was informed that Eliot's New England family claimed descent from one of the conquerors of Hastings, a gentleman named William de Aliot.[20] The marked similarity between the two names – Alhaiot and de Aliot – may of course be no more than a mere coincidence; but if the connection is a deliberate one, then what are we to make of this cryptogram of a meaning 'only visible to the initiate'? Why should Eliot wish to incorporate into his poem such a pecularily private and personal allusion or signature? One possible explanation might be a desire on the part of Eliot to imitate Dante's proud and uniquely personal allusion to himself as a poet in the twenty-second Canto of the *Paradiso*. There, caught up in a moment of ecstasy, the Italian poet finds himself being drawn upwards into the constellation of the Twins, the sphere, as it happens, of his own fixed star:

> O gloriose stelle, o lume pregno
> di gran virtu, dal quale io ricònosco
> tutto, qual che sia, il mio ingegno
>   .   .   .   .   .   .
>
>   quando mi fu grazia largita
> d'entrar nell'alta rota che vi gira,
> la vostra region mi fu sortita.

[O glorious stars. O light pregnant with mighty power from which I acknowledge all my genius whatever it may be. . . . when grace was granted me to enter into the high wheel that bears you round, your region was assigned to me.][21]

If the central image of the Jewish *Cabala* has played some part in Eliot's meditation it is surprising since the few references he makes to the *Cabala* in his prose are in no way complimentary. Speaking on one occasion, for example, of certain sixteenth-century authors whose 'metaphysical systems are often a mere gallimaufry of Plato, Aristotle, Plotinus and the medieval mystics and occultists',[22] Eliot concludes: '[in the sixteenth century] there was too much and too heterogeneous reading available: neoplatonic universes which combined only too well with abracadabric superstitions; cabbalistic studies which were only fomented by genuinely scientific yearnings'.[23] Already, by an unusual coincidence, we have examined in the earlier chapters of this book the influence on *Four Quartets* of Aristotle and the medieval mystics. But the extent to which Eliot allowed his work to be influenced by the occult tradition still remains to be explored.

B.   THE GHOST OF W. B. YEATS

The strange spectre which confronts Eliot in 'Little Gidding' (the ghost of 'some dead master') is, we are informed by the poet, 'both one and many'. It is a 'compound ghost'. And among the many minor and major poets whose presences are evoked by this one apparition, by far the most important for Eliot is not, as we might perhaps have expected, Dante Alighieri but the Irish poet W. B. Yeats.[24] That Yeats – indeed the ghost of Yeats – should be allowed to dominate the scene is unusual from at least one point of view. The problem is that for many years prior to the composition of *Four Quartets* Eliot had expressed not once but many times his disapproval of and even his disdain for Yeats's interests in the occult. 'Ghosts, mediums, leprechauns, sprites', he noted sardonically in 1919, 'are only a few of the elements in Mr Yeats's population.'[25] And later in the same review he observed: 'When an Englishman explores the mysteries of the Cabala, one knows one's opinion of him, but Mr Yeats on any subject is a cause of bewilderment and distress.'[26] Part of the bewilderment was caused by Eliot's awareness that no matter how strenuously he might object on occasion to the spiritualistic content of Yeats' prose he was, nevertheless, often impressed by the *style* of the older poet. 'It is a style of Pater, with a trick of the eye and hanging of the nether lip that come from across the Irish Channel, all the more seductive.'[27] Of Yeats's prose in general Eliot had this to say in a review which appeared in the summer of 1918: 'One is never weary of the voice, though the accents are strange; and as there is no one else living whom one would endure on the subject of gnomes, hobgoblins, and astral bodies we infer some very potent personal charm.'[28]

In a number of Eliot's early poems, in *Gerontion* for example and in *A Cooking Egg*, there are brief allusions made to contemporary occult practice, all of them satirical. And on at least one occasion the immediate object of Eliot's satire is Yeats's fellow initiate, the founder of the Theosophical Society, Madam Helena Petrovna Blavatsky. Yeats himself, in a radio broadcast he gave in 1936, commenting on modern poetry in general and on Eliot's poetry in particular, made the following declaration: 'We older writers disliked this new poetry, but were forced to admit its satiric intensity.'[29] Probably there is no more effective piece of satire in all of Eliot's early work than the short paragraph in *The Waste Land* which introduced Madame Sosostris, the 'famous clairvoyante'. But the cutting edge of Eliot's wit appears all the sharper when we realise that here also, though from well behind the scenes, Eliot may again be attempting to poke fun at 'Mr Yeats' and at the portentious seriousness of his interest in ghosts and mediums. Several years earlier Yeats had attended a unique *séance* in London with a close acquaintance, and he wrote later about his experience in an essay entitled 'Magic'.[30] To read today Yeats's description of that astonishing evening and, alongside it, to read the Madame Sosostris section of *The Waste Land* is instructive in a number of ways, and not least because part of the speech by Eliot's 'famous clairvoyante' contains what appears to be a deliberately mocking echo of Yeats's host and medium. In Yeats's account the *séance* he attended took place 'in a long room that had a raised place on the floor at one end, a kind of dais, but was furnished meagrely and cheaply'.[31]

> I sat with my acquaintance in the middle of the room, and the evoker of spirits on the dais, and his wife between us and him. . . . I remember seeing a number of white figures . . . and then, of a sudden, the image of my acquaintance in the midst of them. . . . It was my acquaintance, the seeress said, as he had been in a past life. . . . My acquaintance saw nothing; I think he was forbidden to see, it being his own life.[32]

When we find in *The Waste Land* the phrase 'forbidden to see' repeated by Madame Sosostris in an almost identical context it seems more than likely that what we are hearing is a deliberately satirical echo by Eliot of his older contemporary:

> . . . and this card,
> Which is blank, is something he carries on his back,
> Which I am *forbidden to see.*
>
> (Emphasis added.)

On the question of religion and the occult in general Eliot was never to be reconciled to Yeats's 'wanderings among Oriental philosophies and dubious mysticisms, journeys unsafe for any but the Christian'.[33] But, interesting to note, it was not only Yeats's spiritualistic practices to which Eliot objected. He also expressed grave reservations about Yeats's theory and practice of poetry. The older poet, in Eliot's view, tended to confuse in his mind poetry with mysticism and to look, therefore, to poetry for what in the end only a religion or an authentic mysticism can provide.

No one can read Mr Yeats's *Autobiographies* and his earlier poetry without feeling that the author was trying to get as a poet something like the exaltation to be obtained, I believe, from hashish or nitrous oxide. He was very much fascinated by self-induced trance states, calculated symbolism, mediums, theosophy, crystal-glazing, folklore and hobgoblins. . . . Often the verse has an hypnotic charm: but you cannot take heaven by magic.'[34]

Much the same criticism of Yeats's theory and practice is repeated by Eliot in *After Strange Gods: A Primer of Modern Heresy*. But conscious though Eliot is of Yeats's 'heresy' his criticism on this occasion is tempered by an awareness that 'there is a good deal of truth in this theory' and that Yeats, in fact, is partly right.[35] In order to illustrate Yeats's 'heretical' theory of poetry, which has, nevertheless, some truth in it, Eliot extracts from 'The Symbolism of Poetry' a short passage of exquisite Yeatsian prose concerning poetry and the practice of meditation, or what he calls the poet's 'deliberate evocation of trance'.[36]

The purpose of rhythm . . . is to prolong the moment of contemplation, the moment when we are both asleep and awake, which is the one moment of creation, by hushing us with an alluring monotony, while it holds us waking by its variety, to keep us in that state of perhaps real trance, in which the mind liberated from the pressure of the will is unfolded in symbols.[37]

Clearly what worried Eliot about this kind of 'spiritual' liberation was that very often, as he says, 'the revelations given in these dissociated states are insufficiently connected with normal experience'.[38] Nevertheless Eliot seems to have realised that, given a more realistic grasp of everyday reality and a truer perception of spiritual values, one could in fact make most valuable use of Yeats's thought and theory concerning meditation.

Yeats's influence on *Four Quartets* is, I think, discernible not so much in certain verbal echoes and allusions but rather in Eliot's occasional use of hypnotic rhythms to hold and 'to prolong the moment of contemplation, the moment when we are both asleep and awake'.

> In that open field
> If you do not come too close, if you do not come too close,
> On a summer midnight, you can hear the music
> Of the weak pipe and the little drum
> And see them dancing around the bonfire . . .

This passage from 'East Coker' and the stanza or paragraph which precedes it, contain 'those wavering, meditative, organic rhythms' which, according to Yeats's theory, are needed to help first the poet himself and then his readers to 'fall into the hypnotic trance'.[39] Yeats's lesson was obviously not lost on Eliot. And it is surely significant that the word 'hypnotised' itself occurs in the passage at present under consideration. For there is, to my knowledge, in all of modern and contemporary European poetry, no more impressive use by a poet of the language of hypnotism. In spite of Yeats's authoritative presence in 'Little Gidding' it is a surprising fact that relatively little has been written so far about his influence on *Four Quartets*. By and large the tendency has been to concentrate on the work of Yeats's mature years. But is it not possible that the work of the younger Yeats, his theory of poetry and the poetry itself, also exercised some influence on *Four Quartets*? The question has in fact been answered by Eliot himself. In a letter written to Montgomery Belgion in July 1940 he openly acknowledged the influence on his second *Quartet*, 'East Coker', of the *early* Yeats.[40]

The passage in 'East Coker' which, in its imagery and cadence, most closely resembles the poetry of Yeats is the short lyric which begins: 'What is the late November doing / With the disturbance of the spring'. In this lyric, as in the short axle-tree meditation of 'Burnt Norton', the underlying theme is again that of the correspondence between what is happening here on earth and what is happening in the heavens.

> Thunder rolled by the rolling stars
> Simulates triumphal cars
> Deployed in constellated wars
> Scorpion fights against the Sun
> Until the Sun and Moon go down
> Comets weep and Leonids fly . . .

As soon as the lyric has been read through, it is dismissed out of hand by its author as 'A periphrastic study in a worn-out poetical fashion'. But one of its themes, namely that of 'the conflict of seasons', is surely worthy of much closer attention.

> What is the late November doing
> With the disturbance of the spring
> And creatures of the summer heat,
> And snowdrops writhing under feet . . .

The theme is one to which Eliot will return later in 'Little Gidding' in his Midwinter spring meditation. But the theme is not, of course, entirely original. Some years earlier, W. B. Yeats, in his famous esoteric work *A Vision*, had expressed the view that this conflict or disturbance among the seasons, is a phenomenon which occurs as soon as someone begins to draw near to another world. He wrote in his book: 'I thought I had discovered this antithesis of the seasons, when some countryman told me that he heard the lambs of Faery bleating in November, and read in some heroic tale of supernatural flowers in midwinter.'[41]

Although Eliot may have remained unimpressed by Yeats's attempt as a poet to 'take heaven by magic' he did realise, as did Hugh Gordon Porteus, one of his reviewers in *The Criterion*, that '[Yeats's] magic is not *all* nonsense' and that 'anyone who dismisses it as a weakness is missing something valuable in his verse – that is to say, in poetry today'.[42] This particular review, which was printed in January 1934, also contains the following brief declaration: 'Yeats really is a magician. And he has definite contributions to make not only to our literature but to our craft of verse.'[43] The link between magician and poet of which Yeats speaks so often in his prose work, is also on occasion noted and underlined by Eliot. Even when he wants to talk about something like the process of poetic composition we find him, and more than once, looking around for metaphors and images in the realm of the occult. The most striking example is a passage Eliot included in the first draft of his essay 'The Function of Criticism' but later deleted before publication. It reads as follows: 'poetic originality does not consist in creation out of nothing . . . it is more like the alchemist's stone turning dross into gold, or sometimes turning one precious substance into another. What is worth remembering is the process.'[44] In another place Eliot speaks of the adolescent author 'writing under a kind of dæmonic possession by one poet'.[45] And in his essay 'The Three Voices of

Poetry' this image of possession recurs again. The poet, Eliot says, 'is haunted by a demon, a demon against which he feels powerless, because in its first manifestation it has no face, no name, nothing; and the words, the poem he makes, are a kind of form of exorcism of this demon'.[46]

The almost magical purpose which Eliot would seem to attribute here to poetry suggests a link between his own work as a poet and those 'early runes and chants, some of which had very practical magical purposes – to avert the evil eye, to cure some disease, or to propitiate some demon'.[47] Once when he was discussing the idea of the artist or poet as magician Eliot took the opportunity to cite with approval Professor Collingwood's definition of magical art or poetry as 'an art which . . . evokes of set purpose some emotions rather than others in order to discharge them into the affairs of practical life'.[48] The idea of the artist or poet as magician will not perhaps serve as a complete description of the poet at work in *Four Quartets*. But one thing is clear: Eliot is obviously concerned 'to evoke of set purpose some emotions rather than others'. He is concerned, that is to say, not only to make his readers 'more aware of what they feel already' but also to make them 'share consciously in new feelings which they had not experienced before'. [49] And in this conscious poetic endeavour Eliot, no less than Yeats, performs like an invisible hypnotist, and is 'really a magician'.

C. A MINOR SOURCE: MAURICE MAETERLINCK

Eliot refers occasionally to the work of Maurice Maeterlinck in his prose, but never with any great enthusiasm.[50] He was critical of the plays; and it is hardly surprising, therefore, that the few echoes from Maeterlinck which we find in his work are not taken from the plays, but from a short prose work entitled *The Treasure of the Humble*.[51] This book, according to Yeats, 'lacks the definiteness of the great mystics', but it shows us many things 'in the light of the great mystics, and a new light that was not theirs beating upon them'.[52]

Like Yeats, Maeterlinck was fascinated by certain preternatural manifestations, and by 'occult powers', all of which he thought could be 'easily verified'.[53] In his book he claimed to possess one of these powers – viz. the gift of premonition – and his curious reflections on the subject were, for some reason, taken up by Eliot fifty years later, and used by him in the portrayal of one of the leading characters in *The Cocktail Party*, Celia Coplestone. Her face – we are told – when she was first introduced to Sir Henry Harcourt-Reilly, 'showed the astonishment / Of the first five minutes after a violent death'.[54] Maeterlinck in *The Treasure of the Humble* also speaks of the 'presentiment' that chilled his blood when he met face to face with those 'for whom *a violent death* was lying in wait'.[55] He writes: 'I remember their faces well. . . . they seemed to be ever beseeching forgiveness for a fault they knew not of, but which was near at hand.'[56] Amazingly, Maeterlinck might almost be describing here, and with unusual accuracy, the spiritual dilemma of Celia Coplestone. 'Why do I feel guilty . . .?' she asks her mentor and friend, Sir Henry Harcourt-Reilly.[57]

> It's not the feeling of anything I've ever *done*,
> Which I might get away from, or of anything in me
> I could get rid of – but of emptiness, of failure
> Towards someone, or something, outside of myself;
> And I feel I must . . . *atone* – is that the word?[58]

Approximately nine years before *The Cocktail Party* was first performed, Eliot completed his second *Quartet*, 'East Coker'. The intensity of vision in this work has often been related – and justifiably so – to the orthodox mystical tradition. But another source for the poem – one less orthodox – now suggests itself: Maurice Maeterlinck's *The Treasure of the Humble*. (In parenthesis here, it is interesting to note that an essay on Maeterlinck, recommended by Eliot in a short review he wrote in July 1916 for *The New Statesman*, treats of the condemnation of Maeterlinck's works by The Holy Congregation of the Index. 'Once more Rome has spoken. . . . She has condemned the works of Maeterlinck, and she has condemned them one and all. The Belgian writer has thus joined the band of the excommunicate authors who are outside the pale of orthodox literature.'[59]) No less than Maeterlinck in *The Treasure of the Humble*, the poet of 'East Coker' is seeking to draw attention to the stark reality of the contemporary spiritual situation. Accordingly, with the assumed authority of a prophet, or of a visionary, he speaks, in his poem, of an imminent Apocalypse. Or, rather, we should say perhaps, he proclaims this new spiritual event as something that is happening now.

> O dark dark dark. They all go into the dark,
> The vacant interstellar spaces, the vacant into the vacant, . . .

Maurice Maeterlinck is likewise struck by the stark immediacy of this 'new' spiritual event. He writes: 'A mass of useless conventions, habits, pretences and intermediaries are being swept into the gulf; and it is by the invisible alone that, though we know it not, nearly all of us judge each other.'[60]

Suspended, as it were, within this terrifying void, we are today made conscious of 'things that are well-nigh unspeakable'; things that even the best and wisest of men in former times seem to have ignored.[61] 'Our ancestors have not spoken of these things, and we realise that the life in which we bestir ourselves is quite other than that which they have depicted. Have they deceived us, or did they not know?'[62] This challenge to 'the elders' is taken up and repeated by Eliot in Section Two of 'East Coker'.

> Had they deceived us
> Or deceived themselves, the quiet-voiced elders,
> Bequeathing us merely a receipt for deceit?
> The serenity only a deliberate hebetude,
> The wisdom only the knowledge of dead secrets
> Useless in the darkness into which they peered
> Or from which they turned their eyes.

Of those who must soon confront the mystery of death Maeterlinck writes in *The Treasure of the Humble*: 'If they could they would deceive us, so that they might the more readily deceive themselves.'[63] Elsewhere in his book, Maeterlinck, like Eliot in 'East Coker', refuses to accept, at its face value, the serene wisdom of 'the ancestors'. He is aware that, in the past, many great and terrible problems were often 'carelessly passed by' and not permitted to 'intrude themselves upon the serenity of the thinker.'[64]

In Eliot's opinion, one of the things 'the elders' are afraid of is actual union or communion with others: the 'fear of possession, / Of belonging to another, or to others, or to God'. Maeterlinck believes that this communion will, in fact, soon be realised. '[T]he souls of mankind', he says, 'seem to be drawing nearer to each other', and 'we seem to feel, more deeply than did our fathers before us, that we are not in the presence of ourselves alone.'[65] The reason why this union or communion with others has not yet been fully realised is explained in a brief sentence by the poet Novalis, whom Maeterlinck quotes towards the end of his essay: 'In truth, it is only *here and there* that the soul bestirs itself; when will it *move* as a whole, and when will humanity begin to feel with one conscience?'[66] The problem then, as Maeterlinck sees it, is the soul's dependence on certain isolated places and conditions, its attachment, in other words, to *here and there*. Eliot, it would seem, is in complete agreement with Maeterlinck on this point, and we find the short phrase of Novalis nicely echoed by Eliot in his own urgent injunction at the close of 'East Coker'.

> Old men ought to be explorers
> *Here and there does not matter*
> We must be still and still moving
> Into another intensity
> For a further union, a deeper communion . . .[67]
>
> (Emphasis added.)

D. P. D. OUSPENSKY AND CHARLES WILLIAMS

John Carswell in his book *Lives and Letters 1906–1957* has recorded that in the autumn of 1920 Eliot was one of a number of poets and writers 'occasionally attending the séances' hosted by Lady Rothermere and James Young and conducted by the philosopher and mystic P. D. Ouspensky.[68] The meetings Ouspensky conducted in London may or may not have been 'séances' in the ordinary meaning of that word but his doctrine was, it has been reported, often 'wrapped in a cocoon of cabalistic, numerological, gymnosophistical jargon about the fourth dimension and the true ratio of zero to infinity'.[69] Why Eliot should have wanted to attend such extraordinary meetings is not clear. Was there perhaps something in the occult philosophy of Ouspensky that attracted his attention? Or did he choose to go along to these 'séances' simply out of intellectual curiosity? Whatever the answer to this question might be, there is evidence to show that Eliot attended at least one other gathering of a similar nature. Approximately three years earlier, in March 1917, he wrote in a letter to his first cousin, Eleanor Hinkley: 'I was at a gathering ['about a fortnight ago'] of a curious zoo of people known as the Omega Club, and was sitting on a mat (as is the custom in such circles) discussing psychical research with William Butler Yeats (the only thing he ever talks about except Dublin gossip).'[70] If it is difficult for us to imagine T. S. Eliot sitting (cross-legged?) on a floor-mat beside the Irish poet, W. B. Yeats, it is surely no less difficult for us to understand how an occult doctrine such as that of P. D. Ouspensky could have held some interest for the young American.

Years later Eliot was prepared to be openly critical of the Ouspensky brand of occultism. Writing in 1937, for example, two years after the death of the editor and essayist A. R. Orage, who was one of Ouspensky's leading disciples in England, Eliot made the following observation: 'his greatest deception was to have been offered a magic when he was seeking a religion'.[71] But Eliot also admitted on another occasion: 'Perhaps my own attitude is suggestive of the reformed drunkard's abhorrence of intemperence; at any rate I deprecate Orage's mysticism as much as anyone does.'[72] The image of 'the reformed drunkard' is an unexpected one, since obviously it could be interpreted to mean that Eliot himself had been susceptible at some stage in his life to the occult mysticism of Ouspensky. But this suggestion, however unusual, is I think worthy of at least some consideration. Eliot's deliberate, public disavowal of allegiance to the Ouspensky camp may seem to us, at first, clear and unambiguous. But it does leave certain questions unanswered about his own earlier attitude to the occult philosopher. And also, unless I am much mistaken, it does not negate the possibility that Orage's and Ouspensky's 'heresy', like that of W. B. Yeats, may have contined for several years to attract and hold Eliot's attention, because of its incisive grasp of some part of the truth.

A major part of the fascination of Four Quartets is the 'naming' by Eliot of what years later in a 'Preface' to Thoughts for Meditation he would refer to as 'those emotions, and states of soul, which are to be found, so to speak, only beyond the limit of the visible spectrum of human feeling, and which can be experienced only in moments of illumination, or by the development of another organ or perception than that of everyday vision'.[73] The exploration or attainment of such rare states of being has always, of course, been considered central to the occult tradition. Here, for instance, is what the occult philosopher P. D. Ouspensky has to say on the subject:

> In theosophical literature, and in books on occultism, it is often asserted that on entering into the 'astral world', man begins to see new colors, colors which are not in the solar spectrum. In this symbolism of the new colors of the 'astral sphere' is conveyed the idea of those *new emotions* which man begins to feel along with the sensation of the expansion of consciousness.[74]

Chapter 20 of Ouspensky's work, *Tertium Organum*, is concerned directly with what the author calls 'moments of the sensation of infinity'. The philosopher's immediate preoccupation, like that of the author of 'Burnt Norton', is not so much with abstract ideas or dogma concerning the Infinite but rather with the sensation of the Infinite. 'Let us imagine for a moment', he writes, 'that a man begins to feel infinity in everything: every thought, every idea leads him to the realization of infinity. This will inevitably happen to a man approaching an understanding of a higher order of reality.'[75] Ouspensky then asks the question: 'But what will he feel under such circumstances?' Even if Eliot never actually read these lines by Ouspensky, the opening section of his first *Quartet* could almost have been written to answer the philosopher's question. But the answer Eliot provides is at one point in his poem so puzzling as to seem almost wilfully obscure. First, there is a sensation of light and accompanying it a vision of the rising lotos:

> And the pool was filled with water out of sunlight,
> And the lotos rose, quietly, quietly,
> The surface glittered out of heart of light, . . .

There follows then a sudden sensation of darkness which in turn leads to a shock of ecstasy at once terrifying and joyful:

> Then a cloud passed, and the pool was empty.
> Go, said the bird, for the leaves were full of children,
> Hidden excitedly, containing laughter.

> Go, go, go, said the bird: human kind
> Cannot bear very much reality.

The unusual conflict in these lines between the feeling of horror and the feeling of ecstatic joy has left many of Eliot's readers distinctly puzzled. But if we examine briefly the answer Ouspensky gives to his own question concerning 'the sensation of the infinite' much that is now obscure in Eliot's lyric will become clear.

> This sensation of *light* and of unlimited joy is experienced at the moment of the expansion of consciousness (the unfoldment of *the mystical lotus* of the Hindu yogi), at the moment of the sensation of infinity, and it yields also the sensation of darkness and of unlimited horror. What does this mean? How shall we reconcile the sensation of light with the sensation of darkness, the sensation of joy with that of horror? Can these exist simultaneously? Do they occur simultaneously? They do so occur, and must be exactly thus. Mystical literature gives us examples of it. The simultaneous sensations of light and darkness, joy and horror, symbolize as it were the strange duality and contradiction of human life. . . . Generally speaking the sensation of light, of life, of consciousness penetrating all, of happiness, gives a new world. But the same world to the unprepared mind will give the sensation of infinite darkness and horror.[76]

This text which Eliot had almost certainly read may or may not have been somewhere at the back of his mind during the composition of his poem. But, at the very least, the parallelism in thought and imagery between it and 'Burnt Norton' Section One is a striking proof of the similarity between Eliot's 'sensation of the infinite' and that of Ouspensky.

The capacity for attaining to certain unknown modes of feeling is precisely the quality or virtue of sensibility which Eliot greatly admired in his friend and fellow author Charles Williams. '[Williams] was almost alone in his generation', Eliot believed, 'for his peculiar understanding of mystical experience.'[77] He was not merely 'a writer *about* mysticism' but 'a mystical writer'.[78] Moreover, 'Williams had an extended spiritual sense: he was like a man who can notice shades of colour, or hear tones, beyond the ordinary range.'[79] Eliot was also aware that Williams employs in his work 'the apparatus of magic' and that 'There is much that he has invented or borrowed from the literature of the occult.'[80] Nevertheless, in so far as he can be considered a mystic, Williams, in Eliot's judgment, is 'first and always a Christian mystic.'[81] What is not so clear, however, is whether or not Eliot was aware that his friend and fellow Anglican had been for years an active member of The Hermetic Order of the Golden Dawn and that on at least one occasion he had been its Magister Templi. (W. B. Yeats and Evelyn Underhill had both belonged to the Order in an earlier phase of its existence.) Williams's particular branch of the Order, The Fellowship of the Rosy Cross, was 'devoted to a study of the principles of magic and the teachings of the Cabbala'.[82] In Williams's occult novel *The Greater Trumps* we find enacted one of the most important principles of magic: 'All things are held together by correspondence, image with image, movement with movement.'[83] And again: 'imagine that every-thing which exists takes part in the movement of a great dance . . . quick or slow, measurable or immeasurable, there is nothing at all anywhere but the dance'.[84] This passage bears an immediate and striking resemblance to one of the phrases in 'Burnt Norton': 'and there is only the dance'. When Eliot was questioned on the subject by Helen Gardner he freely admitted, as Gardner herself tells us, that 'the image of the dance around the "still point" was suggested by Williams's novel *The Greater Trumps*, where in a magical model of the universe the figures of the Tarot pack dance around the Fool at the still centre'.[85] This acknowledgment of a source for 'Burnt Norton' is, it would appear, almost unique. 'There is', Helen Gardner admits, 'very little material available for the study of the composition of *Burnt Norton*'.[86] In the light of this source it may seem that Eliot's immediate aim in 'Burnt Norton' can be identified with that of the occultist. 'C'est, incidemment, le but de toute magie', wrote John Hayward in the footnotes to the French edition of *Four Quartets*, 'que de trouver le point-repos ou point d'équilibre.'[87] But later in his third *Quartet* Eliot will inform us that the point of equilibrium he is seeking to attain is *Incarnation*.

> Here the impossible union
> Of spheres of existence is actual,
> Here the past and future

Are conquered, and reconciled,
Where action were otherwise movement
Of that which is only moved
And has in it no source of movement –
Driven by dæmonic chthonic
Powers.

Unlike W. B. Yeats and Charles Williams, Eliot was obviously not
a practitioner of the occult. His vision and philosophy of stillness
was by and large that of Christian Neo-Platonism. And yet here
in 'Burnt Norton', and elsewhere in *Four Quartets*, we find him
drawing to some significant degree on occult theory and practice.
How are we to explain this phenomenon?

My own conviction is that Eliot belongs to that group of
philosophical poets of whom Denis Saurat writes in his book
Literature and the Occult Tradition.

The philosophical poets, generally speaking [Saurat informs us]
are not occultists: they are not affiliated to any more or less
secret society which could furnish them with their ideas ready-
made. But all are acquainted with occultism and make use of it:
they all take from it, at different epochs, metaphysical ideas,
moral conceptions and above all myths.[88]

Occultism provides the poets, in other words, with 'an almost
inexhaustible mine of new material'. And thus 'It contains, for the
poets, in contrast to the orthodox culture of their time, a whole
world of artistic possibilities.'[89] That Eliot did not hesitate to draw
inspiration from what might be considered unorthodox and even
heretical sources may seem, at first, somewhat surprising. But in
1934 he wrote:

It is characteristic of the more interesting heretics, in the context
in which I use the term, that they have an exceptionally acute
perception, or profound insight, of some part of the truth; an
insight more important often than the inferences of those who
are aware of more but less acutely aware of anything. So far as
we are able to redress the balance, effect the compensation
ourselves, we may find such authors of the greatest value.[90]

The point at which Eliot's concerns as a poet in *Four Quartets* can
be said to fuse and intersect with those of certain occult authors is

first of all his realisation that there exists a supernatural realm, and second his determined struggle to express in words 'the sensation of the infinite'.

Eliot's experience of the Infinite should not, however, be confused with the experience of an occult author such as W. B. Yeats. Yeats, the poet magician, Eliot's chosen master, may well possess, it is true, 'an exceptionally acute perception . . . of some part of the truth' and may therefore assist Eliot as a sort of guide as he sets out in *Four Quartets* to explore beyond the natural boundaries of human perception. But mere magic, in Eliot's opinion, and even the haunting magic of Yeats, is not mysticism. As much for the older Eliot as for the younger, 'Mr Yeats's "supernatural world" was the wrong supernatural world.'[91]

Part Four
'Little Gidding'
An End of Exploration

10

The Language of Patriotism: Rudyard Kipling and Rupert Brooke

Let us take one of the commonest manifestations of natural mysticism, patriotism . . .

(Henri Bremond, *Prayer and Poetry*, 1924)

All the last three Quartets are in a sense war poems . . .

(T. S. Eliot, 'T. S. Eliot Talks about his Poetry', 1958)

The phrase 'spiritual patriots', originally coined by Evelyn Underhill in her 1912 Introduction to *The Cloud of Unknowing*,[1] is perhaps, the most helpful phrase to use when describing the patriotism of someone like T. S. Eliot. But it can also be misleading. Eliot's 'spiritual' patriotism did not prevent him, for example, from an immediate and active involvement in the war effort. And, after 1938, he became, if anything, more concerned than ever with social and political issues. But the full integrity of a civilised life in England (or, perhaps, one should say rather, the *possibility* of such integrity) Eliot saw as being threatened by the general collapse of religious and spiritual values throughout Europe. The war, in his view, with all its attendant horror, was but the merest symptom of this collapse. Eliot's immediate aim was 'to find new spiritual energies to regenerate and vitalize our sick society'.[2] This search led him back to the sources of European wisdom and most notably, at one period, to the English medieval tradition of mysticism.[3] Evelyn Underhill wrote in 1912:

> The little family of mystical treatises which is known to students as 'the Cloud of Unknowing group', deserves more

177

attention than it has hitherto received from English lovers of mysticism; for it represents the first expression in our tongue of that great mystic tradition of the Christian Neoplatonists which gathered up, remade, and 'salted with Christ's salt' all that was best in the spiritual wisdom of the ancient world.[4]

Had Underhill lived to read 'Little Gidding' she would no doubt have been delighted to discover traces and echoes from both the English medieval mystic, Julian of Norwich, and from *The Cloud* itself. Unfortunately, however, she died in June 1941.

Because Eliot has been able to absorb into his poetry so many voices from the distant and the recent past, these voices or 'talents' can be said to have found in him a new opportunity for human speech, and a new kind of immortality. He remarked once in an early essay:

> We dwell with satisfaction upon the poet's difference from his predecessors, especially his immediate predecessors; we endeavour to find something that can be isolated in order to be enjoyed. Whereas if we approach a poet without this prejudice we shall often find that not only the best, but the most individual parts of his work may be those in which the dead poets, his ancestors, assert their immortality most vigorously.[5]

The compound ghost who returns to speak to Eliot in the final *Quartet*, and whose immortality is thereby realised and affirmed, includes, as one might expect, a certain number of historical and literary figures associated with the English Civil War and with the seventeenth-century lay retreat at Little Gidding. But it includes also – if I am not mistaken – two as yet unidentified presences, both of whom are among the best-known English patriots and poets: Rudyard Kipling and Rupert Brooke.

A.   RUDYARD KIPLING: THE PATRIOT AND THE SEER

> . . . *this strange, basilisk personality, which at one moment is like some oriental lizard, and at another as commonplace as a tinned army ration.*[6]

Shortly after completing the first draft of the present chapter I came upon a delightful and informative talk Eliot gave to the

Kipling Society in October 1958. The title of Eliot's talk, 'The Unfading Genius of Rudyard Kipling', clearly reveals the extent of his enthusiasm. Kipling is hailed by Eliot as 'the greatest English man of letters of his generation'.[7]

> Rudyard Kipling, whom I never knew and never saw, and who probably never heard of me, has touched my life at sundry times and in divers manners. . . . [He] has accompanied me ever since boyhood, when I discovered the early verse – 'Barrack Room Ballads' – and the early stories – 'Plain Tales from the Hills'. There are boyhood enthusiasms which one outgrows; there are writers who impress one deeply at some time before or during adolescence and whose work one never re-reads in later life. But Kipling is different. Traces of Kipling appear in my own mature verse where no diligent scholarly sleuth has yet observed them, but which I am myself prepared to disclose.[8]

Curiously, apart from pointing out the influence of Kipling on the title of his poem 'The Hollow Men' ('I could never have thought of this title but for Kipling's poem "The Broken Men" ') Eliot, despite his generous proposal to reveal all, discloses not a single trace of Kipling's influence on his 'mature verse'!

When John Hayward discovered in the summer of 1941 that Eliot was in the process of preparing a selection of Kipling's verse, he remarked to a friend: 'This seems to me a somewhat queer assignment, though I suppose Kipling's verse must be regarded as a kind of stand-by for certain tastes in time of war – no matter what the time or which the war.'[9] Eliot, in his Preface to the selection does have something to say, it is true, about Kipling as a patriotic poet and as a war poet. But he also draws attention to certain other aspects of Kipling's genius:

> An immense gift for using words, an amazing curiosity and power of observation with his mind and with all his senses, the mask of the entertainer, and beyond that a queer gift of second sight, of transmitting messages from elsewhere, a gift so disconcerting when we are made aware of it that henceforth we are never sure when it is *not* present: all this makes Kipling a writer impossible wholly to understand and quite impossible to belittle.[10]

My proposal now is to glance again at each of the *Quartets* in turn to see if Rudyard Kipling's poetry and prose exercised some influence on *Four Quartets*.

(1) 'Burnt Norton'

Eliot regarded Kipling as 'the greatest master of the short story in English'.[11] And when by way of preparation for his own *Choice of Kipling's Verse* Eliot re-read Kipling's 'They' – a story which, apparently, he had not even glanced at for some thirty years – he discovered to his surprise that, five years earlier, it had had an unconscious influence on the composition of 'Burnt Norton'.[12]

The narrator of Kipling's story describes how one day in the countryside he came by chance upon 'an ancient house of lichened and weather-worn stone . . . flanked by semi-circular walls, also rose-red, that closed the lawn on the fourth side, and at their feet a box hedge'.[13] Suddenly he hears behind him a small sound like that of a child.

> I heard a laugh among the yew-peacocks, and turning to make sure (till then I had been watching the house only) I saw the silver of a fountain behind a hedge thrown up against the sun. The doves on the roof cooed to the cooing water; but between the two notes I caught the utterly happy chuckle of a child.[14]

(Compare in 'Burnt Norton' the phrase 'the leaves were full of children, / Hidden excitedly, containing laughter', and also Eliot's reference to the garden and to the box circle.) At the end of the story we discover that the small voices and visions are in fact no more than mere ghosts, appearing to those like the narrator himself who, in the past, have lost their own children. The apparent recovery from the dead of the lost child, Marina, in Eliot's poem of that name, is evoked by these two mysterious lines:

> Whispers and small laughter between leaves and hurrying feet
> Under sleep, where all the waters meet.

Is it not possible that these lines also contain an unconscious echo of Kipling's 'They'? For in the short story we hear of 'the patter of feet – quick feet through a room beyond', and again of 'the tread of small cautious feet stealing across the dead leaves', and of 'a murmur behind us of lowered voices broken by the sudden squeaking giggles of childhood'.[15] Eliot spoke of 'They' as 'one of his [Kipling's] most other-worldly stories'.[16] There are occasions, according to Eliot, when 'Kipling is not merely possessed of penetration, but almost "possessed" of a kind of second sight'.[17] He *knew*, Eliot tells us, 'something of the things which are underneath and of the things which are beyond the frontier'.[18]

(2) 'East Coker'

Intimately related to Kipling's gift of second sight is what Eliot has called the *historical imagination*.

> Kipling, especially in *Puck of Pook's Hill* and *Rewards and Fairies*, aims I think to give at once a sense of the antiquity of England, of the number of generations and peoples who have laboured the soil and in turn been buried beneath it, and of the contemporaneity of the past. Having previously exhibited an imaginative grasp of space, and England in it, he now proceeds to a similar achievement in time.[19]

In Kipling's introduction to *Rewards and Fairies* we read:

> Once upon a time, Dan and Una, brother and sister, living in the English country, had the good fortune to meet with Puck . . . the last survivor of those whom mortals call Fairies. Their proper name, of course, is 'The People of the Hills'. This Puck, by means of the magic of Oak, Ash, and Thorn, gave the children power –
>
> > 'To see what they should see and hear what what they should hear,
> > Though it should have happened three thousand year'.[20]

In *Puck of Pook's Hill* Puck declares that, although he may not be able to take the children to the Hill, 'I may be able to show you something out of the common here on Human Earth . . . it's your meadow, but there's a great deal more in it than your or your father ever guessed.'[21] Eliot, in a short obituary notice for Kipling composed in 1936, spoke of the role of the unconscious in his writings:

> No critic [he remarked] has yet taken the measure of Kipling
> . . . if he was not quite conscious of what he did, how should
> we immediately be wholly conscious of it? He can only be
> judged by those who are able to read the whole of his work,
> and who are capable of entering into his *mystique*, which is
> something larger than a *mystique* of Empire.[22]

It took Eliot himself a lifetime to take the full measure of Kipling.
(In March 1909, for Professor Copeland's course at Harvard, Eliot
composed an essay lugubriously entitled 'The Defects of Kipling'
– a far cry indeed from 'The Unfading Genius of Rudyard
Kipling', the talk which he gave in March 1959, exactly fifty years
later.[23])

Apart from Eliot himself there was at least one literary critic,
contemporary with Kipling, who was, it seems, able to enter into
Kipling's *mystique*. When *Puck of Pook's Hill* was first published it
received an enthusiastic review from Alfred Noyes.

> Mr Kipling has for the first time dug through the silt of modern
> imperialism. He has gone back to the old ground-works and
> seen the inscription upon them. . . . We know of no book in
> the guise of fiction that gives the pageant of our history with
> such breadth and nobility of feeling, and with so sure and easy
> a touch. . . . But let popular Imperialists beware of him. . . .
> Mystics are always dangerous – to materialists, at any rate; and
> Mr Kipling has mysticism in his blood and in his bones.[24]

One of Kipling's most memorable poems of 'second sight' is
entitled 'The Way through the Woods'. Eliot took it from the
collection *Rewards and Fairies* for his own selection of Kipling's
verse. The poem contains, we are told by Eliot, 'some very
remarkable innovations indeed'.[25] Its first stanza describes how
there was once a pathway or a road through the woods, but that
only 'the keeper' can now see where it once passed.

> Yet, if you enter the woods
> Of a summer evening late
> .   .   .   .

> You will hear the beat of a horse's feet
> And the swish of a skirt in the dew.

All through the opening section of 'East Coker' Eliot is likewise striving to give us, his readers, a sense of the antiquity of England, to make us much more conscious than before of the mysterious contemporaneity of the past.

> In that open field
> If you do not come too close, if you do not come too close,
> On a summer midnight, you can hear the music
> Of the weak pipe and the little drum
> And see them dancing around the bonfire.

In another part of *Rewards and Fairies* we read: 'We had a fire of apple-wood, sweet as incense, – and the curtains at the door being looped up, *we could hear the music and see the lights shining on mail and dresses*'.[26] The speaker in this passage is Sir Richard Dalyngridge, a Norman Knight and a follower of William the Conqueror. He is introduced by Kipling into several of the stories in *Puck of Pook's Hill* and *Rewards and Fairies*. Like Kipling himself, Sir Richard, after many arduous journeys throughout the world, decides to settle in England. T. S. Eliot, in his after-dinner speech to the Kipling Society in 1958, talked of a similarity between Kipling's lifelong search and that of the legendary Sir Richard; and he spoke also of 'a similarity, or rather an analogy', between Kipling's background and his own.

> Kipling passed his early childhood in India; he was brought back to England for his schooling; he returned to India at the age of seventeen. Two years of his life were spent in America. Later, he settled in Sussex, but came to pass his winters in the more benign climate of South Africa. . . . Kipling's attitude to things English, like mine, was in some ways different from that of any native-born Briton. I feel this in some of the poems written after Kipling settled in Sussex. For example, 'The Recall':

> > Under their feet in the grasses
> > My clinging magic runs
> > They shall return as strangers
> > They shall remain as sons.

He is referring to the American couple of the story which this
poem accompanies, who settle in England in the village from
which the wife's family had gone to America: but I feel that he
is writing out of his own experience. Similarly, in 'Sir Richard's
Song' the speaker is a Norman knight, a follower of William the
Conqueror, who has settled in England:

> I followed my Duke ere I was a lover,
>   To take from England fief and fee;
> But now this game is the other way over –
>   But now England hath taken me!

Sir Richard, too, I think, is Kipling himself.[27]

The fact that East Coker is the village from which Eliot's own
family had first emigrated to America, and the place also to which
he has chosen, in modern times, to return as a visitor, or as a
stranger, underlines the striking similarity that exists between the
poets, and serves also, I think, to explain why Kipling's presence
is felt to be so strong in 'East Coker'.

(3) 'The Dry Salvages'

In the same year, 1941, in which Eliot compiled and published his
selection of Kipling's verse, he was engaged in the composition of
his own third *Quartet*, 'The Dry Salvages'. The theme of the
poem's first section closely resembles the central theme in
Kipling's short story 'The Bridge Builders'.[28] In both works the
river is depicted as a kind of terrible god, whose wrath or whose
'divinity' the modern world chooses to ignore.

> . . . at first recognised as a frontier;
> Useful, untrustworthy, as a conveyor of commerce;
> Then only a problem confronting *the builder of bridges*.
>   (Emphasis added.)

In Kipling's story there is at one stage a prophecy or a prayer that
those who have defiled and shamed the river 'must come to the
Destroyer'.[29] Findlayson, the engineer who built the bridge, says
to himself, 'What have the Gods to do with my bridge!' But the
River-God itself declares, 'The justice of the Gods on the bridge-

builders!'[30] As it turns out the newly built bridge over the river is not destroyed – in part, it would appear, because of the intervention of Lord Krishna. Addressing himself to the River-God, Krishna declares: 'get thee to thy flood again. . . . What need to slay them [the common people] now? . . . Go now, mother, to the flood again. Men and cattle are thick on the waters – the banks fall – the villages melt because of thee.'[31] After Eliot had completed his first draft of Section Two – the section immediately preceding the Krishna passage in 'The Dry Salvages' – he decided to introduce yet again the image of the river. The lines he added are, to my mind, amongst the most vivid in *Four Quartets*.

> Time the destroyer is time the preserver,
> Like the river with its cargo of dead negroes, cows and
>   chicken coops, . . .

One thinks immediately here of the American Mississippi and not of the Indian Ganges. Eliot, we know, grew up alongside the Mississippi; and, in his Introduction to *The Adventures of Huckleberry Finn* he spoke of the river as 'a treacherous and capricious dictator'.

> At one season, it may move sluggishly . . . at another season, it may obliterate the low Illinois shore to a horizon of water, while in its bed it runs with a speed such that no man or beast can survive in it. At such times, it carries down *human bodies, cattle and houses*. At least twice, at St Louis, the western and the eastern shores have been separated by the fall of bridges, until the designer of the great Eads Bridge devised a structure which could resist the floods.[32]

The obvious and no doubt the primary source of 'The river with its cargo of *dead negroes; cows and chicken coops*' in 'The Dry Salvages' is Eliot's memory of his own childhood experience. But the imagery in this short phrase does, I suspect, owe something also to Kipling's '*Men and cattle* are thick on the waves', and to the following no less horrendous lines, also from 'The Bridge Builders':

> the pent river, once freed of her guide-lines, had spread like a sea to the horizon. Then hurried by, rolling in the water, *dead*

men and oxen together, with here and there *a patch of thatched roof.*[33]

Half way through the central section of 'The Dry Salvages' we read about a group of people on a journey trying to escape from the past into the future. They are warned, however, by the poet, that there can be no escape.

> While the narrowing rails slide together behind you;
> And on the deck of the drumming liner
> Watching the furrow that widens behind you,
> You shall not think 'the past is finished'
> Or 'the future is before us'.

In Rudyard Kipling's short story 'The Wandering Jew' the central character is likewise depicted as 'racing against eternity':

> His days were divided between *watching the white wake spinning behind the stern of the swiftest steamers, or the brown earth flashing past the windows of the fastest trains,* and he noted in a pocket-book every minute that he had railed or screwed out of remorseless eternity.[34]

The calm voice of eternal wisdom which, Eliot informs his hurrying travellers, can be heard singing 'At nightfall, in the rigging and the aerial' is also, I think, vaguely reminiscent of the strange, other-worldly communication transmitted to the helmsman in Kipling's poem, 'In the Matter of One Compass':

> When, foot to wheel and back to wind,
> The helmsman dare not look behind,
> But hears beyond his compass light
> The blind bow thunder through the night.
> And, like a harpspring ere it snaps,
> The rigging *sing* beneath the caps . . .[35]

The central theme of Kipling's poem is that of disappearance and recovery ('By love upheld, by God allowed, / We go, but we return again!'). In the poem's second stanza Kipling speaks of the sea-creatures:

> Who, drowsing, nose the long-lost Ships
> Let down through darkness to their lips —[36]

And in Eliot's invocation to the Virgin ('The Dry Salvages', Section Four) we read:

> Also pray for those who were in *ships*, and
> Ended their voyage on the sand, in the sea's *lips* . . .
> (Emphasis added.)

Kipling's mysterious declaration that there is somehow recovery and return even for those who have been lost or shipwrecked at sea, is also stated explicitly and confidently by Eliot in Section Three of 'The Dry Salvages':

> O voyagers, O seamen,
> You who come to port, and you whose bodies
> Will suffer the trial and judgement of the sea,
> Or whatever event, this is your real destination.

To have discovered in 'The Dry Salvages' certain minor echoes of Rudyard Kipling, chiming, as it were, in unison with the voice of Lord Krishna, and with the voice, therefore, of traditional Indian wisdom, is not I think quite as bizarre or as incongruous as it may at first, perhaps, appear. For Kipling was, after all, born in India, and spent several of his most formative years living and working in India. This aspect of his career is emphasised by Eliot in the long Kipling essay he composed in 1941, the same year in which he also composed and published 'The Dry Salvages':

> [T]here are two strata in Kipling's appreciation of India, the stratum of the child and that of the young man. It was the latter who observed the British in India and wrote the rather cocky and acid tales of Delhi and Simla, but it was the former who loved the country and its people. In his Indian tales [and 'The Bridge Builders' is one of them] it is on the whole the Indian characters who have the greater reality, because they are treated with the understanding of love. . . . Kipling is of India in a different way from any other Englishman who has written, and in a different way from that of any particular Indian, who has a race, a creed, a local habitation and, if a Hindu, a caste. He might almost be called the first citizen of India. And his relation to India determines that about him which is the most important thing about a man, his religious attitude. It is an attitude of comprehensive tolerance.[37]

(4) 'Little Gidding'

The chapel at Little Gidding, the terminus towards which our attention is directed by Eliot in the last *Quartet*, is described by him as 'the world's end'. Although this phrase, being reasonably common, requires no particular explanation as to its origin, it is interesting that it is used twice by Sir Richard Dalyngridge in *Rewards and Fairies*, and used both times on the same page from which I have already quoted above in the section on 'East Coker'.

> Henry [the King] loved to talk gravely with grave men, and De Aquila told him of my travels to *the world's end*. We had a fire of apple-wood, sweet as incense, – and the curtains at the door being looped up, we could hear the music and see the lights shining on mail and dresses. . . . I was telling of our fight . . . at *the world's end*.[38]

The phrase can also be found in another part of the same book. 'You'll do a great many things, and eating and drinking with a dead man beyond *the world's end* will be the least of them. For you'll open a road from the East unto the West, and back again.'[39] Throughout the opening section of 'Little Gidding' we hear repeated over and over again – and with powerful effect – the Kiplinesque incantation heard for the first time in 'East Coker', Section One. I draw the reader's attention here to the comparison made earlier in this chapter between Kipling's 'if you enter the woods / Of a summer evening late . . .' and Eliot's 'If you do not come too close, if you do not come too close, / On a summer midnight'.

> If you came this way,
> Taking the route you would be likely to take
> From the place you would be likely to come from,
> If you came this way in may time. . . .

Eliot knows very well, of course, that Little Gidding is not the only place in the world where the dead are reborn, and where at times they may return to speak with us in a language 'beyond the language of the living':

> But this is the nearest, in place and time,
> Now and in England.

B. RUPERT BROOKE: A VISION OF ENGLAND

If I should die, think only this of me:
  That there's some corner of a foreign field
That is for ever England. There shall be
  In that rich earth a richer dust concealed; . . .

(Rupert Brooke, 'The Soldier'[40])

Where a man dies bravely
At one with his destiny, that soil is his.

(T. S. Eliot, To the Indians who Died in Africa[41])

Rupert Brooke is not a name one is normally inclined to associate with the work of T. S. Eliot. The two poets belong to two entirely different worlds; and, in terms of their natural literary talent, there is between them no comparison to be made. But they do have, all the same, certain notable affinities. C. K. Stead, talking in general about the Georgian period's relation to the Modernist era, says of Rupert Brooke that, in his writings, there was 'an impulse which was driving him in the direction that a poet of his time needed to take. And in taking this direction he met with opposition'.[42] Stead goes on, however, to qualify this remark. 'There is no point', he says, 'in attempting to prove that he would have become a considerable poet had he lived. The point is simply that Brooke, a representative Georgian, was moving in a direction which was advantageous to the development of English poetry. He helped to prepare the ground for the work of better poets.'[43]

Among his own contemporaries the young poet was regarded – and not always with approval – as a kind of *intellectual* poet. To his friend Edwin Marsh he complained: 'They object to my poetry as unreal, affected, complex, "literary", and full of long words.'[44] Tarred, at times, with the same brush as some of the Elizabethan poets and dramatists, Brooke was criticised for the 'coarseness' of part of his work. But this did not deflect him from his purpose. He already possessed – we can see now – the basic knowledge about poetic communication that T. S. Eliot was later to acquire, and later to define, using the celebrated term 'objective correlative'. 'There are', Brooke wrote to his friend Marsh, 'common and sordid things – situations or details – that may suddenly bring all tragedy, or at least the brutality of actual emotions to you.'[45] This was in 1911. Eight years later we come upon the following passage in Eliot's essay on Hamlet:

> The only way of expressing emotion in the form of art is by finding an 'objective correlative'; in other words, a set of objects, a situation, a chain of events which shall be the formula of that *particular* emotion; such that when the external facts, which must terminate in sensory experience, are given, the emotion is immediately evoked. If you examine any of Shakespeare's more successful tragedies, you will find this exact equivalence.[46]

As one might expect, not all Rupert Brooke's English critics objected to what was new in the poet's work. Henry Newbolt, for example, writing in March 1913, responded with considerable enthusiasm. Rupert Brooke, he said, 'is gifted with an intellectual curiosity and a natural and habitual intensity of feeling that recall the work of Donne and of Donne only among the English poets'.[47] Four years later, in September 1917, T. S. Eliot published his 'Reflections on Contemporary Poetry' in *The Egoist*. The immediate object of Eliot's attention was a book of poems by Harold Monro. But in the course of his review Eliot found an opportunity to refer also to the work of Rupert Brooke. 'Mr Harold Monro has', Eliot observed, 'a vocabulary less rich, less astonishing, than Brooke's, but at the same time less rhetorical.'[48] Eliot obviously regretted the 'lapses of rhetoric' in Brooke's poetry; but at the same time he did not hesitate to point out 'a number of lines which', he said, 'show a really amazing felicity and command of language'.[49]

Traces of Brooke's influence on Eliot's earlier work have already been noted by one or two other critics. B. C. Southam in *A Student's Guide to the Selected Poems of T. S. Eliot* mentions Rupert Brooke's famous poem 'The Old Vicarage, Granchester ', and its possible influence on *The Waste Land*. 'This is not', he says, 'in the strict sense, a source. But it is a work which I am sure Eliot wanted to call to the reader's mind. He evokes it through verbal, structural and thematic echoes.'[50] Also worth comparing is the opening of 'The Old Vicarage, Granchester', 'Just now the lilac is in bloom / All before my little room', with these sardonic lines from Eliot's 'Portrait of a Lady': 'Now that lilacs are in bloom / She has a bowl of lilacs in her room'. (The two lines from Brooke were, in fact, quoted in full by Eliot in his 'Reflections on Contemporary Poetry', September 1917.) F. O. Matthiessen has pointed out an interesting similarity between the opening section of *The Waste Land* and Rupert Brooke's description in a letter of the deep impression made upon one of his friends on hearing the announcement, 'We're at war with Germany'. The description includes phrases such as 'the swish of evening air in the face, as one skies down past the pines' and 'the quiet length of evening over the Starnbergersee'.[51] When Eliot was questioned years later by Cleanth Brooks about Rupert Brooke's possible influence on the first section of *The Waste Land*, he replied: 'actually this particular passage approximates more closely to a recollection of a personal experience of my own than anything else, and indeed is as nearly as possible a verbatim report'. On the other hand, it was, he admitted, 'quite possible' that he had read Rupert Brooke's letter, and that it might have been, therefore, somewhere 'at the back of my mind'.[52]

Writing at the close of the Second World War, Eliot spoke once in a short note about the effects of the war on some of the younger British poets, his contemporaries:

> When these poets write about the war, it is mostly about some limited experience, even trivial experience, such as cold, discomfort, or the boredom of waiting at an isolated post. And this is a good thing too, for the bigger experiences need time, perhaps a long time, before we can make poetry of them. You cannot understand war – with the kind of understanding needed for writing poetry – or any other great experience while you are in the midst of it; you can only record small immediate observations.[53]

Many years earlier, during the period of the First World War, Rupert Brooke wrote home to a friend of his on the subject of his own war sonnets. 'It took me', he said, 'an awful long time to hammer them out: you can't think.'[54] And he went on then to say something about his difficulty: 'I think *reading* in war-time's right enough, but writing requires a longer period of serenity, a more certainly undisturbed subconscious.'[55] To another friend, Lascelles

Abercrombie, he confessed: 'One just hasn't, though, the time and detachment to write, I find. But I've been collecting a few words, detaching lines from the ambient air, collaring one or two . . . golden phrases'.[56]

Among the papers Rupert Brooke left uncompleted at his death is a short and somewhat rhetorical 'elegy'. It describes the passage of an individual into Death, and the mystery of the contact still remaining with his spirit in the minds and memories of those who knew him.

> The eyes that met my eyes have looked on night.
> The firm limbs are no more; gone back to earth,
> Easily mingling . . .
> > What he is yet,
> Not living, lives, hath place in a few minds . . .[57]

The juxtaposition of a statement concerning transience with a statement concerning immortality and memory is, one may say, characteristic of the work of both Brooke and Eliot. The text quoted above can be found in a *Memoir* published three years after Brooke's death. Also included in the *Memoir* is the following short passage in which Brooke speaks of his experience of leaving Rugby after several happy years, and of becoming 'for the first time conscious of transience, and parting, and a great many other things'.

> As I looked back at five years, I seemed to see almost every hour golden and radiant, and always increasing in beauty as I grew more conscious; and I could not (and cannot) hope for or even quite imagine such happiness elsewhere. And then I found the last days of all this slipping by me, and with them the faces and places and life I loved, and I without power to stay them.[58]

These lines Eliot would seem to have read and to have remembered well. For we read in 'Little Gidding', Section Three,

> See, now they vanish,
> The faces and places, with the self which, as it could,
> loved them,
> To become renewed, transfigured, in another pattern.

The opening meditation of 'Little Gidding' comes to a mysterious close with these two cryptic lines:

> Here, the intersection of the timeless moment
> Is England and nowhere. Never and always.

This beautiful sonorous statement has always puzzled as much as it has delighted me. And to have come recently upon what I believe to be a possible 'source' in Rupert Brooke has not in any way obscured but rather, I would say, considerably enhanced for me the statement's meaning and its poignancy. Of all the new poems on which Rupert Brooke was working at the time of his death, the most interesting was an Ode-Threnody on England. To Edwin Marsh he wrote: 'My long poem is to be about the existence – and non-locality – of England.'[59] And, in a letter to Violet Asquith, he described his Ode-Threnody as 'a very serene affair, full of major chords and larger outlooks, like an English lawn at sunset'.[60] Unfortunately, Brooke did not live long enough to see his work completed. He died at Scyros on Friday 23 April 1915. But, if one reads through the few scraps of verse that have survived from Brooke's unfinished Threnody, one is, I believe, led gradually to the conviction that the two lines quoted above from Eliot's poem have been in some degree inspired by these Scyros fragments. Certainly, apart from Eliot's 'Little Gidding', I myself know of no other patriotic poem of which the subject is, as it is here, the existence – and non-locality – of England.

> All things are written in the mind
> There the sure hills have station; and the wind
> Blows in that placeless air.
> And there the white and golden birds go flying;
> And the stars wheel and shine; and woods are fair;
> The light upon the snow is there;
> > and in that *nowhere* move
> The trees and hills and waters that we love.
>
> And she for whom we die, she the undying
> Mother of men
> England![61]

Brooke goes on then to speak further about England's spiritual identity, her existence in one place and in one time, 'This local earth, set in terrestrial streams', and yet at the same time her existence in no place and in no time, 'She is with all we have loved and found and known, / Closed in the little nowhere of the brain'.

> She is not here, or now –
> She is here, and now, yet nowhere –
> .   .   .   .
> She was in his eyes, but he could not see her.
> And he was England, but he knew her not.[62]

To discover after many years of reading *Four Quartets* that such a relatively minor poet as Rupert Brooke has had a significant influence on Eliot's major poem may perhaps at first be rather difficult to accept. But, speaking for myself, I can say that I have less and less difficulty in acknowledging Rupert Brooke's 'small' presence in 'Little Gidding'. He also, surely, is part of that 'compound ghost' whose poetic voice is 'tongued with fire beyond the language of the living', and whose 'face still forming' is recognised, or partly recognised, by the living poet as his own – and not his own. 'There are poets', Eliot had occasion once to remark, 'for whom one may have a strong personal feeling, who seem to be speaking privately to oneself: and sometimes these are all the dearer if they are rather small people.'[63]

On one occasion, in the first draft of a talk Eliot delivered in 1953, he made the following somewhat unusual comment: 'The last three of my Quartets', he said, 'are primarily patriotic poems.'[64] This remark was later cancelled. But exactly why Eliot chose to cancel it has not – at least not so far as I am aware – ever been properly explained. Perhaps, after a period of reflection, Eliot came to realise that the remark could, for some people, be seriously misleading. He himself, after all, had some years earlier defined patriotic verse as 'poetry which expresses and stimulates pride in the military virtues of a people'.[65] Now whatever else the last three *Quartets* can be said to represent, their achievement bears, I am sure, little or no relationship to such a straightforward species of propagandist verse. At the same time, however, it is interesting to note that in his poem 'Defence of the Islands' Eliot does not hesitate to link together the poetry of England – 'music's enduring instrument', that 'patient cultivation of the earth, of English verse' – and the war effort.[66] 'Defence of the Islands' was published in 1941 to accompany an exhibition of photographs illustrating the war effort of Britain. One year later, in a short paper entitled 'Poetry in Wartime' Eliot had this to say on the subject of patriotism:

> [W]hile a poet, as a man, should be no less devoted to his country than other men, I distinguish between his duty as a man and his duty as a poet. His first duty as a poet is towards his native language, to preserve and to develop that language. As a man, he has the same duties as his fellow-citizens; as a poet, his duty is to write the best poetry he can, and thereby incidentally create something in which his people can take pride.[67]

The patriotism of a great many of Adolf Hitler's supporters in Nazi Germany was, we now realise, based not so much on any clear political ideology, but rather on a peculiar kind of 'religious' mysticism, an enthralled ecstatic devotion to the Fatherland. The reluctance of T. S. Eliot – after a certain number of years – to acknowledge that the last three of his *Quartets* were 'primarily patriotic poems' may in this context be of some considerable significance. For it may indicate a desire in the poet to disavow any sinister connection between his own deep patriotic devotion to England and his religious mysticism. That there is, however, at least some sort of connection in *Four Quartets* between these two distinct spheres, I have no doubt. Certainly the poet's sense of England, his awareness of England's 'spiritual identity', his feeling for the contemporaneity of England's past, and for the countless numbers of generations and peoples who have laboured the soil, was in the end, I believe, as 'mystical' a sense of England as that of Rupert Brooke or Rudyard Kipling. But I am also equally persuaded that this quasi-mystical enthusiasm on the part of the Christian poet for a Timeless England – his overt yet deep contemplative love of the land and the language he shared with his remote ancestors, and with his immediate contemporaries in the war effort – this love of England and of the English language and of the English people, was never tainted by any form of sinister political or racialist philosophy. Patriotism Eliot always regarded as something virtuous. But at the same time he was well aware that 'it can easily pass into the vices of nationalism, imperialism in the bad sense, collective pride and collective cupidity'.[68] The wave of religious revivalism that swept England towards the end of 1938 Eliot judged to be distinctly suspect and even dangerous. 'It may', he remarked, 'engender nothing better than a disguised and peculiarly sanctimonious nationalism, accelerating our progress towards the paganism which we say we abhor.'[69] And again he noted: 'Our preoccupation with foreign politics during the last few years has induced a surface complacency rather than a consistent attempt at self-examination of conscience.'[70] A. D. Moody has argued recently, and with I think considerable justification, that 'for Eliot "the one great peril" was, not Hitler, but "final and complete alienation from God after death". Atonement with God was what he believed in – a *patria* not of this world'.[71]

11

Mysticism and Myth – I: The Shakespeare Pattern

The essential shortcomings of modern poetry in relation to that of antiquity may be summed up in these words: we have no mythology. But let me add that we are close to acquiring one, or rather it is time that we seriously collaborate in producing one. For it will come to us in a quite opposite way from the original mythology, which was everywhere the first blossoming of youthful imagination, clinging directly to – and rooting itself in – what was most immediate and alive in the sensuous world. The new mythology must, on the contrary, be fashioned out of the profoundest depths of the spirit: it must be the most artificial of all works of art.

(Friedrich Schlegel, 'Dialogue on Poetry', 1800)

'The poet', Eliot remarked once *a propos* of the work of Dante and Shakespeare, 'has something to say which is not even necessarily implicit in the philosophical system, something which is also over and above the verbal beauty.'[1] According to Eliot 'the most extensive, and probably the most inscrutable' pattern of this sort is to be found in the later plays of Shakespeare.

[I]n Dante [on the other hand] the pattern is interwoven chiefly with the systematic pattern which he set himself, and the mystery and excitement lies in trying to trace its relations and differences – the relation, and the personal variations, between for example the Thomist doctrine of Love, the poetic provençal tradition, and the direct experience of Dante with its modifications under philosophical and literary influences.[2]

Our task in this chapter, and in the chapter which follows, will be to elucidate as far as possible the relationship between the pattern

197

to which Eliot has here drawn our attention, in the works of Dante and Shakespeare, and the 'secret' underlying pattern of *Four Quartets*. The task will not be an easy one, but it is, I am persuaded, necessary; since if we avoid speaking about the 'hidden' pattern of *Four Quartets* altogether, we risk ignoring the new method, or new strategy, which Eliot's genius has had to devise during the composition of the poem.

In a lecture which was delivered to a French audience in 1952, Eliot chose to apply the myth of Scylla and Charybdis to the situation of a poet about to begin work on a new poem. 'Je me mis alors à considérer la signification du mythe "Charybde et Scylla" en poésie.'[3] When he begins working on the composition of a fairly long philosophical work, the poet will almost inevitably find himself in the position of Ulysses, the Homeric navigator, caught between two major perils or obstacles. On the one hand he has to think hard about the poem's *intellectual structure*, about what it is he wants to communicate. But, on the other hand, he must also be careful not to forget, or to ignore, the question of the poem's *musical structure*. For to direct himself exclusively in one direction or the other – towards Charybdis, the potential peril of a mere dogmatic propaganda, or towards Scylla, the equal peril of mere Symbolist music and incantation – is to risk in the end an inevitable shipwreck.

In respect of *Four Quartets*, Eliot's critics have so far not been able to agree among themselves as to whether or not the poet-navigator has in fact succeeded in striking a balance between these two extremes. Helen Gardner, although not unaware of the poem's dogmatic and Christian level of meaning, suggests that by relying principally on a musical structure, and on 'certain common symbols', Eliot has created in *Four Quartets* a poem that is 'beautiful, satisfying, self-contained, self-organised, complete'.[4] In marked contrast, another of Eliot's critics, Donald Davie, speaks of 'the high tension' set up between the Mallarméan or Symbolist element and the dogmatic.

> On the one hand a form that is musical, non-discursive, on the other hand a content that for long stretches is painstakingly discursive, even pedestrian; on the one hand Mallarmé, by-word for poetry that is all implication and suggestion, on the other hand Cranmer, bleakly and unsparingly explicit. . . . It is small wonder if the product of such extreme tension is a poem

remarkably uneven in tone if not in quality; a poem which has to make a formal virtue out of its own disparities, by inviting us to think that it switches tone only as Beethoven does when he completes a slow movement and embarks upon a scherzo.[5]

Graham Hough's essay, 'Vision and Doctrine in *Four Quartets*', also brings into sharp focus the apparent unease that exists between the Imagist or Symbolist mode and the dogmatic content. 'The poem as a whole', he declares, 'occupies a position of dogmatism.'[6] And he then goes on to describe this position as nothing less than one of 'sectarian dogmatism'.[7] The poetic method on which Eliot still partly relies, namely the Imagist or the Symbolist method, is completely unsuited (Hough believes) to the kind of poem Eliot is now trying to write. '[T]he *Quartets* . . . present themselves as a philosophical poem; and the images must bear not only more weight, but weight of a different order of magnitude altogether. They must be transformed into something more than images.'[8] The reason he gives for Eliot's failure to achieve this transformation is worth noting. 'How', he asks first of all, 'does traditional poetry accomplish this transformation of the sensory into the symbol of an immaterial reality?' And he replies: 'It is by assigning the sensory images a structural position in a myth, an intelligibly constructed fable – using the words myth and fable in their more neutral sense, the sense that is nearest to plot.'[9] In classical or traditional poetry, 'Power and Meaning are guaranteed by the self-coherence of the myth'. But, 'Imagist poetry renounces this time-honoured source of strength. The images are left to stand alone, or with such fragments of allusive reference as may chance to adhere to them.'[10] Eliot's chosen images in *Four Quartets*, unlike those of his great predecessor Dante in *The Divine Comedy*, 'must work' says Hough, 'by their own immediate impact, unassisted by their place in a total structure'.[11] There are, it is true, 'certain passages of great verbal beauty and precision' in the poem. But because the Imagist mode adopted by the poet is so unsuited to bear the full weight of intellectual and symbolic meaning, even these few outstanding passages are, in the end, considered to be 'fragmentary in content and uncertain in their reference'.[12]

Eliot himself was fully conscious, I suspect, of the nature of the difficulties confronting him in the composition of *Four Quartets*. '[W]e must recognise', he remarked in 1948, 'that the question of

of writing a long poem is not simply that of the
staying power of the individual poet, but may have
conditions of the age in which he finds himself.'[13]
to conclude that there is no fundamental underlying unity in the poem, and that *Four Quartets* has to depend
entirely for its coherence on what has been called its 'pre-
determined doctrine' and its 'pre-determined form'? Is this sphinx
of poems, considered by so many to be the maturest work of
Eliot's genius, no more in fact than an indeterminate mixture of
obscure Symbolist music, of dull moral-doctrinal propaganda, and
of small 'secular epiphanies' and flights of mysticism? Or, is it not
possible that beneath the poem's intricate intellectual and musical
structure, there is concealed yet another kind of pattern, or poetic
strategy, similar in scope to that used by the poet many years
earlier in the composition of *The Waste Land*; a strategy to which
Eliot at that time gave the name 'the mythical method'?

A.   THE MYTHICAL METHOD AND *FOUR QUARTETS*

Exactly one year before the *Quartets* were completed Eliot went to
Dublin to deliver a lecture on the Irish poet W. B. Yeats. During
the course of his lecture he commented on Yeats's *external* and
internal ways of handling myth. The former he saw as exemplified
in the earlier plays and poems in which 'characters are treated,
with the respect that we pay to legend, as creatures of a different
world from ours'. But in Yeats's later work the characters, though
still mythical (e.g. 'the Cuchulain of *The Hawk's Well*, the
Cuchulain, Emer and Eithne of *The Only Jealousy of Emer*') are at
the same time 'universal men and women'.[14] This new heightened
sense of the interpenetration of past and present was due, Eliot
believed, to 'the internal as contrasted with the external way of
handling Irish myth'. In Yeats's more mature work 'myth is not
presented for its own sake, but as a vehicle for a situation of
universal meaning'.[15] The *internal* way of handling myth Eliot had
already discovered many years before in the work of another Irish
author: James Joyce. Of Joyce's novel *Ulysses* Eliot wrote in 1923:

I hold this book to be the most important expression which the
present age has found. . . . In using the myth, in manipulating

a continuous parallel between contemporaneity and antiquity, Mr Joyce is pursuing a method which others must pursue after him. They will not be imitators, any more than the scientist who uses the discoveries of an Einstein in pursuing his own, independent, further investigations. It is simply a way of controlling, of ordering, of giving shape and a significance to the immense panorama of futility and anarchy which is contemporary history.[16]

This original advance in poetic and artistic technique Eliot named *The mythical method*.

Psychology . . . ethnology, and *The Golden Bough* have concurred to make possible what was impossible even a few years ago. Instead of narrative method, we may now use the mythical method. It is, I seriously believe, a step toward making the modern world possible for art, toward order and form. . . . And only those who have won their own discipline in secret and without aid, in a world which offers very little assistance to that end, can be of any use in furthering this advance.[17]

Among the footnotes Eliot appended to *The Waste Land* we find no particular reference made to Yeats or to James Joyce. But we do find an open acknowledgement made to two important twentieth-century studies of myth: Miss Jessie L. Weston's book on the Grail Legend, *From Ritual to Romance*, and Sir James Frazer's *The Golden Bough*. Concerning the latter Eliot wrote: 'I have used especially the two volumes *Adonis, Attis, Osiris*. Anyone who is acquainted with these works will immediately recognise in the poem certain references to vegetation ceremonies.'[18] One year before *The Waste Land* was completed Eliot made an interesting remark on the potential significance of Frazer's work. The occasion was a review of Stravinsky's ballet *Le Sacre du Printemps* ['The Rite of Spring'], the sequences of which are supposed to represent certain primitive vegetation ceremonies. To Eliot the ritual dances, the stage-props and the costumes lacked what he called 'the sense of the present', and seemed to him rather superficial. But Stravinsky's music itself did succeed remarkably well in joining together 'the rhythm of the steppes' and 'the barbaric cries of modern life' into a single musical experience. The mere evocation of the noises of the city ('the

beating of iron and steel, the roar of the underground railway'
etc.) was not enough by itself for the art form; and nor was the
mere tapestry of shadowy ancient myths and rituals. 'In art', Eliot
declared, 'there should be interpenetration and metamorphosis.
Even *The Golden Bough* can be read in two ways: as a collection of
entertaining myths, or as a revelation of that vanished mind of
which our mind is a continuation.'[19]

In *The Waste Land* Eliot strove consciously to point out the link
or the parallel between the objective world of inherited myth and
the world of his own inner subjective experience. In doing this he
was practising that conscious, secret discipline he had named 'the
mythical method'. But its use did not end there. In spite of what
has been said to the contrary by Eliot's critics, exactly twenty
years later, hidden – or at least partly obscured behind an
impressive philosophical and musical structure – we can find, if
we look closely, almost the same discipline being practised by
Eliot in the composition of *Four Quartets*.

Eliot, of all the poets in the modern English literary tradition, is
perhaps the most conscious of what he is doing. The only major
poet with whom he might be compared, in this regard, is the
French Symbolist poet Paul Valéry. We are inclined, normally, to
think that there is a secret, or a mystery, in the making of a work
of art, of which even the artist himself is unaware. So, we are at
first perhaps somewhat surprised, and even shocked, to discover
that in the composition of *Four Quartets* Eliot practised to a
remarkable degree a *conscious*, secret discipline. But, as it happens, there is no reason for us to be surprised. In a volume of
selected papers by Paul Valéry, for which Eliot wrote an Introduction in 1958, we read of 'a totally new and modern conception of
the poet'.

> He is no longer the dishevelled madman who writes a whole
> poem in the course of one feverish night; he is a cool scientist,
> almost an algebraist, in the service of a subtle dreamer. . . . He
> will take care not to hurl on to paper everything whispered to
> him in fortunate moments by the Muse of Free Association. On
> the contrary, everything he has imagined, felt, dreamed, and
> planned will be passed through a sieve, weighed, filtered,
> subjected to *form*, and condensed as much as possible.[20]

Accordingly, to have been made aware, behind *Four Quartets*, of
the labours of 'a cool algebraist', does not necessarily mean that

we must now, as readers, completely erase from our memory the traditional image or idea of the poet as 'a subtle dreamer'. For the use of 'the mythical method' in *Four Quartets* is surely no less arcane, and no less memorable and impressive, for being *conscious*.

The reason why no serious attention has been given, before now, to the question of myth in *Four Quartets* is, I think, because Eliot's handling of the mythical method is much less obtrusive than it was in the earlier poem. What strikes one immediately when reading through *The Waste Land* is the effect of irony that has been achieved by the extremely subtle and deliberate juxtaposition of two distinct worlds. In the later sequence there is also – as I hope to indicate in this chapter and in the chapter which follows – a 'continuous parallel between contemporaneity and antiquity'. But when Eliot came to write *Four Quartets* he had no desire whatsoever to set over against the present age, and its horror, a romantically conceived image of the classical past. And for this reason his use of the mythical method in the poem takes a much more discreet form. The new absorbing surface music, together with the original rich vein of philosophical and religious thought, tend to carry the reader's attention from line to line and from point to point, so that there is hardly time left, as it were, to become conscious of what may also be happening beneath the surface.

Helen Gardner in *The Art of T. S. Eliot*, and Genesius Jones in *Approach to the Purpose*, both conclude that Eliot made no significant use of myth or mythic material in *Four Quartets*. 'The "thematic material" of the poem', writes Gardner, 'is not an idea or a myth.'[21] Accordingly, the poem in her view depends for its coherence *not*, as was the case in *The Waste Land*, on an *underlying myth* 'to which constant reference can be made', but rather on 'certain common symbols' and on an original and brilliantly devised *musical* form. Genesius Jones gives less emphasis to the musical and more to the *dogmatic* nature of *Four Quartets*. He believes that long before the composition of the poem 'Eliot had arrived at a dogmatic position which transcends myth; and that *Four Quartets* is an attempt to realize the perennial dogmas at once in their traditional and contemporary provenance'.[22] It would be unwise, obviously, to undervalue or to ignore the musical and dogmatic dimensions of Eliot's poem. But, at the risk perhaps of appearing to do just that, I intend in this chapter to concentrate almost all my attention on the use Eliot makes of myth and mythic material in *Four Quartets*.

During the composition of *The Waste Land* Eliot received particular aid, as we have seen, from the work of two authors, Sir James Frazer and Miss Jessie L. Weston, both of whom had given serious attention in their books to the question of primitive myth and ritual. Likewise, during the composition of *Four Quartets*, part of the plan and some of the incidental symbolism in the poem may have been suggested to Eliot by the work of two other authors also interested in the question of myth, G. Wilson Knight and Colin Still.

Wilson Knight, in his book *The Wheel of Fire: Interpretations of Shakespearian Tragedy*, talks at one stage about what he calls 'my reading of the Final Plays as mystical representations of a mystic vision'.[23] *The Wheel of Fire* appeared first in 1930. One year earlier its author had already published 'a first sketch' of his ideas in an essay entitled 'Myth and Miracle'.[24] He was not, however, the only critic intent on exploring this new terrain. In 1930 he wrote:

> Since the publication of my essay, my attention has been drawn to Mr Colin Still's remarkable book *Shakespeare's Mystery Play: A Study of The Tempest* (Cecil Palmer, 1921). Mr Still's interpretation of *The Tempest* is very similar to mine. His conclusions were reached by a detailed comparison of the play in its totality with other creatures of literature, myth and ritual throughout the ages; mine are reached solely through seeing *The Tempest* as the conclusion to the Shakespeare Progress. *The Tempest* is thus exactly located as a work of mystic insight with reference to the cross-axes of universal and Shakespearian vision.[25]

The task G. Wilson Knight and Colin Still undertook was obviously fraught with all kinds of difficulties and dangers – and not least the danger to which Eliot alluded more than once, in his criticism, of explaining away the genuine creative achievement of an author 'by literary or other influences . . . or by racial memories and myths of which he is unaware'.[26] And yet in spite of this danger Eliot did not hesitate to assert in an Introduction he composed for Wilson Knight's *The Wheel of Fire*:

> I do not think that Mr Wilson Knight himself, or Mr Colin Still in his interesting book on *The Tempest* called *Shakespeare's*

Mystery Play, has fallen into the error of presenting the work of Shakespeare as a series of mystical treatises in cryptogram, to be filed away once the cipher is read; poetry is poetry, and the surface is as marvellous as the core.[27]

In the remaining two sections of this present chapter I will be concerned with examining in detail the possible influence on *Four Quartets* of Colin Still and G. Wilson Knight. The evidence I intend to bring forward in support of my thesis is not, I think, unimpressive. But it does depend largely on the cumulative effect of a number of resemblances and comparisons, not one of which, perhaps, would be convincing or strong enough to stand on its own. I can hardly expect the reader, therefore, at least in the early stages of my presentation, to feel other than sceptical about what I have to say. But I would ask the reader, especially in these early stages, for his or her forbearance – until, as I trust will be the case, the effect of the evidence has begun to strengthen, by the gradual process of accumulation, and the hidden design or the underlying *mythical* pattern in *Four Quartets* has at last begun to show through.

B.   THE THEME OF DEATH AND REBIRTH: ELIOT AND G. WILSON KNIGHT

In his Introduction to G. Wilson Knight's *The Wheel of Fire: Interpretations of Shakespearian Tragedy* Eliot wrote: 'I believe that there is a good deal in the interpretation of Shakespeare by Mr Wilson Knight which can stand indefinitely for other people. . . . I confess that reading his essays seems to me to have enlarged by understanding of the Shakespeare pattern; which, after all, is quite the main thing'.[28] A few years later, in 1932, in an important and yet still to this day unpublished lecture 'Shakespeare as Poet and Dramatist', Eliot remarked in similar vein: 'Mr Wilson Knight has done a useful service in pointing out the importance of recurring symbolism in all the plays from Shakespeare's maturity, and especially in the later plays.'[29] Wilson Knight himself, in an interesting memoir published shortly after Eliot's death, has recorded for us the details of his early association with the poet, and Eliot's initial reaction to his work.

Now, when my own investigations were beginning, as in my essay 'The Poet and Immortality' in *The Shakespeare Review* of October, 1928, to assert the mystical properties of Shakespeare's last plays, I found . . . Eliot whose critical writings had been, or at least to me appeared, in opposition to mystical interpretations . . . strangely sympathetic. He received my 1929 brochure 'Myth and Miracle: on the Mystic Symbolism of Shakespeare' with a degree of approval.[30]

Apparently this 'degree of approval' was communicated during the course of a telephone call between Eliot and Wilson Knight sometime in the summer of 1929.[31] One year later Eliot wrote:

It happened, fortunately for myself, that when I read some of his [Wilson Knight's] papers I was mulling over some of the later plays, particularly *Pericles, Cymbeline,* and *The Winter's Tale;* and reading the later plays for the first time in my life as a separate group, I was impressed by what seemed to me important and very serious recurrences of mood and theme.[32]

(The papers mentioned include not merely 'Myth and Miracle' but also, very probably, Wilson Knight's first study of Shakespeare's last plays entitled *Thaisa.*[33]) '[T]he idea of the apparently dead found to be alive' is the theme Wilson Knight recognises as the theme common to the three plays *Pericles, Cymbeline* and *The Winter's Tale.*[34] And what is more he even goes so far as to state that the restoration or 'reviving' of Thaisa in *Pericles* is *one of the pinnacles of Shakespeare's art.* '[T]his scene and those of the restoration to *Pericles* of his long-lost daughter [Marina] and consort which follow, are alone sufficient to establish my thesis that the author is moved by vision, not fancy; is creating not merely entertainment, but myth in the Platonic sense.'[35] The 'paradisal radiance of *Pericles*' is due therefore, Wilson Knight believes, to Shakespeare's handling of the old plot or theme of loss and recovery, of death and rebirth. In *Pericles,* he says, 'some mystic apprehension of a life that conquers death has sprung to vivid form, as it were, spontaneously: a shaft of light penetrating into the very heart of death'.[36]

In a note added in 1965 to the monograph, Wilson Knight is not shy to point out,

The grand discovery of *Myth and Miracle* was this – that Shakespeare's autonomous poetry corroborates the death-conquest announced by Christianity. Probably few readers have deeply understood it since Mr T. S. Eliot, as he recorded when introducing *The Wheel of Fire*, found it – or he may have been referring to its unpublished predecessor, *Thaisa* – helpful.[37] [*sic*]

The poetry of 'Little Gidding' does not aim, for the most part, at affirming the reality of an unseen kingdom, or Paradise, where human beings may continue to live on after death. Its aim, rather, is to record, as Shakespeare does in his later plays, 'the poet's intuition of immortality and conquest within apparent death and failure'.[38] Eliot's vision in 'Little Gidding' of those who vanish and die, re-emerging in a new pattern here and now, does corroborate – it is true – the traditional Christian belief in the dogma of Resurrection. But it is, one has to admit, a rather unusual expression of it:

> We die with the dying:
> See, they depart, and we go with them.
> We are born with the dead:
> See, they return, and bring us with them.

The pattern that underlies this vision is the same pattern or theme of death and rebirth that we find in *Pericles*, *Cymbeline* and *The Winter's Tale*. Wilson Knight's 'primary intention' in pointing out this underlying pattern in the later plays of Shakespeare is not, he tells us, 'to insist on the truth of the immortality shadowed forth in these plays; but simply to indicate that they are of this mystic kind'.[39]

Today we hear from theologians that immortality is a matter of quality and value rather than something which can be measured by time. Canon Streeter asserts that its truth can only be expressed by myth or metaphor. Now the supreme value to man is always love. What more perfect form, then, could such a myth take than that of the restoration to Pericles of his Thaisa and Marina, so long and so mistakenly supposed lost? It is, indeed, noticeable that these plays do not aim at revealing a temporal survival of death: rather at the thought that death is a delusion. What was thought dead is in reality alive.[40]

By sheer good fortune the page from the scribbling pad on which Eliot jotted down his first rough notes for 'Little Gidding' has

been preserved. Reading it we can see at once how fundamental
from the beginning, in Eliot's overall plan, was the theme of
immortality or the theme of death and rebirth.

> They vanish, the individuals, and
> our feeling for them sinks into the
> flame which refines. They emerge
> in another pattern and recreated and
>   reconciled
> redeemed, having their meaning to-
> gether not apart, in a union
> which is of beams from the central
> fire. And the others with them
> contemporaneous.[41]

The Christian theme of the Resurrection finds here a perfect
counterpart. But again, as in *The Waste Land*, the underlying
patterns owes, I suspect, as much to the traditional literature of
secular and pagan mythology as it does to the Christian Gospels.[42]
Sometime before 'Little Gidding' was completed, Eliot composed
a Preface for an anthology entitled *The Testament of Immortality*.
This work includes 'testimonies from mystics, initiates, poets,
saints and philosophers' to whom, according to N. Gangulee, the
compiler of the anthology, 'death, although it appears to be the
end of all, is but the prelude to Eternal Life'.[43] Reading these
testimonies, the anonymous author assures us, 'our capacity for
spiritual apprehension is quickened and a process of further
illumination sets in. In our journey through the valley of death,
we then begin to see the pathways to "the Light of Lights".'[44] One
of the 'mystical' authors mentioned in the Introduction is Maurice
Maeterlinck. The single passage from Maeterlinck which is
included in the anthology is, I think, worth comparing with
certain parts of 'Little Gidding'. Here is a short extract from it:
'the dead and the living alike are but moments, hardly dissimilar,
of a single and infinite existence . . . they live in us even as we
die in them'.[45]

More than in any of the previous *Quartets*, the shadow of the
Second World War lies across the pages of the last *Quartet*. In it
we read of death by fire, by air, by water and by earth. There are
direct references made to the German bomber plane ('the dark
dove with the flickering tongue'), to 'epitaph' and 'tombstone';

and we come upon the words 'dead', 'dying' and 'death' no less than twenty times altogether! But in spite of this the poem is not in any sense a melancholy lament for the dead, or for the dying. It is in fact, of all the *Quartets*, perhaps the most lyrical and visionary, the poem of greatest comfort and illumination.

'Little Gidding' was not, however, as it happens, the first of Eliot's poems to be influenced by the Shakespearean critic. In 1930, the same year in which Eliot composed his Introduction to *The Wheel of Fire*, he wrote a short lyrical poem to which he gave the title *Marina*. The poem is today considered by many critics to embody Eliot's most beautiful and most sustained visionary statement. It takes the form of a monologue, spoken by King Pericles, at the precise instant of his own 'recognition', the moment, that is to say, when it begins to dawn on him that his own child and daughter Marina is not dead, after all, but has been restored to him.

Shortly after the poem was completed Eliot sent Wilson Knight a copy of *Marina* inscribed 'for' him, 'with, I hope, some appropriateness'.[46] The 'appropriateness' refers, presumably, to the fact that *Marina* is, to use Wilson Knight's own words, 'a perfect commentary on those Shakespearean meanings which I had unveiled'.[47] In the papers which Eliot read by Wilson Knight during the previous year, 1929, the Shakespearean critic had drawn particular attention to the 'recognition scene' in *Pericles*, the scene in which the King sees his daughter, Marina, whom he had for so long considered lost, being 'miraculously' restored to life.[48] Eliot in his John Ford essay of 1932 also discusses this theme at some length. '[W]e can hardly read the later plays [of Shakespeare] attentively', he writes, 'without admitting that the father-and-daughter theme was one of very deep symbolic value to him in his last productive years: Perdita, Marina and Miranda share some beauty of which his earlier heroines do not possess the secret.'[49] A few years later Eliot again refers explicitly to the mysterious event of Marina's recovery from seeming death. 'To my mind', he declares, 'the finest of all the "recognition scenes" is Act v, scene i of that very great play *Pericles*.'[50] In the same lecture he also remarked: 'To compare Perdita or Miranda or Imogen or Marina with, for instance, Juliet, to call them by comparison insipid or unreal, is to use a wholly irrelevant standard. They belong in a world from which some emotions have been purified away, so that others, ordinarily invisible, may be made apparent.'[51]

For his epigraph line to *Marina* Eliot chose the broken phrases spoken by Hercules when he awoke out of his sleep, and discovered to his great horror that he had murdered his own wife and children. 'Quis hic locus, quae regio, quae mundi plaga?' ('What place is this, what region, what quarter of the globe?' – Seneca's *Hercules Furens*, l. 1138). The bewildered phrases certainly record a moment of recognition, but it is one which is in complete contrast with the 'recognition scene' in *Pericles*. In a postscript to Eliot's letter accompanying the manuscript copy of *Marina* which he presented to Magdalene College, Cambridge, on 9 May 1930, we discover that this contrast is deliberate. 'I intend', the poet explained, 'a crisscross between Pericles finding alive, and Hercules finding dead – the two extremes of the recognition scene.'[52] Eliot's deep sense of horror at human death and at unnatural human vice has found expression in that brief, poignant allusion to *Hercules Furens*. But the feeling, or the emotion, does not end there. For, pulsing still, as it were, through the sinister brilliance of certain dark images and rhythms, at least something of the power of that emotion survives into the poem itself. But even these obsessive nightmare images are, one by one, quietly and miraculously dispelled. The feeling of death and of evil is gradually overcome; and all that remains for us and for 'King Pericles' is a new sense of grace and a new emotion of wonder.

What seas what shores what grey rocks and what islands
What water lapping the bow
And scent of pine and the woodthrush singing through the fog
What images return
O my daughter.

Those who sharpen the tooth of the dog, meaning
Death
Those who glitter with the glory of the hummingbird, meaning
Death
Those who sit in the sty of contentment, meaning
Death
Those who suffer the ecstasy of the animals, meaning
Death

Are become unsubstantial, reduced by a wind,
A breath of pine, and the woodsong fog
By this grace dissolved in place . . .

It is not merely the profound inner structure, or the core, but also, I think, the remarkable surface beauty of *Marina* – its cadences and its imagery – that line by line reveal to us the poem's central paradox or meaning. For the reason why the new life which is here intimated offers such grace and such promise is because its radiance is felt to have been crossed and re-crossed, but never of course extinguished, by the dark, transitory shadow of Death. Some of the elements underlined so far as being characteristic of the vision in *Marina* – the coalescence, for example, of the themes and imagery of death and rebirth – are also to be found repeated in the opening meditation of 'Little Gidding'. Thus, in the passage quoted above from *Marina*, there is a reference made to the death-state of 'Those who sit in the sty of contentment'. And likewise in 'Little Gidding', before we are permitted finally to arrive at the place of true illumination, we are advised to

> . . . leave the rough road
> And turn behind the pig-*sty* to the dull façade
> And the *tombstone*.
>> (Emphasis added.)

The experience of illumination itself takes place 'In the dark time of the year. Between melting and freezing'. And this first intimation of a new life is, we are told, experienced in a place where there is 'no earth smell / Or smell of living thing'. Here, as in *Marina*, we have a deliberate 'crisscross' between the poet coming to a place of death and at the same time to a place of rebirth – 'the two extremes of the recognition scene'. There is of course in 'Little Gidding' no image or symbol of a lost girl being brought back to life from seeming death. And yet, even here the surface vision and the underlying mythic pattern in both poems are, I think, rather similar. Eliot, in the All-Clear passage of 'Little Gidding', sees and recognises the ghost of 'some dead master' coming towards him. And in this event a kind of rebirth is obviously intimated:

> So I find words I never thought to speak
> In streets I never thought I should revisit
> When I left my body on a distant shore.

But the scene's overall visionary atmosphere is not, I have to admit, paradisal but rather purgatorial. There are, however, a small number of other passages in the poem which do, I think, bear close comparison with the resurrection imagery of *Marina*, and with Shakespeare's mystic symbolism in his play *Pericles*. Take for example this passage from the third section of 'Little Gidding':

> See, now they vanish,
> The faces and places, with the self which, as it could,
>   loved them,
> To become renewed, transfigured, in another pattern.

When, in one of his unpublished lectures in Shakespeare, Eliot was explaining why he admired so much the recognition scene in Act v, Scene i of 'that very great play *Pericles*', he remarked,

> It is a perfect example of the 'ultra-dramatic', a dramatic action of beings who are more than human. Shakespeare's consummate dramatic skill is as bright as ever; his verse is as much *speech* as ever; only, it is the speech of creatures who are more than human, or rather, seen in a light more than that of day.[53]

Significantly in his poem *Marina* Eliot prays that he also might attain to that speech which is 'more than human':

> . . . let me
> Resign my life for this life, my speech for that unspoken, . . .

And in the opening section of 'Little Gidding' he delivers what one can only call a short discourse on the true meaning of contemplation:

> . . . prayer is more
> Than an order of words, the conscious occupation
> Of the praying mind, or the sound of the voice praying.
> And what the dead had no speech for, when living,
> They can tell you, being dead: the communication
> Of the dead is tongued with fire beyond the language
>   of the living.

This passage is truly memorable. Not only does its statement emphasise once again the theme of death and rebirth, but also in its discussion of a 'spiritual language' it serves as a kind of gloss or commentary on the actual praying mind of the poet in his earlier lyric *Marina*. The 'more than human' Word which is received in 'Little Gidding' descends in the shape of a dove 'with flame of incandescent terror'. This flame is the flame of God's Holy Spirit – what Eliot calls elsewhere 'pentecostal fire', and it is recalled mysteriously (and horribly) again by the appearance and disappearance, over the streets of London, of the German bomber or fighter plane – 'the dark dove with the flickering tongue'.

Eliot may or may not have realised it at the time, but 'Little Gidding' fulfils in almost every way a dream, or prophecy, made by G. Wilson Knight in his book *Christian Renaissance*:

> Our future poetry must see our city streets tipped with that pentecostal flame, but those cities will for long be areas heavy with suffering, with darkness, illusion and death. These themselves must pulse with life; through these we must burn our way, in spite of these know our freedom, because of these create our hope.[54]

Christian Renaissance was composed in 1933 'in an attempt to harmonize Christian mythology and dogma with Renaissance poetry'. Wilson Knight recalls that when shortly after its publication he met with Eliot, the latter 'showed pleasure at my essay, wherein I had compared his poetry to Dante's and Shakespeare's. For many reasons I scarcely expected him to like the main book, though in an official, publisher's letter he said that he regarded it as important, and expressed no adverse opinion.'[55]

The theme of 'the Descent of the Holy Ghost' is, we are told by Eliot himself, intended to be *an undertone* throughout 'Little Gidding'.[56] In addition, therefore, to one or two other references, we can, I presume, accept that there is a direct allusion to the fire of the Holy Ghost in the phrase, 'the communication / Of the dead is tongued with fire beyond the language of the living'.

> I tell you the truth. [Christ, the Word, said to his disciples shortly before his death on the cross] It is to your advantage that I go away, for if I do not go away, the Counsellor [the Holy Ghost] will not come to you; but if I go I will send him to you. . . . I have yet many things to say to you, but you cannot bear them now. When the Spirit of truth comes, he will guide you into all the truth'.[57]

Seen from this perspective, the 'pentecostal fire' in the first movement of 'Little Gidding' is a symbol of the divine communication beyond death. And it is also, of course, as in *Marina*, a sign of the lost or the dead Word being mysteriously reborn and recreated.

C.   JOURNEY THROUGH DARKNESS INTO LIGHT: ELIOT AND COLIN STILL

Some years before the work of G. Wilson Knight appeared, Colin Still had sought to prove that beneath the surface of Shakespeare's last play, *The Tempest*, there is a single, consistent theme, seldom, if ever, acknowledged by readers and critics, namely 'the story of the upward struggle of the human spirit, individual or collective, out of the darkness of sin and error, into the light of wisdom and truth'.[58] This inner theme is, according to Still, one which is expressed in all authentic initiation rites, in ancient myth and popular legend. The purpose of his study, as he sees it, is

> to show that the inner theme of *The Tempest* is one which is expressed not merely in the pagan initiatory rites, but also in such works as Dante's *Divina Commedia*, Virgil's *Aeneid* VI, Milton's *Paradise Regained*, and Bunyan's *Pilgrim's Progess*; in such stories as the Wanderings of Israel and the Temptation of Christ in the Wilderness.[59]

Within *Four Quartets* there is no consistent narrative, and most of the ordinary connecting links one usually finds in epic verse – as, for instance, in *La Divina Commedia* – seem here deliberately to be suppressed. And yet, is it not the case that Eliot in *Four Quartets*, as Shakespeare in *The Tempest*, has composed a version of the one theme which has unfailingly appealed to the imagination of mankind in every age? In spite of many missing links in the chain, the isolated scenes and images throughout the work concentrate in the end into an intense impression of one man's long and difficult journey through darkness into light. This sense of unity has been achieved, almost certainly, by a conscious discipline on the part of Eliot. One senses throughout the poem that many of the 'subjective' scenes and images were somehow measured by the poet, during the process of composition, against an unseen model or criterion. In this way Eliot judged whether or not the images of his own personal experience corresponded closely enough to the objective, archetypal patterns of imagery that one finds repeated over and over again in the ancient myths. Furthermore, I am, as I have said earlier, persuaded that some of 'the incidental symbolism' in the poem was suggested to Eliot by the English critic Colin Still. Had Eliot never read Colin Still, the resemblances, which I now intend to point out, would be merely coincidental. But Eliot *had* read Still's 'interesting book on *The Tempest*' before 1930; and he took the trouble, at least once, to defend against possible misunderstanding its *mystical* approach to Shakespearean drama.[60] 'The genuine myth', in the view of Still, 'expresses some aspect of inward experience so truthfully and by means of figures that appeal so irresistibly to our instinctive sense of fitness, that it lives on unchanged from age to age.'[61] As a result 'the more a work of imaginative art approximates to myth, the more it has the sanction of the universal mind, not only for the things it says, but also for the manner in which it says them'.[62] Still talks at length about the temptations undergone by the Word in the wilderness. And Eliot's reference in 'Burnt Norton' to a similar drama may well have been, in part, prompted by Still's conviction that the image is, in fact, nothing less than a universal and archetypal symbol. 'The myth [of the Word in the wilderness]', he says, 'is true to the experience, actual or potential, of every man. It deals with that phase in the universal psychology of renunciation in which the aspirant, looking back, muses wistfully and not a little regretfully upon the pleasant things he has forsworn.'[63]

> The Word in the desert
> Is most attacked by voices of temptation,
> The crying shadow in the funeral dance,
> The loud lament of the disconsolate chimera.

Eliot's lines are preceded by a short account of the poet's next-to-impossible struggle with words. Here language itself is understood to bear, with the poet, the full burden of the Fall. Following immediately after the reference to 'the Word in the desert' and its temptations, there is evoked for us a moment of release and transcendence. The aspirant, or initiate, having confronted temptation in the wilderness, and struggled to overcome 'desire', is now able at last to rise above the fallen world of time, and to re-enter and regain, momentarily, the lost, innocent world of Paradise.

The account in the Gospel of Christ's temptation in the wilderness, and the account in *La Divina Commedia* of Dante's pilgrimage up the Mount of Purgatory to Eden, both employ, according to Colin Still,

> the same allegorical medium to express the same subjective experience – namely the rising of the consciousness above sensuous or passional things, the long wanderings in the lonely wilderness of speculation in quest of Truth, and the coming at last to that serenity of pure reason in which the voice of inspiration is heard.[64]

The underlying myth in both cases 'deals with a reversal of the process implied in the myth of the Fall'.[65]

The temptations that the aspirant must undergo can take a number of different forms. But, in almost every case, one can say that 'he is assailed by Desire, tempting him to abandon his quest'.[66] Sometimes the temptation takes the shape of an encounter with 'monstrous apparitions' or Sirens 'baleful and voracious creatures . . . hybrid in form'.[67] But in the case of the temptations in 'Burnt Norton', in spite of a certain suggestion of horror, one also receives a distinct impression that there is something sweet and alluring about the hybrid apparition. It is significant that in the first draft of this passage, Eliot originally spoke of 'the *sweet* disconsolate chimera'.[68] Colin Still, on the subject of the monstrous apparition in *The Tempest*, makes the following interesting observation: 'Like the mythical Sirens, the Strange Shapes in the Play make "gentle acts of salutation" to the accompaniment of "marvellous *sweet* music". They are monstrous and unnatural in form; yet they seem at the first encounter to be pleasing and attractive in their manners, a curious combination of qualities peculiar to the mythical Sirens.'[69] And he notes further: 'these Strange Shapes do not become fierce and violent . . . they only "dance with mocks and mows" '.[70] By placing the mythological image of 'The Word in the desert' alongside a description of his own private struggle as a modern poet, Eliot is obviously making significant use of 'the mythical method'. But here, as elsewhere in the *Quartets*, no irony is intended by this juxtaposition of the two worlds. Instead, what is realised is, I think, simply a new sense of depth and a new perspective.

There are within *Four Quartets* many other instances of Eliot's use of 'the mythical method'. Note, for example, in Section Two of 'The Dry Salvages', how the sudden, unexpected image out of the mythology of the Fall – 'The bitter apple and the bite in the apple' – adds a new depth of meaning to the river's 'cargo of dead negroes, cows and chicken coops'. And notice also in 'The Dry Salvages' the placing side by side of the ancient and modern worlds in Eliot's reference to the primeval River-God on the one hand, and on the other, to the Machine-God of modern industrial society; to 'the torn seine, / The shattered lobsterpot', and to certain 'hints of earlier and other creation'; to the need for wisdom in the mind of the ancient warrior and charioteer Arjuna, and to the same need for enlightenment among our contemporary tourists and travellers, in ships and in trains. That the origin of such wisdom is indeed transcendent is suggested by the use of a curious mythological device. A voice, we are informed, is heard high above the sound of the moving ocean:

> At nightfall, in the rigging and the aerial,
> Is a voice descanting (though not to the ear,
> The murmuring shell of time, and not in any language) . . .

When he was discussing the role of Ariel in relation to the travellers in *The Tempest*, Colin Still remarked that 'Ariel plays in the cosmetic allegory the part which is assigned in the Old Testament to the Angel of the Lord, in the New Testament to the Spirit, and in the pagan mythology to Hermes'.[71] Like Ariel, these 'all belong to the element of air; and, further, they all perform the same function'.[72] Hermes is reputed to be the patron of travellers, primarily because he 'descended from on high, and gave to Perseus the wings which enabled him to mount up into the air'.[73] Furthermore, the Holy Spirit, 'not only by its name, but also by the manner in which it is said to appear, is practically identified with the wind . . . those to whom it comes see tongues parting asunder, like as of fire'.[74] Still immediately then invites us to compare this appearance of the Spirit 'with the appearance of Ariel during the wreck as a fire that divides and burns in many places'.[75] Section Four of the last *Quartet* contains an image of the

Holy Spirit descending 'with flame of incandescent terror'. And this image or symbol may perhaps also have been chosen by Eliot for its great archetypal and universal significance as much as for its more immediate and more obviously restricted dogmatic Christian meaning.

During the composition of the second *Quartet*, Eliot conceived the notion of writing four poems based on the four elements. Fire is, of course, the dominant symbol in 'Little Gidding'. And water, earth and air, the dominant symbols in the first three *Quartets* respectively. Whether Eliot chose to adopt this schema merely for convenience sake, as many of his readers now seem to imagine, or whether he had some other more specific idea in his mind is difficult to say. It is interesting, however, to note in this context the small, yet I think significant, word *perhaps* which occurs in an observation Eliot made on the subject to Professor William Matchett: 'by the time that poem ['East Coker'] was finished I envisaged the whole work as having four parts which gradually began to assume, *perhaps* only for convenience sake, a relation to the four seasons and the four elements'.[76] Colin Still, in his book *The Timeless Theme* (1936), has pointed out that 'the impulse to describe the world within by analogy with the external world is universal and irresistible'.[77] The four external elements, air, earth, water and fire, have always been employed, he tells us, both by Christian and by non-Christian mystics in order to express the changing phases of spiritual and psychological experience, 'the main phases [that is] of actual experience during life' and also 'the main phases of the Soul's supposed experience after death'.[78]

In the Greek initiatory rites, according to Still, the journey that every initiate had to undergo was regarded as a progression, or an ascent, through the four elements, – a journey from an original lost Paradise (associated with the element of *air*), to a new heavenly Paradise (associated with the element of *fire*). Eliot, in *his* description of the journey from the place of air, 'Burnt Norton', to the place of fire, 'Little Gidding' does at times undoubtedly appear to make use of a similar language. So, is it not possible then that some of the authoritative magic and mystery of *Four Quartets* is simply due to the poem's dependence on this traditional language of initiation. Even the myth of 'the Word in the wilderness' is, we are told by Colin Still, itself a symbolic description of one part of the rite of initiation.[79] And likewise, 'the hearing by the ear of a distinctly speaking Voice that bears witness of the mystery which is not yet seen by the eye'[80] is also part of the same ritual process.

By making a journey back through all the elements the initiate is restored, according to pagan belief, to an original state of Paradise. But for Eliot, as a Christian believer, this journey cannot be undertaken without the aid of divine grace. Thus, in one of the typescript drafts for 'Little Gidding', Section Three, we find that the poet relates the theme of the four elements to the prayer *Anima Christi sanctifica me*.

> Soul of Christ, sanctify them,
> Body of Christ, let their bodies be good earth,
> Water from the side of Christ, wash them,
> Fire from the heart of Christ, incinerate them.[81]

The last clause concerning 'fire' Eliot added to the Latin hymn in order, obviously, to support his four-fold schema. And also, in the original manuscript draft, he drew a line connecting 'Soul of Christ' [Anima Christi] with the element of air.[82]

There were, according to Colin Still, two principal stages in the Greek rites of initiation: 'in the Lesser Initiation the candidate passed through Purgatory [a passage normally described as "a descent into Hell"]; in the Greater Initiation he was ritually represented as attaining to Paradise'.[83] When the candidate arrived at the end of his wanderings the hierophant, or high priest, threw open the doors of the temple. '[T]he entry of the neophyte into the brilliantly lighted temple from the gloom . . . where the Monstrous Shapes were encountered obviously expresses', writes Colin Still, 'that passage out of darkness into light which constitutes initiation.'[84] The timeless vision accorded to the initiate was first presented to him 'by means of magical evocation on the part of the hierophant'.[85] This consisted principally in a spoken discourse or 'oral transmission' wherein the candidate received 'some groundwork of teaching and preparation for what was to follow'.[86] The calm, authoritative voice which addresses us at the end of our journey in 'Little Gidding' strives likewise by the same 'magical evocation', to initiate us into a timeless vision:

> You are not here to verify,
> Instruct yourself, or inform curiosity

> Or carry report. You are here to kneel
> Where prayer has been valid.

Furthermore, we are advised to 'put off / Sense and notion'. (Philo, the Greek philosopher, when speaking of the stripping away of bodily passions from the Soul, remarks: 'that is why the High Priest will not enter the Holy of Holies in his sacred robe, but putting off the soul's tunic of opinion and imagery . . . will enter, stripped of all colours and sounds'.[87])

Central to Colin Still's thesis is the idea that whereas the Lesser Initiation was concerned with 'the winding paths of an intricate maze that signified our mortal life', and our constant effort at purification, 'the Greater Initiation was concerned with death and rebirth'.[88] Thus we read: 'in the ecstasy of this direct and full inward perception, the aspirant is temporarily dead to the external world. Hence the ritual ordeal of the Third Degree is a simulated death to represent the closing of the eyes to all things of this world which is a condition precedent to divine revelation.'[89] In the rites at Eleusis, this 'divine revelation', and the ordeals which preceded it, revolved around the myth of the disappearance and return (or the death and rebirth) of Persephone. In other words, the wanderings and searchings of the initiate – his descent first of all into Hell and then his resurrection into the light of Paradise, were for the most part a representation of an ancient myth. '[I]n the Eleusian rites', according to Still, 'the Wisdom [or 'the lost Word'] for which the aspirant goes in search was represented by the mythical Persephone.'[90] This ancient theme of death and rebirth was also, as I have already indicated in this chapter, the underlying theme in Eliot's final Quartet 'Little Gidding' and in his earlier mystical poem *Marina*. The chapel at Little Gidding, like the temple at Eleusis clearly represents for Eliot a privileged place of meeting between the living and the dead. It is 'the world's end', the place of meeting and of separation between the world of time and that of Eternity, between darkness and light, between death and rebirth.

By way of conclusion to this section, I have to acknowledge here that it would be a gross exaggeration to suggest that Eliot had deliberately contrived each one of the resemblances that have been noted so far. But it is by no means unlikely, I think, that in the process of composing *Four Quartets*, Eliot chose at times to test the reality and the expression of his own searchings and his own discoveries against the objective, archetypal model of the spiritual quest for the Word – a model which he found portrayed in the Greek rites of initiation, and in the later plays of Shakespeare. Significantly, in one of his unpublished lectures on Shakespeare, Eliot showed how well aware he was of the connection between the ancient language and liturgy of initiation and Shakespeare's mystical vision in *Pericles* of the 'death' and rebirth of the lost girl Marina: 'Pericles calls for "fresh garments" and "robes": The scene becomes a ritual; the poetic drama developed to its highest point turns back towards liturgy: and the scene could end in no other way than by the vision of Diana.'[91]

D.   THE QUESTION OF BELIEF

One reason – we may presume – why the poet of *Four Quartets* is so interested in the mystical symbolism of Shakespeare's later plays, is because this symbolism 'corroborates', in Wilson Knight's phrase, 'the death-conquest announced by Christianity'.[92] It affords Eliot a unique opportunity, therefore, as a Christian poet, of making his faith more fully real to the secular reader. And, at the same time, it enables him to avoid the obvious pitfall of propagandist verse. This is not to say, however, that simply by harmonising his faith, in 'Little Gidding', with 'the Shakespeare pattern' Eliot has finally solved the problem of belief; a problem which he admitted on one occasion, was 'very complicated and probably insoluble'.[93] But he has I think gone much further in the direction of a solution than any other modern poet of comparable stature.

There is perhaps no better way to begin thinking about the question of belief in *Four Quartets* than with a short statement of paradox which comes from Eliot himself. 'A good poet', he remarked to a French audience in May 1945, 'seems to me to cling closely to his beliefs and convictions, but to be simultaneously detached from them.'[94] To readers of *Four Quartets* who share Eliot's 'beliefs and convictions' it may seem obvious that the poem is rooted in a particular religious and dogmatic tradition. For them, and also, it would appear, for the poet himself, the myths of death and rebirth in 'Little Gidding' are not, in one sense, myths at all, but represent important aspects of revealed truth. They refer, in other words, on at least one level of their meaning, to the death and resurrection of Christ and of humanity. But it should be no less clear to the secular reader who does not share Eliot's beliefs and convictions that the author of *Four Quartets* has no 'palpable design' upon his readers. His intention is not to make them accept some dogmatic belief but to help them 'partake of a kind of experience that he has had'.[95] To that extent, at least, we can say that when Eliot is engaged in writing poetry he is fully justified in being 'detached' from his beliefs and convictions. His poetry – and the poetry of *Four Quartets*, no less than that of *The Waste Land* – is *not*, in spite of its dogmatic content, 'the assertion that something is true, but the making that truth more fully real to us; it is the creation of a sensuous embodiment'.[96]

Directly corresponding to the poet's close *identification* with his own beliefs and convictions, and to his rigorous *detachment* from them, there are in Eliot's opinion – or at least there should be – two successive movements in the reader's critical activity. An effort first of all of *identification* with the work; when, suspending if necessary his own disbelief, he tries to put himself 'in the position of a believer'.[97] And second, an effort of *detachment*, when he seeks to distance himself as much as possible so that he can 'regard the poem from outside the belief'.[98] The effort of detachment will, in practice, be more demanding for those readers who are in close sympathy with the Christian philosophy of the poet. Whereas for others who find this philosophy hard to accept, or uncongenial, the effort of identification will be more difficult. But both identification and detachment are possible; unless, obviously, in some rare case, the poet's particular religion, or his philosophy, appears to be untenable from any point of view.

> Otherwise, when two readers of equal intelligence and sensibility approach a great poem, the one from the starting point of belief in the philosophy of the author, and the other from the starting point of some different philosophy, they should tend towards a point, which they may never quite reach, at which their two appreciations correspond.[99]

In the end, what is I think impressive about *Four Quartets* is Eliot's sustained and intelligent awareness *as a poet* of the problem of belief, and the subtle method or strategy which he developed as a result – namely, the mythical method – in order to help those of his readers whose philosophy is different from this own to 'suspend their disbelief' and thereby make more swift the necessary effort of identification.

The major criticism levelled against *Four Quartets* in recent years is that *the images* Eliot uses to describe his searchings and discoveries – lacking the support of myth – 'are left to stand alone, or with such fragments of allusive reference as may chance to adhere to them'.[100] And, as for the poet's personal intellectual vision, it also, by being left without the protective covering of a myth, is reduced, we are told, to the bare bones of an *a priori* dogmatic vision. This criticism of *Four Quartets* is, however, I believe, valid only if certain individual passages are taken from their place in the poem, and are read and examined by the reader in isolation – as if they were no more than short, separate lyrics. But when these same passages are read *within* their own context in the poem, and when the poem itself has been read through slowly and carefully a number of times, one begins to be aware that the various scenes and images chosen by Eliot to represent his intenser human feelings are not at all as 'fragmentary in content' or as 'uncertain in their reference' as one had first supposed. On the contrary, as the different images are allowed by the reader to fall, one after the other, into his mind, they seem, mysteriously, to compose among themselves a kind of spontaneous pattern and order.

But how are we to explain this phenomenon? Eliot as a modern Symbolist poet has obviously not been able to rely on the device of an objective narrative or story, so to what point of reference, then, are his images related? What is it – setting aside altogether the poem's obvious philosophical core of meaning – that bestows upon them their mysterious unity? And how, finally, are we to account for the fact that these images and scenes of one man's unique, interior journey seem to find a place in our minds already shaped and prepared for them?

Apart from the simple, yet always mysterious, factor of Eliot's natural genius as a poet, the answer to this question lies, I believe, first of all, in Eliot's intuitive grasp of the significance of Sir James Frazer's work as 'a revelation of that vanished world of which our mind is a continuation'.[101] To the young Eliot, who took the trouble to read Frazer's work, and also to study a little in the fields of ethnology and modern depth psychology, the vast universe of primitive myth and ritual, which had for such a long time seemed quite remote from contemporary man's experience, was shown to be in direct continuity with the modern world. As early as 1923 Eliot noted the contribution made by psychology and ethnology, linking it with that of *The Golden Bough*. And almost thirty years later, when he had occasion to discuss the myth of Scylla and Charybdis, he remarked: 'The myth belongs to that Mediterranean world from which our culture springs; it refers to a well-known episode in Mediterranean pre-history; like other myths in the story of Ulysses it is what I believe Professor Jung would call a universal archetype of human experience.'[102]

The idea of the subconscious survival in the modern world of a mythology that can never be erased, and of themes and symbols which are always present, always abundant, was obviously of great potential significance for the modern poet. His reader may have no *conscious* knowledge, for example, of the Eleusian rites of initiation or of the mythical journey through darkness into light; but not far below the surface of the conscious mind there are, or there might well be, the poet now realises – archetypal figures corresponding to these basic myths and rituals, and they perform today much the same function they once did in the ancient world.

The images and symbols available to the modern poet are not then, after all, inevitably private and fragmentary, having only the most tenuous link with the imaginative world of his readers. For, contrary to what numerous critics have so far suggested, is it not, in fact, sometimes the case – whether by grace of a conscious or an unconscious discipline – that the images and the symbols, which emerge out of a given author's or artist's creative struggle, can mysteriously bear the deep impress of certain archetypal and mythical patterns? That this was the case in the later work of Shakespeare, G. Wilson Knight and Colin Still have argued persuasively. And what is more, we now know, or at least we have impressive evidence to suggest, that their arguments concerning the relationship between myth and mysticism in Shakespeare's work made a lasting and deep impression on Eliot.

12
Mysticism and Myth – II: The Dantean Parallel

My purpose has been to persuade the reader first of the importance of Dante as a master – I may even say, the master for a poet writing today in any language.

(T. S. Eliot, 'Preface' to *Dante*, 1929)

His was the true Dantescan voice.

(Ezra Pound, 'For T. S. E.', 1966)

Speaking about Dante in an address delivered at the Italian Institute, London, on 4 July 1950, Eliot remarked: 'I . . . regard his poetry as the most persistent and deepest influence upon my own verse'.[1] And again, later in the same talk, he declared:

Twenty years after writing *The Waste Land*, I wrote, in *Little Gidding*, a passage which is intended to be the nearest equivalent to a canto of the Inferno or the Purgatorio, in style as well as content, that I could achieve. The intention, of course, was the same as with my allusions to Dante in *The Waste Land*: to present to the mind of the reader a parallel, by means of contrast, between the Inferno and the Purgatorio, which Dante visited and a hallucinated scene after an air-raid.[2]

To me it appears unmistakable – yet apparently many readers want to have it otherwise – that what Eliot is talking about here is 'the mythical method'. It is true Eliot does not choose to quote nor even to adapt at length any clearly recognisable passage from Dante, as he did in *The Waste Land*. Yet here, as in the earlier poem, there is the same brilliant manipulation of 'a continuous

225

parallel between contemporaneity and antiquity'. But is this method restricted in its use to the All-Clear passage in 'Little Gidding'? Or does Eliot not perhaps strive, elsewhere in the poem, 'to present to the mind of the reader a parallel by means of contrast' between the mythic journey of Dante through the three states of Hell, Purgatory and Paradise, and his own dogged religious search for meaning in the modern world? Should the answer to this question be positive, how then are we to explain the almost complete silence of Eliot's readers and critics on the question of 'the mythical method' in *Four Quartets*, and in particular their silence on what I have chosen to call the Dantean parallel?

A.   ELIOT 'IN THE MIDDLE WAY'

On 29 June 1927 Eliot was formally received into the Church of England. Shortly afterwards, when the news of his conversion was made public, the largely negative response which it provoked was due, Eliot felt at the time, to a deep misunderstanding of his real situation. 'Most critics appear to think', he wrote, 'that my catholicism is merely an escape or an evasion, certainly a defeat. . . . But it [is] rather trying to be supposed to have settled oneself in an easy chair, when one has just begun a long journey afoot.'[3] To be able to sympathise here with Eliot one must know first of all something more about the nature of this 'long journey' to which he refers. The comment was made in a letter Eliot wrote on 3 August 1929 to his friend and fellow-Anglican Paul Elmer More. Earlier in that same year, in his essay 'Second Thoughts about Humanism', he had talked at length about other possible misunderstandings of the Christian position, and he managed in the process, to cast some light on the nature of the task or the journey to which he now felt himself committed as a Christian believer.

Most people suppose that some people, because they enjoy the luxury of Christian sentiments and the excitement of Christian ritual, swallow or pretend to swallow incredible dogma. For some the process is exactly opposite. Rational assent may arrive late, intellectual conviction may come slowly, but they come inevitably without violence to honesty and nature. To put the sentiments in order is a later, and an immensely difficult task: intellectual freedom is earlier and easier than complete spiritual freedom.[4]

No one, I am sure, would have agreed more with this last statement than the medieval Catholic poet Dante Alighieri. *The Divine Comedy*, although based on certain precise dogmatic convictions, is not primarily an exercise in religious propaganda, but is rather, at least on one level of meaning, an account of Dante's own remarkable struggle as a Christian 'to put [his] sentiments in order'. Much of the strength of Dante's poetry is founded on his resolve to undertake the long and arduous journey necessary to attain 'complete spiritual freedom'. His poetry is, therefore, first and last, a poetry of exploration – *not* a poetry of dogmatism. But can one make this statement with the same justification, or the same validity, about *Four Quartets*?

Professor Graham Hough, in his essay 'Vision and Doctrine in *Four Quartets*', draws a sharp line of division between the situation of Dante as a Christian poet and that of Eliot. On the one hand, 'Dante's system is a majestic and ordered belief; it was once the belief of our whole culture. It is part of the heritage of our civilization to be able to enter imaginatively into this system.'[5] In contrast, 'The Christian view of history, implied throughout the *Quartets*, no longer has the support of the dominant culture. The poem can no longer draw on that vast store of unquestioned assent. It must create out of its own resources a validation that to Dante was simply given.'[6] The sad result of this difference for Eliot is, according to Hough, that a great number of the poet's own contemporaries find it difficult, inevitably, to suspend their natural scepticism and disbelief when reading his work. 'There can be little doubt – simply as a matter of fact, whether it ought to be so or not – that the radical difficulty is doctrinal . . . [Eliot's] poem as a whole occupies a position of dogmatism.'[7]

Denis Donoghue, whom Graham Hough quotes in his article, also states that *Four Quartets* is 'a dogmatic poem in an age hostile to dogma'.[8] The evidence Donoghue brings forward in support of this theory is so cogently presented that one might well be excused for imagining that there is nothing further to be said on the matter. When, however, one returns to the poem itself one beings to sense that there is a level of meaning or 'a pattern' which has almost been overlooked. The most satisfactory way of describing this dimension is to quote a comment of Eliot's to William Force Stead which was remarkably prophetic of *Four Quartets*: 'between the usual subjects of poetry and "devotional" verse there is a very important field still very unexplored by modern poets – the experience of man in search of God, and trying to explain to himself his intenser human feelings in terms of the divine goal'.[9] The immediate subject of this poetry is not Christian dogma, not God, but *'man* in search of God.' The poet's aim is not so much to persuade others of his truth or of his dogma, but to explain first to *himself* and then, perhaps, afterwards to others, 'his intenser human *feelings* in terms of the divine goal'. Eliot's later poetry, like that of George Herbert and that of his chosen master Dante, is, I believe, a poetry of exploration in the sense that it strives to find words to express what he himself called once in a short article on Herbert 'the slow, sometimes almost despairing and always agonising toil of the proud and passionate man of the world towards spiritual life; a toil and agony which must always be the same, for the similar temperament, to the end of the world'.[10] Authentic knowledge about this journey can be found in no catechism of Christian doctrine; it is an experience or a wisdom known only to those who are already 'on the way', and already struggling to achieve some measure of spiritual freedom.

The theme of man's slow and difficult ascent towards God, or towards meaning, is one to which Eliot continued to devote his attention long after the composition of *Four Quartets*. In Act Two, for example, of his verse drama *The Cocktail Party*, we hear the following statement made by Julia Shuttlethwaite. Her immediate subject is the path of self-negation or mysticism chosen by Julia Coplestone:

> yes, she will go far. And we know where she is going.
> But what do we know of the terrors of the journey?
> You and I don't know the process by which the human is
> Transhumanised: what do we know
> Of the kind of suffering they must undergo
> On the way of illumination?[11]

Later in the third and final act of the play the obscure nature of Celia Coplestone's spiritual quest is again referred to, this time by Sir Henry Harcourt Reilly. 'Such experience', he states,

> can only be hinted at
> In myths and images. To speak about it
> We talk of darkness, labyrinths, Minotaur terrors.[12]

If this statement is true, and if, in fact, the spiritual quest can *only* be adequately described or 'hinted at in myths and images' – as in Dante's *Divine Comedy* or in Homer's *Odyssey* – then Eliot's set task within *Four Quartets* of 'trying to explain to himself his intenser human feelings in terms of the divine goal' is, as one or two critics have pointed out, doomed to an inevitable failure. For how can the modern religious poet presume to employ the language of myth, when such language has no meaning, apparently, for the age in which he is living? Eliot's answer to this problem in *Four Quartets* is, as we have already noted in Chapter Eleven, the use of 'the mythical method'. In 'East Coker', Section Two, for instance, the poet is seeking to present to the mind of his reader a kind of parallel between the difficulties of his own search for wisdom or meaning in the modern world, and the experience of Dante, the medieval Christian poet, who like himself in the middle of the journey of his life finds that he is lost 'in a dark wood'.

> In the middle, not only in the middle of the way
> But all the way, in a dark wood, in a bramble,
> On the edge of a grimpen, where is no secure foothold,
> And menaced by monsters, fancy lights,
> Risking enchantment.

Probably very few of Eliot's readers advert consciously to the use of mythical language in this passage – the language, that is, of 'darkness, labyrinths, Minotaur terrors'. Yet, for all that, the evocation of the mythical struggle has a profound impact, I believe, on the emotion of the reader. For far from being a mere superficial ornament, it serves to intensify the interior and exterior drama of the poet's journey. It brings to *Four Quartets* an almost magical sense of depth and perspective, a kind of under-pattern or a *design* – to use a word employed by Eliot in a different context – a 'design which reinforces and is one with the dramatic movement'. The result is, I believe, that when we have come to the end of *Four Quartets* it can be said with justice that this design 'has checked and accelerated the pulse of our emotion without our knowing it'.[13]

lay seem strange Eliot did not draw the attention of
is he did in *The Waste Land*, to this underlying
rn. But here in *Four Quartets*, as I have said before,
itended by the juxtaposition of the contemporary
world and its imagery with that of the classical or ancient world.
The effectiveness, therefore, of the mythical method does not
depend as it did in the earlier poem on the reader's conscious
acknowledgement of what the poet is attempting to achieve.
Furthermore, the fact that Eliot did not trouble to reveal his hand
fully in this case is not surprising, especially when one considers
his use of the Alcestis myth in his verse-drama *The Cocktail Party*.
Several years after the play had been performed Eliot openly
acknowledged that he had gone to the Greek dramatist,
Euripides, for his theme. '[B]ut', he tells us, 'I was determined to
do so merely as a point of departure and to conceal the origins so
well that nobody could identify them until I pointed them out
myself.'[14]

B.   THE JOURNEY TOWARDS SPIRITUAL FREEDOM

Dante Alighieri, in a famous letter to his friend and patron, Can
Grande, distinguishes four different levels of meaning in the
Divine Comedy: the literal, the allegorical, the moral and the
anagogical. Of these four levels the one nearest to the level of
meaning we have isolated so far within *Four Quartets* is the
anagogical. For Dante this term signified 'the passing of the
sanctified soul from the bondage of the corruption of this world to
the liberty of everlasting glory'.[15] Dame Helen Gardner was, I
believe, the first of Eliot's critics to try to relate this Dantean
method of commentary to *Four Quartets*. But for some reason she
speaks only of *three* levels of meaning, the literal, the moral and
the mystical. What she means by 'mystical' carries with it,
unfortunately, little or no suggestion of any parallel between
Eliot's search for meaning and Dante's mythical journey. It is
simply a term used to describe the poem's *dogmatic* aspect or
dimension.[16] And thus, the mysterious underlying pattern in *Four
Quartets* which directly connects the poem, by grace of the
mythical method, to Dante's *Divine Comedy*, has been almost
completely ignored.

Dante's passionate and purposeful journey of the mind to God is intimately related to and dependent on an ascetical schema which we know he took over from mystical authors and theologians such as Pseudo-Dionysius, Richard of St Victor and St Bernard of Clairvaux.[17] Eliot was himself reasonably well informed about this subject. He was aware, for example, of the *rapport* between the poetry of Dante and the ascetical teachings of Richard of St Victor, whose treatise *Benjamin Minor* treats of 'the operations and stages of the mind in its proceeding toward the beatific vision'.[18] As in the *Commedia* of Dante, so also in *Four Quartets*, one is reminded over and over again of the need to begin to work towards the ideal of complete spiritual freedom. The threefold plan or schema for purification which Eliot borrowed from St John of the Cross and to which he referred openly in 'East Coker', Section Three, maps out the territory to be explored. But the plan is not simply taken up by Eliot and enunciated as dogma. In fact what attracts the reader's attention first and last is not so much the ascetical schema itself, but rather the brilliant use which has been made by Eliot of this rather crude form of Scholastic scaffolding. Eliot may well have shared many of the same dogmatic convictions as St John of the Cross but what he is seeking to achieve in *Four Quartets* is *spiritual freedom*, and this demands first of all the voiding and purification of his own faith and hope and love.

(1) The Purification of Faith

Perhaps the most radical form that the purification of faith must take is detachment from thought. And that means, if you are a believer, detachment even from *theological* thought and knowledge.

> . . . there is yet faith
> But the faith and the love and the hope are all in the waiting.
> Wait without thought, for you are not ready for thought.

The 'agnosticism' which is here so urgently recommended is, of course, a vital aspect of the mystical tradition to which Eliot belonged, the tradition of St John of the Cross and of the author of *The Cloud of Unknowing*, of Pseudo-Dionysius and of Richard of St Victor. But Eliot's allegiance and the allegiance of *Four Quartets* to the way of Unknowing, or to the Negative Way, is not demonstrated merely by a few well-chosen quotations. The poems themselves, in their entirety, partake of the discipline of silence and of waiting. They are, in fact, as one commentator, Rowan Williams, succinctly puts it, 'an essay in apophatic statement'.[19] Eliot seems to want to avoid, if possible, making explicit allusions to Christian dogma. His faith in God is real, but like his 'hope' and his 'love' it is 'all in the waiting'.

> [O]nly East Coker [according to Williams] employs directly theistic language, and that with great reticence. The 'theology' of the Quartets is pre-eminently negative, apophatic . . . Little Gidding in particular attempts to mirror the silence of God in the world, and it is this reflected silence that makes the Quartets apophatic. The explicit statements about 'darkness' and destitution, and the more obvious allusions to the mystical writers who stress this element in spirituality, should indicate to us the quality of the whole sequence as a search for the silence *within* speech.[20]

For the mystic, or for the mystical author, the chief enemy of silence is distraction. And it is imperative, therefore, if he hopes through meditation and right action to attain to 'the silence within speech' that he is not deflected by distraction. He must, in fact, always and everywhere be on his guard against false knowledge and deceit.

> In the middle, not only in the middle of the way
> But all the way, . . .

It is not, I think, by accident that within *Four Quartets* our attention is drawn by Eliot to several different kinds of deceitful knowledge – all of them, it would seem, to be carefully and consciously avoided. There is, first of all, that illusion of insight which can sometimes occur under great emotional and spiritual pressure when, for example, instead of trying to accept and to face up to the realities of the past, one attempts to escape back into the garden of one's 'first world'. The fruits and the after-taste of this experience of ecstasy are quite often hollow and illusory. And so one has gradually to learn, the poet admonishes us, to be much more self-disciplined in thought and in imagination. 'You must go by a way wherein there is no ecstasy.'

By the same token we are exhorted, in 'Little Gidding', 'to put off sense and notion', and not to be so much concerned with external and superficial knowledge and information:

> You are not here to verify,
> Instruct yourself, or inform curiosity
> Or carry report.

Similarly in 'The Dry Salvages' many of the different forms of magical and superstituous knowledge which grow and develop out of 'men's curiosity' are, one by one, exposed by Eliot as mere 'pastimes and drugs and features of the press'.

The constant reference throughout Eliot's poem to aspects of our modern civilisation and society make it clear that *Four Quartets* is not a poem of mere devotional interest. But what has not, I think, been noted until now is that the very intensity and sharpness of Eliot's social criticism receives much of its impetus from the fact that he is himself engaged, throughout the poem, in an interior and private struggle for spiritual freedom. Thus, even as he is made aware of his own false ways of thinking and judging, and of his own particular distractions and temptations, he is at the same time gaining more insight into the source of the failure and foibles of his own contemporaries. This process – the interaction between the poet's own experience as he sets out on the path of asceticism and his vocation or role as a social and religious prophet – is one which is especially prominent in the second section of 'East Coker'. There the central subject is once again the problem of deceitful knowledge and wisdom. Eliot obviously believes that to accept that one does not know the way forward, and to undergo here and now the experience of the Dantean 'dark wood' is far better than to make believe one can rely always and everywhere on the few brittle insights gained from past experience. But also, side by side with a determination to confront whatever interior difficulties he may have to face on his own, we find in this same passage a lively and indeed almost a bitter public attack by Eliot on 'the quiet-voiced elders'. For Eliot, as for his master, Dante, before him, the ascetical schema is employed here not so much as an instrument for spiritual growth and exploration, but rather as a medium through which the poet is able to see more clearly and judge more honestly the actual world around him and the people within it.

(2)   The Purification of Hope

Eliot seems almost gladly to welcome what he calls, in 'Little
Gidding', 'the death of hope' i.e. the final disintegration of 'what
was believed in as the most reliable − / And therefore the fittest
for renunciation' ('Dry Salvages', Section Two). There are indicated in the poetry two different kinds of hope which must be
negated: first that of the individual person, and then that of
society in general. Thus 'the long looked forward to, / Long
hoped for calm', which many of us had perhaps been expecting to
experience as we grew older, is rejected out of hand by the poet
as a deceit and an illusion. All that we can expect now is 'bitter
tastelessness of shadow fruit / As body and soul begin to fall
asunder'.

The false hope of society in general on which Eliot focuses his
attention is the complacent idea, prevalent since the nineteenth
century, that somehow everything will be much better in the
future, and that we will all be able, in time, to escape from the
horrors of the past.

(3)   The Purification of Love

Human desire and human love are represented in *Four Quartets*
by the symbol of the rose. And the fire or the flame which burns
within the rose, and yet does not destroy it, is intended to
represent the purifying flame of God's love. But quite apart from
this use of symbolism throughout the poem, the theme of human
love is also openly and explicitly discussed by Eliot in the central
section of 'Little Gidding'. Here we can see more clearly than
anywhere else the interaction between the poet's attempt to
acquire spiritual freedom for himself through detachment 'from
self and from things and from persons', and his insight into the
need of his own contemporaries to be likewise detached and set
free. But by 'detachment' of course Eliot does not mean complete
indifference to the task at hand:

> . . . not less of love but expanding
> Of love beyond desire, and so liberation
> From the future as well as the past. Thus, love of a country
> Begins as attachment to our own field of action
> And comes to find that action of little importance
> Though never indifferent.

In a letter written to a friend in 1936, the year in which the first of the *Quartets* was published, Eliot explained in some detail his theology of detachment. The friend, Bonamy Dobrée, had objected strongly to the quotation from St John of the Cross which Eliot had placed as an epigraph to *Sweeney Agonistes*. The quotation read as follows: 'Hence the soul cannot be possessed of the divine union, until it has divested itself of the love of created beings.' Because Eliot's reply to his friend indicates something of his intellectual and spiritual attitude at this time, and indicates also the profound influence on him of the work of St John of the Cross, it deserves, I think, to be quoted here in full.

> The doctrine that in order to arrive at the love of God one must divest oneself of the love of created beings was thus expressed by St John of the Cross, you know: i.e. a man who was writing primarily not for you and me, but for people seriously engaged in pursuing the Way of Contemplation. It is only to be read in relation to that Way: i.e. merely to kill one's human affections will get one nowhere, it would be only to become rather more a completely living corpse than most people are. But the doctrine is fundamentally true, I believe. Or to put your belief in your own way, that only through the love of created beings can we approach the love of God, that I believe to be UNTRUE. Whether we mean by that domestic and friendly affections, or a more comprehensive love of the 'neighbour', of humanity in general. I don't think that ordinary human affections are capable of leading us to the love of God, but rather that the love of God is capable of informing, intensifying and elevating our human affections, which otherwise have little to distinguish them from the 'natural' affections of animals. Try looking at it from that end of the glass.[21]

In order to perceive the truth, as Eliot perceives it, one must first learn to pass through 'the looking glass' of his vision. And one obviously faces a similar challenge when one takes up the poetry of Dante, who is of course from one point of view, as Eliot himself admitted, 'about as thoroughgoing a didacticist as one could find'.[22] But there are differences, and they are due, I think, principally to the presence in the medieval poem of a secure narrative structure. Thus, instead of always presenting himself in the role of the didactic teacher, Dante can entrust – with ingenious tact and admirable subtlety – the responsibility for teaching in general, and the task of enunciating ascetical and mystical dogma in particular, to certain striking and memorable 'personages' within the drama itself, to St Bernard of Clairvaux, for example, and to Beatrice, to St Thomas Aquinas and to St Peter, and last but not least, to Virgil, the representative voice of human reason.

The use of fictional narrative as a literary device, and of fictional dialogue, is in general denied to the modern religious poet. He has no means, therefore, or at least so it would appear, of ingeniously disguising for the sake of his reader and for the sake of his poetry, the full weight of moral and dogmatic conviction. (One is reminded here, in passing, of the comment John Donne made about one of his own later verses: 'You know my uttermost when it was best, and even then I did best when I had least truth for my subjects. In this present case there is so much truth as it defeats all Poetry.')[23] One obvious way of coming to terms with this difficulty is to reduce the dogmatic content of the poem to a basic minimum. And, at one stage, we know, during the composition of 'The Dry Salvages', Eliot chose to alter a particular passage because he considered it rather too heavily loaded theologically.[24] But this solution, if one had recourse to it too often, would inevitably lead to an impoverishment of the poet's vision. So how then, in the case of *Four Quartets*, did Eliot succeed – if in fact he did succeed – in coming to terms with this problem?

A clue to the sort of solution Eliot devised in the end can be found in a comment he made as early as 1920: 'You cannot create a very large poem', he said, 'without introducing a more impersonal point of view, or splitting it up into various personalities.'[25] The poetry of *Four Quartets* is sometimes described as the poetry of a single voice. But it can, I think, and much more accurately, be described as a poetry containing many voices, each one of which expresses a new and different aspect of Eliot's composite vision. Some of these voices give tongue in a particular way to Eliot's dogmatic and orthodox point of view. But there are others – no less insistent – which betray the emotion of a man manifestly unsure both of himself and of the nature of the task he has undertaken, a man who has just begun a long and difficult journey, but who like Ulysses or like Dante is determined in spite of every risk and obstacle to continue to explore as far as he can beyond the frontiers of the spirit.

> And so each venture
> Is a new beginning, a raid on the inarticulate
> With shabby equipment always deteriorating
> In the general mess of imprecision of feeling,
> Undisciplined squads of emotion.

Eliot noted in his last paper on Dante:

> '*The Divine Comedy*' expresses everything in the way of emotion,
> between depravity's despair and the beatific vision, that man is
> capable of experiencing. It is therefore a constant reminder to
> the poet, of the obligation to explore, to find words for the
> inarticulate, to capture those feelings which people can hardly
> even feel, because they have no words for them.[26]

Although Eliot, unlike Dante, cannot redeem or tone down the
dogmatic element in his poem by entrusting it to a putative
speaker (to the poet Virgil, for instance, or to Beatrice) his poetry
is in the end, I would say, as much a poetry of exploration as that
of his Italian master. For whereas it is true we do hear, at times,
the confident voice of the teacher in *Four Quartets*, and the voice
of the Christian ascetic, and the calm voice of human reason, we
hear also the trembling, questioning voice of 'the wayfarer', and
the sceptical voice of the urbane modern philosopher, and the
voice of the confused and frightened human individual.[27] Almost
immediately following the harsh, unambiguous command in
'Burnt Norton' to descend down into the depths of one's own
being and there experience 'internal darkness' and deprivation,

> Desiccation of the world of sense,
> Evacuation of the world of fancy,
> Inoperancy of the world of spirit; . . .

we hear also, and perhaps at first to our surprise, a voice very
different in its cadence and its feeling:

> Will the sunflower turn to us, will the clematis
> Stray down, bend to us; tendril and spray
> Clutch and cling?
> Chill
> Fingers of yew be curled
> Down on us?

The palpable fear and uncertainty in this voice is answered at once by another voice, far more composed and serene.

> After the kingfisher's wing
> Has answered light to light, and is silent, the light is still
> At the still point of the turning world.

St John of the Cross, in his famous work, *The Spiritual Canticle*, also makes use of this pattern of question and answer in order to describe the different states and stages of the mystical journey: the sense of darkness and abandonment on the one hand, and on the other, the sense of sudden and deep understanding and illumination. But fascinating as the comparison may be with St John of the Cross's poem, a much more helpful comparison is, I suspect, the form of dialogue which takes place between Dante, the wayfarer, and his mentor and guide, the poet Virgil in *The Divine Comedy*.[28] Eliot, as we have said, has had to forego the advantage of a secure narrative structure. But he has succeeded in retaining at least something of the dynamic forward movement and sense of exploration one normally associates with Dante's poem. Those passages in which we seem to detect the dogmatic cadence are not always dull *a priori* discourses delivered as it were *ex cathedra* by the Christian poet to the 'Gentiles'. They are instead, for the most part, urgent messages spoken in an interior monologue by Eliot to Eliot himself, the main protagonist of the poem.

> So I assumed a double part, and cried
> And heard another's voice cry: 'What! are *you* here?'

At least one critic, D. W. Harding, has already, I am glad to say, described this meeting in 'Little Gidding' between Eliot and the ghost of 'some dead master' as 'the logical starting point of the whole poem'.[29] Harding was not thinking, as it happens, of the particular thesis or point of view I have been putting forward in these pages. But what has been said so far will undoubtedly serve to substantiate his claim, and serve also, I trust, to give substance to my own deep conviction that the ghostly conversation or dialogue between the two voices heard here in 'Little Gidding' and elsewhere in *Four Quartets*, is a rhetoric designed to coerce not only Eliot's readers to freedom, but also – and I think one can now say *positively* – Eliot himself.

C. VISIONARY IMAGINATION

The complex and original structure of Eliot's sensibility and the overall nature of his vision in *Four Quartets* are not easy to comprehend, even after long familiarity with his work. But, for an initial understanding of Eliot's visionary achievement, there is in my view no text or series of texts more illuminating than the Dante essays and reviews which Eliot himself composed at intervals during his career. In making this point I intend no disrespect to Professors Praz, Charity, Matthiessen, Moody, Hough, Ward and Higgins – all of whom in different ways have contributed substantially to the topic under consideration.[30] But, in general, with only one or two exceptions, these critics have been slow to acknowledge the accuracy and brilliance of Eliot's understanding of Dante's achievement. The use by the Italian of an allegorical method was one of the two principal factors which, according to Eliot, explain the superb clarity and simplicity of Dante's language and imagery. Thus he observed in 1929 that for a competent poet such as Dante 'allegory means clear visual images'.[31] Eliot's essay on Dante in which this statement occurs was described by Frank Kermode as 'one of the true masterpieces of modern criticism'. More recently, however, the apparent brilliance of Eliot's paper has come under close negative scrutiny. 'For all its virtues it is on occasion', writes A. C. Charity, 'disingenuous, misleading, muddled.'[32] Furthermore we are informed that Eliot 'consistently implies an undervaluation of what Dante owed, not to widespread "Latinity", but to the relatively esoteric traditions of vernacular love poetry in which he trained himself'.[33]

Eliot is instinctively enthusiastic, it is true, about Dante's Latin facility for 'clear visual images'. But is he in fact, inclined to undervalue and even sometimes to ignore the inner processes of Dante's vision and allegory? By way of support for this idea Charity quotes, with seeming approval, Mario Praz's theory that the production of such clear visual images was probably 'the principal influence of Dante's allegory on Eliot'.[34] And Charity also repeats a remark Praz made about the images in 'Ash-Wednesday': 'It is as if Eliot had been reading Dante without giving too much heed to the meaning, but letting himself be impressed by a few clear visual images.'[35] In Eliot's 1929 essay on Dante the poet does state at one point that allegory means clear visual images. But he is at pains also to underline the intimate connection between allegory and the Dantean gift for 'seeing visions', the latter being in his view a kind of 'psychological habit the trick of which we have forgotten'.[36] Eliot asks his reader therefore 'to clear his mind, if he can, of every prejudice against allegory, and to admit at least that it was not a device to enable the uninspired to write verses, but really a mental habit, which when raised to the point of genius can make a great poet as well as a great mystic or saint'.[37] So what then is one to say about the influence of Dante's allegory on Eliot? First of all, it is not so much the production of 'clear visual images', nor even, I have to say, the production of clear and distinct orthodox ideas, but rather the encouragement of a talent for vision in the strict sense of the word, and the impetus, therefore, to explore beyond the ordinary spectrum of human vision, which constitutes the principal influence of Dante's allegory on Eliot.

'Dante's is a *visual* imagination', Eliot noted in his 1929 paper on the Italian poet. 'It is a visual imagination in a different sense from that of a modern painter of still life: it is visual in the sense that he lived in an age when people still saw visions.'[38] Eliot returned to the subject of Dante's gift of vision in the final public talk he gave on his Italian Master in July 1950. One of the lessons, he said, 'one learns and goes on learning from Dante' is the lesson of *width of emotional range*.

> Perhaps it could be best expressed under the figure of the spectrum or of the gamut. Employing this figure, I may say that the great poet should not only perceive and distinguish more clearly than other men, the colours or sounds within the range of ordinary vision or hearing; he should perceive vibrations beyond the range of ordinary men, and be able to make men see and hear more at each end than they could ever see without his help.[39]

Judged by these criteria, Dante emerges as the poet of vision *par excellence*. Other mystical poets or poets of vision may indeed have recorded experiences just as far 'beyond the range of ordinary men', but none of them has kept such a firm hold at the same time on the immediate, visible world. It is this aspect of Dante's poetic genius we find emphasised by Eliot in 'Deux

Attitudes Mystiques: Dante et Donne'. The visible world around us, and also our everyday human emotions, are not negated or forgotten about by the visionary poet of the *Inferno* and the *Paradiso*. It is true, of course, that everything we see and experience now is somehow deepened and expanded through the alchemy of Dante's vision; but the old visible world that is familiar to us is never completely lost to sight. 'A new and wider and loftier world, such as that into which Dante will introduce you, must be built upon a solid foundation of the old tangible world; it will not descend like Jacob's ladder.'[40] Hence the importance and value in Dante's work of 'clear visual images'. But the production of these images – we should always remember – is related first and last to Dante's primary intention, which is to make the unseen or the spiritual visible. Much the same observation can, I think, be made about Eliot's vision of the universe in 'Burnt Norton'. For there, as in *The Divine Comedy*, the poet's vision has as its immediate and primary object

> . . . both a new world
> And the old made explicit, understood
> In the completion of its partial ecstasy,
> The resolution of its partial horror.

Unfortunately, the attainment of this vision, the complete exploration, that is, of the heights and depths of human emotion, is a task fraught with immense difficulty and danger because, as Eliot himself explains in the same passage of 'Burnt Norton', mankind finds it almost impossible to endure the vision of 'heaven and damnation'. For some reason Eliot's statements concerning the expansive and exploratory nature of Dante's vision in 'Deux Attitudes Mystiques: Dante et Donne' (1927), and in 'What Dante means to me' (1950), are passed over in silence by A. C. Charity. This is unfortunate, I think, because together with the 1929 paper on Dante and the review-article composed in 1920, these essays demonstrate just how securely, in fact, Eliot grasped the underlying meaning of Dante's allegorical method. He saw, first of all, that it provided the medieval poet with the scaffolding necessary to support and to express his vision. But this structure or scaffolding of myth is no longer available to the religious poet in a complete form. It is available only in virtue of that useful device or method known to the young author of *The Waste Land* and to the mature genius of *Four Quartets* as 'the mythical method'.

If one were forced to choose a phrase or a word to describe the distinctive quality of Eliot's poetic genius in *Four Quartets* one could not, I think, do better than to choose the word 'expansion' or 'expanding vision'. In 'Deux Attitudes Mystiques: Dante et Donne' Eliot describes the processes of Dante's vision, and that of his fellow poets in the Middle Ages, in terms of going 'beyond the ordinary frontiers of mind'.[41] And in the same essay he refers to the progress of the spirit in the meditative practice of Richard of St Victor, which leads to 'the vision of God'.[42] For Eliot the work of going 'beyond the ordinary frontiers of mind' is not a mere sophisticated literary endeavour. It reflects a spiritual discipline – an extension beyond our ordinary spiritual condition.

> This is the use of memory:
> For liberation – not less of love but *expanding*
> Of love beyond desire, and so liberation
> From the future as well as the past.
>   (Emphasis added.)

The word 'expansion' also appears in a number of Eliot's essays and lectures, and when it does, it is almost always employed as a key-word in the description of that kind of poetry of which he so manifestly approved, namely the poetry of the expansion of reality, or the poetry of vision. Again, in his 1927 essay, 'Deux Attitudes Mystiques', Eliot remarked: 'Among the poets who thus *extended* reality – and I will admit that they are those who interest me the most – I place Dante first absolutely, and Baudelaire first in recent times'.[43] Of Donne, Poe and Mallarmé, Eliot noted in an earlier essay: 'Their work was an *expansion* of their sensibility *beyond the limits of the normal world*, a discovery of new objects calculated to awaken new emotions.'[44] But this gift of vision was never for these poets simply a facility for escaping with a single leap from the real world into a realm of fantasy: 'they do not leap abruptly into a dream world; it is the real world which is enlarged by them and continued'.[45] In the opening section of the second *Quartet*, Eliot's initial evocation of the tiny Somerset village of East Coker is gradually expanded from what we call 'the real world' to become a haunted midnight world of hallucinated vision.

In that open field
If you do not come too close, if you do not come too close,
On a summer midnight, you can hear the music
Of the weak pipe and the little drum
And see them dancing around the bonfire . . .

Here, as so often in Eliot's work prior to *Four Quartets* – as A. D. Moody points out *à propos* of 'The Hollow Men' – the poet is 'following the very modes of Dante's sensibility, from the "simple, direct and even austere manner of speech", to the phantasmagoric and the visionary'.[46]

As it happens, there are also many other instances of this 'expansion of reality' in the *Quartets*. Take, for example, the opening of 'The Dry Salvages'. Eliot's tone is, to begin with, quite prosaic and straightforward.

I do not know much about gods; but I think that the river
Is a strong brown god – sullen, untamed and intractable, . . .

Within the space of no more than twenty lines, however, the voice of the speaker seems to change from being that of an urbane sceptic to being the thrilled voice of a kind of contemporary seer or visionary:

The river is within us, the sea is all about us; . . .

Likewise, in 'East Coker', Section Two, Eliot's vision expands suddenly from the humble, terrestrial world of 'snowdrops' and 'late roses' and 'hollyhocks' to encompass the vast planetary realms of 'the rolling stars'. And again, no less swiftly, at the close of 'East Coker', Section One, Eliot's mind moves from the midnight vision of ghostly dancers to an unexpected and yet profound intimation of another world:

Out at sea the dawn wind
Wrinkles and slides. I am here
Or there, or elsewhere. In my beginning.

In the concluding section of 'East Coker', in the strophe which begins 'Home is where one starts from', there is a similar movement of expansion. After an initial acceptance of the domestic atmosphere of 'the evening under lamplight / (The evening with the photograph album)', there is a sudden almost Ulyssian movement outwards towards an unknown world, far beyond the ordinary frontiers:

> The wave cry, the wind cry, the vast waters
> Of the petrel and the porpoise. In my end is my beginning.

D. THE STATES OF 'HEAVEN AND DAMNATION'

The composition of *Four Quartets* was an act of exploration. From start to finish Eliot strove to pass beyond the limited range of human vision and human communication, a major part of his objective throughout being, like that of Dante, to find a way to make the unseen and the spiritual visible. But can one say that Eliot succeeded in his task? The answer to this question depends a great deal, obviously, on the individual reader's ability to sympathise with the poet's point of view; or, at least, to suspend his or her disbelief long enough to allow the poetry to have its effect. '[P]icturing Paradise', Dante tells us, 'the sacred poem must make a leap like one that finds his path cut off. But he that considers the weighty theme or the mortal shoulder that is burdened with it will not blame it if it trembles beneath the load.'[47]

(1) Paradise: 'our first world'

Although it would be an exaggeration to describe *Four Quartets* as Eliot's *Paradiso*, both the starting point and the term of his journey are, in fact, described within the poem in terms of a Paradise myth. Thus at the close of 'Little Gidding' certain individual images combine so as to evoke or to recall the story of the loss and the recovery of an original heavenly state of innocence and happiness:

> . . . the end of all our exploring
> Will be to arrive where we started
> And know the place for the first time.
> Through the unknown, remembered gate

When the last of earth left to discover
Is that which was the beginning;
At the source of the longest river
The voice of the hidden waterfall
And the children in the apple-tree . . .

'The children in the apple-tree'. This image of an original innocence restored contrasts sharply with the reminder in 'East Coker'
of 'our and Adam's curse', and with that brief allusion Eliot made
in 'The Dry Salvages' to the first cause of man's fall from grace,
namely 'the bitter apple and the bite in the apple'. Furthermore,
the river of time which in 'The Dry Salvages' is seen to carry in its
spate the full burden of human suffering is, when it is tracked
down to its source, discovered to be the timeless river which
flows out of Eden. There are also in 'Burnt Norton' a number of
small verbal echoes from Dante's *Paradiso* worth noting. Compare, for example, the phrase,

And the pool was filled with water out of sunlight,
And the lotos rose, quietly, quietly,
The surface glittered *out of heart of light*,
And they were behind us reflected in the pool
(Emphasis added.)

with Dante's 'del cuor dell'una delle luci nuove' ['from the heart
of one of the new lights'] in *Paradiso*, XII 28.[48] And note also how
the effect of the repetition in Eliot's second line is reminiscent of a
similar effect in Dante's remarkable 'new vision' of the Heavenly
Company in Canto XXX of the *Paradiso*. There Dante sees first of all
a river of light 'pouring its splendour between two banks painted
with marvellous spring'. But then a sudden transformation takes
place. As the poet bends close to the water, the contour of the
river is changed into that of a round pool, and within the pool
Dante sees reflected the two courts of Paradise.

Si, soprastando al lume *intorno intorno*,
    vidi specchiarsi in piu di mille soglie
    quanto di noi lá su fatto ha ritorno.

[Rising up above the light *all around, all around* us, I saw in more
than a thousand tiers as many of us as have returned there
above.][49]

Eliot often expressed an enthusiasm for the last canto of the *Paradiso*: 'Nowhere in poetry', he delcared in 1929, 'has experience so remote from ordinary experience been expressed so concretely, by a masterly use of that imagery of *light* which is the form of certain types of mystical experience.'[50]

> Nel suo profondo vidi che s'interna
>   legato con amore in un volume,
>   ciò che per l'universo si squaderna;
> sustanzia ed accidenti, e lor costume,
>   quasi conflati insieme per tal modo,
>   che ciò ch'io dico è un semplice lume.

[Within its depths I saw ingathered, bound by one love in one mass, the scattered leaves of the universe: substance and accidents and their relations, as though together fused, so that what I speak of is one simple flame.][51]

The image chosen by Dante to represent this marvellous unity in diversity is that of a white rose, with myriads of angels descending upon it like bees 'their faces full of living flame'. And the image he uses to describe the necessary purifying process by which one comes in the end to behold the 'multifoliate rose' is the image of fire. Eliot takes these two images and unites them at the close of the poem in a single resonant line:

> All manner of thing shall be well
> When the tongues of flame are in-folded
> Into the crowned knot of fire
> *And the fire and the rose are one.*
>   (Emphasis added.)

The central section of 'Little Gidding' contains a passage which also brings to mind at once something of the atmosphere of Dante's *Paradiso*. There Eliot is meditating on the bitter political struggles which in the past so often divided England. But, in spite of this, his meditation is not itself agitated or even sorrowful. Indeed whatever the poet's motive for being so engaged in this act of historical memory, his immediate intention is clearly not a polemical one. For within the space of a few lines, he is able to communicate a vision of quite remarkable harmony and reconciliation.

> We cannot revive old factions
> We cannot restore old policies
> Or follow an antique drum.
> These men, and those who opposed them
> And those whom they opposed
> Accept the constitution of silence
> And are folded in a single party.

Again and again throughout *Four Quartets* Eliot rings the changes on this theme of the reconciliation of opposites and contraries. The theme emerges for the first time in that short beautiful lyric which opens the second movement of 'Burnt Norton':

> Garlic and sapphires in the mud
> Clot the bedded axle-tree.
> The trilling wire in the blood
> Sings below inveterate scars
> Appeasing long forgotten wars.
> The dance along the artery
> The circulation of the lymph
> Are figured in the drift of stars
> Ascend to summer in the tree
> We move above the moving tree
> In light upon the figured leaf
> And hear upon the sodden floor
> Below, the boarhound and the boar
> Pursue their pattern as before
> But reconciled among the stars.

The phrase 'in the light upon the *figured leaf*' recalls a short phrase from Tennyson's *In Memoriam* – a poem which Eliot very much admired. Tennyson, in the extremity of his grief for his dead friend, wistfully imagines an unfallen world, a dream-like, terrestrial Paradise in which Death is merely a kind of sleep for the soul; and in which there are somehow preserved forever all the 'silent traces of the past'.

> So then were nothing lost to man;
>   So that still garden of the souls
>   In many a *figured leaf* enrolls
> The total world since life began.[52]
>   (Emphasis added.)

It may be that the recognition of this source can help to guide us to an interpretation of Eliot's lyric, since in 'Burnt Norton' the poet is also concerned to evoke a kind of Paradise restored, a blissful state of being in which time and space are somehow transcended.

This paradisal element in Eliot's vision is further indicated by other small echoes from Dante's *Divine Comedy*. One may recall that in the twenty-second Canto of the *Paradiso*, the poet finds himself being lifted up, among the contemplatives, into 'the high wheel of the Fixed Stars'. Like the poet of 'Burnt Norton', Dante turns around in his ecstasy, 'wheeling with the Eternal Twins', and catches a glimpse far down beneath him of 'the little threshing floor that makes us so fierce'. However, in the composition of 'Burnt Norton', Eliot substitutes in place of Dante's beautiful image of 'the Eternal Twins' an image of 'the boarhound and the boar'.[53]

This change, and the change of the phrase '*threshing* floor', to '*sodden* floor', was almost certainly suggested to Eliot by two short stanzas from the work of quite a different author altogether, the Elizabethan poet George Chapman. Now Chapman was obviously not possessed of the same genius as Dante. But he was, at least in Eliot's judgment, a 'very great poet'.[54]

In Chapman we have a dramatist by accident, who was a poet and a man of thought as well as a scholar. Ideas and the sensibility of thought, meant more to Chapman than to any of his contemporary dramatists; he was much more an 'intellectual' than Ben Jonson, and in a way far more a mystic than any.[55]

Eliot was clearly drawn to Chapman, in part at least, because of the latter's complexity.

Chapman himself is mixed; his classical stoicism is crossed with a strain – perhaps out of Marsilio Ficino and similar writers – of otherworldiness; resulting, here and there in his tragedies, in a sense of double significance which gives him here and there a curious resemblance to Dostoevsky. The analysis and the embryology of this strange fusion of Roman stoicism – which had, undoubtedly, its mystical possibilities – with the diffused hermetic and 'Areopagitic' moods of the time would be an interesting and difficult problem. And how much did Chapman know about Machiavelli? It was a time when anything might join with anything else to produce strange and sometimes beautiful offspring.[56]

George Chapman's magpie gift for lifting out phrases and images from the work of other authors and incorporating them – very often, it seems, completely out of context – into his own original poetry, was a trait which also attracted Eliot's attention.[57] So one has little reason, therefore, to be shocked or in any way perplexed to find repeated in Eliot's lyric George Chapman's fine phrase, 'inveterate scars', and other small phrases from the Elizabethan. Here then is part of a translation by Chapman of one of Petrarch's *Seven Penitential Psalms*.

> . . . As clear as silver, seas shall roar,
>   Descending to that noisome sink
>   Where every hour *hell's horrid Boar*
> Lies plunged, and drown'd, and doth his
>   vomits drink.
>
> Raise, Lord, my sin's *inveterate scars*,
> And take thy new-built mansion up in me:
> Though power fails, see my will's sharp
>   *wars*,
> And let me please even while I anger thee.
>   Let the remembrance of my sin
>   With sighs all night *ascend* thine ear;
>   And when the *moving light* breaks in,
> Let health be seen, and all my skies be
>   clear.[58]
>
>   (Emphasis added.)

In both parts of the second movement of 'Burnt Norton', the much-desired resolution of the 'will's sharp wars' is not made, as in Chapman, the subject of pious devotion and private inter-cessory prayer. Instead, together with the longed-for vision of 'the moving light', it is understood to be something already now being achieved and achieved completely.

> . . . both a new world
> And the old made explicit, understood

> In the completion of its partial ecstasy,
> The resolution of its partial horror.

Notice that even here, at 'the still point' of his vision, Eliot is not so caught up into the blissful 'Paradise' of ecstasy that he forgets altogether about the horror or the 'Hell' which lies beneath him. The still point which he has attained, or would attain in 'Burnt Norton', is a point which includes, by resolving and completing both horror *and* ecstasy. And it is, moreover, a state of such freedom that in it the poet believes he has, at last, transcended the usual oscillation between these two extremes of human experience.

> The human mind [Eliot wrote in 1937] is perpetually driven between two desires, between two dreams each of which may be either a vision or a nightmare: the vision and nightmare of the material world, and the vision and nightmare of the immaterial. Each may be in turn, or for different minds, a refuge to which to fly, or a horror from which to escape. We desire and fear both sleep and waking: the day brings relief from the night, and the night brings relief from the day; we go to sleep as to death, and we wake as to damnation.[59]

(2)   Hell: 'the place of disaffection'

Belief in the future states of Heaven and Hell was for Eliot something absolutely fundamental to Christianity. But the states of 'heaven and damnation' to which he refers explicitly in 'Burnt Norton' are not descriptions of man's future condition after death. They are, instead, intended to represent those states of ecstasy and horror which at least a certain number of men and women can expect to enjoy and suffer even in this life. On the subject of Hell, Eliot wrote to Paul Elmer More on 10 August 1930:

> in this life one makes, now and then, important decisions; or at least allows circumstances to decide; and some of these decisions are such as have consequences for all the rest of our mortal life. Some people find themselves consequently in circumstances such that the whole of their mortal life *must* be a torment to them. And if there is no future life then Hell is, for such people, here and now.[60]

With this somewhat disturbing observation still fresh in our minds, let us turn our attention back now to the first *Quartet*.

> Here is a place of disaffection
> Time before and time after
> In a dim light: . . .

These lines introduce the poem's third section. Later in the same passage Eliot goes on to paint a vivid picture of people seen in the London City Underground:

> . . . the strained time-ridden faces
> Distracted from distraction by distraction
> Filled with fancies and empty of meaning
> Tumid apathy with no concentration . . .

Soon it becomes clear to us that what is being presented extends far beyond a mere empirical description of urban city life. For under the pressure of Eliot's vision we see the temporal image of the Underground merge gradually into an image of that place or state of torment which we call the state of 'eternal damnation'.

> Men and bits of paper, whirled by the cold wind
> That blows before and after time.

Although there is here no direct quotation from Dante's *Divine Comedy* the link between the contemporary world of London ('the torpid / Driven on the wind that sweeps the gloomy hills of London') and the haunting visionary world of Dante's *Inferno* becomes more insistent as the poem continues. One is reminded in particular of *Inferno*, Canto v, and of its terrible vision of the souls of the damned being borne and 'driven' on the winds of Hell. In his 1929 Dante essay, Eliot quoted the following phrase from Canto v: 'I saw the wailing shadows come, wailing, carried on the striving wind'.[61] And in the same essay, referring to an impressive comparison or simile in the Brunetto Latini episode (*Inferno*, Canto xv) he spoke of 'the crowd in Hell who peered' at Dante and his companion 'under a dim light'.[62] The fact that this short expression or phrase – 'under *a dim light*' – recurs also in the passage from 'Burnt Norton' we have been considering, is surely more than mere coincidence. For there the vision of damnation 'which flesh cannot endure' is somehow endured. And by the same token 'the partial horror' of urban city existence is resolved into the final horror of the *Inferno*. What Eliot remarked on one occasion about the work of Fyodor Dostoevsky can, I think, be applied also to Dante and to himself.

> If you examine some of Dostoevsky's most successful and most imaginative 'flights', you find them to be projections, continuations of the actual, the observed . . . Dostoevsky's point of departure is always a human brain in a human environment, and the 'aura' is simply the continuation of the quotidian experience of the brain in seldom explored extremities of torture. Because most people are too unconscious of their own suffering to suffer much, this continuation appears fantastic. But Dostoevsky begins with the real world as Beyle does; he only pursues the reality further in a certain direction.[63]

In the third movement of 'East Coker' Eliot demonstrates, as he did in 'Burnt Norton', and with no less disturbing authority, his bleak perception of damnation. He sees at the very edge of our contemporary political and industrial society the void of Hell itself. And, in his eyes, the darkness into which 'the statesmen and the rulers . . . Industrial lords and petty contractors' are now seen to enter, is nothing less than the darkness of an Apocalypse:

> . . . dark the Sun and Moon, and the Almanach de Gotha . . .

The phrase 'dark the Sun and Moon' recalls at once to mind the central theme in the short lyric which opens the poem's second section ('Scorpion fights against the Sun / Until the Sun and Moon go down'). But here one has the impression that the apocalyptic vision is not actually believed in by Eliot, but is merely entertained by him, as it were, for as long as the lyric lasts. In contrast, the vision of final desolation and death in the third section of 'East Coker' impresses one at once as being an *immanent* reality, and an *immediate* threat.

The visionary despair in Section Three of 'East Coker' leads, of course, in the end, to a vision of new hope and new illumination. The state of darkness is clearly, therefore, regarded by Eliot as being a necessary prelude to the experience of illumination: 'So the darkness shall be the light, and the stillness the dancing'. This is a point well worth underlining. For on numerous occasions the expression in *Four Quartets* of Eliot's almost obsessive sense of horror and loathing – what one might call the hate theme in the poem – has been attacked by readers and critics. It is, however, of some interest to note here in passing that several years before the composition of the *Quartets* Eliot composed what now seems, in retrospect, to have been a kind of prophetic *apologia* or defence of his poem. Writing in 1930 of Cyril Torneur's 'intense and unique and horrible vision of life' as portrayed in that 'isolated master-piece' *The Revenger's Tragedy*, Eliot observed that 'its motive is truly the death motive, for it is the loathing and horror of life itself'.[64] But he then goes on to say and without even the slightest scruple or hesitation: 'To have realized this motive so well is a triumph; for the hatred of life is an important phase – even, if you like, a mystical experience – in life itself.'[65] Later, in the following year, 1931, Eliot reiterates this theme in his essay on Pascal:

> His [Pascal's] despair, his disillusion, are, however, no illustration of personal weakness; they are perfectly objective, because they are essential moments in the progress of the intellectual soul; and for the type of Pascal they are the analogue of the drought, the dark night, which is an essential stage in the progress of the Christian mystic. . . . [Furthermore] our heart tells us that it [Pascal's despair] corresponds exactly to the facts and cannot be dismissed as mental disease . . . it was a despair which was a necessary prelude to, and element in, the joy of faith.[66]

If Eliot's visionary despair in 'East Coker', Section Three, is likewise to be regarded as a necessary prelude to, and element in, the joy of his faith, it must also surely be regarded as the expression of a deeply disturbed sensibility and as the revelation of a mind 'void with the utter vacuity of the knowledge of death'. G. Wilson Knight uses this phrase in his book *The Wheel of Fire* in order to describe 'the sick soul' of Hamlet, Prince of Denmark.[67] And there are other phrases, also descriptive of Hamlet's state of soul, in *The Wheel of Fire*, which can be applied equally well to Eliot's vision in 'East Coker'. Section Three of 'East Coker', in particular, reads like the soliloquy of a twentieth-century urban Hamlet. There is the same sense of horror expressed at the rottenness of the state and at its functionaries. Eliot talks, or

raves, after the manner of the Prince 'like one loosed out of Hell /
To speak of horrors'. His prayer in darkness,

> I said to my soul, be still, and let the dark come upon you
> Which shall be the darkness of God.

echoes, even while it changes, Hamlet's 'would the night were
come! / Till then sit still, my soul' (Act I, Scene iii). And of course
the phrase 'lost the motive of action' might well, we know, have
come straight from the 'affrighted' lips of Hamlet.[68] Woven into
the magnificent opening strophe of the third movement,

> O dark dark dark. They all go into the dark,
> The vacant interstellar spaces, the vacant into the vacant,

we find a deliberately discordant echo from Henry Vaughan's
Ascension Hymn ('They have all gone into the world of light'), and
also a number of echoes from John Milton's dramatic poem
Samson Agonistes:

> O dark, dark, dark, amid the blaze of noon,
> Irrecoverably dark, total eclipse
> Without all hope of day
>   .   .   .   .
> The sun to me is dark
> And silent as the moon,
> When she deserts the night
> Hid in her vacant interlunar cave.[69]

The only phrase not immediately inspired, it would seem, by
either Henry Vaughan or John Milton, is the modest, yet, I think
perfectly chosen, phrase, 'interstellar spaces'. A. D. Moody
suggests that 'Eliot was perhaps superimposing upon Milton's
image Pascal's "Le silence éternal de ces espaces infinis
m'effraie" '.[70] I am more inclined to think, however, that the
immediate source of Eliot's phrase is a passage from Wilson
Knight's *The Wheel of Fire*. (Eliot, we remember, composed an
Introduction to this work in 1930.) The passage which, I suspect,
may well have remained somewhere at the back of Eliot's mind
long after he read it, occurs in the book's second chapter, which is
entitled 'The Embassy of Death: An Essay on Hamlet'. Wilson

Knight is concerned in this chapter to speak about what he calls Hamlet's 'spiritual atrophy'. And on page 24 he expresses a judgement about the true meaning of Hell and Paradise; a judgement similar to that which was expressed by Eliot himself in his letter to Paul Elmer More on 10 August of the same year. Here then is the relevant passage from Wilson Knight's *The Wheel of Fire*:

> Between the sick soul and the knowledge of love are all the *interstellar spaces* that divide Hell from Heaven: for Hell and Heaven are but spatial embodiments of these two modes of the spirit.[71]

A final comment: the poet of *Four Quartets*, like the poet of *The Divine Comedy*, is a man on a journey, a man in search of God and meaning. His principal task as poet is, he believes, to be a pioneer of human consciousness, an explorer investigating those states of human awareness and feeling which exist at and beyond the ordinary frontiers of the spirit. And if, in the end, it can be said that Eliot, like his master Dante before him, has been able to attain to the two extreme poles of the emotional spectrum and come back to express for us in words his intenser feelings of horror and ecstasy, it is, I believe, in large part because of the unobtrusive yet almost continuous 'contrast and parallel' established in the poem between these two intense states of feeling and the great archetypal and mythological states of 'heaven and damnation'. In the final analysis 'Hell and Heaven are' for the poet of *Four Quartets*, 'but spatial embodiments of these two modes of the spirit'.[72]

Conclusion

Four Quartets is a poem which defies attempts at classification. It exhibits in turn the characteristics of music, meditation, occult literature, philosophy, mystical and visionary poetry, doctrine, lyric poetry, and all of these together. It remains first and foremost a poem – not a philosophical treatise, nor a prose passage of mystical theology – just as Eliot himself remains first and foremost a poet. So profoundly, however, has the poem been influenced by the mystical attitude of its author and by the poet's own astonishingly wide-ranging knowledge of mystical literature and philosophy that at times one can say: the mysticism, the philosophy and the music have become one thing. And – though it may be necessary at a moment of critical assimilation – it is no longer enough to separate analytically the music of his words from the philosophical and mystical vision which takes shape in their sound. The poem must be allowed to work its own immediate alchemy on the reader, and communicate its own disturbing vision and utterance in being recited, heard and turned over in memory. What the critic of music has to offer in the end – as Søren Kierkegaard remarked on one occasion concerning a work by Mozart – 'has a meaning only for those who have heard, and who keep on hearing. To such I may be able to give a suggestion here and there for renewed hearing.'[1]

(1) Mysticism of the Poem

In addition to quotations from the works of St John of the Cross and Julian of Norwich, from *The Cloud of Unknowing* and from the *Bhagavad-Gita*, Eliot has woven into the fabric of *Four Quartets* themes and symbols from a variety of Christian and non-Christian mystical sources. These themes and symbols, which include, for example, the search for enlightenment and the use of memory in meditation, the waiting in darkness on God and the ascetical journey, the voiding of the spiritual faculties and the yoga of disinterested action – to name but a few – are not always present in the work in the form of explicit and easily recognisable quotations. But they are manifestly present all the same, in certain complex metaphors, in patterns of thought, and even in the overall intellectual framework of the poem. Throughout *Four Quartets*, in fact, even if sometimes only implicitly, the passage from Eliot's theological vision to his poetry, and vice versa, is continuous.

Because of this rich complexity of vision the task undertaken in the present study of interpretation and elucidation has not always been an easy one. This does not mean, however, that the statement of the mystical experience within the poem is opaque or esoteric, 'a sort of cryptogram of a mysticism only visible to the initiate'.[2] The mysticism of *Four Quartets* is as much on the surface of the work (i.e. in the firmly textured music and imagery of the poem and in the immediate drama of the poem's structure) as in the subtle and rich play of allusion. And it is conveyed, therefore, in some degree, to every reader who can genuinely respond to the poem as a poem.

(2) Mysticism of the Poet

T. S. Eliot, it hardly needs to be said, was more a distinguished poet and a great man of letters than a great mystic. But 'the mystical impulse' in his temperament and make-up was, I think, far stronger and far more importunate than is generally acknowledged. Notes taken while he was still a student at Harvard University demonstrate a precociously strong interest in the subject of religious mysticism. And this interest, on the part of the young Eliot, as later on the part of the mature Christian poet, was by no means purely academic. Although one cannot with any justification classify Eliot as a mystic in the strict sense of the word, nor even perhaps as a visionary, the vision communicated in his poetry of the Timeless Moment is, I think, an authentic expression of a state of soul that one can only call mystical.

(3) Distinctive Character of Eliot's Mystical Attitude

One part of our task in this study has been to distinguish Eliot's mystical attitude from other forms and types of mysticism. *Four Quartets*, we have remarked from the beginning, unlike numerous

other mystical texts in the Western tradition, is not informed by
an intense, erotic-devotional atmosphere. The poem represents,
in fact, a conscious and deliberate correction by Eliot of the
unrestrained 'emotionalism' of the baroque mystical attitude and
sensibility. And it also represents an equally conscious and
purposeful rejection by the poet of the mystical attitude of Henri
Bergson. The experience of vision within *Four Quartets* is not
attained by a deliberate stripping of the mind of its rational modes
of thinking in order thereby to enter naked into the flow of
immediate experience. On the contrary, ecstatic or visionary
experience is almost always preceded by, and is even seen in
some way to be dependent on, a process of disciplined philosophical reflection and meditation.

In the assimilation of his poetry to music, Eliot's method and
intention, within *Four Quartets*, can be compared with the method
and intention of certain French Symbolist poets. But there is one
important difference to be noted. Eliot is not content simply to
create for himself, and for his reader, an arcane, dazzling and
lyrical *mysticism of nothingness*. His aim, or one of his aims within
the poem, is 'to state a vision' and a vision which includes the
articulate formulation of his own distinctive religious and mystical
attitude. Accordingly, Eliot's attention appears at times to shift
away from the poet's concern with the purification of language
and with the beauty of sound to the mystic's concern with
asceticism and with 'the purification of the motive'.

Within the Western tradition there are two distinct forms under
which Christian poets have been accustomed to conceive Divine
Reality. The first of these, the doctrine or the poetry of immanence, invited the believer to look outwards towards the material
universe that surrounds him, and through all his senses to
perceive in the power and beauty of Nature the immanent
presence of God. This doctrine of immanence is nowadays, of
course, associated in particular with the work of Gerard Manley
Hopkins. But it is the second form of Christian doctrine and
experience – namely that of Transcendence – which can be said to
characterise the poetic and mystical vision of *Four Quartets*. This
doctrine insists on an almost total separation of the human and
the divine, of the temporal and the eternal worlds. God, or the
Supreme Being, is thought of as being separated from our world
of multiplicity by an immeasurable distance. And thus the path of
the man who is in search of spiritual perfection, or in search of

God, must of necessity be a path of interior darkness and of determined self-denial, a journey 'inward and upward'.

(4) The Collocation of East and West

Although there are few direct or explicit allusions to Christian belief in 'Burnt Norton' the underlying philosophy of mysticism or mystical attitude is undoubtedly that of Christian neo-Platonism, the tradition mediated to Eliot through the works of St Augustine of Hippo, Pseudo-Dionysius, Richard and Hugh of St Victor, and St John of the Cross. In the West it is this intellectual and spiritual tradition which is nearest in character and in spirit to the great mystical traditions of the East; and this helps to explain how it was possible for Eliot, both as philosopher and as poet, to incorporate into the inner structure of *Four Quartets* so many echoes and traces of Hindu and Buddhist mysticism.

In spite, however, of this extraordinary eclectic instinct, and the positive acknowledgement of the spiritual depth of other religions which it implies, Eliot was not at heart a Universalist. Neither in his prose work, nor in the poetry directly influenced by the East, does Eliot suggest to his reader that it is a matter of indifference to which creed or religion or philosophy one adheres.

> I am aware [he remarked in 1951] . . . that there are readers who persuade themselves that there is an 'essence' in all religions which is the same, and that this essence can be conveniently distilled and preserved, while every particular religion is rejected. Such readers may perhaps be reminded that no man has ever climbed to the higher stages of the spiritual life, who has not been a believer in a particular religion or at least a particular philosophy.[3]

Side by side with this declaration, however, Eliot also noted in his 'Preface' to *Thoughts for Meditation: A Way to Recovery from Within* that contemplatives and mystics of different religions, creeds and civilisations, are very often 'saying the same thing'. And he expressed his regret that some Christian believers in the West 'perhaps under the prejudice that mysticism is something morbid or perverse, refuse to venture further than a narrow Christian tradition'.[4] By allowing his work to be directly influenced by the literature of mysticism, Eliot was pursuing something more fundamental than an intellectual or a literary tradition. *Four Quartets*, in fact, we now realise, was composed under the impulse of certain traditional methods of meditation, both Western and Eastern, and from these 'hidden sources' was provided with a basic discipline and a fundamental inner structure.

(5) Incarnation, 'the point of intersection'

During the period immediately preceding the composition of *Four Quartets* the subject of mysticism held a peculiarly strong fascination for Eliot. And yet, characteristically, he was at times almost as suspicious as he was fascinated. One of the points we have underlined in the present study is that this conflict in Eliot's mind concerning mysticism was still active during the composition of *Four Quartets*. Within 'Burnt Norton' Eliot's desire had been to raise himself as far as possible above the flux of time, through prolonged self-denial, calm meditation and the experience of ecstasy. But this initial mystical attitude did not remain Eliot's fundamental attitude throughout the rest of the *Quartets*. Already at the close of 'East Coker' and in the central section of 'The Dry Salvages' Eliot begins to question his own earlier understanding of the relationship between time and the Timeless. He is, however, careful not to reject outright as an illusion the experience of illumination itself. All that is required, he tells us, is that the original meaning we gave the experience be revised. The moments of illumination and the small experiences of ecstasy are no longer to be regarded in themselves as being capable of 'redeeming the time'. They are 'only hints and guesses'. The real contemplative task and the vocation, therefore, of the saint, is not to transcend or to escape from the horror and the burden of 'time past and time future', but rather 'to apprehend the point of intersection of the Timeless with time' – a task which cannot be fulfilled without the assistance of divine grace. This new awareness of the mystic's need for the grace of Incarnation, an awareness no doubt heightened by Eliot's reading at this time of Søren Kierkegaard, is the explanation for the increasing number of allusions to Christian dogma and belief in the later *Quartets*.

Of all Eliot's themes, the theme of the experience of illumination, although perhaps the most difficult to grasp, is the most striking and beautiful. At the close of 'The Dry Salvages' it is linked explicitly by Eliot to the theme of Incarnation, and this mysterious linking of 'the moments of happiness' with the Christian dogma is for many readers one of the poem's most impressive achievements. But within *Four Quartets* there is another mode or method employed by Eliot for comprehending through words the mystery and meaning of Incarnation, and of the two it is the second which is for Eliot perhaps the more fundamental: the terrible linking of Incarnation and Annunciation with the experience of immeasurable human dread, and with the fear of death itself, and with 'the moments of agony'. By using this unexpected and courageous strategy Eliot succeeds in giving *poetic* form to his theological thought and vision. He communicates, in other words, not merely an abstract understanding of his Christian dogma but also what it feels like in practice to believe in Incarnation.

(6) The Poetry of Exploration

If *Four Quartets* can be said to represent an attempt by Eliot to explore beyond the ordinary frontiers of human emotion and human consciousness, and 'to report of things unknown', the principal subject of this inquiry – strange though it may sound at first – is Eliot himself; or rather, to be more precise, those intenser states of consciousness and emotion which Eliot lived and worked through during his long and tireless search for meaning and for God.

As a religious poet and a modern poet of vision, Eliot was confronted by two major obstacles or temptations: first, the temptation to write a poetry which is illuminating and informative but, perhaps, 'rather too heavily loaded theologically'[5] – a poetry of moral and religious edification; and second, the temptation to write a poetry whose meaning is so private it is almost esoteric, but whose music holds us all the same because it sounds 'like statements made in our dreams'[6] – a poetry of pure sound and incantation. A major part of the inner life of *Four Quartets* is born of the struggle between these two alternatives. And so we should, perhaps, be grateful that in the end neither of the two succeeded in cancelling out the other. But it would be a mistake to approach *Four Quartets* exclusively in terms of these polarities, and to ignore completely the use by Eliot within the poem of 'the mythical method' which adds to the work an almost magical sense of depth and perspective, a sort of under-pattern. Here in

Four Quartets, as in *The Waste Land*, Eliot has learned how to practise a conscious, secret discipline, and has devised a hidden pattern of myth which acts throughout as a reconciler between the opposing demands of music and dogma, and helps to make possible, in the end, the poetry of exploration.

In order to lend greater significance and meaning to his own individual religious search within *Four Quartets*, Eliot has deliberately drawn upon related patterns of thought and experience in the fields of anthropology, mystical philosophy, occult literature, poetry and myth. It is particularly noteworthy that in his evocation of the two extremes states of horror and ecstasy, or of Hell and Paradise, we find many echoes and traces of other poets and authors, e.g. George Chapman, Alfred Lord Tennyson, John Milton, Shakespeare and Dante. But the feelings or the emotions Eliot expresses in the poem are always his own. He does not seek to glamorise his sense of 'partial ecstasy' or 'partial horror' by erroneously naming the experience mysticism or Carmelite asceticism. He may, it is true, and with an astonishing originality of vision, seek to exploit at times the points of similarity between the darkness of secular despair and the interior or mystical darkness of the *via negativa*. But his intention on these occasions is never to equate the mystical experience of self-emptying, or 'voiding', with his own private sense of loss and emptiness. Indeed, far from presenting the *via negativa* tradition as a mere mirror image of his own distress, Eliot sees it clearly as the path or the teaching which will lead him forward step by step out of the darkness into the light, out of the states of Hell and of Purgatory into the state of Paradise.

(7)   Between Two Worlds: Eliot and the Occult

In his exploration of the heights and depths of human consciousness and emotion, Eliot never loses his hold on the immediate, visible world around him. His point of departure is always 'a human brain in a human environment' – as the place-names in the titles of the individual *Quartets* indicate. It is an actual garden at Burnt Norton, therefore, which in his mind is expanded to become an image of the garden of Eden; and it is an actual station in the London City Underground which, under the pressure of his vision, becomes an image of damnation. As a poet of vision Eliot has tried – and with considerable success – to follow in the steps of his Italian master, Dante Alighieri. But his poetry of vision has also been directly inspired – or so at least it would appear from our study – by works of literature much nearer to hand. One thinks immediately of the obvious spectre in 'Little Gidding' of W. B. Yeats. But there are also, we have discovered, a number of previously unidentified and half-unidentified 'ghosts' haunting the *Quartets* as minor sources. These include a small number of Eliot's own contemporaries, for example, the poets Rudyard Kipling, Rupert Brooke and Charles Williams, the occult philosopher P. D. Ouspensky and the Belgian playwright Maurice Maeterlinck, who was himself a sort of theosophist. Eliot is attracted to these authors, it would seem, because in their writings they are possessed at times of a kind of second sight. They seem to know 'something of the things which are underneath and of the things which are beyond the frontier'.[7] And thus they are able, with an almost preternatural ease, to cross and re-cross the borderline that divides the visible from the invisible world.

In an essay which he composed in 1932 on Wordsworth and Coleridge, Eliot remarked that 'the great poet is, among other things, one who not merely restores a tradition which has been in abeyance, but one who in his poetry re-twines as many straying strands of tradition as possible'.[8] Within the context of mystical poetry and literature the tradition 'restored' by Eliot in *Four Quartets* is that of Christian Neo-Platonism. We are, perhaps, inclined nowadays to associate this tradition exclusively with mystics and theologians such as St John of the Cross and St Augustine of Hippo. But in the past, and particularly in the sixteenth century, this tradition also included among its followers many Christian thinkers and believers who, it must be said, were anything but orthodox. Take, for example, the scholar-magicians of the fifteenth and sixteenth centuries. These remarkable people allowed themselves to be influenced not merely by Christian mysticism but also by Hermeticism and by the Cabala. According to their way of thinking it seemed likely that the Wise Men, the magicians of antiquity, had been Christ's first disciples. And so they came to regard their own magic and occult philosophy as 'true Christianity, a Christianity which was the religion of eternity'.[9] Given Eliot's rejection of this sort of philosophy as 'often a mere gallimaufry of Plato, Aristotle, Plotinus and the medieval mystics and occultists',[10] it may come as something of a shock to us to discover that one of 'the straying strands' which he has woven into the pattern of *Four Quartets* is that of the occult.

How is this peculiarity to be explained? Is it perhaps the case that Eliot's public quarrel with the world of the occult, and with its most interesting modern representative, W. B. Yeats, is in some hidden and obscure way really a quarrel with himself and with his own distinctive religious sensibility? And are we to conclude, therefore, that certain impulses or energies, latent in the poet from the first but held under control for years by the vigilant exercise of his will, have at last been given some scope to work within *Four Quartets*? Whatever the answer to this question may be, and it is a question almost impossible to answer, it is certainly the case that by some circuitous route the occult world has found its way into the pages of *Four Quartets*. Whether the important influence is from actual occult sources or from quasi-occult sources, one thing is clear: Eliot has allowed his mystical attitude in the poem to be crossed by a strain of spirituality which we do not find in the work of orthodox Christian mystics. But Eliot has not, thereby, become an occultist or become heterodox. The authors to whom, on occasion, he looks for inspiration in his work may well be regarded as 'heretics' by the orthodox. But such authors, in Eliot's opinion, can sometimes possess 'an exceptionally acute perception, or profound insight, of some part of the truth'.[11] They may never, it is true, be listed by critics among the most important of Eliot's sources. But they are sources, all the same, and of such importance to Eliot that if, during the composition of *Four Quartets*, he had not been willing as a Christian poet to learn from the occult tradition, and from the writings of some of its 'more interesting heretics', he might never perhaps have composed a work of such unusual power and magic.

(8) 'At the source of the longest river'

'At what point in its course does the Mississippi become what the Mississippi *means*? It is both one and many. . . .'[12] This short phrase – 'both one and many' – which occurs here in Eliot's Introduction to *The Adventures of Huckleberry Finn*, was first used by the poet to describe 'the compound ghost' in 'Little Gidding', that 'familiar' yet 'unidentifiable' representative of the many sources behind his work, the many springs of his inspiration. But the sources of *Four Quartets*, when they are tracked down to their separate origins, are not of course the poem itself. They do not constitute the living current of the poem's meaning any more than the sources and confluents of the River Mississippi constitute the moving river itself.

In this study we have many times taken the trouble to travel back up-stream, as it were, to uncover some of the hidden mystical sources and springs of *Four Quartets*. But our intention has always been to return back quickly to the poem, and to stay close to its shores, to follow its loops and its bends, and to commit ourselves once again to its living current.

. . . the River itself has no beginning or end. In its beginning, it is not yet the River; in its end, it is no longer the River. What we call its headwaters is only a selection from among the innumerable sources which flow together to compose it.[13]

Notes

Notes to the Preface

1. T. S. Eliot, 'A Note of Introduction' to *In Parenthesis* by David Jones (London, 1961) p. viii.
2. T. S. Eliot, 'Dante' (1929) in *SE* (London, 1932) p. 277.
3. Goethe to Eckermann, 28 March, 1827. See *Goethe: Conversations and Encounters*, ed. and trans. by D. Luke and R. Pick (London, 1966) p. 155.

Notes to the Introduction

1. T. S. Eliot, 'The Mysticism of Blake', *Nation and Athenaeum*, XLI.24 (17 September 1927) p. 779.
2. Interview, 'Talking Freely: T. S. Eliot and Tom Greenwell', *Yorkshire Post* (Leeds), 29 August 1961, p. 3.
3. Words used originally by Eliot to describe the mystical talent of his friend Charles Williams. See 'Introduction' in *Charles Williams: All Hallows' Eve* (New York, 1984) p. xvii.
4. Quoted in B. A. Harries, 'The Rare Contact: a Correspondence between T. S. Eliot and P. E. More', *Theology*, 75 (1972) p. 144.
5. See 'Appendix I: Eliot's Reading in Mysticism (1908–14)' in Lyndall Gordon, *Eliot's Early Years* (Oxford, 1977) pp. 141–2. And see also Peter Ackroyd, *T. S. Eliot* (London, 1984) pp. 51–2.
6. Gordon, *Eliot's Early Years*, p. 15. Eliot's poem still remains unpublished.
7. Ibid., p. 53.
8. 'Although his Harvard reading notes mention both Dionysius and St John of the Cross – especially in the cards on James's *Varieties of Religious Experience* and Underhill's *Mysticism* – his interest in them', writes Eloise Knapp Hay, 'was plainly counterbalanced by scepticism and his readings on religious neuroses' (see her *T. S. Eliot's Negative Way* (London, 1982) pp. 156–7).
9. T. S. Eliot, 'Eeldrop and Appleplex I', *Little Review* (Chicago, Ill.), IV.1 (May 1917) p. 7.
10. Ibid., p. 7.

11. E. R. Dodds, *Missing Persons: An Autobiography* (Oxford, 1977) p. 40.
12. See Herbert Howarth, *Notes on Some Figures Behind T. S. Eliot* (London, 1965) pp. 272–7.
13. T. S. Eliot, '[A Review of] *A Defence of Idealism'*, *New Statesman*, ix.233 (22 September 1917) p. 596.
14. M. Sinclair, *A Defence of Idealism* (London, 1917) p. 273.
15. Ibid., p. 276.
16. T. S. Eliot, 'Orage: Memories', *New English Weekly*, vi.5 (15 November 1934) p. 100.
17. T. S. Eliot, 'A Commentary', *Criterion*, xiv.55 (January 1935) p. 261.
18. T. S. Eliot, 'An Emotional Unity', *Dial*, lxxxiv.2 (February 1928) p. 112. Eliot's review of von Hügel has been severely criticised by F. A. Burrell; see his 'English Catholic Mystics in Non-Catholic Circles III', *Downside Review*, xciv.316 (July 1976) p. 230.
19. Quoted in B. A. Harries, 'The Rare Contact', p. 144.
20. The phrase 'ecstasy of thought' occurs in *A Song for Simeon* (1928): 'Not for me the martyrdom, the ecstasy of thought and prayer, / Not for me the ultimate vision'. See *The Complete Poems and Plays of T. S. Eliot* (London, 1969) p. 105.
21. See T. S. Eliot, 'Mystic and Politician as Poet: Vaughan, Traherne, Marvell, Milton', *Listener*, iii.64 (2 April 1930) p. 590.
22. T. S. Eliot, 'Religion without Humanism', in Norman Foerster (ed.), *Humanism and America* (New York, 1930) p. 110. For more general and extended observations on the nature of mysticism see, by the present author, *The Mysticism Debate* (Chicago, 1977).
23. T. S. Eliot, 'The Author of "The Burning Babe" ', *Times Literary Supplement* (London), 1278 (29 July 1926) p. 508.
24. See Hay, *Eliot's Negative Way*, p. 99.
25. T. S. Eliot, 'Thinking in Verse: a Survey of Early Seventeenth-Century Poetry', *Listener*, iii.61 (12 March 1930) p. 443. Eliot acknowledges openly in *The Clark Lectures* (1926) the need for a deeper study of St Teresa of Avila. He would, in fact, like to be able 'to defend the memory of a great saint against calumny and degradation'. See Hay, *Eliot's Negative Way*, p. 99. Six years later, in February 1932, Eliot was prepared to speak out in defence of St John of the Cross. See Harries, 'The Rare Contact', p. 144.
26. T. S. Eliot, 'An Italian Critic on Donne and Crashaw', *Times Literary Supplement* (London), 1248 (17 December 1925) 878 (a review of *Secentismo e Marinismo in Inghilterra: John Donne, Richard Crashaw* by Mario Praz). The title of *The Clark Lectures* – 'On the Metaphysical Poetry of the Seventeenth Century, with special reference to Donne, Crashaw and Cowley' – further underlines the link with Mario Praz's book.
27. T. S. Eliot, *The Sacred Wood: Essays on Poetry and Criticism* (London, 1920) p. 170.
28. T. S. Eliot, 'The Silurist', *Dial*, lxxxiii.3 (September 1927) p. 259. (A review of *On the Poems of Henry Vaughan: Characteristics and Intimations* by Edmund Blunden.)
29. Eliot, 'Mystic and Politician as Poet', p. 590.

30. T. S. Eliot, 'Rhyme and Reason: the Poetry of John Donne', *Listener*, III.62 (19 March 1930) p. 503. It is unfortunately outside the scope of the present study to pursue in any great detail the development of Eliot's attitude to mysticism after the completion of *Four Quartets*. I would, however, like to recommend one short explanatory reflection, which touchs on the subject, and which reveals in Eliot a tension between his 'need for self-transcendence in love' and his religious mysticism. It is 'The Playwright's Late Revisions of the Poet's Vision' – a section in A. D. Moody's *Thomas Stearns Eliot: Poet* (Cambridge, 1979) pp. 268–85.

31. For a useful and interesting study of asceticism in Eliot's poetry and plays, see Hay, *Eliot's Negative Way*. Moody's *Thomas Stearns Eliot*, although it is not concerned exclusively or primarily with the question of Eliot's mysticism, makes a most valuable contribution to the subject. Fayek M. Ishak's *The Mystical Philosophy of T. S. Eliot* (New Haven, 1970), in spite of its rather promising title, is for the most part disappointing. Chapter Three of Staffan Bergsten's *Time and Eternity: A Study of the Structure and Symbolism of T. S. Eliot's Four Quartets* (Stockholm, 1960) deals directly with the question of the poem's mysticism. And also worth reading is William Johnston S.J., 'The Mysticism of T. S. Eliot', in *T. S. Eliot: A Tribute from Japan* (Tokyo, 1966) pp. 144–46.

32. *CFQ*, p. 30.

33. D. Daiches, 'T. S. Eliot', *Yale Review*, XXXVIII (1949) p. 460.

34. Flint's paper is included by Bernard Bergonzi in *T. S. Eliot, 'Four Quartets': A Selection of Critical Essays* (London, 1969) p. 107. The paper was originally published in the *Sewanee Review*, LVI.1 (1948).

35. Bergonzi, *T. S. Eliot, 'Four Quartets*, p. 17.

36. Ibid., pp. 19–20.

37. E.g. Denis Donoghue, 'T. S. Eliot's *Quartets*: a New Reading' (1965), in Bergonzi, *T. S. Eliot, 'Four Quartets*, pp. 212–36; Graham Hough, 'Vision and Doctrine in *Four Quartets*', *Critical Quarterly*, 15 (1973) pp. 107–27.

38. E.g. Peter G. Ellis, 'T. S. Eliot, F. H. Bradley and *Four Quartets*', *Research Studies: Washington State University*, 37 (June 1969) pp. 93–111; Elizabeth Drew, *T. S. Eliot: The Design of His Poetry* (New York, 1949).

39. Sister Mary Gerard, 'Eliot of the Circle and John of the Cross', *Thought*, 34 (Spring 1959) pp. 107–27.

40. Paul Kenneth Kramer, 'The Waiting Self: A Study of Eliot's 'Quartets' as Meditative Poetry' (1971), unpublished thesis, Temple University.

41. Interview, in Kristian Smidt, *Poetry and Belief in the Work of T. S. Eliot* (London, 1949) pp. 155–6.

42. R. Aldington, *Ezra Pound and T. S. Eliot* (Hurst, Berks, 1954) pp. 14, 17.

43. *Letters on Poetry from W. B. Yeats to Dorothy Wellesley* (London, 1964) p. 68.

44. W. B. Yeats, *Essays and Introductions* (New York, 1961) p. 522.

45. T. S. Eliot, 'Introduction', in *Ezra Pound: Selected Poems* (London, 1928) pp. x–xi.
46. *SE*, p. 346.
47. *PP*, p. 108, Eliot's statement here calls into question the common Romantic viewpoint as expressed, for example, in, 1759 by Edward Young. See his 'Conjectures on Original Composition', in E. D. Jones (ed.), *English Critical Essays* (London, 1975) pp. 270–311.
48. T. S. Eliot, 'Reflections on Contemporary Poetry', *The Egoist*, vi.3 (July 1919) p. 39.
49. H. Servotte, 'T. S. Eliot's *Four Quartets* and the Language of Mystics', in *Handelingen van het vier en dertigste Nederlands Filologencongres* (Amsterdam, 1976) p. 97.
50. Ibid., p. 96.
51. Ibid., p. 96.
52. K. Nott, *The Emperor's Clothes* (London, 1953) p. 112.
53. A. Schökel, *The Inspired Word* (London, 1965) p. 200.
54. On the subject of Dante's 'borrowings' Eliot remarked that in the *Vita Nuova* the Italian poet 'follows closely a form of vision which has a long history'. But this does not, Eliot argues, leave him open to the charge of being a 'fake': '[P]ossibly Dante, in his time and place, was following something more essential than merely a "literary" tradition.' See 'Dante' (1929) *Selected Essays*, p. 274.
55. T. S. Eliot, 'The Function of Criticism', *SE*, p. 33.
56. See T. S. Eliot, 'Introduction', in G. Wilson Knight, *The Wheel of Fire: Interpretations of Shakespearean Tragedy* (London, 1930) pp. xviii–xix.
57. S. Bergsten, 'Illusive Allusions: Some Reflections on the Critical Approach to the Poetry of T. S. Eliot', *Orbis Litterarum*, 14 (1959) p. 13.
58. Ibid., p. 13.
59. Ibid., p. 14.
60. Eliot, 'The Function of Criticism', p. 33.
61. B. Everett, 'A Visit to Burnt Norton', *Critical Quarterly*, 16 (1974) pp. 199–224.

Notes to Chapter 1: Mysticism and Music

1. T. S. Eliot, 'Conclusion', in *The Use of Poetry and the Use of Criticism* (London, 1933) p. 145.
2. Evelyn Underhill, *Mysticism* (London, 1930; first published 1911) p. 76.
3. Ibid., pp. 76–7.
4. Paul Valéry, *The Art of Poetry*, trans. Denise Folliot (New York, 1958) p. 43.
5. Quoted by A. Hartley in his 'Introduction' to the Penguin edition of *Mallarmé* (London, 1970) pp. xxii–xxiii.

6.   Valéry, *The Art of Poetry*, p. 42.
7.   Ibid., p. 41.
8.   See Stephen Spender, 'Remembering Eliot', in Allen Tate (ed.), *T. S. Eliot: The Man and His Work* (London, 1967) p. 54.
9.   See T. S. Eliot, 'The Music of Poetry' (1942) in *PP*, p. 36.
10. Helen Gardner, *The Art of T. S. Eliot* (London, 1949) p. 48.
11. Grover Smith, *T. S. Eliot's Poetry and Plays* (Chicago, 1968), p. 56.
12. Peter Milward, *A Commentary on T. S. Eliot's 'Four Quartets'* (Tokyo, 1968) p. 56.
13. T. S. Eliot, 'The Silurist', *Dial*, LXXXIII.3 (September 1927) pp. 259–60. (A review of *On the Poems of Henry Vaughan: Characteristics and Intimations* by Edmund Blunden.)
14. See Eliot, 'The Music of Poetry', p. 38.
15. H. Jaegar, *La Mystique Protestante et Anglicane* (Paris, 1965) p. 280. Translation by the author.
16. Ibid., p. 278.
17. Ibid., p. 278.
18. See T. S. Eliot, 'Introduction', in Valéry, *The Art of Poetry*, p. xiv. In the same passage we read: 'if the other arts may be thought of as yearning for duration, so Music may be thought of as yearning for the stillness of painting or sculpture'.
19. See T. S. Eliot, 'Poetry and Propaganda', in M. D. Zabel (ed.), *Literary Opinion in America* (New York, 1951) p. 105. Eliot's essay was originally published in 1930 in the *Bookman*.
20. Ibid., p. 105.
21. Edgar Allan Poe, 'Song-Writing', in *Edgar Allan Poe: Selected Writings* (London, 1967) p. 493.
22. T. S. Eliot, *The Sacred Wood: Essays on Poetry and Criticism* (London, 1920) p. 170.
23. Gardner, *The Art of T. S. Eliot*, p. 38.
24. See Paul Valéry, 'Spiritual Canticles', in *The Art of Poetry*, p. 282. Valéry's essay first appeared thirty years after he had read the works of St John. When in 1958 the essay, alongside other essays by Valéry, was made available to English-speaking readers, Eliot wrote an introduction to the collection.
25. Ibid., pp. 283–4.
26. Ibid., p. 283.

Notes to Chapter 2: The Philosophy of Stillness

1.   H. Servotte, 'T. S. Eliot's *Four Quartets* and the Language of Mystics', in *Handelingen van het vier en dertigste Nederlands Filologencongress* (Amsterdam, 1976) p. 96.
2.   T. S. Eliot, 'The Mysticism of Blake', *Nation and Athenaeum*, XLI.24 (September 1927) 779. (A review of six books by or about William Blake.)
3.   Weitz's article first appeared in *Sewanee Review*, LX.1 (1952). It is reprinted in B. Bergonzi (ed.), *T. S. Eliot, 'Four Quartets': A Selection of Critical Essays* (London, 1975) pp. 138–52.

4. The Clark Lectures were delivered by Eliot in Cambridge in 1926. A. D. Moody, who has had access to the unpublished manuscripts in the library of King's College, Cambridge, has not been slow to grasp their importance for a full understanding of the 'new form and style' of Eliot's later poetry. See A. D. Moody, *Thomas Stearns Eliot: Poet* (Cambridge, 1979) pp. 124–31.

5. T. S. Eliot, 'Deux Attitudes Mystiques: Dante et Donne', *Chroniques* (Paris), 3 (1927) p. 171 (Le Roseau d'or, p. 14). Translation by the author. The original French text reads as follows: 'En résumé j'ai chercher á poser le rapport entre la mystique de Richard de Saint-Victor et la poésie de Dante d'une part, et de l'autre, la mystique du seizième siècle et la poésie de John Donne.' This particular sentence is not included in Eliot's original Clark Lectures.

6. Ibid., p. 155. The version of the lecture which I have quoted in my text is taken from the original, unpublished *Clark Lectures* in King's College Library, Cambridge, Lecture 111, p. 8.

7. Ibid., p. 158 (*Clark Lectures*, Lecture 111, p. 12).

8. Ibid., pp. 157–8 (*Clark Lectures*, Lecture 111, p. 10).

9. Ibid., p. 154 (*Clark Lectures*, Lecture 111, p. 7).

10. See *The Works of Aristotle*, ed. and trans. W. D. Ross (London, 1928) vol. VIII: *Metaphysica*, book A.7, pp. 1072A and 1072B.

11. Ibid., p. 1072B. For an instructive commentary on this section in the *Metaphysica*, see G. E. R. Lloyd, *Aristotle: The Growth and Structure of His Thought* (Cambridge, 1968) pp. 142–7.

12. *The Works of Aristotle*, vol. VIII: *Metaphysica*, book A.7, p. 1072B.

13. Paul Valéry, *The Art of Poetry*, trans. Denise Folliot (New York, 1958) p. 284.

14. St John of the Cross, *The Dark Night of the Soul*, Book 11, ch. 18 and ch. 19.

15. John Hayward, note in T. S. Eliot, *Quatre Quatuors* (Paris, 1950) p. 133.

16. Jacques Maritain, *Art and Scholasticism*, trans. J. W. Evans (London, 1974; originally published in French in 1935) p. 68. Eliot quoted from *Art and Scholasticism* in March 1933. See his 'The Modern Mind' in *The Use of Poetry and the Use of Criticism* (London, 1933) p. 121.

17. See *SE*, p. 430.

18. Gustave Flaubert, *La Tentation de Saint Antoine*, with Introduction, Notes and Variations by Edouard Mayniad (Paris, 1954).

19. Ibid., p. 258. Translation by the author.

20. Ibid., p. 261.

21. See T. S. Eliot's review of *The Philosophy of Nietzsche* by A. Wolf in *International Journal of Ethics*, XXVI.3 (April 1916) p. 427.

22. See T. S. Eliot's review of *God: Being an Introduction to the Science of Metabiology* by Middleton Murray, in *Criterion*, IX.35 (January 1930) p. 335.

23. See Jacques Maritain, *Bergsonian Philosophy and Thomism* (New York, 1955). This book includes studies published from 1913 to 1954. Note especially pp. 176–8, 232–6, 289 and 293–4. See also T. E. Hulme, *Speculations: Essays on Humanism and the Philosophy of Art*, ed. G. Herbert (New York, 1924).
24. Wyndham Lewis, *Time and Western Man* (London, 1927) p. 166.
25. Ibid., p. 27.
26. See T. S. Eliot, *After Strange Gods: A Primer of Modern Heresy* (London, 1934) p. 43.
27. See W. A. Thorpe's review of *Time and Western Man* by Wyndham Lewis in *Criterion*, vii.1 (January 1928) pp. 70–3. Eliot referred years later to *Time and Western Man* in a Foreword he wrote introducing W. Lewis's *One-Way Song* (London, 1960) p. [8].
28. Thorpe, review of *Time and Western Man*, p. 70.
29. See Henri Bergson, 'The Perception of Change' (lectures given at the University of Oxford in 1911) in *The Creative Mind* (New York, 1946) p. 176.
30. Ibid., p. 176.
31. T. S. Eliot, 'A Commentary', *Criterion*, xii.46 (October 1932) p. 74.
32. T. S. Eliot, 'Deux Attitudes Mystiques', p. 154 (*Clark Lectures*, Lecture 111, p. 7).
33. Ibid., p. 154.
34. Pierre Auriol, *Commentarii in Primum Librum Senteniarum, Pars Prima* (Rome, 1596) p. 829. Quoted by George Poulet, 'The Metamorphoses of the Circle', in John Freccero (ed.), *Dante: A Collection of Critical Essays* (Englewood Cliffs, N.J., 1965) p. 154. The immediate source of Eliot's image of the *dance* around the 'still point' was a passage in Charles Williams's novel *The Greater Trumps* (London, 1932). See chapter 9, p. 171 of this book.
35. See G. Poulet, 'Metamorphoses', pp. 151–69.
36. See T. S. Eliot, 'Charybde et Scylla: Lourdeur et Frivolité', *Annales du Centre Universitaire Méditerranéen* (Nice) v (1951–2) pp. 78–9. Although, in this paragraph, I do not quote directly from 'Charybde et Scylla', my statements are at times little more than a rough translation, or a paraphrase, of part of Eliot's essay.
37. F. R. Leavis, 'T. S. Eliot's Later Poetry', in Hugh Kenner (ed.), *T. S. Eliot: A Collection of Critical Essays* (Englewood Cliffs, 1962) p. 111. Leavis's article was originally published in 1943.
38. Ibid., p. 111.
39. Ibid., p. 110.
40. Ibid., p. 111.
41. D. W. Harding, 'A Newly Created Concept', in B. Bergonzi (ed.), *T. S. Eliot, Four Quartets: A Selection of Critical Essays* (London, 1975) p. 30. Harding's article was first published in *Scrutiny* (1936).
42. See *Dionysius the Areopagite: The Divine Names and the Mystical Theology*, trans. by C. E. Rolt (London, 1920) p. 200.
43. See Eloise Knapp Hay, *T. S. Eliot's Negative Way* (London, 1982) p. 98.

44. Eliot also refers to the influence of Pseudo-Dionysius in his 'Clark Lectures'. See Hay, *T. S. Eliot's Negative Way*, p. 98.
45. Paul Elmer More, *Hellenistic Philosophies* (Princeton, N.J., 1923) p. 250.
46. T. S. Eliot, 'Paul Elmer More', *Princeton Alumni Weekly*, xxxviii.17 (5 February 1937) p. 373.
47. T. S. Eliot 'The Mysticism of Blake', *Nation and Athenaeum*, xli.24 (17 September 1927) p. 779.
48. H. C. White, *The Mysticism of William Blake* (Madison, 1927) p. 61.

Notes to Chapter 3: Eliot in Meditation

1. T. S. Eliot, 'Preface' in *Thoughts for Meditation: A Way to Recovery from Within*, selected and arranged by N. Gangulee (London, 1951) pp. 11–14.
2. Ibid., p. 12.
3. Ibid., p. 12.
4. See Stephen Spender, 'Remembering Eliot' in Allen Tate (ed.), *T. S. Eliot: The Man and His Work* (London, 1967) p. 59; Leon Edel, 'Abulia and the Journey the Lausanne', in *Stuff of Sleep and Dreams: Experiments in Literary Psychology* (London, 1982) pp. 182–6.
5. T. S. Eliot, 'Tradition and the Individual Talent', *The Sacred Wood*, p. 49.
6. See Chapter 2 for a discussion of this question; see pp. 28–9.
7. T. S. Eliot, 'Thinking in Verse: a Survey of Early Seventeenth-Century Poetry', *Listener*, iii.61 (12 March 1930) p. 443.
8. Louis Martz, *The Poetry of Meditation: A Study in English Religious Literature of the Seventeenth Century* (New Haven, Conn., 1971) pp. 1–2.
9. *Listener*, iii.63 (26 March 1930) pp. 552–3.
10. *Listener*, iii.64 (2 April 1930) pp. 590–1.
11. Martz, *The Poetry of Meditation*, p. 324.
12. One notable exception is Paul Kenneth Kramer's unpublished thesis, 'The Waiting Self: A Study of Eliot's Quartets as Meditative Poetry' (Temple University, 1971).
13. Martz, *The Poetry of Meditation*, p. 330. In 'The Music of Poetry', when discussing the inadequacy of the term 'lyric Poetry' Eliot concluded: 'I should prefer to say meditative verse' (*PP*, p. 33).
14. Martz, *The Poetry of Meditation*, p. 326.
15. Louis Martz, *The Paradise Within: Studies in Vaughan, Traherne and Milton* (New Haven, Conn., 1964) p. 33.
16. Ibid., p. 23.
17. Ibid., p. 25.
18. St. Augustine, *The Confessions*, trans. Sir Tobie Matthew (London, 1935) book xi, ch. 18.

19. Ibid., book x, ch. 23. There is a brief discussion of Eliot's relation to St Augustine in David Ward's *T. S. Eliot Between Two Worlds* (London, 1973) p. 230.

20. Kristian Smidt, *Poetry and Belief in the Work of T. S. Eliot* (London, 1961) p. 215.

21. Leonard Unger, 'The Rose Garden' in *T. S. Eliot: Moments and Patterns* (London, 1956) p. 80.

22. Philip Wheelwright, 'Eliot's Philosophical Themes', in B. Rajan (ed.), *T. S. Eliot: A Study of His Writing by Several Hands* (London, 1947) p. 99.

23. David Hirch, 'Eliot's Rose-garden: Illumination or Illusion?', *Christian Scholar's Review*, 4 (1975) p. 202.

24. See Derek Traversi, *T. S. Eliot: The Longer Poems* (London, 1976) p. 98.

25. Graham Hough, 'Vision and Doctrine in *Four Quartets*', *Critical Quarterly*, 15 (1973) pp. 117–19.

26. St Augustine, *Confessions*, book xi, ch. 7.

27. Ibid., book xi, ch. 11.

28. See T. S. Eliot, 'Second Thoughts about Humanism' (1929) *SE*, p. 491.

29. St Augustine, *Confessions*, book xi, ch. 11.

30. T. S. Eliot, 'A Dream within a Dream' (on Edgar Allan Poe) *Listener*, xxix.737 (25 January 1943) p. 243.

31. The quotation is from a description by Stephen Spender of the 'Angel' in Rilke's *Duino Elegies*. See Rainer Maria Rilke, *Duino Elegies*, trans. Stephen Spender and J. B. Leishman (New York, 1960) p. 102.

32. Philip H. Wickstead, *Dante and Aquinas* (London, 1913) pp. 237–8.

33. Dom Cuthbert Butler, *Western Mysticism* (New York, 1966) p. 34.

34. '[Mens mea] pervenit ad id quod est in ictu trepidantis aspectus' (St Augustine, *Confessions*, book vii, ch. 17).

35. Ibid., book ix, ch. 10.

36. See St François de Sales, *Introduction to the Devout Life*, trans. and ed. J. K. Ryan (New York, 1952) p. 61.

37. Helen Gardner, *The Art of T. S. Eliot* (London, 1949) p. 37.

Notes to Chapter 4: The Ascetic Vision

1. 'Mr T. S. Eliot's Confession', *Times Literary Supplement*, 14 September 1940. Quoted by B. Bergonzi in *T. S. Eliot, 'Four Quartets': A Selection of Critical Essays* (London, 1975) pp. 34–5.

2. F. R. Leavis, 'T. S. Eliot's Later Poetry', in Hugh Kenner (ed.), *T. S. Eliot: A Collection of Critical Essays* (Englewood Cliffs, 1962) pp. 110–24. The article was first published in *Scrutiny* xi.1 (Summer 1942).

3. Ibid., p. 124.

4. See F. R. Leavis, *The Living Principle: English as a Discipline of Thought* (London, 1975) pp. 155–264.
5. On the question of the *religious* aspect of Leavis's criticism, see R. P. Bilan, *The Literary Criticism of F. R. Leavis* (London, 1979) p. 301.
6. Leavis, *The Living Principle*.
7. Eric Neumann, *Art and Creative Unconscious* (Princeton, N.J., 1974) pp. 136–7.
8. See H. W. Haüsermann, '"East Coker" and *The Family Reunion*', *Life and Letters Today*, xlvii (1945) p. 35.
9. Ibid., p. 35.
10. See Lyndall Gordon, *Eliot's Early Years* (Oxford, 1977) p. 52.
11. T. S. Eliot, 'Blake', in *The Sacred Wood: Essays on Poetry and Criticism* (London, 1920) p. 157.
12. T. S. Eliot, 'What Dante Means To Me', in *To Criticize the Critic and Other Writings* (London, 1965) pp. 132, 126.
13. See *CFQ*, p. 187.
14. T. S. Eliot, 'Dante', in *SE*, p. 245.
15. T. S. Eliot, 'Tradition and the Individual Talent', *The Sacred Wood*, p. 55.
16. See Eliot, 'Dante', in *The Sacred Wood*, p. 166.
17. A. C. Charity, *Events and their After-life: The Dialectics of Christian Typology in the Bible and Dante* (Cambridge, 1966) p. 217.
18. Ibid., p. 221.
19. Ibid., p. 224.
20. Ibid., pp. 214–15.
21. See *CFQ*, p. 42.
22. Eliot, 'Dante', in *SE*, p. 274. Emphasis added.
23. T. S. Eliot, 'The Christian Concept of Education', in *Malvern: The Life of the Church and the Order of Society, being the Proceedings of the Archbishop of York's Conference* (1941) p. 207.
24. Samuel Taylor Coleridge, *Essays On Shakespeare and Some Other Old Poets and Dramatists* (London, Everyman Edition) p. 275.
25. Ibid., p. 287.
26. Ibid., p. 287.
27. Ibid., p. 287.
28. See Raymond Preston, 'T. S. Eliot as a Contemplative Poet', in Neville Braybrooke (ed.), *T. S. Eliot: A Symposium for his Seventieth Birthday* (London, 1958) p. 161.
29. T. S. Eliot, 'The Devotional Poets of the Seventeenth Century: Donne, Herbert, Crashaw', *Listener*, iii.63 (26 March 1930) p. 552.
30. Ibid., p. 552.
31. In his first draft of the corresponding lyric in 'Little Gidding', Eliot sought to draw on the new mythology of economics, the language of 'stocks and shares'. See *CFQ*, p. 215.
32. *Times Literary Supplement*, 1337 (15 September 1927) p. 620.
33. T. S. Eliot, 'A Note on Crashaw', in *For Lancelot Andrewes* (London, 1928) p. 96.
34. G. W. Williams (ed.), *The Complete Poetry of Richard Crashaw* (New York, 1972) p. 512.

35.   A. D. Moody, *Thomas Stearns Eliot: Poet* (Cambridge, 1979) pp. 218–19.
36.   See *CFQ*, p. 95.
37.   The lyric is quoted by the Spanish mystical theologian, Padre J. G. Arintero O.P., in the seventh and last volume of his *Cuestiones Misticas*. Alongside the text of the lyric, Arintero notes that the author was clearly suffering from 'the disease of love'. When Arintero's book was first published in 1916, it was well received in England. The seventh volume was subsequently translated and published as a separate book. See Arintero, *Stages in Prayer* (London, 1957) pp. 153–4.
38.   The phrase in quotation marks occurs in Section Three of 'Little Gidding'.
39.   A. Rudrum (ed.), *Henry Vaughan: The Complete Poems* (London, 1976) p. 142.
40.   This quotation from 'The Garland' and the quotation which follows in the text can be found in Rudrum (ed.), *Henry Vaughan*, pp. 255–6.
41.   Ibid., p. 204.
42.   See T. S. Eliot, 'The Post-Georgians', *Athenaeum*, 4641 (11 April 1919) p. 171.
43.   Thomas Merton, *The Sign of Jonas* (New York, 1956) p. 56.
44.   'I by T. S. Eliot', in Gustaf Aulén, Karl Barth *et al.*, *Revelation* (London, 1937) p. 1.
45.   Note also, for example, these lines which occur in *Choruses from 'The Rock'*, Part I (in *Complete Poems and Plays of T. S. Eliot* (London, 1969) p. 149). Here, the stark image of the desert, a traditional mystical symbol, is cleverly transported by Eliot into a modern secular context:

> The desert is not remote in southern tropics
> The desert is not only around the corner,
> The desert is squeezed in the tube-train next to you,
> The desert is in the heart of your brother.

46.   Lines from the poem 'God's Grandeur': see *Gerard Manley Hopkins: A Selection of his Poems and Prose* (Middlesex, 1963) p. 27.
47.   Lines from the poem 'A, a, a, Domine Deus': see 'David Jones: Special Issue', *Agenda*, v.1–3 (Spring–Summer 1967) p. 5.

Notes to Chapter 5: Mysticism and Incarnation

1.   See *CFQ*, p. 145.
2.   Graham Hough, 'Vision and Doctrine in *Four Quartets*', *Critical Quarterly*, 15 (1973) p. 113.

3. Ibid., p. 127.
4. Ibid., pp. 113–14; emphasis added.
5. Ibid., p. 127.
6. For further reflections on the distinction between the poetry of Immanence and Transcendence, see Helen C. White's *The Metaphysical Poets* (New York, 1956) pp. 22–5, 405–6.
7. *Poems of Gerard Manley Hopkins* (London, 1938) pp. 70–1.
8. Ibid., pp. 74–5.
9. Evelyn Underhill, *Mysticism* (London, 1911) p. 169.
10. St Augustine, *The Confessions*, book x, ch. 6, trans. R. S. Pine-Coffin (Middlesex, 1961) pp. 211–12.
11. Henri Bremond, *Prayer and Poetry*, trans. Algar Thorold (London, 1927) p. 90. Bremond's work was favourably commented upon by Eliot in his 'Conclusion' in *The Use of Poetry and the Use of Criticism* (London, 1933): 'That there is an analogy' he remarked, 'between mystical experience and some of the ways in which poetry is written I do not care to deny; and I think that the Abbé Brémond [*sic*] has observed very well the differences as well as the likenesses' (p. 144).
12. Ibid., p. 90.
13. Ibid., p. 95; emphasis added.
14. 'I by T. S. Eliot', in Gustaf Aulén, *et al.*, *Revelation* (London, 1937) p. 1.
15. Graham Hough, 'Vision and Doctrine in *Four Quartets*', *Critical Quarterly*, 15 (1973) p. 109.
16. Ibid., p. 110.
17. See 'Appendix I: Eliot's Reading in Mysticism (1908–14)', in Lyndall Gordon, *Eliot's Early Years* (Oxford, 1977) p. 141.
18. See CFQ, pp. 69–70
19. See, for example, R. W. Flint, '*Four Quartets* Reconsidered', in B. Bergonzi (ed.), *T. S. Eliot, 'Four Quartets': A Selection of Critical Essays* (London, 1969) p. 116; F. O. Matthiessen, 'Eliot's Quartets', *Kenyan Review*, v(1943) p. 171; Elizabeth Drew, *T. S. Eliot: The Design of his Poetry* (New York, 1949) p. 187.
20. Underhill, *Mysticism*, p. 118.
21. In Hopkins's early Journal we read for example: 'I do not think I have ever seen anything more beautiful than the bluebell I have been looking at. *I know the beauty of our Lord by it*' (*Notebooks*, 134, May 1870).
22. See Holograph Index Cards, the Houghton Library. This point is noted by Gordon in *Eliot's Early Years*, p. 63.
23. See T. S. Eliot, 'The Aims of Poetic Drama', *Adam*, xvii.200 (November 1949) p. 12; emphasis added.
24. Underhill, *Mysticism*, p. 120.

Notes to Chapter 6: The Influence of St John of the Cross

1. Lyndall Gordon, *Eliot's Early Years* (Oxford, 1977) p. 60.
2. See Eliot's letter to Sister Anne Cyril, S.N.D. The letter is quoted in a doctorate thesis by A. C. Delaney, 'Anagogical Mirrors: Reflections on the Poetry of T. S. Eliot and the Doctrine of St John of the Cross' (Boston, Mass., 1954) pp. 288–9.
3. T. S. Eliot, 'The Silurist', *Dial*, LXXXIII, 3 (September 1927) p. 260.
4. T. S. Eliot, 'Thinking in Verse', *The Listener*, III, 61 (12 March 1930) p. 443. Towards the end of his life Eliot became much more enthusiastic about St John as a poet. He remarked in 1961: 'I can't think of any mystic who was also a fine poet except St John of the Cross'. See the Interview 'Talking Freely: T. S. Eliot and Tom Greenwell', *Yorkshire Post* (29 August 1961) p. 3.
5. James Johnson Sweeney was the first critic to make the observation. See 'East Coker: a Reading', *Southern Review*, VI (1941) pp. 771–91 (reprinted in Bernard Bergonzi (ed.), *T. S. Eliot, 'Four Quartets': A Selection of Critical Essays* (London, 1969) pp. 36–57).
6. See Haüsermann , 'East Coker by T. S. Eliot', *English Studies*, XXIII.4 (August 1941) p. 109.
7. St John of the Cross, *The Ascent of Mount Carmel* in *The Complete Works of Saint John of the Cross*, ed. and trans. E. Allison Peers (Hertfordshire, 1974; first published 1935) book I, ch. 8, p. 59. Although Eliot was able to read some of St John's writings in Spanish, he depended to a great extent on the translation of the Saint's works by Professor Allison Peers. On this point, see Eliot's letter writen to Sister Anne Cyril and quoted in Delaney, 'Anagogical Mirrors', pp. 288–9.
8. See the letter Eliot wrote to More on 17 February 1932. The letter is quoted by B. A. Harries in 'The Rare Contact: a Correspondence between T. S. Eliot and P. E. More', *Theology*, 75 (1972) p. 144. For similar comments by Eliot on More's treatment of St John of the Cross in *The Catholic Faith*, see T. S. Eliot, 'Paul Elmer More', *Princeton Alumni Weekly*, XXXVIII.17 (5 February 1937) p. 373. And also, T. S. Eliot, 'An Anglican Platonist: the Conversion of Elmer More', *Times Literary Supplement* (London), 1865 (30 October 1937) p. 792.
9. Paul Elmer More, *The Catholic Faith* (Princeton, N.J., 1931) p. 264.
10. St John of the Cross, *Ascent*, book II, ch. 6, p. 82.
11. Ibid., book I, ch. 2, p. 19. Cf. book I, ch. 8, p. 59.
12. More, *The Catholic Faith*, pp. 268–9.
13. St John of the Cross, *Ascent*, book II, ch. 8, p. 109.
14. Later, in Chapter 12, pp. 231–5, I hope to demonstrate how Eliot makes use of St John's ascetical schema as a medium through which to sharpen his own perception of the actual world around him.
15. Eloise Knapp Hay, *Eliot's Negative Way* (London, 1982) p. 156.
16. Ibid., p. 155.

17. See St John of the Cross, *The Dark Night of the Soul*, book I, chs 1–16.
18. When St. John speaks of 'beginners', the term refers primarily to certain enclosed contemplatives of the Carmelite Order who have already begun to be led by the Lord in the way of perfection, and who are, as he tells us himself in his Prologue to *The Ascent* 'already detached from the temporal things of this world'.
19. Hay, *Eliot's Negative Way*, p. 174.
20. St John of the Cross, *Ascent*, book I, ch. 13, p. 59.
21. St John of the Cross, *Ascent*, book I, ch. 1, p. 17.
22. T. S. Eliot, 'Mystic and Politician as Poet: Vaughan, Traherne, Marvell and Milton', *Listener*, III.64 (2 April 1930) p. 590.
23. St John of the Cross, *Ascent*, book I, ch. 2, pp. 19–20.
24. Ibid., book I, ch. 4, p. 25.
25. Ibid., book II, ch. 7, p. 83.
26. Thomas Merton, 'Introduction', *Counsels of Light and Love of St John of the Cross* (London, 1953) pp. 10–11. The reference to *Living Flame of Love* is vol. III in Allison Peer's *Complete Works of St John of the Cross*.
27. St John of the Cross, *Ascent*, book I, ch. 4, p. 24.
28. Ibid., book I, ch. 4, p. 23.
29. Ibid., book I, ch. 3, p. 23.
30. Ibid., book I, ch. 1, p. 18.
31. Ibid., 'Argument', *Ascent*, book I, p. 10.
32. T. S. Eliot, 'Religion without Humanism', in Norman Foerster (ed.), *Humanism and America: Essays on the Outlook of Modern Civilization* (New York, 1930) p. 110. And see also Eliot's comments on St John's negative way which I quote in Chapter 12, p. 235.
33. The letter is quoted by B. A. Harries in 'The Rare Contact', p. 141.
34. Quoted in Delaney, 'Anagogical Mirrors', pp. 288–9, Eliot spoke in another place of possessing 'a Catholic cast of mind, a Calvinistic heritage, and a Puritan temperament'. See 'Goethe as the Sage' in *PP*, p. 209.

Notes to Chapter 7: Mysticism under Scrutiny: The Influence of Søren Kierkegaard

1. F. R. Leavis, *The Living Principle* (London, 1975) pp. 232, 235.
2. Ibid., p. 223.
3. See Hans Urs von Balthasar, *Prayer* (New York, 1967) p. 64.
4. C. A. Bodelsen, *T. S. Eliot's 'Four Quartets': A Commentary* (Copenhagen, 1966) p. 80.
5. A. D. Moody, *Thomas Stearns Eliot: Poet* (Cambridge, 1979) pp. 203–22.

6.   T. S. Eliot, *The Idea of a Christian Society and Other Writings* (London, 1982; first published 1939) p. 88.

7.   Moody, *Thomas Stearns Eliot*, p. 206. See also p. 220.

8.   Quoted by B. A. Harries, 'The Rare Contact: a Correspondence between T. S. Eliot and P. E. More', *Theology*, 75 (1972) p. 140.

9.   Ibid., p. 144. See also 'I by T. S. Eliot', in Gustaf Aulén *et al.*, *Revelation* (London, 1937) p. 1.

10. Harris, 'The Rare Contact', p. 140.

11. Ibid., p. 139.

12. See T. S. Eliot, 'Paul Elmer More', *Princeton Alumni Weekly*, xxxviii.17 (5 February 1937) p. 373.

13. See Ranjee Shahani, 'T. S. Eliot Answers Questions', *John O'London's Weekly* (London), lviii.1369 (19 August 1949) p. 498.

14. T. S. Gregory, a review of *Kierkegaard: His Life and Thought* by E. L. Allen, in *Criterion*, xv.59 (January 1936) pp. 306–7.

15. For example, *The Diary of a Seducer* (New York, 1932); *A Kierkegaard Anthology* (New York, 1936); *Selections* (Texas, 1923); *Philosophical Fragments* (Oxford, 1937). (Eliot's friend and fellow-Anglican Charles Williams penned an 'Introduction' to *The Present Age* and *Two Minor Ethico-Religious Treatises* by Kierkegaard in 1940. One of these minor treatises is subtitled *The Posthumous Papers of a Solitary Individual: A Poetic Experiment*. In a modest 'Preface' to the two treatises, Kierkegaard states that they 'will no doubt, only be of essential interest to theologians'.)

16. See the T. S. Eliot Collection of the University of Texas at Austin (1975), compiled by A. Sackton. See G.309 (letter).

17. Rayner Heppenstall, review of *Purify Your Hearts* by Søren Kierkegaard, *Criterion*, xviii.70 (October 1938) pp. 107–11.

18. T. S. Eliot Collection at the University of Texas, G.310 (letter).

19. T. S. Eliot, 'Types of English Religious Verse', in *Miscellaneous Essays and Reviews*, the Hayward Collection, King's College Library, Cambridge, H.I.C., p. 20.

20. Ibid., p. 2.

21. Ibid., p. 3. Compare Eliot's comment ten years earlier in 'Thinking in Verse: a Survey of Early Seventeenth-Century Poetry', *Listener*, iii.61 (12 March 1930) p. 442.

22. T. S. Eliot, 'An Emotional Unity', *Dial*, lxxxiv.2 (February 1928) p. 110.

23. See James M. Connolly, *Human History and The Word of God* (New York, 1963) pp. 109–10.

24. T. S. Eliot, *After Strange Gods* (London, 1934) p. 48.

25. T. S. Eliot, 'Types of English Religious Verse', p. 20.

26. T. E. Hulme, *Speculations: Essays on Humanism and the Philosophy of Art*, ed. Herbert Read (New York, 1924) pp. 70–1; quoted by Eliot in 'Second Thoughts about Humanism', in *SE*, pp. 490–1.

27. Ibid., p. 71.

28. See Søren Kierkegaard, *Either/Or*, vol. II, trans. Walter Lowrie (New York, 1959) p. 249. In spite of the fact that this volume was published by Kierkegaard under an assumed name, the judgements expressed *on the subject of mysticism* do roughly correspond to Kierkegaard's own attitude of mind. 'Mysticism', he wrote in one of his private journals, 'has not the patience to wait for God's revelation'. See *The Journals of Søren Kierkegaard* (Oxford, 1938) p. 321. Kierkegaard did, however, find time to make a study of Gorres's *Mystik*, and he was acquainted also with mystical writers such as Tauler, Boehme and the Victorines.
29. Kierkegaard, *Either/Or*, vol. II, pp. 251–2.
30. Ibid., pp. 253–4.
31. Ibid., pp. 246–7.
32. Ibid., p. 247.
33. Ibid., p. 251; emphasis added.
34. Ibid., p. 249.
35. Walter Lowrie, *Kierkegaard* (Oxford, 1938) p. 170.
36. See *CFQ*, p. 118.
37. Kierkegaard, *Either/Or*, vol. II, p. 251.
38. Alessandro Pellegrini, 'A London Conversation with T. S. Eliot', trans. Joseph Frank, *Sewanee Review*, 57 (Spring 1949) p. 288.
39. Ibid., pp. 288–9.
40. F. R. Leavis, *The Living Principle* (London, 1975) p. 239.
41. E. L. Allen, *Kierkegaard: His Life and Thought* (London, 1935) pp. 144–5.
42. Ibid., pp. 145–7.
43. See *Kierkegaard*, selected and introduced by W. H. Auden (London, 1955) p. 129.
44. 'I by T. S. Eliot', pp. 31–2.
45. Søren Kierkegaard, *Efterladte Papirer* (Copenhagen, 1881) p. 31. The passage was quoted by Walter Lowrie in *Kierkegaard*, p. 562.
46. Walter Lowrie, for example, in *Kierkegaard* (pp. 171 and 562), draws attention to the link made by Erich Przywara S.J. in his book *Das Geheimnis Kierkegaards* (1929) between Kierkegaard and St John of the Cross. And Melville Chaning-Pearce discusses Kierkegaard's mysticism in *Søren Kierkegaard: A Study* (London, 1945).
47. Søren Kierkegaard, *The Point of View for my Work as An Author: A Report to History*, trans. Walter Lowrie (New York, 1962) p. 18.
48. The letter is quoted by B. A. Harries in 'The Rare Contact', p. 141.
49. See Allen, *Kierkegaard*, p. 147.
50. T. S. Eliot, 'Introduction', in Djuna Barnes, *Nightwood* (London, 1963; first published 1937) pp. 5–6.
51. See *Kierkegaard*, selected and introduced by W. H. Auden, p. 129.
52. Allen, *Kierkegaard*, p. 146; emphasis added.
53. Ibid., p. 182.
54. Donoghue's essay, originally published in 1965, is included in Bernard Bergonzi (ed.), *T. S. Eliot, 'Four Quartets': A Selection of Critical Essays* (London, 1969) pp. 212–36.

55. Ibid., p. 234.
56. Gregory, a review of *Kierkegaard: His Life and Thought*, in *Criterion*, xv.59 (January 1936) pp. 306–7.
57. Allen, *Kierkegaard*, p. 192. The possibility that this particular passage in Allen's book may have had some influence on Eliot is indicated by one or two small yet perhaps significant verbal echoes in 'The Dry Salvages'. In particular I am thinking of the phrase: 'The *Incarnation* is the *actualisation* of *the impossible*'. Compare: 'The hint half guessed, the gift half understood, is Incarnation. / Here the impossible union / Of spheres of existence is *actual*.
58. Ibid., p. 181.
59. Ibid., p. 67.

Notes to Chapter 8: The Brahmin and Buddhist Influence

1. T. S. Eliot, 'Appendix', in *Notes Towards the Definition of Culture* (London, 1948) p. 113. (This 'Appendix' was originally published in book form in German in Berlin in 1946.)
2. Ranjee Shahani, 'T. S. Eliot Answers Questions', *John O'London's Weekly* (London), LVIII.1369 (19 August 1949) p. 498.
3. See Lyndall Gordon, *Eliot's Early Years* (Oxford, 1977) p. 57. For further information concerning Eliot's studies of Eastern literature, see Peter Ackroyd, *T. S. Eliot* (London, 1984) p. 47.
4. See *CFQ*, p. 54, note 49.
5. See B. A. Harries, 'The Rare Contact: a Correspondence between T. S. Eliot and Paul Elmer More', *Theology*, 75 (1972) p. 136.
6. Ibid., p. 136.
7. *The Complete Poems and Plays of T. S. Eliot* (London, 1969) p. 80. For an analysis of Eliot's use of Brahmin sources in *The Waste Land*, see G. Nageswara Rao, 'T. S. Eliot's Use of the Upanishad', *The Aryan Path*, 38 (1967) pp. 19–32.
8. Stephen Spender, 'Remembering Eliot', in Allen Tate (ed.), *T. S. Eliot: The Man and His Work* (London, 1967) p. 40.
9. T. S. Eliot, *After Strange Gods* (London, 1934) pp. 40–1. (The book consists of lectures Eliot gave in 1933 at the University of Virginia). Ten years later he remarked in similar vein: 'our sensibility . . . is not the same as that of the Chinese or the Hindu'. See 'The Social Function of Poetry' (an address delivered at the British–Norwegian Institute in 1943) in *PP*, p. 20.
10. Eliot, *After Strange Gods*, pp. 40–1.
11. T. S. Eliot, *The Use of Poetry and the Use of Criticism* (London, 1933) p. 132, note 1.
12. T. S. Eliot, 'Education in a Christian Society', in *The Idea of a Christian Society and Other Writings* (London, 1982; first published 1939) p. 142.

13. T. S. Eliot, 'The Christian Conception of Education', in *The Idea of a Christian Society*, p. 153, note 1.
14. T. S. Eliot, 'Goethe as the Sage', in *PP*, p. 226.
15. A phrase used by Eliot in his 'Preface' in Simone Weil, *The Need for Roots* (London, 1952) p. ix.
16. T. S. Eliot, 'Thinking in Verse: a Survey of Early Seventeenth-Century Poetry', *Listener*, iii.61 (12 March 1930) p. 443.
17. See Chapter 2, p. 39.
18. J. Estlin Carpenter, *Buddhism and Christianity: A Contrast and a Parallel* (London, 1923) p. 265.
19. See *Brihad-Aranyaka Upanishad*, book iii.viii, para. 8: 'It is not coarse or fine; not short nor long . . . it has no face or measure; it has no within, no without. Nothing does it consume nor is it consumed by anyone at all.' *Hindu Scriptures*, trans. R. C. Zaehner (London, 1966) p. 56.
20. May Sinclair, 'Jones's Karma', *Criterion*, ii.5 (October 1923) p. 43.
21. See *Criterion*, xi.45 (July 1932) p. 681, note 1.
22. A phrase in Eliot's 'Preface' to *Thoughts for Meditation* (London, 1951) p. 13. Other readers before now have been struck by the apparent meeting and coalescence of Eastern and Western sources in 'Burnt Norton'. See Staffan Bergsten, *Time and Eternity: A Study of the Structure and Symbolism of T. S. Eliot's Four Quartets*, Studia Litterarum Upsaliensia, i (Stockholm, 1960) pp. 78–84; Harold E. McCarthy, 'T. S. Eliot and Buddhism', *Philosophy East and West*, 2 (April 1952) pp. 48–9; Narsingh Srivastava, 'The Ideas of the *Bhagavad Gita* in *Four Quartets*', *Comparative Literature*, 29 (1977) pp. 101–2; Eloise Knapp Hay, *T. S. Eliot's Negative Way* (London, 1982) pp. 166–9; Cleo McNelly Kearns, *T. S. Eliot and Indic Traditions* (Cambridge, 1987) pp. 232–9. Of all the studies which have appeared so far on the subject of Eliot's Eastern antecedents, McNelly Kearns's book is by far the most substantial and the most interesting.
23. 'I by T. S. Eliot', in Gustaf Aulén *et al.*, *Revelation* (London, 1937) pp. 1–2.
24. In Chapter 3, pp. 51–2, and in Chapter 12, pp. 244–55, I discuss other allusions in 'Burnt Norton' to the states of 'heaven and damnation'.
25. T. S. Eliot, 'Scylla and Charybdis', *Agenda*, xxiii.1–2 (Spring–Summer 1985) p. 17. (This paper was originally delivered by Eliot at a conference in Nice on 29 March 1952). Emphasis added.
26. W. B. Yeats, 'Preface' in *The Ten Principal Upanishads'*, trans. Shree Purohit Swami and W. B. Yeats (London, 1937) p. 9.
27. Ibid., p. 10.
28. See *CFQ*, p. 112.
29. John Dowson, *A Classical Dictionary* (London, 1888) p. 21.
30. See 'The Upanishads', in Abhishiktananda, *The Further Shore* (Delhi, 1975) p. 98.
31. Dowson, *Classical Dictionary*, p. 21.

32. See *Hindu Scriptures*, trans. R. C. Zaehner (London, 1966) p. 72. J. J. Sweeney proposed an almost identical text from the *Isa Upanishad* as a possible source. See his '"East Coker": a Reading', in Bernard Bergonzi (ed.), *T. S. Eliot, 'Four Quartets': A Selection of Critical Essays* (London, 1975) p. 48.
33. It is not inconceivable that the *blind* darkness in the Upanishadic text recalled to Eliot's mind the cry of *blind* Samson in Milton's dramatic poem *Samson Agonistes*:

    O dark, dark, dark, amid the blaze of noon,
    Irrevocably dark, total Eclipse
    Without all hope of day!

34. *Brihad-Aranyaka Upanishad*, book II.i. See *Hindu Scriptures*, pp. 43–4.
35. See the statement by Mr B. P. N. Sinha in *CFQ*, pp. 55–6.
36. See Paul Elmer More, *The Catholic Faith* (Princeton, N.J., 1931) pp. 294–5.
37. B. N. Chaturvedi, 'The Indian Background of Eliot's Poetry', *English* 15 (1965) p. 222.
38. See Aldous Huxley's 'Introduction', in *The Song of God: Bhagavad-Gita*, trans. Swami Prahhavananda and Christopher Isherwood (Hollywood, Calif.: 1944) pp. 13–14.
39. *Brihad-Aranyaka Upanishad*, book I.iv, paras. 1 and 2 (*Hindu Scriptures*, pp. 35–7). See also book IV (*Hindu Scriptures*, pp. 64–5).
40. *Brihad-Aranyaka Upanishad*, book IV.iii (*Hindu Scriptures*, p. 68). Also in the *Brihad-Aranyaka Upanishad* we read: 'As all the waters meet in one place only, – in the sea . . . so too, I say, is this Being, – infinite, boundless, a mass of understanding', book II.iv (*Hindu Scriptures*, pp. 46–7).
41. *CFQ*, p. 113.
42. Compare 'East Coker', Section One, with this passage from Act I, Scene ii of *The Cocktail Party*:

    The self that can say 'I want this – or want that' –
    The self that wills – he is a feeble creature;
    He has to come to terms in the end
    With the obstinate, the tougher self; who does not speak,
    Who never talks, who cannot argue;
    And who in some men may be the *guardian* . . .

43. Eliot used the phrase 'the temporal aspect of the soul' in the first draft of 'The Dry Salvages'. See *CFQ*, p. 147.
44. See Sweeney, 'East Coker: a Reading', p. 40. The phrase 'In my beginning is my end' is also, of course, an inversion of Mary Stuart's motto: 'En ma fin est mon commencement'.
45. Arthur Osborne (ed.), *The Collected Works of Ramana Maharshi* (London, 1980) p. 8. See also Arthur Osborne (ed.), *Ramana Maharshi and the Path of Self-Knowledge* (London, 1970) p. 19. An article entitled 'Hindu Music' appeared in Eliot's *Criterion* in 1926.

46. Helen Gardner, *The Art of T. S. Eliot* (London, 1949) p. 173, note 1.
47. *CFQ*, p. 57.
48. See T. S. Eliot, 'Dante' (1929) in *SE*, p. 258.
49. The phrase 'right action' occurs in 'The First Sermon' of the Buddha, otherwise known as 'Sutta of Turning the Wheel of the Doctrine'. The Buddha is speaking about the Middle Way: 'Now this, O monks, is the noble truth of the way that leads to the cessation of pain: this is the noble Eightfold Path, namely, right views, right intention, right speech, *right action*, right livelihood, right effort, right mindfulness, right concentration' (emphasis added). See Edward J. Thomas, *The Life of the Buddha* (London, 1975; first published 1927) p. 87.
50. The phrase 'right action' is, of course, associated particularly with Buddhism. Other Buddhist allusions in Section Three of 'The Dry Salvages' have been noted by Grover Smith. See his *T. S. Eliot's Poetry and Play: A Study in Sources and Meaning* (Chicago, 1968) p. 282.
51. *The Complete Poems and Plays of T. S. Eliot* (London, 1969) p. 79.
52. Ibid., p. 79.
53. Ibid., p. 411.
54. Ibid., p. 420.
55. Ibid., p. 421.
56. Harold E. McCarthy, 'T. S. Eliot and Buddhism', *Philosophy East and West*, 2 (April 1952) p. 38.
57. Eliot's Harvard lecture notes show that he was quite familiar with Buddhaghosa's Commentary on the *Anguttura Nikaya*. See Eloise Knapp Hay, *T. S. Eliot's Negative Way* (London, 1982) p. 71.
58. See Henry Clarke Warren, *Buddhism in Translations* (Harvard, 1900) pp. 215–16. I discussed this source already in my article 'The Unidentified Ghost: Arthur Hugh Clough and T. S. Eliot's *Four Quartets*', *Studies*, LXX, 227 (Spring 1981) p. 48.
59. See 'The first draft of *Little Gidding*', in *CFQ*, pp. 228–9.
60. See *Saundaranandakavya* in *Buddhist Scriptures*, trans. Edward Conze (Middlesex, 1959) pp. 110–11. 'Nanda the Fair' was a text on meditation intended for use by laymen.
61. T. S. Eliot, *The Use of Poetry and the Use of Criticism* (London, 1933) p. 91.
62. *The Complete Poems and Plays*, p. 384.
63. Ibid., pp. 384–5.
64. See *Buddhaghosa, Visuddhimagga*, book XIII, in *Buddhist Scriptures*, p. 131.
65. *CFQ*, p. 228.
66. T. S. Eliot, 'What is Minor Poetry', in *PP*, p. 42.
67. James S. Whitlark, 'More Borrowings by T. S. Eliot from *The Light of Asia*', *Notes and Queries*, 220 (May 1975) pp. 206–7. See also Christopher Clausen, 'A Source for Thomas Becket's Temptation in *Murder in the Cathedral*', *Notes and Queries*, 219 (October 1974) pp. 373–4.

68. See Valerie Eliot (ed.), *T. S. Eliot, 'The Waste Land': A Facsimile and Transcript of the Original Drafts* (London, 1971) p. 31.
69. Edwin Arnold, *The Light of Asia* (London, 1932; originally published 1879) p. 20.
70. Ibid., p. 26.
71. See *CFQ*, pp. 228–9.
72. 'I by T. S. Eliot', in Gustaf Aulén *et al.*, *Revelation* (London, 1937) p. 24.
73. Ibid., p. 22.
74. Ibid., p. 25.
75. Ibid., pp. 22–3.
76. Ibid., p. 25.
77. *CFQ*, p. 229.
78. Eliot, 'Education in a Christian Society', p. 142.
79. *CFQ*, p. 230.
80. The first quotation is from the thirteenth revelation (ch. 27): 'Synne is behovabil, but al shal be wel & al shal be wel & al manner of thyng shal be wel'; and the second is based on a phrase from the fourteenth revelation (ch. 41): 'I am Ground of thy beseeching'. See Grace Warrack's 1901 version of the *Revelations*, pp. 56 and 84.
81. T. S. Eliot, 'The Christian Conception of Education', p. 153.

Notes to Chapter 9: Mysticism and Magic

1. T. S. Eliot, 'Letter to the Editor', *Time and Tide*, xvi.3 (19 January 1935) p. 95.
2. T. S. Eliot, 'From Poe to Valéry', in *To Criticize the Critic and Other Writings* (London, 1948) p. 31.
3. T. S. Eliot, 'To Walter de la Mare', in *The Complete Poems and Plays of T. S. Eliot* (London, 1969) p. 205.
4. G. Wilson Knight, *Neglected Powers* (London, 1971) p. 396. See also John Senior, *The Way Down and Out: The Occult in Symbolist Literature* (New York, 1959) pp. 170–98.
5. Evelyn Underhill, *Mysticism* (London, 1930) p. 70.
6. Ibid., p. 71.
7. Ibid.
8. See 'Introduction by T. S. Eliot', to Charles Williams, *All Hallows' Eve* (New York, 1948) p. xvii.
9. Dion Fortune, *Sane Occultism* (London, 1921) p. 43.
10. Ibid., p. 44.
11. Fred Gettings, *The Encyclopaedia of the Occult* (London, 1986) p. 202.
12. C. A. Bodelsen, *T. S. Eliot's 'Four Quartets'* (Copenhagen, 1966) p. 100.

13. Quoted in 'Preface to Second Edition', in C. A. Bodelsen, *T. S. Eliot's 'Four Quartets'* (Copenhagen, 1966) p. 8.
14. See Elizabeth Drew, *T. S. Eliot: The Design of His Poetry* (London, 1950) p. 190.
15. Dion Fortune, *The Mystical Qabalah* (London, 1935) p. 18.
16. Ibid., p. 191.
17. Ibid., p. 205.
18. Ibid., p. 75.
19. See R. P. Festugière O.P., *L'Astrologie et les Sciences Occultés* (Paris, 1950) p. 166.
20. See Peter Ackroyd, *T. S. Eliot* (London, 1984) p. 15.
21. This possible allusion to Dante's Paradiso in 'Burnt Norton' is discussed further in Chapter 12, pp. 247–8.
22. T. S. Eliot, 'Humanist, Artist, and Scientist', *Athenaeum*, 4667 (10 October 1919) p. 1015. (A review of *La pensée italienne au XVIme siècle et le courant libertin*, by J. Roger Charbonnel, and *L'éthique de Giordano Bruno et le deuxième dialogue du Spaccio*.)
23. Ibid., p. 1015.
24. See *CFQ*, pp. 65–9.
25. See T. S. Eliot, 'A Foreign Mind', in *The Athenaeum*, 4653 (4 July 1919) p. 552 (a review of *The Cutting of an Agate* by W. B. Yeats).
26. Ibid., p. 552.
27. See T. S. Eliot, 'Shorter Notices', in *the Egoist*, v.6 (June–July 1918) p. 87 (a review of *Per amica silentia lunae* by W. B. Yeats).
28. T. S. Eliot, 'A Foreign Mind', p. 553.
29. W. B. Yeats, 'Modern Poetry: a Broadcast' (1936) in *Essays and Introductions* (New York, 1977) p. 499.
30. W. B. Yeats, 'Magic' (1901) in *Essays and Introductions*, pp. 28–52.
31. Ibid., p. 29.
32. Ibid., pp. 29–31.
33. Quoted by A. Walton Litz in 'Introduction and Afterword to *Tradition and the Practice of Poetry* by T. S. Eliot', *Southern Review*, xxi.4 (October 1985) p. 873. (Eliot made the remark on 23 January 1936 at the inaugural meeting of the English Literary Society of University College, Dublin.)
34. T. S. Eliot, 'The Modern Mind' in *The Use of Poetry and the Use of Criticism* (London, 1933) p. 140.
35. T. S. Eliot, *After Strange Gods* (London, 1934) p. 45.
36. Ibid., p. 45.
37. Ibid.
38. Ibid., p. 46.
39. See W. B. Yeats, 'The Symbolism of Poetry' (1900), in *Essays and Introductions*, pp. 159, 163.
40. See Ackroyd, *T. S. Eliot*, p. 255 and p. 357, note 10; emphasis added.
41. W. B. Yeats, *A Vision* (New York, 1966; first published in definitive form in 1938) p. 210. Cleo McNelly Kearns was the first among Eliot's readers to draw attention to this passage from Yeats. See her *T. S. Eliot and Indic Traditions* (Cambridge, 1987) p. 255, note 16.

42. Hugh Gordon Porteus, a review of *The Winding Stair* by W. B. Yeats, *Criterion*, XIII.51 (January 1934) p. 314.

43. Ibid., p. 313.

44. T. S. Eliot, 'Author and Critic' (later title: 'The Function of Criticism'), in T. S. Eliot Collection, King's College, Cambridge, H.I., p. 10.

45. T. S. Eliot 'From Poe to Valéry', in *To Criticize the Critic*, p. 34.

46. T. S. Eliot 'The Three Voices of Poetry' (1953), in *PP*, p. 98.

47. T. S. Eliot, 'The Social Function of Poetry' (1943), in *PP*, p. 16.

48. T. S. Eliot, 'Rudyard Kipling' (1941), in *PP*, pp. 239–40, note 2.

49. T. S. Eliot, 'The Social Function of Poetry', p. 20.

50. See T. S. Eliot, ' "Rhetoric" and Poetic Drama' (1919), in *SE*, pp. 41–2; 'The Possibility of a Poetic Drama' (1920), in *The Sacred Wood: Essays on Poetry and Criticism* (London, 1920) p. 66; 'John Marston' (1934), in *SE*, p. 229; 'Poetry and Drama' (1951), in *PP*, pp. 77–8.

51. Maurice Maeterlinck, *The Treasure of the Humble*, trans. Alfred Sutro (London, 1897).

52. See W. B. Yeats, a review of *The Treasure of the Humble* in *Uncollected Prose by W. B. Yeats* (New York, 1975) p. 46. (Yeats' review was first published in *The Bookman* for July 1897.)

53. Maeterlinck, *Treasure of the Humble*, p. 31.

54. T. S. Eliot, *Collected Poems and Plays*, p. 437.

55. Maeterlinck, p. 58; *Treasure of the Humble*, emphasis added.

56. Ibid., p. 58. Elsewhere in *Treasure of the Humble* we read: 'Whence comes the shadow of a mysterious transgression that at times creeps over our life and makes it so hard to bear? What are the great spiritual sins of which we can be guilty?' (pp. 71–2).

57. Eliot, *Collected Poems and Plays*, p. 417.

58. Ibid., p. 416.

59. See Charles Sarolea, 'The Condemnation of Maeterlinck', in *The French Renaissance* (London, 1916) p. 262. Sarolea refers to the unorthodox mysticism of *The Treasure of the Humble* (see p. 263).

60. Maeterlinck, *Treasure of the Humble*, p. 416.

61. Ibid., pp. 35, 37.

62. Ibid., p. 40.

63. Ibid., p. 50. Maeterlinck is thinking here of people fated or predestined to die young: 'was it that we avoided them because though younger than ourselves, they were still our elders?'

64. Ibid., p. 36.

65. Ibid., pp. 62–3.

66. Ibid., p. 73; emphasis added.

67. The phrase 'here and there' occurs in all the printed editions of *Four Quartets* until the 1974 edition. Helen Gardner suggests that it is an error overlooked by Eliot in the correction of proofs and that the text should read: 'Here or there does not matter'. See *CFQ*, p. 113.

68. John Carswell, *Lives and Letters, 1906–1957* (London, 1978) pp. 171–2.

69. Ibid., p. 172.
70. T. S. Eliot to Eleanor Hinckely, 23 March 1917, in Valerie Eliot (ed.), *The Letters of T. S. Eliot*, vol. I: *1898–1922* (London, 1988) p. 169.
71. T. S. Eliot, 'A Commentary', *Criterion*, XVI.63 (January 1937) p. 293.
72. T. S. Eliot, 'A Commentary', *Criterion*, XIV.55 (January 1935) p. 261.
73. T. S. Eliot, 'Preface', in *Thoughts for Meditation: A Way to Recovery from Within*, selected and arranged by N. Gangulee (London, 1951) p. 11.
74. P. D. Ouspensky, *Tertium Organum, the Third Canon of Thought: A Key to the Enigmas of the World* (London, 1934; first published, 1921) pp. 258–9.
75. Ibid., p. 243.
76. Ibid., p. 259.
77. T. S. Eliot, 'Mr Charles Williams' (an obituary notice), *Times*, 17 May 1945, p. 7.
78. T. S. Eliot, 'The Significance of Charles Williams', *Listener*, XXXVI.936 (19 December 1946) p. 895.
79. Ibid., p. 894.
80. 'Introduction by T. S. Eliot', in Charles Williams, *All Hallows' Eve* (London, 1948) p. xv.
81. Eliot, 'The Significance of Charles Williams', p. 895.
82. Glen Cavaliero, *Charles Williams: Poet of Theology* (Cambridge, 1983) p. 4.
83. Charles Williams, *The Greater Trumps* (London, 1932) p. 44.
84. Ibid., p. 95.
85. *CFQ*, p. 85.
86. Ibid., p. 79.
87. John Hayward, note in T. S. Eliot, *Quatre Quatours* (Paris, 1950) pp. 132–3.
88. Denis Saurat, *Literature and the Occult Tradition: Studies in Philosophical Poetry* (London, 1930) p. 61.
89. Ibid., p. 62.
90. Eliot, *After Strange Gods*, pp. 24–5.
91. Ibid., p. 46.

Notes to Chapter 10: The Language of Patriotism: Rudyard Kipling and Rupert Brooke

1. See Evelyn Underhill 'Introduction', in *A Book of Contemplation the which is called The Cloud of Unknowing* (London, 1912) p. 6. *The Cloud of Unknowing* is a mystical text from the Middle Ages composed in the vernacular by an anonymous English author.

2. A phrase from a letter by J. H. Oldham quoted with approval by Eliot in 'Notes' to 'The Idea of a Christian Society' in *The Idea of a Christian Society and Other Writings* (London, 1982; first published 1939) p. 98.

3. In his essay 'The Idea of a Christian Society', first issued in 1939, Eliot remarked: 'I should not like it to be thought that I considered the presence of the higher forms of devotional life to be a matter of minor importance for such a society' (p. 79).

4. Underhill, 'Introduction', p. 5.

5. T. S. Eliot, 'Tradition and the Individual Talent', *The Sacred Wood* (1920) p. 48.

6. See T. S. Eliot, a review of *Poetry at Present* by Charles Williams, in *Criterion*, IX.37 (July 1930) p. 786.

7. T. S. Eliot, 'The Unfading Genius of Rudyard Kipling', in Elliot L. Gilbert (ed.), *Kipling and the Critics* (London, 1966) p. 123.

8. Ibid., pp. 118–19.

9. See *CFQ*, pp. 20–1.

10. T. S. Eliot (ed.), *A Choice of Kipling's Verse* (London, 1941) p. 22. Among the 'half a dozen aspects of Kipling' in which Eliot declares himself to be particularly interested, in his address to the Kipling Society, we find listed 'the curious seeker into the abnormal and paranormal, and the seer'. See Eliot, 'The Unfading Genius', p. 121.

11. See T. S. Eliot, 'A Commentary', *Criterion*, IV.4 (October 1926) p. 628.

12. See *CFQ*, pp. 29, 39.

13. Rudyard Kipling, 'They' (London, 1905) p. 10.

14. Ibid., pp. 11–12.

15. Ibid., pp. 61, 30, 34.

16. Eliot (ed.), *A Choice of Kipling's Verse*, p. 28.

17. Ibid., p. 19.

18. Ibid., p. 20.

19. Ibid., p. 32.

20. Rudyard Kipling, *Rewards and Fairies* (London, 1920) p. xx.

21. Rudyard Kipling, *Puck of Pook's Hill* (London, 1920) p. 12.

22. See T. S. Eliot, 'A Commentary', *Criterion*, XV.60 (April 1936) pp. 462–3.

23. Seven paragraphs from the 1909 essay are included in J. Donald Adams, *Copey of Harvard: A Biography of C. T. Copeland* (Boston, Mass., 1960) pp. 159–62.

24. See 'Alfred Noyes on Kipling the Mystic', *Bookman*, XXXI (November 1906) pp. 80–1. Noyes's review is reprinted in Roger Lancelyn Green (ed.), *Kipling: The Critical Heritage* (London, 1971) pp. 298–301.

25. See Eliot (ed.), *A Choice of Kipling's Verse*,. p. 17. The poem itself can be found in Kipling's *Rewards and Fairies*, pp. 242–3.

26. Ibid., p. 324; emphasis added.

27. Eliot, 'The Unfading Genius', p. 120.

28. See Rudyard Kipling, 'The Bridge Builders' in *The Day's Work*, vol. XIII of *The Writings in Prose and Verse of Rudyard Kipling* (London, 1899) pp. 3–55.

29. Ibid., p. 36.

30. Ibid., pp. 33–5.

31. Ibid., p. 43.

32. See T. S. Eliot, 'Introduction', in Samuel L. Clemens (Mark Twain), *The Adventures of Huckleberry Finn* (London, 1950) pp. xii–xiii; emphasis added.

33. Kipling, 'The Bridge Builders', p. 235; emphasis added.

34. Rudyard Kipling, 'The Wandering Jew', in *The Phantom Rickshaw and Other Stories*, vol. V of *The Writings in Prose and Verse of Rudyard Kipling* (London, 1898) p. 318.

35. See *Rudyard Kipling's Verse* (London, 1940) p. 168; emphasis added.

36. Ibid., p. 168.

37. T. S. Eliot, 'Kipling', in *A Choice of Kipling's Verse* (London, 1941) pp. 23–4.

38. Kipling, *Rewards and Fairies*, p. 234; emphasis added.

39. Ibid., p. 292; emphasis added.

40. See *Collected Poems of Rupert Brooke* (London, 1918) p. 9.

41. See *The Complete Poems and Plays of T. S. Eliot* (London, 1969) p. 203.

42. See C. K. Stead, *The New Poetic: Yeats to Eliot* (London, 1964) p. 83. On a more superficial level Eliot's likeness to the English poet is suggested by Lyndall Gordon in *Eliot's Early Years* (Oxford, 1977): 'At times he seemed like a Harvardian Rupert Brooke with a Gioconda smile, dimples, and a graceful neck!' (p. 75).

43. Stead, *The New Poetic*, p. 84.

44. See 'Memoir', in *Collected Poems of Rupert Brooke* (London, 1918) p. lxviii.

45. Ibid., p. lxvii.

46. See *SE*, p. 145.

47. Quoted by Stead, *The New Poetic*, p. 83.

48. See T. S. Eliot, 'Reflections on Contemporary Poetry [I]', *The Egoist*, IV.8 (September 1917) p. 119.

49. Ibid., p. 119. Eliot refers again to Rupert Brooke in a later review of the same year: 'Reflections on Contemporary Poetry [III]', *The Egoist*, IV.10 (November 1917) p. 151. See also 'A Preface to Modern Literature', *Vanity Fair*, XXX.3 (November 1923) p. 44. No critic, to my knowledge, has remarked before now on these unique references to Brooke's poetry by T. S. Eliot.

50. B. C. Southam, *A Student's Guide to the Selected Poems of T. S. Eliot* (London, 1981) p. 25. See also p. 86.

51. See F. O. Matthiessen, *The Achievement of T. S. Eliot* (New York, 1958) pp. 92–3.

52. For this information see Southam, *A Student's Guide*, p. 87.

53. See 'T. S. Eliot on Poetry in Wartime', *Common Sense* (New York) XI.10 (October 1942) p. 351.

54. See Christopher Hassal, *Rupert Brooke: A Biography* (London, 1964) p. 504. (The letter in question was written to Sybil Pye.)
55. Ibid., p. 504.
56. See 'Memoir', in *Collected Poems*, p. cxlviii.
57. Ibid., p. clii.
58. Ibid., p. xii.
59. Ibid., p. cxlix.
60. See Hassal, *Rupert Brooke*, p. 504.
61. See 'Memoir', in *Collected Poems*, p. cxlix; emphasis added.
62. Ibid., p. cl.
63. See T. S. Eliot, 'John Dryden', *Listener*, iii.66 (16 April 1930) p. 689.
64. The finished draft of the talk is included in the collection *On Poetry and Poets* (London, 1957). See A. D. Moody, *Thomas Stearns Eliot: Poet* (Cambridge, 1979) p. 203.
65. 'T. S. Eliot on Poetry in Wartime', p. 351.
66. See *Complete Poems and Plays*, p. 201.
67. 'T. S. Eliot on Poetry in Wartime', p. 351.
68. T. S. Eliot, 'Christian and Natural Virtues' (part of the *Christian Newsletter*, 3 September 1941) in *The Idea of a Christian Society and Other Writings* (London, 1982; first published 1939) p. 125.
69. Eliot, *The Idea of a Christian Society*, p. 78.
70. Ibid., p. 78.
71. See Moody, *Thomas Stearns Eliot*, p. 204. The two phrases in inverted commas are taken from Eliot's *The Idea of a Christian Society*, p. 104.

Notes to Chapter 11: Mysticism and Myth – I: The Shakespeare Pattern

1. T. S. Eliot, 'Introduction', in G. Wilson Knight, *The Wheel of Fire: Interpretations of Shakespearean Tragedy* (London, 1978; first published 1930) p. xiii.
2. Ibid., pp. xiii–xiv.
3. See T. S. Eliot, 'Charybde et Scylla: lourdeur et frivolité', *Annales du Centre Universitaire Méditerranéen* (Nice) v (1951/52) p. 72. The lecture was first published in English in *Agenda*, xxiii.1–2 (Spring–Summer 1985) pp. 5–21.
4. Helen Gardner, *The Art of T. S. Eliot* (London, 1949) p. 185.
5. See Donald Davie, 'Anglican Eliot', in A. Walton Litz (ed.), *Eliot in His Time: Essays on the Occasion of the Fiftieth Anniversary of The Waste Land* (Princeton, N.J., 1973) p. 195.
6. Graham Hough, 'Vision and Doctrine in *Four Quartets*', *Critical Quarterly*, 15 (1973) p. 110.
7. Ibid., p. 110.
8. Ibid., pp. 114–15.

Notes 293

Notes 293

9. Ibid., p. 115.
10. Ibid., p. 115.
11. Ibid., p. 115.
12. Ibid., p. 115.
13. T. S. Eliot, 'From Poe to Valéry', in *To Criticize the Critic* (London, 1965) p. 34.
14. T. S. Eliot, 'Yeats', in *PP*, p. 260.
15. Ibid., p. 260.
16. See T. S. Eliot, 'Ulysses, Order and Myth', as reprinted in Richard Ellmann (ed.), *The Modern Tradition: Backgrounds of Modern Literature* (Oxford, 1964) pp. 679–81.
17. Ibid., p. 681.
18. *The Complete Poems and Plays of T. S. Eliot* (London, 1969), p. 76.
19. T. S. Eliot, 'London Letter', *Dial*, LXXI.4 (October 1921) p. 453.
20. Paul Valéry, *The Art of Poetry*, trans. Denise Folliot (New York, 1958) pp. 315–17.
21. Gardner, *The Art of T. S. Eliot*, p. 44.
22. Genesius Jones, *Approach to the Purpose* (London, 1964) p. 294, note 1.
23. Knight, *Wheel of Fire*, p. 16.
24. The essay is reproduced in G. Wilson Knight's *The Crown of Life* (London, 1965) pp. 9–31.
25. Knight, *Wheel of Fire*, p. 16.
26. 'Preface by T. S. Eliot', in Leone Vivante, *English Poetry* (London, 1950) p. xi.
27. T. S. Eliot, 'Introduction', in Knight, *Wheel of Fire*, p. xx.
28. Ibid., p. xviii.
29. 'Shakespeare as Poet and Dramatist', a lecture in two parts, was delivered first at Edinburgh in 1937, and then at Bristol University in 1941. It was subsequently adopted for delivery in Germany in 1949. A version of part of it was published under the title 'Shakespeares Verskunst' in *Der Monat*, II.20 (May 1950) 198–207. The short extract quoted above can be found in the Appendix to G. Wilson Knight's *Neglected Powers* (London, 1971) p. 489.
30. G. Wilson Knight, 'T. S. Eliot: Some Literary Impressions', in Allen Tate (ed.), *T. S. Eliot: The Man and His Work* (London, 1967) p. 246.
31. See Appendix to Knight, *Neglected Powers*, p. 489.
32. T. S. Eliot, 'Introduction', in Knight, *Wheel of Fire*, p. xviii. Eliot spoke again of 'those late plays of Shakespeare about which Mr Wilson Knight has written illuminatingly' in his essay 'To Criticize the Critic' (see *To Criticize the Critic*, pp. 19–20). For further evidence of Eliot's positive acceptance of Wilson Knight's contribution, see 'The Music of Poetry', in *PP*, p. 36; 'John Ford', in *SE*, p. 194; review of *Shakespeare* by John Middleton Murray, *Criterion*, XV.61 (July 1936) p. 710.
33. See Knight, 'T. S. Eliot: Some Literary Impressions', p. 247. *Thaisa* was completed in 1928 and was submitted to Faber and Faber. It was not, however, accepted for publication. The typescript is at present lodged in the Shakespeare Memorial Library in the Birmingham Reference Library.

34. See 'Myth and Miracle' as reprinted by Knight in *The Crown of Life* (London, 1965) pp. 19 and 14.
35. Ibid., p. 15.
36. Ibid., p. 17.
37. Ibid., p. 31.
38. Ibid., p. 13.
39. Ibid., p. 22.
40. Ibid., p. 22.
41. *CFQ*, p. 157.
42. Grover Smith has pointed out, quite conclusively in my view, that throughout *The Waste Land* Eliot 'employs the primordial imagery of death and rebirth in accordance with the Grail Legend'. (See his *T. S. Eliot's Poetry and Plays: Studies in Sources and Meanings* (Chicago, 1968) p. 69.) And Charles Moorman, in an interesting study of literature and myth, has spoken of 'the constant pervading and unifying influence of the death-rebirth pattern' in Eliot's later work (see *Arthurian Tryptich* (London, 1960) p. 143).
43. *The Testament of Immortality*, an anthology selected and arranged by N. Gangulee (London, 1940) p. 11.
44. Ibid., pp. 12–13.
45. Ibid., p. 136. Eliot's reflections on 'the pattern of dead and living' here in 'Little Gidding' and also in 'East Coker', Section Five, bear some resemblance to Maeterlinck's discussion of the same theme in *The Treasure of the Humble*, trans. Alfred Sutro (London, 1897). See pp. 108–9, 142–3.
46. See Knight, *T. S. Eliot: The Man and his Work*, p. 247.
47. Ibid., p. 247.
48. See Knight, 'Myth and Miracle', pp. 14–15.
49. *SE*, pp. 194–5.
50. See the extract from Eliot's 'Shakespeare as Poet and Dramatist' quoted in the Appendix to Knight, *Neglected Powers*, p. 490.
51. Ibid., p. 490.
52. The postscript is quoted by B. C. Southam, *A Student's Guide to the Selected Poems of T. S. Eliot* (London, 1981) p. 146.
53. See Appendix to Knight, *Neglected Powers*, p. 490.
54. Knight, *Christian Renaissance*, p. 264 (see also p. 120).
55. Knight, *Neglected Powers*, p. 387.
56. See *CFQ*, p. 126.
57. 'Gospel according to St John' in *The Holy Bible*, Revised Standard Version (London, 1952) 16:7–13.
58. See Colin Still, *Shakespeare's Mystery Play: A Study of the Tempest* (London, 1921) p. 234.
59. Ibid., p. 84.
60. See 'Introduction', in *The Wheel of Fire*, p. xx.
61. Colin Still, *The Timeless Theme* (London, 1936) p. 63.
62. Ibid., p. 63.
63. Still, *Shakespeare's Mystery Play*, p. 143.
64. Ibid., p. 126.

65. Ibid.
66. Ibid., p. 123.
67. Ibid., p. 138.
68. *CFQ*, p. 88; emphasis added.
69. Still, *Shakespeare's Mystery Play*, p. 141; emphasis added.
70. Ibid., p. 142.
71. Ibid., p. 208.
72. Ibid., p. 208.
73. Ibid., p. 209.
74. Ibid., p. 209.
75. Ibid., p. 209.
76. *CFQ*, p. 18, note 8; emphasis added.
77. Still, *The Timeless Theme*, p. 20.
78. Ibid., p. 22.
79. Still, *Shakespeare's Mystery Play*, p. 122.
80. Ibid., p. 123.
81. *CFQ*, p. 207.
82. Ibid., p. 197, note 2.
83. Still, *Shakespeare's Mystery Play*, p. 45.
84. Ibid., p. 149.
85. Ibid., p. 45.
86. Ibid., p. 110.
87. See *Legum Allegoriae*, 2.56; quoted by E. R. Dodds, *Pagan and Christian in an Age of Anxiety* (Cambridge, 1965) p. 95.
88. Still, *Shakespeare's Mystery Play*, p. 58.
89. Ibid., p. 111.
90. Ibid., p. 217.
91. Quoted by Knight in Appendix to *Neglected Powers*, p. 490.
92. Knight, 'Myth and Miracle', p. 31.
93. T. S. Eliot, 'Shakespeare and the Stoicism of Seneca' (1917) in *SE*, p. 138.
94. See 'Extracts from "Le Rôle Social du Poète" ', in P. Lal (ed.), *T. S. Eliot: Homage from India* (Calcutta, 1965) p. 164. (Translation of the 'Extracts' by J. de Bonhome, S.J.) Eliot's lecture was delivered in Paris on 11 May 1945.
95. See T. S. Eliot, 'Introduction', in Charles Williams, *All Hallows' Eve* (New York, 1948) p. xiv.
96. The phrase is Eliot's. In its original context it is descriptive of poetry in general. See T. S. Eliot, 'Poetry and Propaganda' in Morton D. Zabel (ed.), *Literary Opinion of America* (New York, 1951) p. 106. The essay was first published in *Bookman*, LXX.6 (February 1930) pp. 505–602.
97. T. S. Eliot, 'Goethe as the Sage' (1955), in *PP*, p. 225.
98. Ibid., p. 225.
99. Ibid., pp. 225–6.
100. G. Hough, 'Vision and Doctrine in *Four Quartets*', *Critical Quarterly*, 15 (1973) p. 115.
101. T. S. Eliot, 'London Letter', *Dial*, LXXXI.4 (October 1921) p. 453.

102.   T. S. Eliot, 'Scylla and Charybdis', *Agenda*, xxiii.1–2 (Spring–Summer 1985) p. 6. (This lecture was originally delivered by Eliot at a conference in Nice on 29 March 1952.)

Notes to Chapter 12: Mysticism and Myth – II: The Dantean Parallel

1.   T. S. Eliot, 'What Dante Means to Me' (1950), in *To Criticize the Critics and Other Writings* (London, 1965) p. 125.
2.   Ibid., p. 128.
3.   Quoted by J. D. Margolis, *T. S. Eliot's Intellectual Development* (Chicago, 1972).
4.   *SE*, p. 491.
5.   Graham Hough, 'Vision and Doctrine in *Four Quartets*', *Critical Quarterly*, 15 (1973) p. 109.
6.   Ibid., p. 109.
7.   Ibid., pp. 108–10.
8.   Denis Donoghue, 'T. S. Eliot's *Four Quartets*: a New Reading', in Bernard Bergonzi (ed.), *T. S. Eliot, 'Four Quartets': A Selection of Critical Essays* (London, 1969) p. 212.
9.   Quoted by Helen Gardner, *CPQ*, p. 29.
10.   T. S. Eliot, 'George Herbert' ('Studies in Sanctity VIII'), *Spectator* (London) cxlviii.5411 (12 March 1932) p. 361.
11.   *The Complete Poems and Plays of T. S. Eliot* (London, 1969) p. 421.
12.   Ibid., p. 438.
13.   T. S. Eliot, 'Poetry and Drama' (1951) in *PP*, p. 76.
14.   Ibid., p. 85.
15.   *Dantis Alagherii Epistolae: The Letters of Dante*, trans. and ed. Paget Toynbee (Oxford, 1920) Ep.x,7 and 8, pp. 134ff. For an illuminating discussion of Dante's four levels of meaning, see Joseph Anthony Mazzeo, 'Dante's Conception of Poetic Expression', *Romantic Review*, xlvii (1956) pp. 241–58.
16.   See Helen Gardner, *The Art of T. S. Eliot* (London, 1949) pp. 164, 170, 176 and 184. The usefulness of reading *Four Quartets* in the light of Dante's four levels of meaning has been discussed by other critics, most notably Sister Mary Cleophas, R.S.M., 'Notes on Levels of Meaning in *Four Quartets*', *Renascence*, 2 (Spring 1950) pp. 102–16, and Staffan Bergsten, *Time and Eternity* (Stockholm, 1960) pp. 141–5.
17.   See Giorgio Petrocchi, 'Dante and Thirteenth Century Asceticism', in T. G. Bergin (ed.), *From Time to Eternity: Essays on Dante's Divine Comedy* (New Haven, 1967) pp. 39–64.
18.   See T. S. Eliot, 'Deux Attitudes Mystiques: Dante et Donne', *Chroniques* (Paris) 3 (1927) p. 155 (*Clark Lectures*, Lecture III, p. 8).
19.   The quotation is from the text of an unpublished talk on 'Little Gidding' by Rowan Williams.

20. Ibid.
21. See Bonamy Dobrée, 'T. S. Eliot: a Personal Reminiscence', in Allen Tate (ed.), *T. S. Eliot: The Man and His Work* (London, 1967) p. 81.
22. See T. S. Eliot, 'Shelly and Keats' in *The Uses of Poetry and the Use of Criticism* (London, 1933) p. 95.
23. See Grierson (ed.), *Poems* (Oxford, 1912), p. i.288.
24. *CFQ*, p. 147.
25. *The Sacred Wood*, p. 156.
26. Eliot, 'What Dante Means to Me', p. 134.
27. It is interesting to note that the questioning voice of the poet, Arthur Hugh Clough, is echoed a number of times in *Four Quartets*. See Paul Murray, 'The Unidentified Ghost: Arthur Hugh Clough and T. S. Eliot's *Four Quartets*', *Studies*, LXX.227 (Spring 1981) pp. 35–54.
28. And note also in the *Bhagavad-Gita* the dialogue which takes place between the young warrior, Arjuna, and his master, the Lord Krishna.
29. D. W. Harding, 'Little Gidding: a Disagreement in Scrutiny', in Bergonzi (ed.), *T. S. Eliot, 'Four Quartets'*, p. 64.
30. See Mario Praz, *The Flaming Heart* (New York, 1958) pp. 348–74; A. C. Charity, 'The Dantean Recognition', in A. D. Moody (ed.), *The Waste Land in Different Voices* (London, 1974) pp. 117–56; F. O. Matthiessen, *The Achievement of T. S. Eliot* (Oxford, 1958); A. D. Moody, *Thomas Stearns Eliot: Poet* (London, 1979); G. Hough, 'Dante and Eliot', *The Critical Quarterly* 16 (1974) pp. 293–305; David Ward, *T. S. Eliot between Two Worlds* (London, 1973); D. H. Higgins, 'The Power of the Master: Eliot's Relation to Dante', *Dante Studies* LXXXVIII (1970) pp. 129–47.
31. T. S. Eliot, '*Dante*', in *SE*, p. 242.
32. Charity, 'The Dantean Recognitions', p. 118.
33. Ibid., p. 119.
34. Ibid., p. 137.
35. Ibid., pp. 136–7.
36. *SE*, p. 243. As one might expect, given this emphasis by Eliot on the importance of seeing visions, the debt Dante owes to 'the ancient tradition of vision literature' and to 'the poetry of his Provençal predecessors', is by no means ignored or overlooked by Eliot (see pp. 272 and 275). And see also his 'Introduction' in G. Wilson Knight, *The Wheel of Fire: Interpretations of Shakespearean Tragedy* (1930) p. xiv.
37. *SE*, p. 243. Contrast the following statement made by Eliot in the same year when reviewing E. K. Rand's *Founders of the Middle Ages*: 'A sure path to mysticism is through allegory he [Dr Rand] says. Mysticism is frequently applied to allegory; but it was a slip to call allegory a path to mysticism.' (See 'The Latin Tradition', *Times Literary Supplement* (London) 1415 (14 March 1929), p. 200.)
38. *SE*, p. 243.
39. Eliot, 'What Dante Means To Me', p. 134.

40.	Eliot, 'Deux Attitudes Mystiques: Dante et Donne', p. 149 (*Clark Lectures*, Lecture 111, p. 3).
41.	Ibid., pp. 150–1 (*Clark Lectures*, Lecture 111, p. 4).
42.	Ibid., pp. 156–8 (*Clark Lectures*, Lecture 111, p. 10).
43.	Ibid., pp. 149–50 (*Clark Lectures*, Lecture 111, p. 3). Emphasis added.
44.	T. S. Eliot, 'Note sur Mallarmé et Poe', *La Nouvelle Revue Française* (Paris), XIV.158 (1 November 1926) p. 524 (English text not published): 'Leur oeuvre était une *expansion* de leur sensibilité *au-delà des limites du monde normal*, une découverte de nouveaux objets propres à susciter de nouvelles émotions' (emphasis added).
45.	Ibid., p. 525: 'ils ne sautent pas brusquement dans un monde de rêve; c'est le monde réel qui est par eux agrandi et continué.'
46.	Moody, *Thomas Stearns Eliot*, p. 125. One should make an effort, Eliot believed, to accept 'the forms of imagination, phantasmagoria and sensibility' of Dante. See *SE*, p. 277. And note also pp. 246 and 256.
47.	Dante, *Paradiso*, Canto XXIII, trans. J D. Sinclair (Oxford, 1971) p. 333.
48.	This source was first noted by John Hayward in his footnotes to the French edition of Eliot's poem. See *Quatre Quatours* (Paris, 1950) p. 132.
49.	The same device of repetition is used by Dante in *Purgatorio* XXVIII.5: 'prendendo la campagna *lento lento*'.
50.	*SE*, p. 267.
51.	Eliot quotes this passage from Canto XXXIII of the *Paradiso* in *SE*, p. 267.
52.	'In Memoriam XLII', *Poems of Tennyson* (London, 1929) p. 342.
53.	This allusion to Dante's *Paradiso* is also discussed in Chapter 9, pp. 157–8.
54.	See T. S. Eliot, *Elizabethan Dramatists* (London, 1963) p. 7.
55.	See T. S. Eliot, 'Wanley and Chapman', *Times Literary Supplement* (London), 1250 (31 December 1925) p. 907.
56.	Ibid., p. 907.
57.	See Eliot, 'The Stoicism of Seneca', *SE*, p. 139.
58.	Psalm Two of Petrarch's *Seven Penitential Psalms* in *The Works of George Chapman: Poems and Minor Translations* (London, 1875) p. 137; emphasis added. (Eliot's phrase 'familiar compound ghost' is almost certainly an echo of Shakespeare's Sonnet no. 86, in which George Chapman is referred to as 'that affable familiar ghost'.)
59.	'I by T. S. Eliot', in Gustaf Aulén *et al.*, *Revelation* (London, 1937) pp. 31–2.
60.	Quoted by B. A. Harries in 'The Rare Contact: a Correspondence between T. S. Eliot and P. E. More', *Theology*, 75 (1972) p. 143.
61.	*SE*, p. 245.
62.	Ibid., p. 243.
63.	See T. S. Eliot, 'Beyle and Balzac', *Athenaeum*, 4648 (30 May 1919) p. 392.

64. *SE*, p. 190.
65. Ibid., p. 190.
66. *SE*, p. 412.
67. Knight, *Wheel of Fire*, p. 20.
68. There is a deliberate allusion to the ghost of Hamlet's father at the close of the All-Clear passage: 'He left me with a kind of valediction / And faded on the blowing of the horn.' It is perhaps significant that in spite of pressure from John Hayward, Eliot showed himself determined not to forego this minor echo. See *CFQ*, p. 196.
69. *Samson Agonistes and the Shorter Poems of Milton* (New York, 1966) p. 164. Both the Vaughan and Milton sources are mentioned by Grover Smith, *T. S. Eliot's Poetry and Plays: A Study in Sources and Meaning* (Chicago, 1968) p. 272.
70. Moody, *Thomas Stearns Eliot*, p. 344, note 20.
71. Knight, *Wheel of Fire*, p. 24.
72. Ibid., p. 24.

Notes to the Conclusion

1. Kierkegaard on *Don Juan*. Quoted by Alfred Einstein in *Mozart: His Character, His Work*, trans. A. Mendel and N. Broder (London, 1977) p. 7. Exact source of S. K.'s remark is not given.
2. T. S. Eliot, 'The Silurist', *Dial*, LXXXIII.3 (September 1927) p. 259.
3. T. S. Eliot, 'Preface', in *Thoughts for Meditation: A Way to Recovery from Within* (London, 1951), p. 13.
4. Ibid., p. 13.
5. A phrase used by Eliot in a letter to Hayward, 12 February 1941. See *CFQ*, p. 147.
6. A phrase used by Eliot in his essay 'Swinburne as Poet'; see *The Sacred Wood: Essays on Poetry and Criticism* (London, 1920) p. 149.
7. T. S. Eliot (ed.), *A Choice of Kipling's Verse* (London, 1941) p. 20.
8. T. S. Eliot, 'Wordsworth and Coleridge', in *The Use of Poetry and the Use of Criticism* (London, 1933) p. 85.
9. See Francis King, *Magic: The Western Tradition* (London, 1975) p. 14.
10. T. S. Eliot, 'Humanist, Artist and Scientist', *Athenaeum*, 4667 (10 October 1919) p. 1015.
11. T. S. Eliot, *After Strange Gods* (London, 1934) p. 24.
12. T. S. Eliot, Introduction in Samuel L. Clemens, *The Adventures of Huckleberry Finn* (London, 1950) p. xvi.
13. Ibid., p. xvi.

Selected Bibliography

The standard bibliography of Eliot's writing is Donald Gallup, *T. S. Eliot: A Bibliography* (London, 1969). There is also a helpful selected bibliography in Caroline Behr, *T. S. Eliot: A Chronology of his Life and Works* (London, 1983) pp. 89–120. Three useful reference books for writings *on* Eliot are, in order of publication:

Martin, Mildred, *A Half-Century of Eliot Criticism: An Annotated Bibliography of Books and Articles in English, 1916–1965* (London, 1972);

Frank, M. and D. P., and Jochum, K. P. S., *T. S. Eliot Criticism in English, 1916–1965: A Supplementary Bibliography* (Edmonton, 1978);

Ricks, Beatrice, *T. S. Eliot: A Bibliography of Secondary Works* (New Jersey, 1980).

1.   PRIMARY SOURCES: WORKS BY T. S. ELIOT

(A)   Unpublished Material

Literary manuscripts in the T. S. Eliot Collection bequeathed to King's College, Cambridge, by John Hayward in 1965. These MSS include essays, addresses, sermons, letters and the original typescript copies of *Four Quartets.*

(B)   Books

The Sacred Wood: Essays on Poetry and Criticism (London, 1920).

For Lancelot Andrewes (London, 1928).

Selected Essays, 3rd enlarged edn (London, 1951; first published 1932).

The Use of Poetry and the Use of Criticism (London, 1933).

After Strange Gods: A Primer of Modern Heresy (London, 1934).

The Idea of a Christian Society and Other Writings, 2nd edn (London, 1982; first published 1939).

Four Quartets, 1st edn (New York, 1943; London, 1944).

Notes Towards the Definition of Culture (London, 1948).

Quatre Quatuors, a translation by Pierre Leyris of *Four Quartets*, with notes supplied by John Hayward (Paris, 1950).

On Poetry and Poets (London, 1957).

George Herbert, Writers and Their Work, no. 152 (London, 1962).

Elizabethan Dramatists (London, 1963).

To Criticize the Critic and Other Writings (London, 1965).

The Complete Poems and Plays of T. S. Eliot (London, 1969).

The Waste Land: A Facsimile and Transcript of the Original Drafts including the Annotations of Ezra Pound, ed. Valerie Eliot (London, 1971).

Four Quartets, new and revised edn, ed. Valerie Eliot (London, 1979).

The Letters of T. S. Eliot, vol. 1: *1898–1922*, ed. Valerie Eliot (London, 1988).

(C) Essays and Articles

'The Borderline of Prose', *New Statesman*, ix.215 (19 May 1917) pp. 157–9.

'Eeldrop and Appleplex, I', *Little Review* (Chicago, Ill.) iv.1 (May 1917) pp. 7–11.

'London Letter', *Dial*, lxxi.2 (August 1921) pp. 213–17.

'Note sur Mallarmé et Poe', *La Nouvelle Revue Francaise* (Paris), xiv.158 (1 November 1926) pp. 524–6. (Translated by Ramon Fernandez; English text not published.)

'Deux attitudes mystiques: Dante et Donne', *Chroniques* (Paris), 3 (1927) pp. 149–73 (Le roseau d'or, 14). A translation by Jean de Menasce of one of the unpublished Clark lectures.

'A Note on Poetry and Belief', *Enemy* (London), i (January 1927) pp. 15–17.

'The Prose of the Preacher: the Sermons of Donne', *Listener*, ii.25 (3 July 1929) pp. 22–3.

'Religion without Humanism', in Norman Foerster (ed.), *Humanism and America: Essays on the Outlook of Modern Civilization* (New York, 1930) pp. 105–12.

'Poetry and Propaganda' in Morton D. Zabel (ed.), *Literary Opinion of America* (New York, 1951) pp. 97–107. The essay was first published in *Bookman*, LXX.6 (February 1930) pp. 595–602.

'Thinking in Verse: a Survey of Early Seventeenth Century Poetry', *Listener*, III.61 (12 March 1930) pp. 441–3.

'Rhyme and Reason: the Poetry of John Donne', *Listener*, III.62 (19 March 1930) pp. 502–3.

'The Devotional Poets of the Seventeenth Century: Donne, Herbert, Crashaw', *Listener*, III.63 (26 March 1930) pp. 552–3.

'Mystic and Politician as Poet: Vaughan, Traherne, Marvell, Milton', *Listener*, III.64 (2 April 1930) pp. 590–1.

'The Minor Metaphysicals: From Cowley to Dryden', *Listener*, III.65 (9 April 1930) pp. 641–2.

'John Dryden', *Listener*, III.66 (16 April 1930) pp. 688–9.

'George Herbert', *Spectator* (London), CXLVIII.5411 (12 March 1932) pp. 360–1: 'Studies in Sanctity VIII'.

'The Modern Dilemma', *Christian Register* (Boston, Mass.), CII.41 (19 October 1933) pp. 675–6.

'Orage: Memories', *New English Weekly*, VI.5 (15 November 1934). T. S. Eliot's is the last of five tributes to A. R. Orage printed under this general title, pp. 97–100.

'Paul Elmer More', *Princeton Alumni Weekly* (Princeton, N.J.), XXXVII.17 (5 February 1937) pp. 373–4.

'I by T. S. Eliot', in Gustaf Aulén *et al.*, *Revelation*, ed. John Baillie and Hugh Martin (London, 1937) pp. 1–39.

'Preface to the English Tradition', *Christendom* (Oxford), X.38 (June 1940) pp. 101–8.

'T. S. Eliot on Poetry in Wartime', *Common Sense* (New York) XI.10 (October 1942) p. 351.

'A Dream within a Dream', T. S. Eliot on Edgar Allan Poe, *Listener*, XXIX.737 (25 February 1943) pp. 243–4.

'Mr Charles Williams: An Obituary Notice', *Times* (17 May 1945) p. 7.

'The Significance of Charles Williams', *Listener*, XXXVI.936 (19 December 1946) p. 895.

'The Aims of Poetic Drama', *Adam*, XVII.200 (November 1949) pp. 10–16.

'Charybde et Scylla: Lourdeur et Frivolité', *Annales du Centre Universitaire Méditerranéen* (Nice) V (1951–2) pp. 71–82. The original English text of this lecture was published in *Agenda*, XXIII.1–2 (Spring–Summer 1985) pp. 5–21.

'The Unfading Genius of Rudyard Kipling', in Elliot J. Gilbert (ed.), *Kipling and the Critics* (London, 1966) pp. 118–23.

'Tradition and the Practice of Poetry', Introduction and Afterword by A. Walton Litz, *Southern Review*, XXI.4 (October 1985) pp. 873–88. Eliot's lecture was delivered at Dublin in January 1936.

(D) Introductions and Prefaces

'A Brief Introduction to the Method of Paul Valéry', *Le Serpent par Paul Valéry* (London, 1924) pp. 7–15.

'Introduction', G. Wilson Knight, *The Wheel of Fire: Interpretations of Shakespearian Tragedy*, 4th edn (London, 1978; first published 1930) pp. xiii–xx.

'Introduction', Djuna Barnes, *Nightwood*, 2nd (English) edn (London, 1963; first published New York, 1937) pp. vii–xiv.

'Preface by T. S. Eliot', *The Testament of Immortality*, an anthology selected and arranged by N. G.[angulee] (London, 1940) pp. 9–10.

'Introduction', Charles Williams, *All Hallows' Eve* (New York, 1948) pp. ix–xviii.

'Preface', Leone Vivante, *English Poetry* (London, 1950) pp. vii–xi.

'Introduction', Samuel L. Clemens (Mark Twain), *The Adventures of Huckleberry Finn* (London, 1950) pp. vii–xvi.

'Preface', *Thoughts for Meditation: A Way to Recovery from Within*, an anthology selected and arranged by N. Gangulee (London, 1951) pp. 11–14.

'Preface', Simone Weil, *The Need for Roots* (London, 1952) pp. v–xii. This book is a translation by Arthur Will of *L'Enracinement* (first published Paris, 1949).

'Foreword by T. S. Eliot', Joseph Chiari, *Symbolism from Poe to Mallarmé* (London, 1956) pp. v–viii.

'Introduction', *Paul Valéry: The Art of Poetry*, trans. Denise Folliot; vol. VII of *The Collected Works of Paul Valéry* (Bollingen Series XLV) (New York, 1958).

'Preface', *Selected Poems: Edwin Muir* (London, 1965) pp. 9–11.

(E) Reviews and Commentaries

Review of *The Philosophy of Nietzsche*, by A. Wolf, in *International Journal of Ethics*, XXVI.3 (April 1916) pp. 426–7.

Review of *The Ultimate Belief*, by A. Clutton Brock, in *International Journal of Ethics*, xxvii.1 (October 1916) p. 127.

Review of *Mens Creatrix*, by William Temple, in *International Journal of Ethics*, xxxvii.4 (July 1917) pp. 542–3.

'Reflections on Contemporary Poetry [1]', *Egoist*, iv.8 (September 1917) pp. 118–19. In part, a review of *Strange Meetings*, by Harold Monro.

Review of *A Defence of Idealism*, by May Sinclair, in *New Statesman*, ix.223 (22 September 1917) p. 596.

Review of *A Manual of Scholastic Philosophy*, vol. i, by Cardinal Mercier and other professors of the Higher Institute of Philosophy, Louvain, in *International Journal of Ethics*, xxviii.1 (October 1917) pp. 137–8.

'Reflections on Contemporary Poetry [III]', *Egoist*, iv.10 (November 1917) p. 151. In part, a review of *The New Poetry*, ed. by Harriet Monroe and A. C. Henderson.

'A Contemporary Thomist', *New Statesman*, x.247 (29 December 1917) pp. 312, 314. A Review of *Episemology*, by P. Coffey.

'Style and Thought', *Nation* (London) xxii.25 (23 March 1918) pp. 768–9. A review of *Mysticism and Logic*, by Bertrand Russell.

'Shorter Notices', *The Egoist*, v.6 (June–July 1918) p. 87. A review of *Per amica silentia lunae*, by W. B. Yeats.

'Kipling Redivivus', *Athenaeum*, 4645 (9 May 1919) pp. 297–8. A review of *The Years Between*, by Rudyard Kipling.

'Beyle and Balzac', *Athenaeum*, 4648 (30 May 1919) pp. 392–3. A review of *A History of the French Novel, to the Close of the Nineteenth Century*, vol. ii, by George Saintsbury.

'A Foreign Mind', *Athenaeum*, 4653 (4 July 1919) p. 552. A review of *The Cutting of an Agate*, by W. B. Yeats.

'Humanist, Artist, and Scientist', *Athenaeum*, 4667 (10 October 1919) p. 1015. A review of *La pensée italienne au XVI me siècle et le courant libertin*, by J. Roger Charbonnel, and *L'éthique de Giordano Bruno et le deuxième dialogue du Spaccio*.

'Dante as a "Spiritual Leader"', *Athenaeum*, 4692 (2 April 1920) pp. 441–2. A review of *Dante*, by H. D. Sidgwick; revised and reprinted as 'Dante' in *The Sacred Wood*.

'An Italian Critic and Donne and Crashaw', *Times Literary Supplement* (London), 1248 (17 December 1925) p. 878. A review of *Secentismo e Marinismo in Inghilterra*: John Donne–Richard Crashaw, by Mario Praz.

'Wanley and Chapman', *Times Literary Supplement* (London), 1250 (31 December 1925) p. 907. A review of *Essays and Studies by Members of the English Association*, vol. xi, collected by Oliver Elton.

'The Author of "The Burning Babe" ', *Times Literary Supplement* (London), 1278 (19 July 1926) p. 508. A review of *The Book of Robert Southwell*, by C. M. Hood.

'A Commentary', *Criterion*, iv.4 (October 1926) pp. 627–9.

'Poet and Saint', *Dial*, lxxxii.5 (May 1927) pp. 424–31. A review of *Baudelaire: Prose and Poetry*, trans. by Arthur Symons.

'The Silurist', *Dial*, lxxiii.3 (September 1927) pp. 259–63. A review of *On the Poems of Henry Vaughan: Characteristics and Intimations*, by Edmund Blunden.

'The Mysticism of Blake', *Nation and Athenaeum*, xli.24 (17 September 1927) p. 779. A review of six books by or about William Blake.

'An Emotional Unity', *Dial*, lxxxiv.2 (February 1928) pp. 108–12. A review of the *Selected Letters of Baron Friedrich von Hügel (1896–1924)*, ed. by B. Holland.

'The Poems English Latin and Greek of Richard Crashaw', *Dial*, lxxxiv.3 (March 1928) pp. 246–50. Reprinted as 'A Note on Richard Crashaw' in *For Lancelot Andrewes*.

'Mr P. E. More's Essays', *Time Literary Supplement* (London), 1412 (21 February 1929) p. 136. A review of *The Demon of the Absolute*, by Paul Elmer More.

'The Latin Tradition', *Times Literary Supplement* (London), 1415 (14 March 1929) p. 200. A review of *Founders of the Middle Ages*, by E. K. Rand.

Review of *God: Being an Introduction to the Science of Metabiology*, by J. Middleton Murray, *Criterion*, ix.35 (January 1930) pp. 333–6.

Review of *Poetry at Present*, Charles Williams, *Criterion*, ix.37 (July 1930) p. 786.

'A Commentary', *Criterion*, xi.45 (July 1932) pp. 676–83.

Review of *The Winding Stair*, by W. B. Yeats, *Criterion*, xiii.51 (January 1934) p. 314.

Review of *Selected Shelburne Essays*, by Paul Elmer More, *Criterion*, xv.59 (January 1936) p. 363.

'A Commentary', *Criterion*, xv.60 (April 1936) pp. 458–63.

'Mr Murray's Shakespeare', *Criterion*, xv.61 (July 1936) pp. 708–10.

'A Commentary', *Criterion*, xvi.65 (July 1937) pp. 666–70.

'An Anglican Platonist: The Conversion of Elmer More', *Times Literary Supplement* (London), 1865 (30 October 1937) p. 792. A review of *Pages from an Oxford Diary*, by Paul Elmer More.
'A Commentary: That Poetry is Made with Words', *New English Weekly*, xv.2 (27 April 1939) pp. 27–8. Chiefly on *Situation de la poésie*, by Jacques and Raissa Maritain.
'A Lay Theologian', *New Statesman and Nation* (London), xviii.459 (9 December 1939) pp. 864, 866. A review of *The Descent of the Dove*, by Charles Williams.

(F) Interviews

'T. S. Eliot Answers Questions', by Ranjee Shahani, *John O'London's Weekly* (London), lviii.1369 (19 August 1949) pp. 497–8.
'T. S. Eliot Talks about Himself and the Drive to Create', by John Lehmann, *New York Times Book Review*, 29 November 1953, pp. 5, 44.
'The Aged Eagle Spreads His Wings: a 70th Birthday Talk with T. S. Eliot' by Helen Gardner, *Sunday Times*, 21 September 1958, p. 8.
'The Art of Poetry I: T. S. Eliot, an Interview', *Paris Review* (Paris), 21 (Spring–Summer 1959) pp. 47–70. An interview, transcribed from tape recorder, by Donald Hall.
'Talking Freely: T. S. Eliot and Tom Greenwell', *Yorkshire Post* (Leeds), 29 August 1961. Includes T. S. Eliot's tape-recorded answers to questions posed by Tom Greenwell.
'An Interview with T. S. Eliot, Donald Carroll, Interviewer', *Quagga* (Austin), ii.1 (1962) pp. 31–3.

2.   OTHER PRIMARY SOURCES

(A) Mysticism

Bremond, Henri, *Prayer and Poetry*, trans. Algar Thorold (London, 1927).
The Cloud of Unknowing and Other Treatises by a Fourteenth-Century English Mystic, revised, edited and introduced by Justin McCann, O.S.B. (London, 1924).

Julian of Norwich, *Revelations of Divine Love*, a version by Grace Warrack (London, 1901).

[Pseudo-] Dionysius the Areopagite, *The Divine Names and the Mystical Theology*, trans. C. E. Rolt (London, 1920).

Richard of St Victor, *Opera Omnia*, Migne, *P.L.*, vol. cxcvi (Paris, 1855).

St Augustine of Hippo, *The Confessions*, trans. Sir Tobie Matthew (London, 1935).

St John of the Cross, *The Complete Works of St John of the Cross*, 4th edn, trans. and ed. E. Allison Peers (Wheathampstead, 1974; first published 1935).

Underhill, Evelyn, *Mysticism* (London, 1911).

(B) Philosophy and Religion

Allen, E. L., *Kierkegaard: His Life and Thought* (London, 1935).

Arnold, Sir Edwin, *The Light of Asia* (London, 1932; first published 1879).

Gregory, T. S., review of *Kierkegaard: His Life and Thought*, by E. L. Allen, *Criterion*, xv.59 (January 1936) pp. 305–7.

Heppenstall, Rayner, review of *Purify Your Hearts*, by Søren Kierkegaard, and *Kierkegaard*, by Walter Lowrie, *Criterion*, xviii.70 (October 1938) pp. 107–11.

Lewis, Wyndham, *Time and Western Man* (London, 1927).

Maeterlinck, Maurice, *The Treasure of the Humble*, trans. Alfred Sutro (London, 1908).

More, Paul Elmer, *The Greek Tradition*, vol. i: *The Catholic Faith* (Princeton, N.J., 1931).

Ouspensky, P. D., *Tertium Organum, The Third Canon of Thought: A Key to the Enigmas of the World* (London, 1934; first published 1921).

Sinclair, May, *A Defence of Idealism* (London, 1917).

Sinclair, May, 'Jones's Karma', *Criterion*, ii.5 (October 1923) pp. 43–56.

Thorpe, W. A., review of *Time and Western Man*, by Wyndham Lewis, *Criterion*, vii.1 (January 1928) pp. 70–3.

Warren, Henry Clarke, *Buddhism in Translations* (Cambridge, Mass., 1900).

Yeats, W. B., *A Vision* (New York, 1966; first published 1938).

(C) Poetry and Prose

Brooke, Rupert, *Collected Poems of Rupert Brooke with a Memoir*, ed. E. Marsh (London, 1918).

Chapman, George, *The Works of George Chapman: Poems and Minor Translations*, Introduction by Algernon Charles Swinburne (London, 1875).

Crashaw, Richard, *The Complete Poetry of Richard Crashaw*, ed. G. W. Williams (New York, 1972).

Dante (Alighieri), *The Divine Comedy*, 3 vols, Italian text with translation and commentary by John D. Sinclair (London, 1975).

Flaubert, Gustave, *La Tentation de Saint Antoine*, Introduction, Notes and Variations by Edouard Mayniad (Paris, 1958).

Kipling, Rudyard, *The Writings in Prose and Verse of Rudyard Kipling*, vol. v, *The Phantom Rickshaw and Other Stories* (London, 1898).

Kipling, Rudyard, *The Writings in Prose and Verse of Rudyard Kipling*, vol. xiii, *The Day's Work* (London, 1899).

Kipling, Rudyard, 'They', with illustrations by F. H. Townsend (London, 1905).

Kipling, Rudyard, *Puck of Pook's Hill* (London, 1920; first published 1906).

Kipling, Rudyard, *Rewards and Fairies* (London, 1920; first published 1910).

Kipling, Rudyard, *Rudyard Kipling's Verse*, Definitive Ed. (London, 1940).

Kipling, Rudyard, *A Choice of Kipling's Verse*, T. S. Eliot with an essay on the author (London, 1941).

Milton, John, *Samson Agonistes and the Shorter Poems of Milton* (New York, 1966).

Tennyson, Alfred Lord, *Poems of Tennyson, 1829–1868* (London, 1929).

Williams, Charles, *The Greater Trumps* (London, 1932).

(D) Literary Criticism

Knight, G. Wilson, *The Wheel of Fire: Interpretations of Shakespearean Tragedy*, with an Introduction by T. S. Eliot (London, 1978; first published 1930).

Knight, G. Wilson, *Christian Renaissance* (London, 1933).

Knight, G. Wilson, *The Crown of Life* (London, 1965); includes 'Myth and Miracle' (first published 1929).

Knight, G. Wilson, *Neglected Powers* (London, 1971).

Praz, Mario, *Secentismo e Marinismo in Inghilterra: John Donne, Richard Crashaw* (Florence, 1925).

Still, Colin, *Shakespeare's Mystery Play: A Study of The Tempest* (London, 1921).
Still, Colin, *The Timeless Theme* (London, 1936).

3. SECONDARY SOURCES: STUDIES OF THE WORKS OF T. S. ELIOT

(A) Books

Ackroyd, Peter, *T. S. Eliot* (London, 1948).
Alldritt, Keith, *Eliot's Four Quartets: Poetry as Chamber Music* (London, 1978).
Bergonzi, Bernard (ed.), *T. S. Eliot, 'Four Quartets': A Selection of Critical Essays* (London, 1969).
Bergsten, Staffan, *Time and Eternity: A Study of the Structure and Symbolism of T. S. Eliot's 'Four Quartets'*, Studia Litterarum Upsaliensia, I (Stockholm, 1960).
Bodelsen, C. A., *T. S. Eliot's 'Four Quartets': A Commentary* (Copenhagen, 1966; first published 1958).
Braybrooke, Neville (ed.), *T. S. Eliot: A Symposium for His Seventieth Birthday* (New York, 1958).
Bush, Ronald, *T. S. Eliot: A Study in Character and Style* (Oxford, 1984).
Drew, Elizabeth, *T. S. Eliot: The Design of His Poetry* (New York, 1949).
Gardner, Helen, *The Art of T. S. Eliot* (London, 1968; first published 1949).
Gardner, Helen, *The Composition of 'Four Quartets'* (London, 1978).
George, A. G., *T. S. Eliot: His Mind and Art* (Bombay, 1969).
Gordon, Lyndall, *Eliot's Early Years* (Oxford, 1977).
Gordon, Lyndall, *Eliot's New Life* (Oxford, 1988).
Grant, Michael (ed.), *T. S. Eliot: The Critical Heritage*, 2 vols (London, 1982).
Hay, Eloise Knapp, *T. S. Eliot's Negative Way* (London, 1982).
Howarth, Herbert, *Notes on Some Figures Behind T. S. Eliot* (London, 1965).
Ishak, Fayek M., *The Mystical Philosophy of T. S. Eliot* (New Haven, 1970).
Jones, Genesius, *Approach to the Purpose* (London, 1964).

Kearns, Cleo McNelly, T. S. Eliot and Indic Traditions: A Study in Poetry and Belief (Cambridge, 1987).

Kenner, Hugh (ed.), T. S. Eliot: A Collection of Critical Essays (Englewood Cliffs, N.J., 1962).

Kenner, Hugh, The Invisible Poet: T. S. Eliot (New York, 1965; first published 1959).

Kirai, Nasao and Tomlin, E. W. F., T. S. Eliot: A Tribute from Japan (Tokyo, 1966); includes 'The Mysticism of T. S. Eliot' by W. Johnston, S.J., pp. 144–66.

Kojecky, Roger, T. S. Eliot's Social Criticism (London, 1971).

Lal, P. (ed.), T. S. Eliot: Homage from India (Calcutta, 1965).

Lobb, Edward, T. S. Eliot and the Romantic Critical Tradition (London, 1981).

Lucy, Sean, T. S. Eliot and the Idea of Tradition (London, 1960).

Margolis, John D., T. S. Eliot's Intellectual Development, 1922–1939 (Chicago, 1972).

Matthiessen, F. O., The Achievement of T. S. Eliot (New York, 1958).

Maxwell, D. E. S., The Poetry of T. S. Eliot (London, 1952).

Moody, A. D. (ed.), The Waste Land in Different Voices (London, 1974).

Moody, A. D., Thomas Stearns Eliot: Poet (Cambridge, 1970).

Patterson, Gertrude, T. S. Eliot: Poems in the Making (Manchester, 1973).

Preston, Raymond, 'Four Quartets' Rehearsed (New York, 1946).

Rajan, B. (ed.), T. S. Eliot: A Study of his Writings by Several Hands (London, 1947).

Ricks, Christopher, T. S. Eliot and Prejudice (London, 1988).

Smidt, Kristian, Poetry and Belief in the Work of T. S. Eliot, 2nd edn (London, 1961).

Smith, Grover C., T. S. Eliot's Poetry and Plays: A Study in Sources and Meaning (Chicago, 1968).

Smith, Grover C., The Waste Land (London, 1983).

Southam, B. C., A Student's Guide to the Selected Poems of T. S. Eliot, 4th edn (London, 1981).

Tate, Allen (ed.), T. S. Eliot: The Man and His Work (London, 1967).

Traversi, Derek, T. S. Eliot: The Longer Poems (London, 1976).

Unger, Leonard (ed.), T. S. Eliot: Moments and Patterns (London, 1966).

Ward, David, T. S. Eliot: Between Two Worlds (London, 1973).

(B) Articles

Bergsten, Staffan, 'Illusive Allusions: Some Reflections on the Critical Approach to the Poetry of T. S. Eliot', *Orbis Litterarum*, 14 (1959) pp. 9–18.

Blisset, William, 'The Argument of T. S. Eliot's *Four Quartets*', *University of Toronto Quarterly*, 15 (January 1946) pp. 115–26.

Bradbury, John M., '*Four Quartets*: The Structural Symbolism', *Sewanee Review*, 59 (Spring 1951) pp. 254–70.

Brett, R. L., 'Mysticism and Incarnation in *Four Quartets*', *English*, xvi (Autumn 1966) pp. 94–9.

Butter, P. H., '*Four Quartets*: Some yes-buts to Dr Leavis', *Critical Quarterly*, 18 (1976) pp. 31–40.

Chaturvedi, B. N., 'The Indian Background of Eliot's Poetry', *English*, xv (Autumn 1965) pp. 220–3.

Cleophas, Sister Mary, 'Notes on Levels of Meaning in *Four Quartets*', *Renascence*, 2 (Spring 1950) pp. 102–16.

Davis, Jack L., 'Transcendental Vision in *The Dry Salvages*', *Emerson Society Quarterly*, 62 (1971) pp. 38–44.

Donoghue, Denis, 'T. S. Eliot's *Four Quartets*: A New Reading', *Studies*, 54 (Spring) 41–62; reprinted in B. Bergonzi (ed.), *T. S. Eliot: A Selection of Critical Essays* (London, 1969) pp. 212–36.

Everett, Barbara, 'A Visit to Burnt Norton', *Critical Quarterly*, 16 (1974) pp. 199–224.

Fowler, Russel T., 'Krishna and the Still Point: a Study of the Bhagavad-Gita's Influence in Eliot's *Four Quartets*', *Sewanee Review*, 79 (1971) pp. 407–23.

Gerard, Sister Mary, 'Eliot of the Circle and St John of the Cross', *Thought*, 34 (Spring 1959) pp. 107–27.

Hanshell, Deryck, 'L'Ascesa di T. S. Eliot', *Letture* xx (1965) pp. 755–68.

Harries, B. A., 'The Rare Contact: a Correspondence between T. S. Eliot and P. E. More', *Theology*, 75 (1972) pp. 136–44.

Hay, Eloise, 'T. S. Eliot's Virgil: Dante', *Journal of English and Germanic Philology*, LXXXII.1 (January 1983) pp. 50–65.

Higgins, David H., '"The Power of the Master": Eliot's Relation to Dante', *Dante Studies*, LXXXVIII (1970) pp. 129–47.

Hough, Graham, 'Vision and Doctrine in *Four Quartets*', *Critical Quarterly*, 15 (1973) pp. 107–27.

Hough, Graham, 'Dante and Eliot', *Critical Quarterly*, 16 (1974) pp. 293–305.

Leavis, F. R., 'T. S. Eliot's Later Poetry', *Scrutiny*, XI.1 (Summer 1942) pp. 60–71; reprinted in Hugh Kenner (ed.), *T. S. Eliot: A Collection of Critical Essays* (Englewood Cliffs, N.J., 1962) pp. 110–24.

McCarthy, H. E., 'T. S. Eliot and Buddhism', *Philosophy East and West*, 2 (April 1952) pp. 31–55.

Miller, James E., 'Whitman and Eliot: the Poetry of Mysticism', *South West Review*, 43 (Spring 1958) pp. 113–23.

Moody, A. D., 'The Secret History of *Four Quartets*', *Cambridge Quarterly*, VIII (1978) pp. 164–79.

Murray, Paul, 'The Unidentified Ghost: Arthur Hugh Clough and T. S. Eliot's *Four Quartets*', *Studies*, LXX.227 (Spring 1981) pp. 35–54.

Nageswara Rao, G., 'T. S. Eliot's Use of the Upanishads', *The Aryan Path* (Bombay) 38 (1967) pp. 19–32.

Pellegrini, Alessandro, 'Arts and Letters: London Conversation with T. S. Eliot', trans. by Joseph Frank, *Sewanee Review*, 57 (Spring 1949) pp. 287–92.

Pérez Gallego, Candido, 'Las etapas espirituales de T. S. Eliot', *Arbor*, 4 (1966) pp. 283–90.

Rao, K. S. Narayana, 'T. S. Eliot and the Bhagavad-Gita', *American Quarterly*, 15 (1963) pp. 572–8.

Robinson, David, 'Eliot's Rose Garden: Illumination or Illusion?', *Christian Scholar's Review*, 4 (1975) pp. 201–10.

Schmidt, G., 'An Echo of Buddhism in T. S. Eliot's "Little Gidding" ', *Notes and Queries*, 218 (1973) p. 330.

Servotte, H., 'T. S. Eliot's *Four Quartets* and the Language of Mystics', *Handelingen van het vier en dertigste Nederlands Filologencongres:* Gehouden te Amsterdam op dinsdag 13, woensdag 14 en donderdag 15 April 1976 (Amsterdam, 1976) pp. 93–7.

Sharp, Sister Corona, ' "The Unheard Music": T. S. Eliot's *Four Quartets* and John of the Cross', *University of Toronto Quarterly*, LI.3 (Spring 1982) pp. 264–78.

Srivastava, Narsingh, 'The Ideas of the Bhagavad Gita in *Four Quartets*', *Comparative Literature*, 29 (1977) pp. 97–108.

Stenger, G. L., 'Notes on "Burnt Norton" ', *Notes and Queries*, 19 (September 1972) pp. 340–41.

Tinsley, E. J., 'Aldous Huxley and T. S. Eliot: a Study in Two Types of Mysticism', *Life of the Spirit*, 6 (October 1951) pp. 119–30.

Weatherhead, A. Kingsley, '*Four Quartets*: Setting Love in Order', *Wisconsin Studies in Contemporary Literature*, 3 (Spring–Summer 1962) pp. 32–49.

Weigand, Elsie, 'Rilke and Eliot: the Articulation of the Mystic Experience', *Germanic Review*, 30 (October 1955) pp. 198–210.

Whitlark, James S., 'More Borrowings by T. S. Eliot from "The Light of Asia"', *Notes and Queries*, 220 (May 1975) pp. 206–7.

4. OTHER SECONDARY SOURCES

(A) Mysticism and Philosophy

Abhishiktananda, *The Further Shore* (Delhi, 1975).

Arintero, J. G., *Stages in Prayer*, trans. K. Pond (London, 1957).

Burrell, F. A., 'English Catholic Mystics in Non-Catholic Circles III', *Downside Review*, 94 (July 1976) pp. 213–31.

Butler, Cuthbert, *Western Mysticism* (New York, 1966; first published, 1926).

Carpenter, J. Estlin, *Buddhism and Christianity: A Contrast and a Parallel* (London, 1923).

Conze, Edward (ed.), *Buddhist Scriptures* (Middlesex, 1959).

Dodds, E. R., *Pagan and Christian in an Age of Anxiety: Some Aspects of Religious Experience from Marcus Aurelius to Constantine* (Cambridge, 1965).

Festugière, O.P., R. P., *L'Astrologie et les Sciences Occultés* (Paris, 1950).

Fortune, Dion, *Sane Occultism* (London, 1921).

Fortune, Dion, *The Mystical Qabalah* (London, 1935).

Gardner, Edmund, *Dante and the Mystics* (London, 1913).

Hulme, T. E., *Speculations: Essays on Humanism and the Philosophy of Art*, ed. Herbert Read (New York, 1924).

Jaeger, H., *La Mystique Protestante* (Paris, 1965).

King, Francis, *Magic: The Western Tradition* (London, 1975).

Knowles, David, *The Nature of Mysticism* (New York, 1966).

Lloyd, G. E. R., *Aristotle: The Growth and Structure of His Thought* (Cambridge, 1968).

Maharshi, Ramana, *The Collected Works of Ramana Maharshi*, ed. Arthur Osborne (London, 1980).

Milner, Max, *Poésie et Vie Mystique chez Saint Jean de la Croix* (Paris, 1947).

Murray, Paul, *The Mysticism Debate* (Chicago, 1977).

Stace, W. T., *Mysticism and Philosophy* (New York, 1960).

Thomas, Edward J., *The Life of the Buddha* (London, 1975; first published 1927).

Thurston, S.J., Herbert, *The Church and Spiritualism* (Milwaukee, 1933).

Von Balthasar, Hans Urs, *Prayer*, trans. A. V. Littledale (New York, 1967).

White, Helen C., *The Metaphysical Poets: A Study in Religious Experience* (New York, 1956).

Zaehner, R. C., *Hindu Scriptures* (London, 1966).

(B) Literary Criticism

Berger, Pierre, *William Blake: Mysticism et Poésie*, trans. D. H. Conner (Paris, 1907).

Bodkin, Maud, *Archetypal Patterns in Poetry: Psychological Studies in Imagination* (Oxford, 1934).

Carswell, John, *Lives and Letters, 1906–1957* (London, 1978).

Charity, A. C., *Events and their Afterlife: The Dialectic of Christian Typology in the Bible and Dante* (Cambridge, 1966).

Donoghue, Denis, *The Ordinary Universe: Soundings in Modern Literature* (London, 1968).

Foster, Kenelm, *God's Tree: Essays on Dante and other Matters* (London, 1957).

Knight, G. Wilson, *Neglected Powers* (London, 1971).

Leavis, F. R., *The Living Principle: English as a Discipline of Thought* (London, 1975).

Martz, Louis L., *The Poetry of Meditation: A Study in English Religious Literature of the Seventeenth Century* (Yale, 1971).

Neumann, Eric, *Art and the Creative Unconscious* (Princeton, N.J., 1974).

Nott, Kathleen, *The Emperor's Clothes* (London, 1953).

Schökel, Alonso, *The Inspired World: Scripture in the Light of Language and Literature*, trans. F. Martin (London, 1965).

Saurat, Denis, *Literature and the Occult Tradition: Studies in Philosophical Poetry* (London, 1930).

Senior, John, *The Way Down and Out: The Occult in Symbolist Literature* (New York, 1959).

Tuve, Rosemund, *Elizabethan and Metaphysical Imagery: Renaissance Poetic and Twentieth-Century Critics* (Chicago, 1947).

Weatherby, Harold C., *The Keen Delight: The Christian Poet in the Modern World* (Athens, 1975).

Wickstead, Philip K., *Dante and Aquinas* (London, 1913).

Yeats, W. B., *Letters on Poetry from W. B. Yeats to Dorothy Wellesley* (London, 1940).

Yeats, W. B., *Essays and Introductions* (New York, 1961).

Yeats, W. B., *Uncollected Prose*, vol. II, ed. J. P. Frayne and C. Johnson (New York, 1976).

Index